Taylor's Guides to Gardening

Roger Holmes, Editor

Frances Tenenbaum, Series Editor

HOUGHTON MIFFLIN COMPANY
Boston • New York   1995

Taylor's Guide to Container Gardening

Copyright © 1995 by Houghton Mifflin Company
Drawings copyright © 1995 by Steve Buchanan

All rights reserved

For information about permission to reproduce selections from this book, write to Permissions, Houghton Mifflin Company, 215 Park Avenue South, New York, New York 10003.

Taylor's Guide is a registered trademark
of Houghton Mifflin Company.

CIP data is available

ISBN 0-395-69829-4

Printed in Japan

DNP 10 9 8 7 6 5 4 3 2 1

Cover photograph © by Derek Fell

Contents

Contributors vi
How to Use This Guide viii

Introduction: Essentials of Container Gardening 1
Pots and Planters 5
Plants for Containers 17
Designing the Containers 35
Containers in the Landscape 51

The Plant Gallery
Annuals 98
Perennials 124
Bulbs 148
Vines 160
Deciduous Trees and Shrubs 170
Evergreen Trees and Shrubs 182

Encyclopedia of Plants
Plant Descriptions A–Z 204

Acquiring Plants 389
Potting Soils 397
Planting a Container 401
Caring for Container Gardens 414
Planting and Caring for Trees and Shrubs 424

Hardiness Zone Map 436
Photo Credits 438
Index 439

Contributors

Rita Buchanan made the final selection of plants for the encyclopedia and was a valued consultant on editorial and horticultural matters. She has worked as a botanist and horticulturist in Texas, Colorado, Virginia, Connecticut, England, and Costa Rica. A co-editor of *Taylor's Master Guide to Gardening* and several other Taylor's Guides, she is a former editor of *Fine Gardening* magazine. She now edits and writes gardening books from her home in Winsted, Connecticut.

John R. (Dick) Dunmire helped select plants for the encyclopedia and provided information for the descriptions of a number of those plants. He was a senior editor in the gardening department of *Sunset Magazine* at his retirement in 1990. During his 27 years with *Sunset*, he edited three editions of the *Western Garden Book*. A resident of Los Altos and Inverness, California, Dunmire has long been active in horticultural organizations on the West Coast.

John Elsley helped select plants for the encyclopedia and provided information for the descriptions of a number of those plants. He is vice president of George W. Park Seed Company and Wayside Gardens, with special responsibility for the selection of plants. He trained as a horticulturist in England at Kew and was the botanist at the Royal Horticulture Society's garden at Wisley before taking an appointment as a curator at the Missouri Botanical Gardens.

Roger Holmes, this book's editor, was a co-editor of *Taylor's Master Guide to Gardening*. He has edited several other Taylor's Guides and was the founding editor of *Fine Gardening* magazine. He is now a freelance editor and writer based in Lincoln, Nebraska.

Gary Keim helped select plants for the encyclopedia and provided information for the descriptions of a number of those plants. A graduate of the professional gardener's program at Longwood Gardens, he has worked in England with Penelope

Hobhouse, has been an estate gardener in Connecticut, and has written for gardening magazines. He is presently working at Longwood Gardens.

Tovah Martin helped select plants for the encyclopedia and provided information for the descriptions of a number of those plants. She is staff horticulturist for Logee's Greenhouse in Danielson, Connecticut, and the author of several books, including *Tasha Tudor's Garden* and *Once Upon a Windowsill*, as well as a regular contributor to leading garden magazines.

Tom Peace consulted on the selection of trees and shrubs for the book. Trained in forest biology and botany, he served in a forestry program in the Peace Corps and managed commercial greenhouses before starting his own business as a "garden creator." He splits his time between Denver, Colorado, and the Austin, Texas, area.

Rob Proctor, who wrote the essay chapters, also helped select plants for the encyclopedia and provided information for the descriptions of a number of those plants. Author of several gardening books, including *Annuals* and *The Outdoor Potted Bulb*, he is also an accomplished botanical illustrator and photographer. He lives in Denver, Colorado, and teaches at the Denver Botanic Gardens.

How to Use This Guide

Growing plants in containers can extend your gardening horizons, allowing you to try plants you don't have the space or the climate to grow in the ground, as well as bringing your garden right onto the patio, deck, or your bedroom windowsill. Some folks are happy with a few pots or boxes of annuals, perhaps varying the contents every year. Others create complex container gardens, rich in the variety of plants, colors, textures, and combinations. Whether you're a dabbler or an enthusiast, this book will help you along your way.

How This Guide Is Organized

Like many of the books in this series, this one contains articles on the many aspects of this type of gardening as well as a large selection of plants shown on color plates and described in an encyclopedia.

The Articles

The book's nine chapters present an overview of container gardening, including examinations of containers, plants, and design, as well as practical information on growing and caring for plants in containers. You'll learn the relative merits of various types of containers, qualities to look for when selecting plants, strategies for effective plant combinations, how to start plants from seed, what constitutes good potting soil and how to make your own, when and how to water and feed your plants, and how to help long-lived plants through the winter.

The Plants

A great many plants can be successfully grown in containers—annuals, perennials, bulbs, vines, trees, shrubs, and others. From this vast pool, we have selected nearly 200 that we feel exhibit qualities that make them especially valuable for containers. Lovely flowers, handsome foliage, striking form, attractive texture, enticing fragrance—we looked for all these qualities and more. The plants that we selected usually have more than one quality to recommend them. In addition, we wanted our list to offer a range of plants that would lend themselves to a variety of uses—as specimens or in combination with others, for small pots and large, upright plants or trailers, and so on. We looked for plants that are likely to be readily available from major local nurseries or established mail-order suppliers.

Color plates

To give you a sense of the many possibilities for container gardening, we include nearly 100 color photos that illustrate what we discuss in the chapters. Then, to help you choose individual plants, we provide a collection of plant portraits in the gallery section. These will give you a good idea of a plant's foliage, flowers, and, often, growth habit. The portraits are arranged by plant type: annuals, perennials, bulbs, vines, evergreen trees and shrubs, and deciduous trees and shrubs. A short comment on the plant's use or character accompanies each plate, along with its botanical and common names, its height, its hardiness-zone rating, and the page on which you'll find its written encyclopedia entry.

Plant encyclopedia

If you're intrigued by a plant that is mentioned in a chapter, is shown in the plant gallery, or you see on a friend's patio, consult this section. The encyclopedia contains descriptions of each plant shown in the color plates as well as a great many additional cultivars and related species. The listings are arranged alphabetically by genus. (If you don't know the botanical name, consult the index, where botanical and common names are cross-referenced.)

Each genus is briefly described, followed by detailed profiles of selected species and cultivars. These entries present the plant's desirable characteristics (foliage, flowers, growth habit), provide suggestions for using it, and comment on how to grow it in a container.

Plants vary considerably in their ability to withstand cold temperatures. Those native to high-elevation northern regions, for instance, can survive bitter cold, many degrees below zero, whereas some tropical plants may die when touched by the slightest frost. In the early years of the 20th century, horticulturists began to correlate the cold hardiness of plants with gradients of temperature as plotted on a map. The zone map on p. 436 is based on one recently revised by the U.S. Department of Agriculture, which represents 10 temperature zones for North America. The zone ratings given for each plant indicate the lowest temperatures the plant can usually be expected to survive. A plant rated zone 5, for example, should survive minimum temperatures between –10° and –20° F.

When selecting plants, remember that zone ratings are collected for plants grown in the ground, not in containers. In general, plants grown in containers will not be as hardy as when they're planted in the ground. (On the other hand, container plants can be moved to protected quarters during the winter.) Remember also that hardiness-zone ratings don't account for other important factors, such as heat and wind. These factors are mentioned in the plant descriptions; if you're in doubt about a plant's suitability for your location, ask a knowledgeable staff person at your local nursery.

Introduction: Essentials of Container Gardening

Almost everyone can grow plants in containers. Potted gardens grace homes in every region of the country, from the deserts of New Mexico to the forests of Maine, from the mild climes of coastal southern California to the extreme climates of the Great Plains. They're as enjoyable for the owner of an acreage in the country as for the city gardener whose "land" extends no farther than the edge of the roof or the ledge of the kitchen window.

With ingenuity and imagination, it is possible to enliven every one of your outdoor living spaces with plants in containers. They can line walkways and balconies, decorate decks and patios, and greet visitors at the door. Hung on fences or under windows, flanking a secluded bench, or mingling with in-ground plantings, in sunny spots or shady, plants in containers add color, fragrance, and eye-catching enjoyment to your property.

Container gardening also expands your gardening options beyond the confines of your site and climate. Because you can maintain tight control of certain conditions—soil, water, nutrients, and exposure—within a pot, container gardening makes accessible a range of plants that would otherwise be difficult or impossible to grow in your garden. And treating a single pot or a group of pots as a miniature garden allows you to experiment with more styles and combinations than you might have space or energy to attempt in a full-scale garden. With a little know-how, patience, and practice, you can grow what you fancy, be it a collection of culinary herbs, continuously blooming annuals, tender tropicals, tiny trees and shrubs, or tasty fruits and vegetables.

Plants in Pots versus Plants in the Ground

There are differences between growing plants in containers and growing them in the garden. Most of these favor the container gardener. The obvious advantage is being able to select the soil mixture to suit each individual plant. For example, cacti and succulents thrive in a gritty, porous loam, whereas Oriental lilies prefer an acidic, friable mixture enhanced with liberal amounts of organic matter. A garden that offers both types of soil is unusual, but pots with the two different soils can coexist on the same patio.

Container-grown plants may also be positioned where they receive the optimum amount of sunlight. The cacti and succulents just mentioned, for instance, are best placed where they can bake under the sun, whereas the lilies will thrive where they receive only the morning rays. Since areas of light and shadow created by buildings and trees change throughout the growing season (trees leaf out; the sun shifts its path incrementally each day), pots can be moved around to provide just the right exposure, something not possible in the garden itself.

The mobility of most (though not all) containers also makes easier the protection of plants from early or late frosts and damaging storms. Some pests, such as slugs, snails, rodents, and other wildlife, can be effectively countered by growing plants in containers. Bulb-eating rodents can't gnaw their way through a terra-cotta pot, and grazing deer can't reach favorite plants growing in containers on a second-story balcony.

Container gardening does present some difficulties. Because the container environment is much smaller and more artificial than that in the garden, the gardener has more responsibility. Most container-grown plants require more attention than those in the garden. Consistent watering is the key to growing beautiful container plants. Soil in pots dries out quickly (particularly in smaller pots), and a few days of watering neglect can cause serious damage. Careful attention to the "diet" of a container garden is also important. Nutrients in potted soil are depleted by plants (quickly by some, over a longer period by others), and nature doesn't replenish them. Timely applications of appropriate fertilizers help ensure healthy plants, whether they're annuals grown for only a season or trees and shrubs that are decades-long residents of container homes.

While stresses of water or nutrient deficiency are brought on by an inattentive gardener, the physical limitations of the container itself create others. Plant roots are not free to roam, and eventually they hit the pot wall. Perennials, trees, and shrubs need to be repotted periodically, either shifted to a larger pot or pruned, roots and top growth, to return comfortably to the same pot. Annuals needn't be repotted, but when they're crowded together in small containers, even more vigilance regarding water and nutrients is needed to compensate for their cramped quarters.

Performance varies considerably when plants are confined in containers. Most annuals will grow as high and wide and will flower as much as their counterparts in the garden if given rich soil, adequate moisture and fertilizer, and the right amount of light. The same can be said for many bulbs and smaller perennials. In the spring, soil in containers warms faster than garden soil, so container-grown specimens sometimes grow more quickly and outperform garden-grown ones. But the amount of growth and flowering of most larger perennials, shrubs, and trees will be somewhat inhibited when they're confined in containers. This does not necessarily make a plant unsuitable for container culture. When the alternative is not growing the plant at all, a slower growth rate and fewer flowers are a small price to pay. A few plants, such as agapanthus, may even perform best in crowded conditions. For others (bonsai plants, for example), stunted growth is desired.

Pots and Planters

People grow plants successfully in almost any kind of container, from traditional terra-cotta to old toilet bowls. Aside from minimal practical requirements, candidates for containers are limited only by your taste and imagination.

Drainage and size are the prime practical considerations. For all but bog plants, overly moist soil can spell disaster. Drainage holes of some kind in the container are therefore essential. Pot size has an effect on plant health in somewhat more complicated ways. An undersized pot can crowd roots, affecting the plant's supply of water (too much or too little) and nutrients, leading to stifled growth and increased susceptibility to disease. A container that is too big holds extra soil that the plant's roots will be slow to penetrate. This soil will stay wet, and roots in an overly soggy pot begin to rot.

In a "true" hanging basket, such as this, a variety of annuals are planted in sphagnum moss that fills a wire framework.

The root systems of plants sold at nurseries or garden centers often come close to filling their plastic pots. A good rule of thumb for purchased plants grown for summer display is to select a pot about 2 inches wider and deeper than the one the plant is sold in. Like all rules, this has exceptions, which we'll discuss in chapters 3 and 4. Certainly avoid cramming a plant into a smaller container.

Terra-Cotta

The pot of choice for more than a century has been one made of clay. Terra-cotta (Italian for "baked earth") is valued for more than sentiment and its good looks. Fired clay is porous, allowing air from outside to penetrate and supply oxygen to plant roots. At the same time, excess moisture inside the pot evaporates through the wall. Terra-cotta readily absorbs and conducts heat, so high daytime temperatures can cause excessive evaporation and raise soil temperatures to unhealthy levels. (In spring, however, the clay will keep the roots of plants somewhat warmer, allowing for a slight jump on the season.) Small pots are particularly susceptible to too much evaporation; the greater mass of soil inside larger pots mitigates the effects of heat absorption. Regardless of size, terra-cotta pots in hot, sunny, or windy spots need special attention to watering.

Pots and Planters

Clay flue tiles, which come in a range of sizes, can be striking containers.

Terra-cotta pots come in any number of sizes and shapes, from the very simple to the ornate. The color of the clay also varies according to where the pots are produced, from deep brick red to blond buff to almost white. While no particular style of pot affects plant performance, some features are desirable. Pots with thick walls are more durable. Those made with too much sand in the mix (detectable by a coarser surface) will start to disintegrate after a few seasons. Terra-cotta pots don't overwinter well in cold climates—their porous walls can be cracked when moist soil inside expands as it freezes.

Used thoughtfully, inexpensive plastic pots can look just as good as their pricier cousins.

Plastic

Often designed to mimic terra-cotta, plastic pots also come in a wide range of sizes, shapes, and colors. They are inexpensive and lightweight. Because their walls aren't porous, soil in them retains moisture longer, which is an advantage for many container plants but not for those, such as herbs or succulents, that prefer drier conditions. The color of the pot is a factor in how much heat it will absorb—soil in lighter-colored pots will remain cooler than soil in dark pots. Plastic pots are less likely to fracture when overwintered outdoors.

Cast Concrete

Pots made from cast concrete are very popular because of their good looks. Cast-concrete urns add charm flanking porch steps, especially of Victorian-style homes. Large cast-concrete pots or troughs hold plenty of soil, making extravagant annual displays possible. Many will last for years outside, although their thick walls can still be damaged by the expansion of moist soil as it freezes. Concrete heats up in the sun, like clay, but not quite as quickly, and the larger size of most cast-concrete containers helps moderate overheating.

As for other containers, those made of cast concrete should have drainage holes to avoid waterlogged soil. If the container doesn't, you can bore holes yourself (or have the job done for you) with an electric drill and a $1/2$-inch masonry bit. If that isn't possible, consider planting in plastic pots resting on a layer of gravel or small stone spread at the bottom of the concrete container, which will keep the potted soil above runoff from watering. Many concrete pots are quite heavy, so you may need to have them delivered and placed for you.

Metal

Containers of brass, copper, iron, aluminum, or lead are highly ornamental. Ornate cast-iron urns were especially popular in the 19th century, and they fetch a high price today. Contemporary copies, often cast in aluminum and painted black or forest green, mimic the originals at a fraction of the price. All make lovely focal points when planted with cascading annual flowers. To protect containers made of ferrous metals from rust, their interiors may be coated with pitch, paint, or wax, which must be reapplied every few years. The thicker the walls of these containers, the longer they will generally last.

Metal containers with an Oriental motif are frequently used for bonsai specimens.

10 Pots and Planters

Recycled Italian cookie and olive-oil cans are a perfect choice for a miniature herb garden.

It is relatively easy to bore drainage holes in many metal containers; alternatively, you can plant in plastic pots or liners resting on stones, as described previously for cast concrete. Avoid placing metal containers (other than lead) in hot afternoon sun, where they'd heat up quickly and cook plant roots.

Stone

Many kinds of stone have been fashioned into garden containers over the years. Granite, marble, limestone, and alabaster pots and urns are expensive. Recent technology has

Pots and Planters 11

made less expensive replicas available in synthetic stone. The imitations are often as lovely as the stone they simulate and are frequently much lighter in weight. You can make your own "stone" trough of a material called hypertufa. (See p. 408.) Many plants appreciate the heat and lower humidity common in stone and stonelike containers. (Drainage, of course, is important; a drill and masonry bit or gravel and liner pots can remedy a deficiency of holes.)

A classical stone urn provides interest on its own, in addition to the plants it contains.

Homemade hypertufa troughs are a suitable foil for landscapes of tiny alpine plants.

A growing segment of the gardening public is discovering the joys of growing miniature plants in hypertufa troughs. These jewels of the mountain world are all the more treasured by those who don't have the space for a rock garden. Many trough enthusiasts make miniature landscapes for their plants, using rocks within the troughs similar to those found in the plants' natural habitat. The reason is not merely an aesthetic one: many alpine plants perform best when their roots grow between the crevices of rocks as they do in nature.

Wood

Because of the ease with which wood can be worked and painted, wooden containers can be made to complement almost any style of architecture or landscape design. From large, freestanding planters to small balcony boxes, wood also serves a wide range of plants and planting styles.

Wooden containers offer many advantages. Wood is a natural insulator, and it keeps roots relatively cool compared with those of plants growing in terra-cotta pots. Because soil temperatures inside wooden containers fluctuate less from day to day, plants in them suffer less long-term stress. Wooden boxes allow less evaporation than terra-cotta, so

A mix of colorful plants is ideal for a bushel-basket planter; this one has been treated with wood preservative and lined with plastic.

Pots and Planters 13

Easily made wooden boxes have potential beyond the traditional window box.

Sawn in half and hollowed out, this weathered log makes a striking planter.

A cargo of begonias, petunias, and other annuals brightens an old wooden rowboat beached on a pebble "shore."

they're easier to keep watered. They are also durable. Less rigid and brittle than clay or concrete, they aren't as easily broken up by the expansion of freezing soil and may be left outside in winter with little damage. Some types of wood, such as redwood and cedar, are resistant to rot and will last without treatment for many years. When painted or otherwise waterproofed, other types of wood can also make durable planters. Wooden containers are a good choice for large plants. They're more affordable than enormous clay pots and easier to move, especially if equipped with casters.

Permanent planters, such as this one of brick, can be planted like large containers or small garden beds.

Permanent Planters

Large, immobile planters made of stone, brick, or heavy timber can be thought of as big, deep pots or small self-contained garden beds. Some are built with the house; others are added later, perhaps with a patio or deck. Permanent planters offer opportunities for mass plantings of one or two types of large plants, such as black-eyed Susans or big hostas. They can be treated as small beds composed of various combinations of annuals, perennials, shrubs, and trees. Narrow planters might provide space to grow a hedge or screen or may be treated like window boxes. They may also be the center of a container garden that includes plants grown in smaller, portable pots.

"Found" containers like this recycled grill can add surprise and humor to a garden.

"Found" Containers

Gardeners have long made use of all sorts of castoffs as plant containers. Ingenuity can turn a rusting wheelbarrow, old crock, hollow tree stump, or vintage coal bucket into a perfect home for summer plants. Half whiskey barrels planted with everything from roses to peaches to lilies can make striking focal points; this American innovation is increasingly copied overseas. Bushel-basket planters, another uniquely American idea, are back in vogue. Most of our grandparents grew at least a geranium or two in the inexpensive wooden baskets, and a new generation is enjoying them again. The baskets last for only a few years, but the slatted sides drain well and allow plenty of air penetration.

Not all innovations have staying power. The peeled-back tractor tires that once adorned many gardens are out of favor today. But much of the fun is in getting the nerve to try something new. Who knows what eye-catching container lurks in the shadows of your shed or basement, waiting to be filled with plants?

Plants for Containers

Annuals, perennials, vines, trees, and shrubs—all kinds of plants are grown in containers. Given the rather severe constraints placed on plants in containers, it's surprising how many are suitable. The obvious limitation is size, but sizable trees are container-grown in public places. Rather than the size of the container, it is more often the available space that limits the size of container-grown plants—few of us have room on our patio for a container 4 feet wide and tall housing a 20-foot-tall tree.

Container plants, like their garden-grown kin, must be selected with an eye to the conditions in which they will grow. While you have considerable control over soil type, moisture, nutrients, and exposure, providing a different environment for each of dozens of container-grown plants can be time-

Plants for Containers

Life can be a barrel of roses with a little imagination and effort.

consuming. By all means, pamper a special few, but select most to accommodate a single type of potting soil and the particular conditions of sun, shade, heat, and wind on your patio or deck or in your entryway. When choosing long-lived plants, be aware of their requirements for winter care—can they survive on the deck, or will you need to haul them inside? If you're cautious, plants you intend to leave outside over the winter should be hardiness-rated one and sometimes two zones colder than your zone. (In zone 6, for example, you're less likely to lose plants rated zone 5 or 4.) Keep practical considerations such as these in mind while we explore the attractions and uses of various types of plants.

Annuals

The most popular category of plants for container gardening is annuals—plants that grow, bloom, and die in a single season. Most annuals are grown for their heavy, all-season flowering, although some are valued primarily for their leaves. Others are prized for producing a spectacular floral display for a relatively short time, such as the spring-blooming schizanthus, nemophila, and English daisies, or zinnias and woodland tobacco in late summer.

Perennials that survive winter outdoors only in the mildest of climates are often grown and treated as annuals. These "tender" perennials include such well-known plants as geraniums, begonias, coleus, and impatiens. Many of these are carried through the winter indoors on windowsills and sun porches. A cool greenhouse, a cold frame, or a trench in the garden can accommodate somewhat hardier tender perennials through the winter.

Gardening conditions vary considerably from region to region, but many annuals demonstrate remarkable adaptability. And because they're grown for only a season, hardiness and overwintering are not important considerations. (Some annuals are "overwintered" in the form of rooted cuttings to produce next season's display.) It's easy to experiment with annuals—you risk only a few seeds and some effort. Try a few new annuals each year, and you'll soon have a varied palette for container combinations and compositions.

Most annuals grow beautifully in pots. Some are star performers, whereas others are best used to complement showier plants. One of the secrets to beautiful containers is to combine a wide variety of annuals with different attributes. To ensure continuity throughout the season, select some known for reliable flowering (such as marigolds and impatiens) and others with noteworthy foliage (such as dusty-miller and coleus). Verbenas, lobelias, and other sprawling and trailing annuals soften the edges of pots and planters. Vertical plants such as blue salvia or flowering tobacco add structure to a composition.

Most vegetables are annuals, and some offer ornamental qualities as well as tasty produce. These double-duty plants are ideal for containers, where you must get a lot of mileage from limited space. Peppers, patio tomatoes, cabbage, lettuce, and more earn their keep among pots of posies. The same can be said for herbs, including everything from basil and parsley to dill and savory.

An obvious advantage of planting annuals in containers is being able to change them each year or, if you're ambitious, each season (pots for spring, summer, and fall). Trying out a

Peppers and marigolds demonstrate the charm of "edible" container gardening.

color scheme is a delightful process. You may opt for the "explosion in the paint factory" theme, where anything goes, or decide to limit your colors. Some gardeners select all pastels, while others go for brilliant primary colors. You might restrict yourself to one or two colors, such as yellow and blue, or pink and purple, or focus on only one flower color and its various tints. Leaves, of course, figure into the composition, whether in shades of green; in grays, bronzes, or yellows; or in variegated forms and multicolored hues.

Perennials

Although not as widely grown in pots as annuals, perennials can be equally effective. Perennials are plants that persist from year to year. Some die back to the ground and regenerate from their roots each spring, while others carry their leaves through the winter. Climate and the severity of winter determine how they will react for you.

Perennials are valued for their diversity, offering a vast range of color and form in flowers and foliage as well as a wide variety of growth habits. In general, perennials bloom for shorter periods than annuals. Different plants bloom at different times, allowing you to make a selection that ensures perennial flowers spring, summer, and fall. Some perennials, such as coralbells, coreopsis, and daylilies, provide an extended season of bloom or repeat performances. Others, such as cranesbill or border jewel, are handsome in leaf as well as in flower. Because space is precious, it makes sense to choose perennials with more to offer than just a few weeks of flower—look for attractive foliage or interesting seed heads.

Perennials make excellent specimens; a sunlit tub of daylilies or a pot of hostas in a shady nook can be equally eye-catching. Annuals and perennials coexist well in large containers, the shallow-rooted annuals occupying the top few inches of soil, while the roots of the perennials delve deeper.

Perennials in containers can grace patios or walkways as easily as garden beds. Euryops pectinatus, *a tender perennial (zone 9), is shown here.*

As in a garden bed, quick-growing annuals in a mixed container can provide interest while the perennials leaf out. When the perennials bloom, annuals form a pretty backdrop, then resume center stage after the perennial show.

Vines and Bulbs

Some vines are truly perennial, whereas others are tender or truly annual. Annual vines, such as morning glories or scarlet runner beans, are relatively easy to grow. Other vines—perennial clematis or tender bougainvillea, for example—need winter protection. Tender vines that must be moved for overwintering pose a special problem—you must be able to move the structures on which they grow or be willing to cut the plant off the trellis.

The joy of vines is their rambling, rambunctious nature and their loose, relaxed habit. A single vine can provide a fountain of leaves and flowers amidst other pots of plants, or a backdrop to showcase others. A trellised vine can furnish shade for plants, or it can relieve boredom on a flat patio by dividing the space and introducing a quality of "hide and seek" to it. Most vines make unwilling trailers—they will simply climb back on their own shoots in their drive to grow upward. You can train container vines up a wooden or metal trellis inserted in or placed next to the container, or you can erect a tepee of brush over the pot to support them.

Rising from three half-barrels, a vibrant display of bougainvillea is set off by geraniums, lobelias, and other plants in adjacent tubs.

Plants for Containers 23

Tulips and hyacinths in small tubs brighten a patio in springtime.

Bulbs (for our purposes we include plants that grow from corms, tubers, and rhizomes as well as true bulbs) offer a special pizzazz that many container gardeners find appealing. Like perennials, they are easy to combine with annual companions in the same pot; the annuals carry the show before and after the bulbs have flowered. Bulbs may also be grown in their own pots to be displayed when they are at their best and removed afterward.

Bulbs are so varied in flower types and timing that they can be part of the patio landscape for long periods, even throughout the entire year where winters are mild. Spring features traditional favorites, such as tulips, daffodils, crocuses, and hyacinths. These are especially engaging with cold-tolerant annuals such as pansies. Northern gardeners can get a jump on spring by "forcing" spring bulbs indoors and setting them out when temperatures warm sufficiently.

Summer-flowering bulbous plants, such as lilies, cannas, and dahlias, are attractive grown in containers on their own or used as accents with annuals and perennials. As summer gives way to fall, cyclamens, amarcrinums, colchicums, tuberoses, and nerines are lovely on the patio. Dahlias and cannas produce until the first frost. In mild-winter areas, many bulbs flower from fall to spring, including calla lilies, clivia, cyclamen, paperwhite narcissus, and anemones.

Cacti and Succulents

Cacti and succulents offer exciting forms in leaf, structure, and flower. Besides being highly ornamental, most are easy-care plants that can survive watering negligence. Most, but not all, thrive in full sun and provide an interesting, bold contrast to more traditional plants typically found on balconies and decks. Where winters are mild, cacti and succulents can decorate your outdoor living area throughout the year, but they need protection where cold winter weather prevails. Large specimens require special attention when they are moved (especially if they sport menacing needles), since they are often brittle and easily damaged. Smaller cacti and succulents lend themselves to trough or dish gardens, forming miniature landscapes of considerable interest. The chart below lists some of the many cacti and succulents now available.

Succulents and Cacti for Container Gardens

Succulents

Aeonium arboreum
Rosette tree
Height: 3 ft.
Rosettes of shiny, succulent green leaves top thick bare stems. 'Atropurpureum' is dark purple. Part shade, well-drained soil, moderate water. Frost-tender.

Agave spp.
Century plant
Height: varies with species
Rosettes of pointed, sharp-toothed, fleshy leaves produce slender flower stalks after several years, depending on species. *A. utahensis* grows to 9 in., *A. victoriae-reginae* reaches 2 ft., and *A. americana* attains 3–6 ft. All require full sun, porous soil, and winter protection in all but frost-free areas. See also encyclopedia entry.

Aloe spp.
Aloe
Height: varies
Spiny, triangular, overlapping leaves may be green or gray-green, sometimes with bands or streaks of contrasting color. Flowers are orange, yellow, red, or cream. Tiger aloe (*A. variegata*) grows to 1 ft.; candelabra aloe (*A. arborescens*) may reach 2 ft. Medicinal aloe (*A. barbadensis*, a.k.a. *A. vera*) grows 2 ft. or more, and the sap from its leaves helps heal minor scrapes and burns. All grow best in full or part sun with minimum water. Must be wintered indoors where temperatures drop below freezing.

Cacti and succulents lend themselves particularly well to pot culture.

***Crassula* spp.**
Jade, silver-dollar plant
Height: varies with age and container size
Succulent shrubs with rounded, fleshy leaves. Silver-dollar plant (*C. arborescens*) has silver-blue, often red-edged, leaves; may reach 12 ft. Propeller plant (*C. falcata*) has long gray leaves twisted like a propeller and can grow 3 ft. tall. The common jade plant (*C. ovata*) can grow to 6 ft. or more. All thrive in bright shade with regular moisture and fertilizer during the summer. Frost-tender.

***Delosperma* spp.**
See encyclopedia.

***Echeveria* spp.**
Many species of small succulent plants, usually less than 6 in. tall, with attractive rosettes and orange, red, or yellow flowers on thin stems. Some species have smooth glossy leaves, others are hairy. All need full or part sun and dry conditions. Winter indoors.

Euphorbia milii
Crown-of-thorns
Height: to 2 ft.
Spiny shrubs with red flowers. Lomi hybrids bloom yellow, pink, red, or purple. Full or part sun, well-drained soil; keep fairly dry. Frost-tender.

Graptopetalum paraguayense
Mother-of-pearl plant
Height: 4 in.
Silver rosettes with pink and lavender tones like its namesake; grows much like

(continued on next page)

Succulents and Cacti for Container Gardens (continued)

hen-and-chicks. Best in part sun, dry conditions. Frost-tender.

Haworthia spp.
Star cactus
Height: to 6 in.
Spread: varies with age and container size
Clump-forming basal rosettes of spiny to smooth leaves. Small white tubular flowers on thin stems appear periodically. Grow in part shade and well-drained soil; water regularly. Frost-tender.

Kalanchoe tomentosa
Panda plant
Height: 20 in.
Bushy upright perennial with rounded velvety gray leaves edged with brown. Full or part sun, porous soil, moderate water. Frost-tender.

Lampranthus spp.
Ice plant
Height: to 1 ft.
Prostrate creepers with indefinite spread, gray-green leaves, and attractive daisylike flowers in red, yellow, orange, or cerise. Flowers over a long period. Grow in full sun with moderate water. Frost-tender.

Nematanthus glabrus
(*Hypocyrta glabrus*)
A trailer with round, puffy orange flowers and leathery dark green leaves that hold up well in hanging baskets in dry air. Part or full shade. Moderate water in summer, very dry in winter. Frost-tender.

Sansevieria spp.
Mother-in-law's tongue
Height: to 3 ft.
Variegated sword-shaped leaves in thick clumps; make effective container plants in part or full shade with moderate water. Winter indoors.

Sedum spp.
See encyclopedia.

Sempervivens spp.
See encyclopedia.

Cacti

These are smaller, easy-care, summer or spring bloomers that do well in container gardens. In general, they need moderate water from May to September and dry conditions in winter. Feed during blooming season with a fertilizer formulated for cacti and succulents. All prefer sunny locations; all are frost-tender and should be overwintered indoors in cold climates.

Plants for Containers

***Cleistocactus* spp.**
Pillar cactus
Height: to 3 ft.
Upright pillars with fine needles; tubular flowers of red, magenta, or orange from spring to summer. Keep on the dry side.

Echinocactus grusonii
Barrel cactus, golden ball
Height: 3–4 ft.
Round cactus characterized by golden yellow thorns. Yellow flowers appear in summer on mature specimens.

***Echinofossulocactus* spp.**
Brain cactus
Height: under 6 in.
Wavy ribs on rounded spheres. Spring flowers are white, yellow, or purple with darker center stripes. Let dry out between waterings.

***Gymnocalycium* spp.**
Height: 6–8 in.
Rounded form with profuse yellow, red, pink, cream, or white flowers up to 2 in. across from spring to summer. Water thoroughly, but let soil dry between waterings; water sparingly in winter.

***Lobivia* spp.**
Height: usually under 1 ft.
Prominent ribs feature showy flowers up to 4 in. across from spring to summer in orange, red, yellow, pink, or violet. Let dry out between waterings.

***Mammillaria* spp.**
Pincushion cactus
Height: to 20 in.
Variable in shape, these cacti have characteristic pincushion spines. Clusters of flowers are produced in spring.

***Notocactus* spp.**
Short pillar cactus
Height: 6–8 in.
Round to pickle-shaped, these cacti have flowers up to 3 in. across in yellow, pink, or red. Bloom spring to summer.

***Parodia* spp.**
Height: to 8 in.
Variable shapes, usually with woolly crowns; yellow or red flowers from spring to summer.

***Rebutia* spp.**
Height: most under 3 in.
Small, spring-blooming cacti with profuse yellow, purple, or red flowers 3/4–2 in. across.

Containers can make adding a water feature to the garden easy; here water lilies and a striking container are guarded by a bronze beast.

Water Plants

It doesn't take a full-scale pond or pool to grow and enjoy water lilies, water hyacinths, papyrus, and many other water and bog plants. Half-barrels, ceramic Oriental fishbowls, and a myriad of watertight containers can serve as miniature ponds on the terrace or porch. You may even be able to enjoy the glint of darting goldfish in your portable pool. For more on container water gardens, see the chapters "Designing the Containers" and "Containers in the Landscape."

Plants for Container Water Gardens

Canna glauca and hybrids
Water cannas. Zone 9
Height: 4–6 ft.
Spread: 2–3 ft.
Available with flowers of yellow, orange, red, or pink. Place potted rhizomes 4–6 in. below water surface. Grow in full sun and minimum water temperature of 65°–70° F. Overwinter in pots in tubs of water in greenhouse or sunroom.

Cyperus alternifolius
Umbrella plant. Zone 9
Height: 1–4 ft.
Set potted plants slightly above or below water surface, or plant in nondraining container kept very moist. Water temperature 65°–70° F. *C. papyrus*, papyrus, grows 4–10 ft. Select dwarf varieties of both species for containers. Overwinter like canna.

Eichhornia crassipes
Water hyacinth. Zone 9
Height: 6–9 in.
Spread: 8–12 in.
A floater with pale lavender flowers and inflated leaves. Grow in full or part sun. "Float out" into water after danger of frost is past. Take care to keep confined to your container—they have become pests in southern waterways.

Iris kaempferi
Japanese iris. Zone 4
Height: 2 ft.
Spread: 10–20 in.
Large flowers (4–10 in. across) come in purple, blue, pink, and white. Plant in pots of acidic soil; set rims at water surface in full or part sun. Allow pots to dry out somewhat over winter.

Nelumbo nucifera
Lotus. Zone 6
Height: 2–5 ft.
Spread: 3–6 ft.
Huge flowers (1 ft. wide) in pink, yellow, or white. Large blue-green leaves look like parasols. Place pot 10–20 in. beneath water surface in full sun with minimum water temperatures of 60°–70° F. Roots must never freeze. Store indoors in tubs, or cut off leaves and store tuber in damp sand at 35°–45° F.

Nymphaea spp.
Water lilies. Some to zone 4
Hundreds of varieties of hardy and tropical water lilies are available in white, yellow, red, purple, pink, and all shades in between. Choose dwarf varieties with spreads of less than 2 ft. for half-barrels or Oriental fishbowls. Set out hardy varieties in spring in water 50° F or warmer; tropical varieties in water 70° F.

(continued on next page)

Plants for Container Water Gardens (continued)

Gradually lower potted plants in water as they grow to a depth of 8–12 in. in full sun. Store in sand in cool basement.

Pistia stratiotes
Water lettuce. Zone 9
Height: 6 in.
Spread: 6–8 in.
A floater with attractive rosettes of pale mint green. Place in full or part sun in water at least 70° F. Winter indoors in small tubs.

Pontederia cordata
Pickerel weed. Zone 3
Height: 1–4 ft.
Spread: 10–20 in.
Large, heart-shaped leaves and spikes of lavender-blue flowers. Place in full or part sun, with pot rim at water surface.

Sagittaria montevidensis
Giant arrowhead. Zone 9
Height: 2–3 ft.
Spread: 1–2 ft.
Pointed leaves and spikes of white flowers. Submerge pot to within 4–8 in. of rim in water at least 50° F. Full or part sun.

Trees and Shrubs

Gardeners whose horticultural activities are confined to small areas or who don't have any actual ground are the biggest beneficiaries of growing shrubs and trees in containers. But most outdoor living areas, regardless of size, can be enriched by these plants. A small ornamental tree can bring grace to a group of plants in pots and add a contrast in scale. You may welcome its shade for a chair or bench or as habitat for growing pots of shade-loving plants. Dwarf fruit trees offer the additional attractions of spring blossoms and tantalizing fruit.

Because of their size and their longevity, trees and shrubs are challenging container plants. The most important practical concerns are the plant's ability to survive in your climate and the selection of an appropriate container. Growing trees and shrubs in containers requires long-term commitments of space and time. You want to make sure the plants you select will survive with a level of care that doesn't exceed your resources or energies. Exposure to heat, wind, sun, or shade is important, but the main concern for many gardeners is winter temperatures. Fewer trees and shrubs will survive outdoors in containers in northern regions than in the South, but a great many can be grown outdoors year-round where temperatures rarely drop below freezing.

Plants for Containers 31

Grown in containers, evergreen trees and shrubs, such as this Hinoki cypress, can be handsome specimens.

One of the enticements of container gardening is being able to grow plants outside their ordinary limits. Many trees and shrubs that would be too tender to grow in the ground can be grown in containers if, and this is a very large if, you are willing and able to provide an appropriate winter home. To do so, you'll need storage space in a sunroom, basement, or, possibly, garage (depending on the plant), and you'll need to be able to move the plant and its container.

A container for a tree or large shrub must meet the same requirements as those for other plants—but on a larger scale. It must accommodate a substantial root system, provide adequate drainage, and be sturdy in the weather. In addition, it may need to have room for stakes that support trunks. And if the plant needs to be moved to winter quarters, it may need wheels, casters, or handles. It's not so difficult to move a hi-

*Deciduous trees and shrubs, such as this holly (*Ilex verticillata *'Sparkleberry'), can provide year-round interest.*

A broad-leaved evergreen shrub brings interest to an awkward corner.

biscus, small palm, or dwarf citrus tree in a 5- or 10-gallon pot, but sizes larger than that present a challenge. How much will plant, pot, and soil weigh? Does the path to winter storage include steps, narrow doors, or low ceilings? Answering questions such as these before you choose a tree or shrub can save you a lot of trouble later.

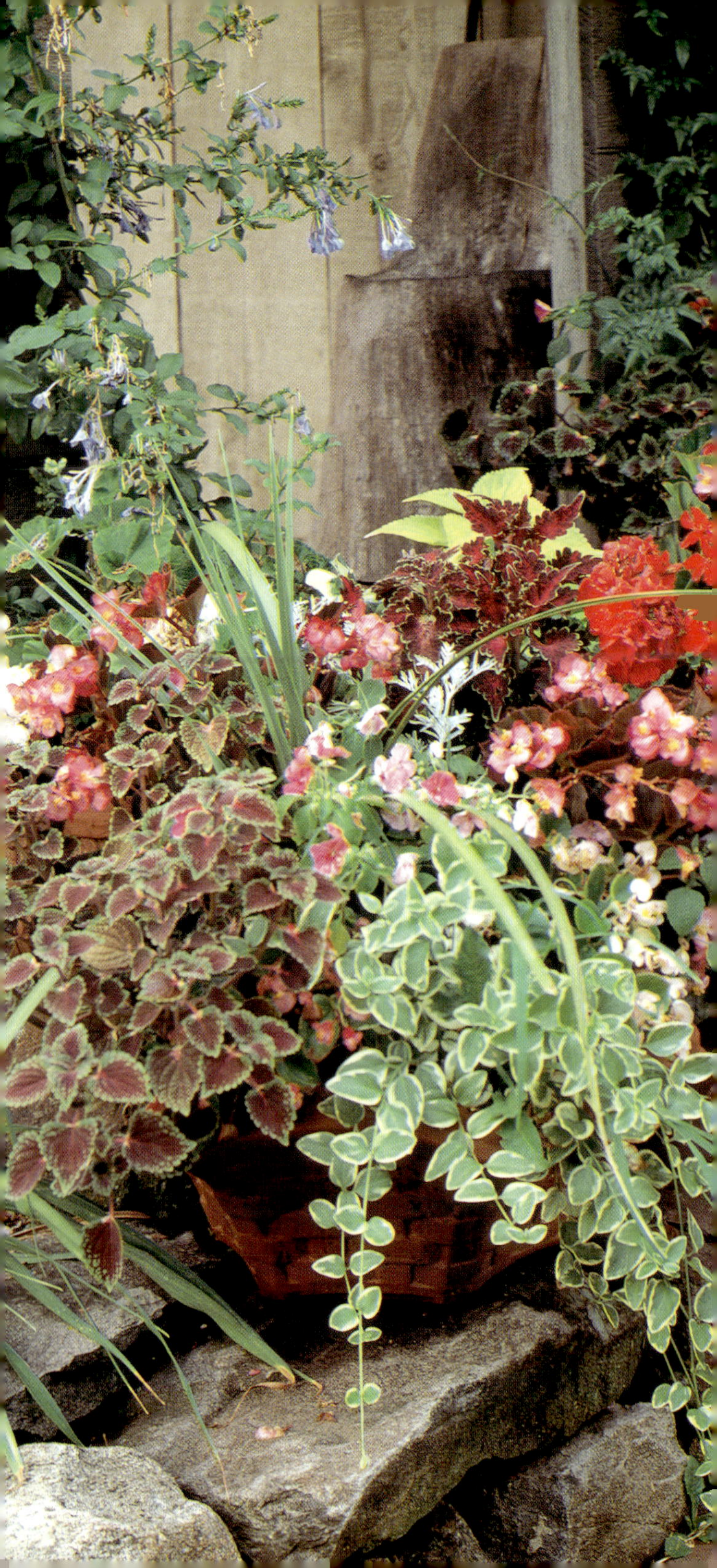

Designing the Containers

Container design ranges from the display of a single plant in a single pot to the orchestration of scores of plants in dozens of pots. For both extremes and in between, success requires forethought. We can't discuss all the possible combinations of plants, pots, and locations, but we can present some basic ideas that will serve in a variety of situations.

Many plants recommend themselves for the color, form, or fragrance of their flowers or foliage. An array of shapes adds variety, whether the plants are grown together in the same container or potted up separately and staged together. Round, mounded plants are enhanced by spiky, linear plants or by sprawlers and trailers. Airy, feathery plants need the contrast of dense, compact companions. Vase-shaped plants add grace, while fanciful shapes such as clipped topiary balls lend a degree of formality. Tall plants and vines serve as screens or focal points.

36   *Designing the Containers*

Whether you're displaying one plant or many, success depends as much on how they relate to their surroundings as on the qualities of the plants and pots themselves. Choose colors, shapes, and textures that complement your home and personality. Old-fashioned annuals and perennials suit a cottage-garden approach; striking, dramatic flowers and foliage enhance the lean look of modern architecture. Scale is as im-

Rhythmic repetition of colors and forms unifies a long container.

Designing the Containers 37

portant as style. A small pot of pansies on its own outside a large formal entrance will be lost; a flowering tree, a tall clump of ornamental grass, or a staged grouping of a half dozen pots would be more effective. Consider also the mood you wish to create. Reinforce the tranquillity of a shady nook with an all-white-and-green potted display; enliven a sunny patio or deck with a riotous blend of hot-colored flowers.

Where pots rest on the same level, plants of different heights as well as textures create an effective composition.

Common to these two distinctly different but equally striking compositions is a fine sense of color and texture; the result is the right pot and the right plant in the right place.

Individual Plants

The effective display of a single plant in a single pot (or a number of the same plants in a single pot) has much to do with selecting the right pot for the plant. Perhaps one of the least effective displays is a tall pot planted with short annuals. As a general guideline for pleasing plant-to-pot proportions, single-specimen plants should be as tall as the pot they in-

Designing the Containers 39

habit. (This is true of window boxes, urns, and other containers as well.) There are, of course, many exceptions to this principle. Succulents are often displayed in short, wide pots with their foliage forming low, thick clumps. Ornamental grasses and shrubs may be seven or eight times as tall as their containers. The idea is to select the container that best displays the distinctive form of the plant.

Less is more: This juxtaposition of red hollyhocks, red geraniums in an interesting box, adobe walls, and blue trim seems just right.

More is more: It's difficult to imagine fitting one more plant in this hanging basket, and the effect is delightful.

Mixing Plants in One Pot

A pot of mixed flowers and foliage is essentially a living bouquet. The number and variety of plants are limited by the size of the container, though you can generally put more plants in a pot designed for just a single season. Because annuals (and other plants grown as annuals) need only enough soil to see them through a few months, they can be spaced more closely than would otherwise be prudent. This is true also of annuals mixed with a single dominant perennial, shrub, or bulb. You will need to be generous with water and fertilizer to help alleviate conditions in their cramped quarters.

Designing the Containers 41

In a mixed container, consider plants that occupy different levels as well as orchestrating a color scheme. Here salvia, dusty-miller, petunia, and ivy form a pleasing composition.

Create an eye-catching pot by combining plants with attributes that complement or contrast one another in a pleasing manner. Start by choosing a dominant plant as the centerpiece. Depending on the size of the container, this could be anything from a rosebush to a marguerite daisy to a fuchsia. Then design around this plant, just as you would plan a room around an important feature such as a sofa, rug, or china cabinet. Large permanent planters or long, narrow containers such as window boxes may have several focal points.

Begin, for example, with an upright fuchsia in a pot with an opening measuring a foot across. Consider the fuchsia's flowers (perhaps deep pink and white) and their graceful, weeping manner. What annuals could complement them? Remember, all the plants in the pot must share the fuchsia's preferences for bright morning sun, afternoon shade, and plenty of water. Noting that the leaves of most fuchsias are not all that exciting, you may wish to add some coleus near the base of the fuchsia, perhaps with pink bands of color on their leaves, or a variety that is beet red. You might choose the polka-dot plant, whose deep green rounded leaves are freckled with red, deep pink, or white spots, a nice match for the fuchsia's flowers. By way of contrast, you might select gray-leaved dusty-miller as a foliage accent.

A plant with a spiked, upright form would add height and interest to the composition. A spike dracaena might be the answer, especially the tricolor form with pink margins on its leaves. The maroon version of standard bedding salvia or the straight spikes of another salvia, white mealy-cup sage, would be appropriate; choose the blue form of the mealy-cup if you want to expand the pink-and-white color theme.

Next, consider something round to contrast with the upright forms of the fuchsia and the spiked plants. Blue, pink, or white ageratum offers rounded shapes of both the plant and its flower heads. The finely textured, puffy flowers would also underscore the satinlike sheen of the fuchsia. Impatiens, too, have a rounded shape, and the colors of their blossoms in the pink and red tones is quite variable, so it would be easy to select ones close to the color of the fuchsia.

Finally, think about adding a sprawling or trailing plant to weave its way through the other plants and spill over the sides of the pot. Trailing lobelia has a pleasant meandering manner, and the masses of tiny blue, white, lavender, or carmine pink flowers would sparkle in this grouping. Plant a cream-edged vinca vine or silver-marked lamiastrum to cascade over the pot's rim. If you've still got room, work in a trailing fuchsia.

Groups of Pots

One beautifully designed container may stand on its own, or it may become part of a larger grouping clustered on stairs, a windowsill, or a patio. A line of identical pots and plants can edge a driveway or the railing of a deck, as well as leading the eye and visitors to your door or to an area of entertainment or recreation. Massed, multipot plantings of a single plant type can provide a bold accent near an entryway or by a garden seat.

Staging groups of pots is an art in itself. If you start with the pot of fuchsia and annuals cited above, the next step is

Designing the Containers 43

Simple combinations, such as this one of nicotiana, impatiens, and red fountain grass in a ceramic bowl, can be very pleasing.

Introducing a difference in height adds something special to an attractive but ordinary planting scheme.

44 *Designing the Containers*

Massed pots containing poor-man's orchid (Schizanthus spp.) in a coordinated range of colors march up a stairway.

This vibrant collection of bulbs and annuals is enhanced by being displayed at a variety of heights.

An underplanting of geraniums and lantana transforms an unruly potted California bay tree.

to add more pots to form a group. Consider the same sorts of things we've been discussing—the colors and forms of flowers and foliage, plant texture and growth habit, types of pots, surroundings, and so on. The process is not unlike planning a bed or border in the garden.

Remember that in the confines of a small deck or balcony, a single large plant serves the same purpose a tree does in the yard—adding structure to the area, inviting an assortment of smaller companion plants. A few large specimens also add a more permanent feeling to a collection of potted plants. Large plants can serve as backdrops for smaller plants or as focal points, especially if they offer a flush of bloom, interesting leaves, or striking branching patterns.

For an informal look, select pots of varying sizes—some deeper than others, one or two perhaps that are quite a bit bigger than the rest. Mix square, rectangular, or other shapes with the round pots. Add a metal, stone, or wood container as an accent in a group of terra-cotta pots.

Tucked in attractive slate containers, these exquisite miniature landscapes demonstrate the appeal of a special form of container gardening.

Since pots filled with soil and plants are heavy, position larger pots when they're empty. Take your time to place all the pots, arranging them in clusters with several dominant, bigger pots in back (or in the center, if the grouping is meant to be viewed from all sides). You might try the "hen and chicks" approach, thinking of a mother hen pot with randomly staggered smaller pots at her feet.

Raise some of the pots well above others. A variety of heights gives you more opportunity to display plants to best advantage, and it can make the grouping attractive to both seated and standing viewers. Bricks, concrete blocks, sturdy wooden platforms, purpose-made pot holders, or "found" pedestals and stands can all provide support. Smaller pots placed at the edges of the grouping disguise staging that lacks visual interest of its own.

Sooner or later, your enthusiasm for container plants may get the best of you and you'll discover that every square inch of the balcony or patio is covered in a jumbled hodgepodge of pots. The solution is to bring order out of chaos by careful grouping. Plant stands help. Reproductions of tiered Victorian stands, usually made of wire or metal, make handsome showcases. Some are modular, with straight and curved components that can be put together to suit your site and needs. Put four quarter-round "ends" together and you have a circular unit. Use two straight pieces and one end to wrap around a corner. It's a little like putting toy railway tracks together.

Other options depend on your imagination and taste. A tea cart or old Radio Flyer wagon becomes a portable garden. A stepladder with boards laid spanning the distance between steps and braces, or a pair of straight ladders with boards resting on the rungs make interesting display space. Wooden stools, simple benches, or wooden boxes of varying heights are effective pedestals for prize specimens. Open-end clay flue tiles, which come in various lengths, make sturdy pedestals, or you can fill them with soil and plants (ensuring excellent drainage).

Large numbers of plants in a collection are often more attractive when grouped into sections, rather than strung uniformly around the patio. Leave some area blank for visual relief. Imagine you are hanging a number of small pictures on your wall. The "one here and one there" approach looks busy, but group them together, with plenty of wall to "frame" them, and the whole collection is enhanced.

Themes and Seasons

Gardeners with a passion for particular colors may use all styles of plant groupings—mixed pots, massing, and planters—to carry a theme throughout their property. For example, an aficionado of yellow flowers may feature that color everywhere, in sun or shade, and in every season, by positioning containers in strategic spots. Marigolds, lilies, and zin-

A lovely silver garden like this is much easier to accomplish in containers than in a garden bed.

nias blaze in their sunny pots, while yellow tuberous begonias bloom in the shade. Primroses and daffodils grace the garden for winter or spring accents (depending on climate); golden mums glow in autumn.

    Not only can you change the look of your garden with different plants and colors (almost like new slipcovers for indoor furniture), but you can echo the change of seasons. A springtime grouping of tulips and daffodils, for instance, gives way to bright petunias or bold cannas, concluding with chrysanthemums or ornamental kale. Designing container gardens is not solely a once-a-year activity. A creative gardener can paint an ever-changing picture through the year.

Planned carefully, container plantings can change dramatically with the seasons. Here geraniums give way to nicotiana as spring moves to summer, both seasons spiced by white salvias and alyssum. In fall, the pots can be changed to provide a tapestry of chrysanthemums.

Designing the Containers 49

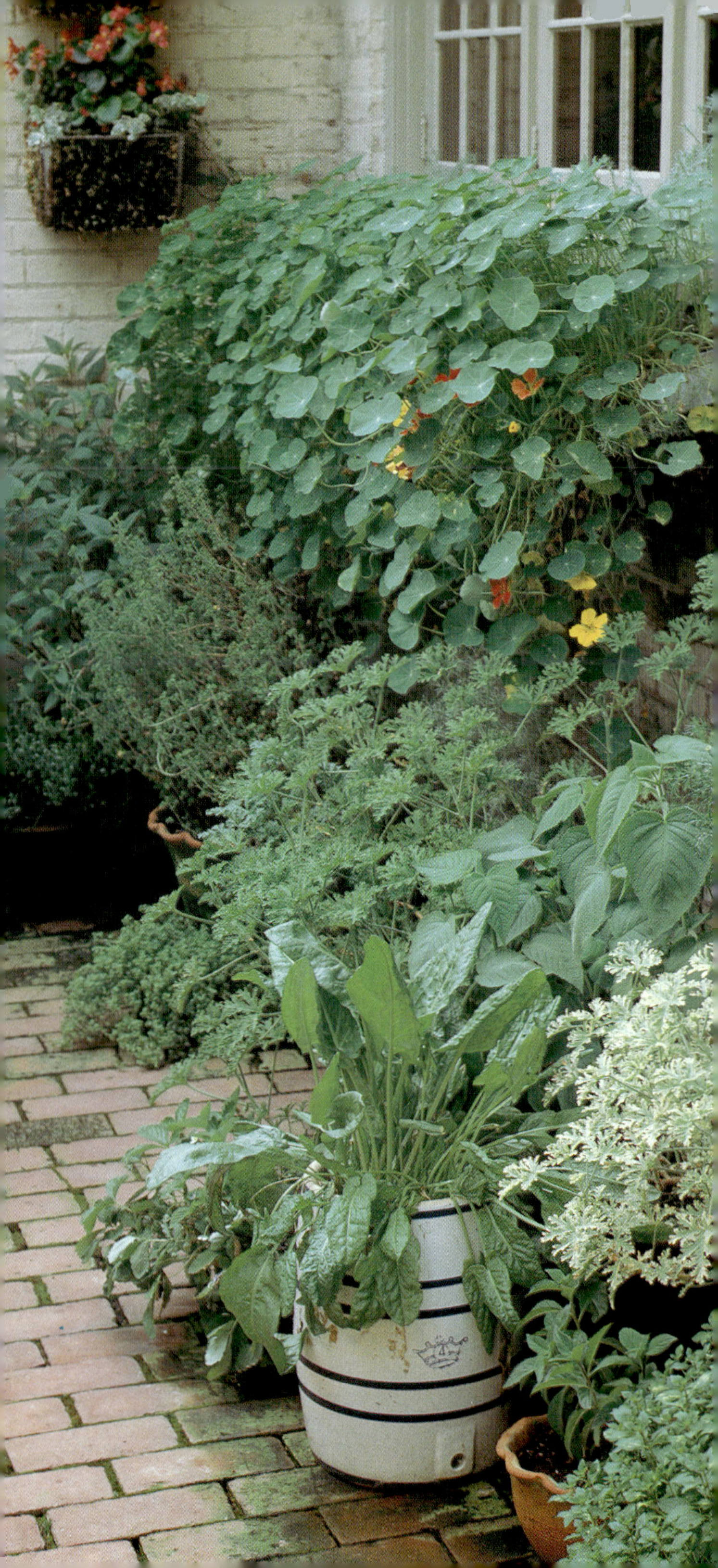

Containers in the Landscape

Plants in containers can enhance every part of your home landscape. The possibilities for containers on your patio, entryway, balcony, or other area depend in large part on the size and configuration of the available space, on the furnishings and activities sharing that space, and on your gardening ambitions, energies, and budget.

While much design revolves around matters of taste, one critical factor does not. Just as you consider the climate in your garden when selecting appropriate plants for different areas, you must consider the "climate" on your patio or entryway when choosing plants for containers. Each area can be said to have its own little climate, varying according to its exposure to the elements.

Most important is sunlight—its timing, duration, intensity, and the heat it generates. Other than thinning or removing trees, there may not be much you can do to increase the amount of sunlight on a particular spot—it's tough to move a shade-casting building. If your favorite plants are shade lovers, however, you can screen a sunny patio with a simple lattice and vines and entirely change its character. Consider also exposure to winds, driving rain, or, in cold-winter areas, snow, all of which can damage plants. Fortunately, it's not difficult to shelter containers from these elements.

When choosing plants it's important to match, as much as possible, their preferences for climate with conditions on the site. The encyclopedia section of this book provides information on the conditions preferred by several hundred plants recommended there for containers. In addition, take note as you travel around town or walk through your neighborhood of what plants seem to do well in containers.

Carefully coordinated with the color of the vine-covered wall behind, this begonia and its formal stand (above) are a perfect accent and focal point at the end of this terrace. Pots and hanging baskets lend substance as well as interest to the otherwise austere posts of this lath-roofed garden room (left).

Patios and Decks

Patios are as varied as the rooms in a house and the people who inhabit them. Some are formal, the outdoor equivalent of an elegant living room. (In keeping with their tony nature, these patios are often called terraces.) Others promote a more relaxed atmosphere, akin to a family room, and host a variety of activities. In each instance, container plantings can play a major role in establishing character, setting the mood, and adding beauty to the scene.

Though most often associated with backyards, patios may also occur in side yards or in front of the house. They are frequently close to the house, typically accessible through the kitchen or an informal dining room, although sometimes paired with a living room, family room, or other room. Association with activities inside the house and exposure to sun or shade dictate, to a degree, the patio's uses. A shady spot

54   *Containers in the Landscape*

A simple combination of daisies, impatiens, and geraniums marks the transition from patio to garden and lawn.

A pot full of colorful petunias makes a striking accent in this adobe courtyard.

off the study or bedroom provides a retreat for reading, quiet conversation, and rest. A sunny site linked by French doors with the kitchen or family room is ideal for outdoor dining, entertaining, games, and family recreation.

Symmetry and balance are usually ingredients of a formal outdoor setting. A pair of matching urns might accent a bench or architectural feature. Topiary balls and cones are the height of formal symmetry. Standards—plants such as roses, geraniums, and lantana trained so that they perch atop a single "trunk" or multiple intertwining long bare stems—can be an elegant touch in pairs or larger numbers. Shrubs with a looser habit, such as citrus or hibiscus, lend a slightly more relaxed feeling.

Repetition can reinforce formality. Several large, identical containers with matching contents can complement porch or wall columns. On a smaller scale, you can repeat a flowering annual, perhaps in one color only, in matching pots. You can unify a formal terrace by placing a number of pots of elegant plants—purple China asters, white Asiatic lilies, or fancy-leaved caladiums, for instance—in strategic spots.

The repetition of a favorite bold plant can also unite an informal patio, but with a difference—the plant appears in

Container plants play a role in creating a secluded spot in a corner of a patio.

conjunction with many plants and many pots in different styles. Many of us gravitate toward this loose, informal style because it fits the way we garden. We don't rush out and buy all of our pots and flowers at one time. Pots are accumulated over time, replaced as they break, or acquired when a unique one catches our eye. Our plants come and go in the same way: some are bought with a plan in mind, whereas others are impulse purchases. How many of us can leave a nursery without at least one new plant that we just have to try?

Containers should complement the plants they hold and reflect the quality and style of the other patio furnishings, whether formal or informal. Ceramic, metal, stone, or embellished terra-cotta pots in classic shapes emphasize clipped junipers or boxwood. Well-made wooden planters, neatly painted white or traditional hunter green, reinforce a formal ambiance. "Found" containers can add a delightful touch to an informal patio.

Potted trees, shrubs, annuals, perennials, hanging baskets—all these make this low deck a pleasant spot for relaxing or entertaining.

Remember scale when you choose planters and plants for your patio or terrace. A pair of tiny pots on either side of a large patio has very little visual impact; they are out of scale. Replace them with a handsome pair of terra-cotta pots, 2 feet tall or more, and they begin to take on significance. They also hold enough soil to grow plants with some stature of their own. Elevate the pots on sturdy pedestals, plant them with a mixture of tall plants and ones that cascade flowers over the rims, and the effect is dramatic. Think also of pots at many levels, not just on the patio floor. Bring some of them up at least to waist height, so you won't always be bending over to admire them.

Consider placement of containers. Positioned near a dining table, a baker's rack of begonias, impatiens, ferns, and browallia can turn an evening meal into a feast for the eye as well. Situated close to a seating area, fragrant plants, such as lilies and tuberoses, add a new dimension to conversation.

58   *Containers in the Landscape*

Mounds of daisies in big pots give this bench a cozy feeling.

Without its mantle of potted plants, this spa would stick out like a sore thumb in its small courtyard.

Containers tend to line the perimeter of patios, perhaps because our traffic and seating areas occupy the middle, but this need not be the case. Use benches and tables to bring plants into the thick of things, where they can be sniffed and closely admired.

Much of what has been said applies equally to decks, which can be thought of as elevated patios, often lined with railings for safety. Because of their height, decks may feature

Potted plants add character and divide space on this terrace.

a prominent view that you would not wish to hide with large containers. A grouping of low pots with attractive plantings can lead the eye toward the vista without distracting from it. Conversely, a highly visible and unattractive tangle of telephone poles can be screened from sight by placing large containers of tall plantings on the edge of the deck. Heavy containers can pose problems for decks—place them on or near supporting beams to minimize stress, or support them on a wooden pallet to spread the weight. In addition, water collects beneath pots resting directly on the wood and can warp the boards. Use saucers at least, or elevate pots on trivets similar to those used in the kitchen.

Balconies and Rooftops

Views are commonly the very reason for being on a balcony or rooftop, perhaps surveying the sky above or the city skyline beyond and below. It's possible to showcase this view through the use of carefully positioned container plants. Tall spiral plants, such as junipers, can frame a scene when placed on either side of a seating area.

Balcony and rooftop gardens are frequently too cramped to hold furniture, people, and large pots of flowers. Establish a focal point with one large or medium-size pot, then supplement with smaller ones, carefully placed to take up the least space. Take advantage of vertical surfaces. Outfit railings with hangers that hold a number of smaller pots, or install brackets to support box planters. Add shelves and racks to partitions and walls and create a hanging garden, which affords a pleasant backdrop for furniture without obscuring views.

Small spaces require plants that won't outgrow their welcome. Some gardeners enjoy a junglelike ambiance; others re-

To survive the winter on an exposed windy rooftop, trees, shrubs, and perennials need the security of very large tubs.

sent devoting half their balcony or rooftop garden to a shrub that has gained too much girth. In general, plants for these sites should be chosen for their small stature. Fortunately, there is a nice selection of dwarf trees and shrubs from which to pick. You might consider a containerized rock garden of diminutive perennials, and many of today's annuals are bred for a compact growth rate. In addition, plants with a trailing habit don't take up much room cascading from a balcony or from a wall-mounted container.

When selecting plants, remember that they must thrive in sometimes difficult conditions. Balcony and rooftop gardens can be whipped by strong winds, which can shred large-leaved plants and upend top-heavy ones. Fasten hanging containers securely. Drying winds require extra watering chores. If you live in a cold-winter area and your balcony or rooftop is more than a few stories high, temperatures are likely to be colder than at ground level.

Besides considerations of climate, remember too that soil is heavy, as are some containers. Who is going to haul soil, plants, and pots up the stairs? Be sure your rooftop or bal-

Large tubs with generous amounts of soil also cut down on the water plants need to get through a hot summer.

A crowd of small pots arranged in tiers provides this narrow roof garden with brilliant color all summer long.

cony is structurally able to support the load you're asking it to carry. Evaluate older buildings carefully. Remind yourself of the load as you accumulate pots large and small over time—the weight adds up.

Entryways

Gardeners don't spend a great deal of time at the front door, but making a gardening statement there goes a long way. "Saying it with flowers" at the entryway is a time-honored tradition, and there's no easier way to say welcome than with carefully planned containers.

Many houses have only a relatively small pad of concrete, brick, or wood immediately in front of the door. The obvious choice for maximum impact is to flank the door with large containers and imposing plants, say, 3-foot-tall jars filled with tall, bushy dahlias, or a miniature garden combining plants of several heights and shapes as well as trailers. A formal entrance can be enhanced by topiary or a neatly clipped specimen, perhaps underplanted with smaller blooming annuals for contrast.

Containers in the Landscape 63

Two colorful mounds of geraniums brighten this foliage-dominated entry.

Just imagine this austere entry without its color-coordinated accent of bright flowers and hanging peppers.

Rows of daffodils in plastic pots make this rather somber stairway welcoming.

You can expand a small entryway by setting pots on the steps and/or path that leads to the door. Larger entry areas can accommodate more plants and more pots, perhaps staged on a variety of levels. An unfortunate consideration of modern life is that front-porch containers should be heavy enough that they can't be stolen; if you use small pots, fix them securely to the porch or railing with epoxy, cement, or stout wire.

A recent trend in entryway containers is to vary the plantings by season. Perhaps the most obvious beneficiary of this idea is the mail carrier, who may be greeted by pots of bulbs in springtime, vibrant annuals or shrubs such as oleander in summer, asters and grasses in autumn, and evergreens and berried shrubs in winter. Add flowering branches in the spring or cornstalks at harvest. Vary the containers, as well as the plants, from wicker baskets holding tulips and primroses to a hollow pumpkin hosting a pot of chrysanthemums.

Whether it's a pair of sculpted junipers in Victorian urns or pansies in a hollow log, have some fun enlivening your entry with potted plants. Your visitors (and your mail carrier) will appreciate it, as will you and your family every time you go in or out the door.

Containers in the Landscape 65

Where pavement extends right to the front door, containers provide an entire garden.

66   Containers in the Landscape

Window Boxes and Hanging Baskets

Window boxes bring cascades of foliage and flowers to otherwise unexciting walls. Some are designed to be enjoyed at close range, but most are meant to be viewed from farther away. The tradition is firmly established in Europe, where brilliant window boxes brighten city and country homes alike. In America we've adapted the boxes for use on the railings and walls of decks and patios as well.

Window boxes are commonly made of wood, but you can buy versions in plastic or fiberglass. They can be rustic, fashioned out of reclaimed barn wood, or formal, with precise joinery and paintwork. As with other containers, boxes are most effective when they suit the style of the house. (For information on constructing, planting, and maintaining window boxes, see the chapter "Planting a Container.")

Window boxes are planted in a wide variety of styles. Some window-box gardeners opt for a unified look, includ-

Abundant foliage and flowers of tuberous begonias make a lush traditional window box planting.

ing plants in only a few colors. This can be highly effective or merely unimaginative, depending on the choice of plants. The old red, white, and blue trio of scarlet geraniums, white petunias, and blue lobelias is still useful, but with a little thought it can be freshened up. Change the geraniums to peachy pink and the petunias to soft lavender-blue, and keep the cobalt blue lobelia, for example, to whip up a pleasing pastel froth.

Other gardeners like to go beyond the bounds of tradition. You might create a small "wildflower" garden of annual gaillardia, black-eyed Susans, poppies, and ornamental grasses or a bright, Monet-inspired planting of nasturtiums, zinnias, and celosia. If you treat the box as a shelf that houses a collection of plants in individual pots, you can change the display as things go into and come out of bloom. Use milled sphagnum moss or similar material to hide the pots and to cut moisture loss.

68   Containers in the Landscape

The successful window-box plantings shown in these photos depend on skillful selection of plants, box, and color scheme to contrast with or complement the style and character of the surroundings.

   Whatever scheme you select, from cool to hot, tried and true to off the wall, remember to use flowers of varying sizes, shapes, and textures for maximum impact. Long-blooming plants are important, but so is good foliage. Consider the color and texture of the wall, window curtains, and other nearby elements when choosing colors, plants, and materials. If the box is to be viewed close up, you can use subtle colors and delicate flowers and forms. A box meant to be appreciated from a distance, such as one hung at a second-floor window, needs bolder forms and colors. Trailing plants also help cover the sides and bottom of a box hung above eye level.

Because window boxes are usually long and narrow, they pose some design problems and opportunities. To ensure that the narrow planting space doesn't lead to a two-dimensional composition, combine upright, bushy, mounding, and trailing forms to create a sense of depth. You can make use of the length by repeating certain plants, colors, or forms at intervals, much as you would in a garden border.

Hanging baskets are one of the most delightful forms of container gardening—little floating islands of flowers and foliage. Successful baskets often combine plants chosen primarily for their flowers with some chosen for their handsome leaves and interesting shape. Trailing and cascading plants are essential components. One of the biggest mistakes in

A color-coordinated hanging basket and window box containing petunias, ivy geranium, strawflower, and other plants greet visitors to this English row house.

A hanging basket of colorful flowers and foliage accents a vine-covered wall.

Containers in the Landscape 71

making hanging baskets is to use plants, such as marigolds, that have no desire to cascade down the side. Viewed from below, or even at eye level, all you see is the pot, while the flowers face the sky. Commercially made plastic baskets and pots suspended by some sort of hanger need rambunctious trailing plants to provide as much show as possible below the rim of the basket or pot or, best of all, to disguise the pot altogether.

Orbiting a majestic tree like cartoon spaceships, baskets of donkey's-tail (Sedum morganianum) sway gently in the breeze.

A hanging garden of recycled tin cans makes a striking sight.

The traditional hanging basket doesn't have this problem. Made of a wire frame lined with sphagnum moss and filled with potting soil, this basket is planted all over—top, sides, even on the bottom. (See p. 405 for how to make and plant a traditional hanging basket.) Even plants that don't trail, such as impatiens, appear to trail when planted on the sides or bottom of the basket. Combining these with some trailers, such as cascading petunias, lobelias, nasturtiums, ivy geraniums, vinca vine, rhodochiton, lotus vine, clock vine, wandering Jew, ground ivy, and bougainvillea, produces a fascinating interplay. Sphagnum-lined baskets need a lot of plants to be effective; with plants trailing at different levels, obscuring the moss liner, the result is a ball of hanging flowers.

Baskets can be used in a variety of situations. You can space them at regular intervals along a roofline, railing, or on or between columns. They make excellent focal points dangling from tree limbs or arbors above a patio. A hanging basket can brighten up a gazebo or potting shed as well as lampposts and tall fences. Half-round baskets made of plastic or

A row of boxed geraniums is the perfect cap for this lattice-work fence.

terra-cotta, or wire and sphagnum, can be attached to a house or garage wall, solid fences, and similar spots. Baskets positioned too high lose their visual impact. Those at head height can be a downright hazard in a trafficked area; move them either up out of the way or down to chest height so that no one can possibly overlook them.

Permanent Planters

As the name implies, permanent planters are containers that cannot be moved. Built of a durable material such as stone, brick, or wood, planters are frequently part of the overall design of the house. They flank entries and define terraces and other outdoor living areas, integrating them visually and functionally with the house as a whole. Planters can also delineate areas away from the house, perhaps setting a different tone and style from that of the main building.

Practically speaking, planters are similar to other containers; they're just larger. There are several differences, however.

Made of brick or other solid material, permanent planters complement and extend the architecture of a house while tying it to the garden.

Large masses of soil and heavy materials such as stone and brick don't heat up or lose moisture as quickly. Many planters are constructed without bottoms, so if the native soil beneath drains well, they don't need drainage holes.

When designing a planting for a permanent planter, size is important. You can treat a small permanent planter as you would a large pot, planting anything from a single tree to a profusion of annuals. Larger planters offer greater scope and can be designed like small garden beds or borders. Many permanent planters are intended to be viewed from more than one side, so you can treat them as you would an island bed.

As for any container, proportions are crucial. Architects and builders don't always have the gardener in mind when constructing a permanent planter, and some kinds are very narrow. A tall, narrow planter of brick or stone filled with only short plants looks bottom heavy, a perception emphasized by the weight, both visual and actual, of the construction material. Plants that provide their own visual "weight" in a variety of heights and forms can balance the composition; plants that spill over the edges of the planter help make

A lead-covered trough planter is perfect for this shady spot.

it seem broader than it is. A long planter often looks better when "broken up" by taller annuals, perennials, or shrubs spaced at regular intervals or grouped in an informal manner. Taller plants can also camouflage an eyesore or provide a sense of privacy for a patio or porch.

Because permanent planters are normally in spots where they're seen daily all year long, they need to look presentable in every season. Bare soil and frozen geraniums don't offer a pleasing picture in midwinter. If the planter is deep enough and wide enough, you can incorporate shrubs, perennials, bulbs, and annuals that will produce something of interest in every season.

Shrubs are a good foundation. There are a number of attractive evergreens, both needle-leaved and broad-leaved, with compact growth habits, including dwarf conifers and small azaleas or rhododendrons, as well as holly, mahonia, and nandina. Consider deciduous shrubs that offer attractive seeds, fruit, bark, or branching patterns in winter, such as hip-bearing roses, barberries, or Harry Lauder's walking stick. Perennial evergreen ground covers, such as dianthus, ice plants, ivy, and pachysandra, look good year-round. Include perennials, such as ornamental grasses, that can be enjoyed for their winter foliage or seedpods.

Don't neglect annuals and what they add to the "border" in summer. Tucking trailing verbena or miniature zinnias into a combination of shrubs and perennials is an easy process, as is removing them after frost. Annuals are especially useful for unifying a composition. By incorporating several annuals in a single color, such as verbenas, snapdragons, and dianthus all in red, a planter can have just as strong a "theme" as any area of the garden. A single favorite annual, used repeatedly in and amongst the other plants, also solidifies a composition.

The line between permanent planter and raised bed isn't always clear, as this planter/bed full of tulips demonstrates.

Like a tasseled sentry, a permanent planter full of fuchsias stands guard at a gate.

Having labored to achieve a white border, this gardener decided that a touch of color was needed—just the job for a pot on a stand.

Containers in the Garden

While the obvious use for containers is in transforming a hard surface into a landscape, they can also enhance an existing garden. Containers can bring exotic plants where we least expect them. You wouldn't ordinarily find a lemon tree in a northern herb garden, but coming across a potted one, with its fragrant blossoms, glossy leaves, and colorful fruit, in such hardy surroundings is a delight. In similar situations, other tender plants introduce a pleasing interplay of texture and color. Tropical flowering shrubs that are too large to treat as annuals can nonetheless join the perennial border for the summer. Rather than dig holes for them each spring and repot them each autumn, move a large potted specimen into place—this may take some elbow grease, but it's much easier.

Container plants can expand a small garden by making use of vertical space. Any wall or tall fence can become a spec-

A large pot full of daisies provides a colorful accent in a spot dominated by foliage.

tacular display of pots, either set on shelves or mounted on the wall. Repeat the same container and its cascading contents in a long line, or vary the containers, contents, and positions. The former idea has good impact from a distance, whereas the latter invites lingering and closer inspection.

A large container plant can serve as the focal point in a garden composition, adding structure and mass to a bed where many small-leaved, fine-textured plants grow. In a bed of larger plants, positioned near the front and tucked in among lower-growing flowers, it can provide an accent. Where the terrain is unrelentingly flat, large containers or containers on stumps or pedestals can break up the monotonous level. Groups of potted flowers can draw attention to principal features, such as a reflecting pool. (They can also

Water and lush foliage are complemented nicely by a colorful container.

A splendid urn full of geraniums is the linchpin of this handsome formal design.

do the reverse, diverting attention from the water spigot or garbage enclosure.)

Garden containers are often highly ornamental. An urn or a decorated terra-cotta pot doubles as a piece of sculpture. And, with flowers spilling from their sides, they can be more interesting than a static statue, since their contents grow and change like the surrounding garden. Containers can also enhance garden ornaments, clustered at the feet of fountains or birdbaths. An old-fashioned water pump is much more attractive if buckets and watering cans beneath hold sprays of flowers instead of water. Keep an eye out for containers suitable for this sort of high visibility. Set aside an unusual pot that doesn't blend in with a grouping of containers; it may shine if given star treatment. Imagine the old cart or wheelbarrow planted with a bounty of beautiful blossoms and placed in congenial surroundings.

This small composition inextricably combines plants grown in the ground and in a container.

Pots of pansies usher us from one part of this garden to another. Note how effectively the empty pots add structure and architectural interest.

Shallow pots of begonias are more effective and easier in this situation than trying to establish an in-ground bed.

Pots can also enrich garden paths. Matching containers with similar plantings can tie together an area alongside a path. Container plants can provide transitions between areas of the garden. Lining a walkway leading from one section to another, they can signal a change in color schemes or use of plants. Pots of shiny eggplant or scarlet cherry tomatoes, for instance, can be highly ornamental and hint at the vegetable garden just around the corner. If your garden paths are lit, why not make the most of their circles of light by placing potted plants in them? Plants with white or very pale pastel blossoms, as well as variegated leaves, show up especially well when lit by night lights.

In an awkward shady spot where not much else would thrive, this potted fern provides some greenery.

Containers in the Shade

Some gardeners work diligently to brighten their shady areas with colorful annuals, but there is something to be said for the tranquillity that shade gardens offer. Many shade-loving plants make relatively easy-care container plants, though the number of annuals, perennials, and bulbs that flower in a shady setting is not as large as the spectrum of plants that thrive in sun. Shade gardeners make the most of the opportunity for subtlety that shade affords, relying on the fascinating interplay of variously colored and textured leaves for interest, as well as the ever-changing interplay of light and shadow.

Very dense shade, such as that beneath many evergreen trees and dense deciduous trees or in the shadow of a structure, supports little plant life. Tropical plants that evolved in the gloomy light beneath a rain-forest canopy can brighten up these spots. Often equipped with broad leaves that capture as much filtered light as possible, plants such as philodendron, pothos, sansevieria, or peace lily are commonly grown indoors in areas of low light. You can move them outdoors for seasonal interest in northern climates and year-round beauty in mild ones.

Where brighter light is available—under less dense trees or where the north side of the home is open to the sky—your options expand. They increase on the east side of the house or where sunlight is blocked only part of the day. A wide range of flowering and foliage plants, usually grown as annuals in northern states, can enliven a shady patio or garden. Perhaps the most popular are those with bright blossoms, lead by impatiens and fibrous and tuberous begonias. Many other flowers, such as browallia, calla lilies, and fuchsias, lend a colorful note; foliage plants such as coleus, caladiums, ferns, and fancy-leaved begonias are equally valuable.

Large permanent planters or pots designed to withstand the rigors of winter weather can support a wide variety of

Boston ferns and geraniums hanging in the tree and patio pots enrich this shady spot.

perennials and even shrubs and trees that thrive in shade. Favorite perennials include hostas, astilbes, jack-in-the-pulpit, cardinal flower, ligularia, and goatsbeard as well as a vast array of ferns. Depending on your region, shrubs might include dwarf conifers (especially hemlocks and junipers), dwarf azaleas and rhododendrons, sorbaria, Harry Lauder's walking stick, and daphnes. Larger specimens include shrubs such as yew, serviceberry, Carolina allspice, and dogwoods as well as small trees such as redbud, Japanese maples, fringe tree, laburnum, and Japanese snowbell. All do best in light shade and with attention to watering so that they are not stressed.

When designing containers for a shady location, draw on the widest possible array of plant shapes, colors, and textures. Employ trailers such as ground ivy, ivy, asparagus fern, lotus vine, wandering Jew, and vinca vine for your shade-garden pots for the same impact and softening effect in containers as in sunshine. Group containers to emphasize the contrasts between trailing and upright plants, as well as between broad and fine-textured leaves. Plants with variegated or otherwise marked leaves add interest; these markings show up all the better in shade.

Water Gardens

The fascinating world of aquatic plants is not just for those with a stream or pond. A number of these plants can be easily grown in a container on the patio or balcony. Many gardeners' first love will be water lilies—for good reason—but other plants can share the same container pond. There are dramatic, large-leaved aquatic cannas, horsetail, elephant's-ear, arrowhead, reeds, cyperus, pickerel, and monkey flower. A few moisture-loving perennials can also join this group, such as purple loosestrife, ligularia, cardinal flower, Japanese and Louisiana irises, and houttuynia.

Use your imagination when choosing containers. A dab of epoxy and a plastic plug can convert a handsome terra-cotta pot into a miniature pond. The larger the pot the better, since evaporation will keep you busy topping up the water level. Glazed ceramic pots, sometimes called Oriental fishbowls, make a perfect home for floating water hyacinths or a miniature water lily. These graceful pots are often decorated in beautiful patterns and add a strong presence to a patio or balcony even before the plants are added.

Perhaps the most popular container for a small water garden is the half whiskey barrel. Moderate price and large size recommend it for home use. Small containers may support only a few plants, but a single half-barrel can accommodate

Containers in the Landscape 85

Running water is a soothing presence in the garden. Two very different styles are shown here, one employing a wooden half-barrel, the other a more elaborate pond about the size of a permanent planter.

a small water lily, several bog plants such as pickerel or cyperus, and a few small floating plants such as water lettuce, duckweed, and water clover. Even goldfish are possible if you ensure that they have enough oxygen to survive. Depending on the size of the container and the number of fish and plants, this can be accomplished by growing oxygenating

Perched on the edge of a larger water garden, a pot full of moisture-loving sweet flag irises fits right in.

Water lilies grace this small water garden created from a galvanized metal tank stuccoed and embedded with ceramic tiles.

water plants, such as anacharis, or by installing a fountain or oxygenating pump.

A small pump, suitable for an aquarium, may be all you need and can be purchased from a store specializing in tropical fish. To run a fountain, you will need a more powerful unit, although the constant motion in a small container is not beneficial to many aquatic plants. It will inhibit the flowering of water lilies, for example. For the soothing sound of splashing water, buy a simple recirculating pump to trickle water from the mouth of a fish, frog, or cherub statue. Be sure you have a grounded, waterproof source of electricity for pumps—it is unsafe to simply run an extension cord out the bedroom window. (For more on planting and caring for container water gardens, see p. 412.)

Edible Gardening

Gardeners are exploring new territory in making fruits, vegetables, and herbs integral elements of their container gardens. Some simply tuck in the lettuce, basil, or eggplant with the marigolds and daisies—there's no reason why the beautiful pot of plants you admire in the morning can't provide tonight's salad as well. Other gardeners are geared toward high-yield container production.

Like their garden counterparts, container edibles offer homegrown flavor and the peace of mind that comes from knowing what (if anything) has been sprayed on them. In addition, container growing allows some gardeners to extend

As attractive as it is tasty, this little vegetable garden includes 'Quickpick' tomatoes, 'Holiday Chili' peppers, and 'Lemon Gem' marigolds.

A range of fruit-bearing plants, such as the peach tree shown here, do well in containers.

the growing season by being able to move their gardens to shelter when cold snaps threaten at one end of the season or the other. Containers provide gardeners plagued by poor soil the opportunity for immediate crops while long-term soil improvement goes on in the garden. Weeds and certain pests are easier to control in containers, and you can move containers if necessary to capture as much available sunlight as possible. Positioned close to the kitchen door, a container of mixed herbs or a hanging basket of cherry tomatoes or mint puts fresh flavor only a snip away.

In suitable pots, most vegetables grow as well as or better than they do in the ground. There are a few notable exceptions, such as corn, and some types of vegetables may not be worth your effort. In recent years, many edible plants, especially vegetables, have been bred for container growing. Efforts have been concentrated on producing dwarf, space-saving plants with high yields. The most promising and productive vegetables for container gardening include the leaf crops—lettuce, spinach, chard, and cabbage; root crops, such as radishes, carrots, green onions, and beets; and bush varieties of squash and cucumbers, tomatoes, peppers, and egg-

Strawberry jars are ideal for miniature herb gardens—this one contains Cuban oregano, rosemary, Oriental chives, purple sage, and lemon variegated thyme.

plant. Most herbs take readily to container culture, and many fruits, particularly dwarf varieties, can succeed in containers.

All edible plants can be combined with flowers, and many are ornamental in their own right. For maximum yield, most vegetables should be grown separately so that they do not have to compete with other plants for water and nutrients. There's little harm, however, in tossing in a few marigolds at the base of an eggplant or tomato plant. Some gardeners enjoy designing containers that hold several varieties of herbs or vegetables. The pockets of the classic strawberry jar, for instance, can house a number of trailing or small-size culinary herbs, such as thyme, savory, and chives.

Single potted specimens of some edible plants are handsome additions to container groupings. Rosemary, lemon verbena, bay, and parsley are tasty and attractive. Dwarf fruit trees are pretty in both their flowering and fruiting stages. Add pots of edible flowers, such as nasturtiums, pot marigolds, and pansies, and no one will know that your highly ornamental garden can be nibbled on as well. If you mix ornamentals with edibles, be careful about pesticides— it's safest to rely on proven organic pest and disease controls.

Specialties

Several important types of container plants have devoted followings. Standards, topiary, and bonsai require a mastery of techniques and skills more involved than those needed to grow most plants in containers. These techniques are beyond the scope of this book, but if the photos shown here inspire you, most libraries will have books devoted to each subject.

A standard is a plant, usually woody or semiwoody, trained to treelike form. A single bare stem (or multiple stems twined to look single), sometimes supported by a stake, is topped by a mass of foliage and flowers. Many plants can be trained as standards. Perhaps the most familiar is a standard rose, handy for bringing blossoms up to nose level. Other candidates include citrus, bay, lantana, geraniums, African mallow, hibiscus, and herbs such as rosemary and scented geraniums.

Standards traditionally have been used to flank entries, such as the 'Showbiz' rose standards shown here.

Topiary is the art of training plants into ornamental shapes. When the growth on top of a standard takes on a geometric shape through careful clipping, it becomes a form of topiary. Many shapes are possible, including balls, domes, and cones and combinations thereof; fanciful animals and creatures are popular. Training woody plants to assume these shapes unsupported takes patience (a topiary may be years in the training). It takes practice to learn which branches to keep and which to discard, as well as a good eye. Woody plants with small leaves and dense growth, such as junipers and boxwood, lend themselves to topiary creations.

Another form of topiary, where climbing plants such as ivy or creeping fig are trained into wire forms, produces results faster. One method is to weave stems around a wire support in the shape you desire. Another is to fill a wire skeleton with

Standards also make fine focal points on a patio or terrace, as shown by this fuchsia ('Lord Byron').

organic matter such as sphagnum moss, onto which clinging vines are trained. Sometimes soil fills the interior, and the whole operation is very much like a wire-cage hanging basket. With a quick-growing creeper and a little imagination, you can have green dinosaurs, roosters, and reindeer roaming your patio in a short time.

Standards and topiary lend a decidedly formal look to outdoor areas. Large specimens have a commanding presence. They can be used to enhance a doorway or gate or to stand guard on a fountain or birdbath. The geometric shapes are

Containers in the Landscape 93

Top: With wire, a dependable vine, and a little patience, you can create simple topiaries like this pair of rosemary hearts. Above: If you're more ambitious, you might try something like the teddy bear's picnic.

94 Containers in the Landscape

Carefully shaped and pruned over many years, bonsai plants are fascinating creations. Shown here are a 39-year-old crape myrtle (top) and an 89-year-old Atlas cedar (above).

You needn't be a bonsai devotee to enjoy the striking shapes of small trees and shrubs in your garden. Knowledgeable training and pruning can create handsome specimens such as the cypress shown here.

effective at night, either backlit by floodlights or decorated with tiny lights (which you would be wise to unplug during routine trimming). A single standard, such as a rose, can add height and substance to a grouping of flowering annuals and perennials. To help maintain their shape, all standards and topiary need a quarter turn weekly; otherwise, the growth on the side facing the sun will thrive while the other side thins out.

The art of bonsai springs from Asia, but gardeners around the world embrace it. It is said that the inspiration for bonsai was evergreens growing at the timberline, dwarfed by the harsh climate and shaped by prevailing winds. Limiting and shaping the growth of trees and shrubs by careful pruning and training, the bonsai artist attempts to capture the essence of a plant on a very small scale. The relationship between the plant and its container, which is often small and shallow, is very important. Commonly cultivated bonsai plants include evergreens (especially junipers), Japanese maples, and some flowering shrubs and trees.

Your garden need not have an Oriental theme for you to enjoy bonsai. One specimen may make a delightful accent. A number of bonsai containers can be somewhat more difficult to display. Since each is a story in itself, they may not be at their best in a group. Individual shelves mounted on a wall or simple pedestals provide for group display but individual viewing. Aficionados often create entire environments designed to show their prize bonsai to best advantage. Check with local garden clubs or your extension agent to see if there is a bonsai organization in your area; members are usually happy to help novices get started.

The Plant Gallery

The plant portraits that follow will help you put a "face" to the plant names in the essays and encyclopedia. They are grouped according to plant type: annuals, perennials, bulbs, vines, deciduous trees and shrubs, and evergreen trees and shrubs. A short description accompanies each plate, along with the plant's botanical and common names, its height, its hardiness zone rating, and the page on which you'll find its written encyclopedia entry.

A Word About Color

Color, more than many other visual attributes, is in the eye of the beholder. What one person describes as blue, another may call lavender or even purple. And it's not just the names that vary. Light and shade, time of day, and other colors nearby can all affect what we actually see. A leaf that appears rich red in the midday sun may be a deep lavender in late-afternoon shade.

As you look at the photos on the following pages, remember that the camera, no less than the eye, captures the color as it appears at a certain moment. Add to that the natural variation among plants and the difficulties of printing colors precisely, and you'll see why it doesn't pay to count on your plant having exactly the color you see in the photograph.

Annuals

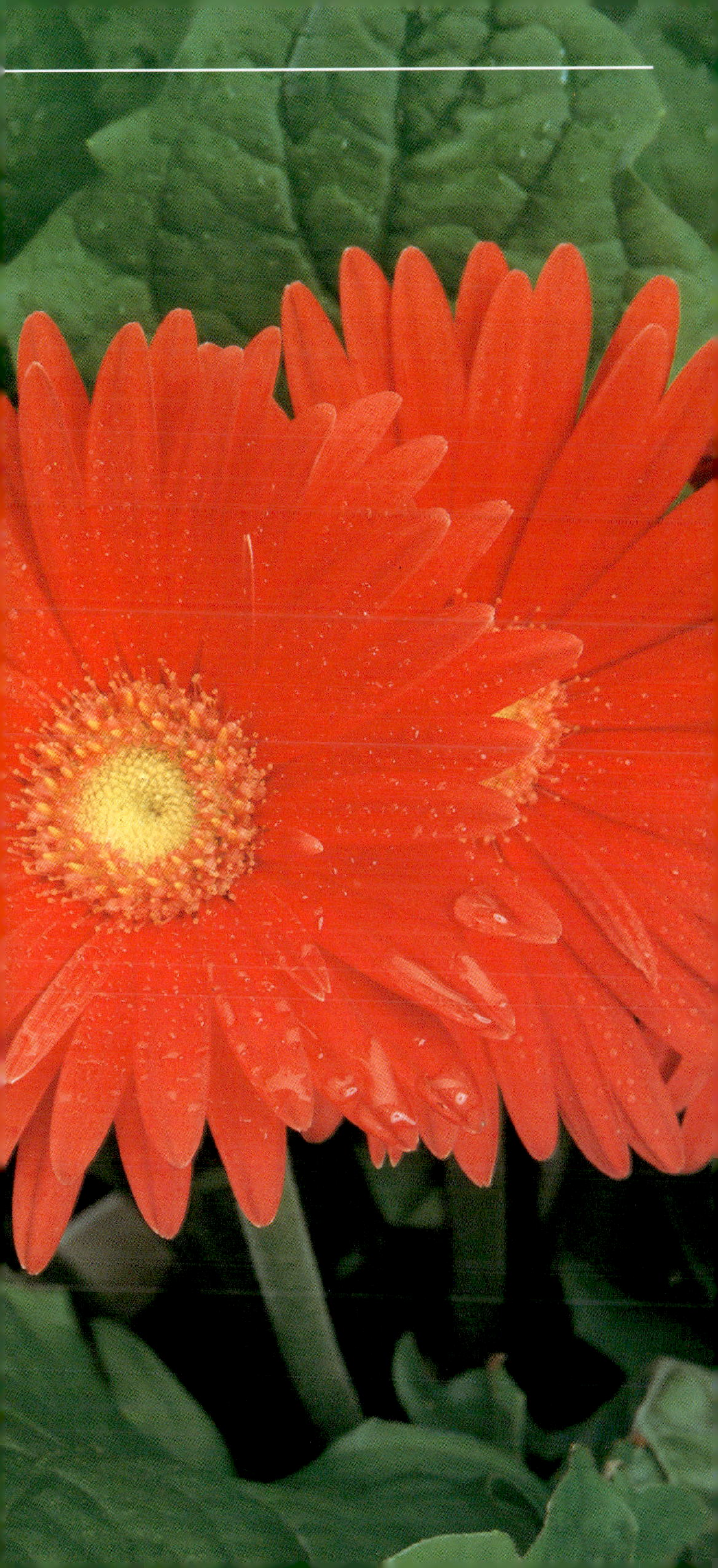

100 Annuals

Aloysia triphylla

*Lemon verbena
Height: 3–4 ft.
Tender woody herb
grown as annual in
cold climates
Zone 8*

*Full sun
p. 210*

***Antirrhinum
majus***

*Snapdragon
Height: 6–36 in.
Cheerful plant;
grows year-round
in mild climates*

*Full or part sun
p. 212*

Annuals 101

***Arctotis* garden hybrids**

*African daisies
Height: 12–18 in.
Cheerful as edging
for mixed
containers*

*Full or part sun
p. 213*

***Asparagus
densiflorus***

*Asparagus fern
Height: 2 ft. or
more
'Myers' shown here
Zone 9*

*Full or part sun
p. 215*

102 Annuals

Begonia* × *semperflorens-cultorum

Wax begonia
Height: 6–12 in.
Bushy mounds covered with flowers for months on end

Sun to shade
p. 218

Brassica oleracea

Flowering kale
Height: 12 in.
Effective in spring or fall container plantings

Full or part sun
p. 223

Annuals 103

Browallia speciosa

Bush violet
Height: 12–24 in.
Terrific trailer for hanging baskets
Zone 10

Part sun to shade
p. 224

Calendula officinalis

Pot marigold
Height: to 2 ft.
Easy to grow;
'Family Circle' mix shown here

Full or part sun
p. 228

104 Annuals

Capsicum annuum

Ornamental pepper
Height: 8–14 in.
Brightens a mixed container; easy from seed; 'Red Missile' shown here

Full sun
p. 233

Catharanthus roseus

Madagascar periwinkle
Height: 1–2 ft.
Long-blooming; 'Magic Carpet Pink' shown here

Full or part sun
p. 235

Annuals 105

Celosia argentea Cockscomb Full sun
Height: to 2 ft. p. 236
Thrives in heat

Chrysanthemum multicaule

Height: 6–8 in.
Cheerful window-box or hanging-basket plant

Full sun
p. 240

106 Annuals

Chrysanthemum parthenium

*Feverfew
Height: 1–3 ft.
Long-blooming;
pungent leaves*

Full or part sun
p. 241

Coleus blumei hybrids

*Coleus
Height: 1–2 ft.
Complements
many plants; 'Fiji
Red' shown here*

Part sun or filtered shade
p. 246

Annuals 107

Cosmos *sulphureus* — *Yellow cosmos*
Height: to 3 ft.
'Lady Bird Orange' shown here
Full sun
p. 249

Dahlia hybrids — *Dahlias*
Height: 1–6 ft.
Colorful flowers from midsummer on
Full sun
p. 253

108 Annuals

Dianthus chinensis hybrids

China pinks
Height: 6–9 in.
Easy from seed;
quick to flower

Full sun
p. 257

Exacum affine

Persian violet
Height: 1–1½ ft.
Good window-box
plant; flowers for a
long period

Full sun
p. 261

Annuals 109

***Fuchsia* hybrids**

Height: varies
Use in hanging baskets, as standards, as specimens

Part sun to shade
p. 267

Gerbera jamesonii *Gerbera daisy* *Full or part shade*
Height: to 18 in. *p. 269*
Perennial grown as annual; 'Happy Pot' shown here
Zone 9

110 *Annuals*

Gomphrena globosa

Globe amaranth
Height: 8–16 in.
Loves hot weather;
flowers can be
dried

Full sun
p. 271

Heliotropium arborescens

Heliotrope
Height: 12–36 in.
Long-blooming;
can be strongly
scented; 'Marina'
shown here
Zone 10

Full sun
p. 277

Annuals 111

Hibiscus rosa-sinensis

Rose-of-China
Height: 3–4 ft.
Perennial shrub
often grown as
annual
Zone 10

Full or part sun
p. 283

Impatiens New Guinea hybrids

Patient Lucy
Height: 2–3 ft.
Year-round flowers
outdoors and in

Part sun
p. 291

112 Annuals

Impatiens wallerana

Impatiens
Height: to 2 ft.
Fine specimen plant; 'Grand Prix' shown here

Shade
p. 291

Lantana camara Common lantana
Height: 2–4 ft.
Perennial grown as annual; 'Variegata' shown here
Zone 8 or 7

Full sun
p. 302

Annuals   113

Lantana montevidensis

Trailing lantana
Height: 6–18 in.
Perennial grown as annual; good for hanging baskets
Zone 7

Full sun
p. 303

Lobelia erinus | Edging lobelia
Height: 4–8 in.
Superb trailer or edger; 'Blue Cascade' shown here | Full sun or part shade
p. 311

114 Annuals

Lobularia maritima

Sweet alyssum
Height: to 6 in.
Superb container plant with many uses

Full sun
p. 312

Nicotiana alata

Flowering tobacco
Height: 1–3 ft.
Some are sweetly fragrant

Full or part sun
p. 327

Annuals 115

Ocimum basilicum

*Sweet basil, common basil
Height: to 2 ft.
Shown from left:
'Golden Bouquet',
lemon basil, 'Fine Vert Nain'*

*Full or part sun
p. 328*

Papaver nudicaule

*Iceland poppy
Height: 1–2 ft.
'Champagne Bubbles' shown here
Zone 2*

*Full sun
p. 331*

116 Annuals

Pelargonium × hortorum

Common or zonal geranium
Height: 6–48 in.
Versatile tender perennial grown as annual

Full sun
p. 333

Pelargonium peltatum

Ivy geranium
Height: 1 ft.
Excellent trailer for hanging baskets

Full sun
p. 334

Annuals 117

***Pelargonium* spp.**

*Scented geraniums
Height: varies
Pleasing fragrance;
P. tomentosum
shown here*

*Full sun
p. 334*

Petunia × *hybrida* | *Common garden petunia
Height: 1–3 ft.
For pots, window boxes, hanging baskets, and more* | *Full or part sun
p. 335*

Portulaca grandiflora

*Moss rose
Height: under 1 ft.
Cheerful cascading plant; 'Sunglow' shown here*

*Full sun
p. 341*

Salvia elegans

*Pineapple sage
Height: 4–5 ft.
Flavorful leaves; hummingbirds like flowers
Zone 9*

*Full sun
p. 357*

Annuals 119

Salvia farinacea

Mealy blue sage
Height: to 2–3 ft.
Blooms for months
Zone 8 or 7

Full or part sun
p. 357

Salvia splendens Salvia Full or part sun
Height: 1–3 ft. p. 359
Nonstop flowers;
dwarf, medium,
and tall strains

120 Annuals

Senecio cineraria   Dusty-miller
Height: to 12 in.
Makes clashing
colors compatible,
more or less

Full or part sun
p. 364

Tagetes lucida

Mexican mint
marigold
Height: to 1 ft.
Grown for rich
anise fragrance of
foliage
Zone 8

Full sun
p. 366

Tagetes patula

*French marigold
Height: 6–14 in.
T. patula
foreground;
T. tenuifolia on left*

*Full sun
p. 366*

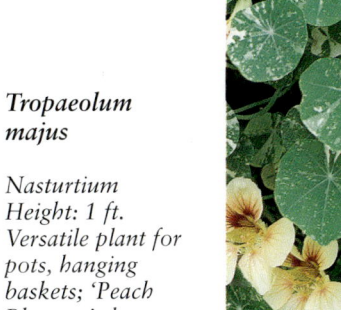

Tropaeolum majus

*Nasturtium
Height: 1 ft.
Versatile plant for
pots, hanging
baskets; 'Peach
Blossom' shown
here*

*Full or part sun
p. 374*

122 Annuals

Verbena × hybrida

*Garden verbena
Height: 6–12 in.
Mixes well in
containers; some
types trail*

*Full sun or
afternoon shade
p. 377*

Viola × wittrockiana

*Pansy
Height: to 12 in.
A favorite offering
many colors*

*Full sun or
afternoon shade
p. 381*

Annuals 123

Zinnia angustifolia

Height: 12 in. Billows of small flowers through hottest weather; 'Classic' shown here

Full sun
p. 386

Zinnia elegans cultivars

Common zinnias Height: 1–3 ft. Easy to grow; wide range of colors and sizes; 'Yellow Marvel' shown here

Full sun
p. 387

Perennials

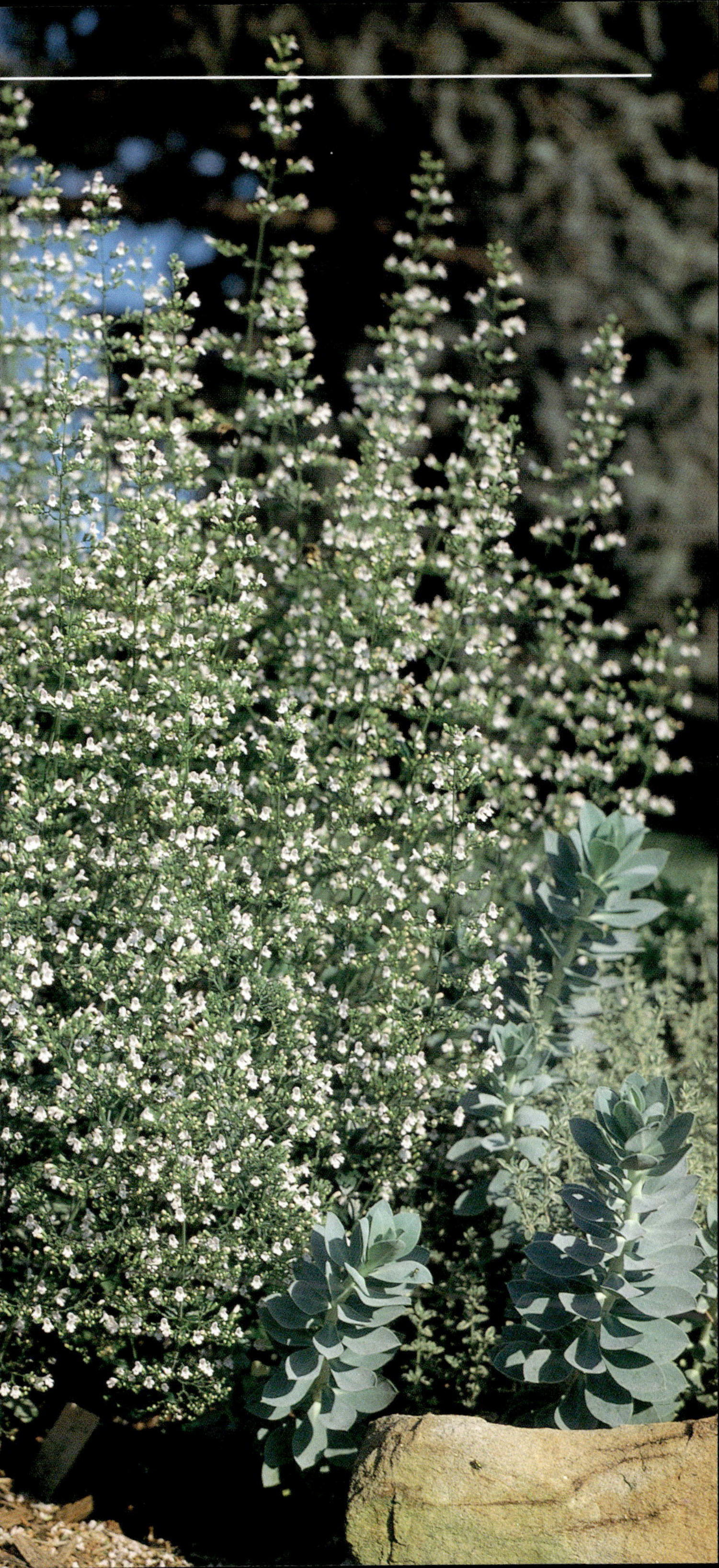

126 Perennials

Acanthus mollis

*Bear's-breeches
Height: 1½–2 ft.
Lush foliage; spring and early-summer flowers
Zone 6*

*Sun to shade
p. 204*

Achillea 'Moonshine'

*Yarrow
Height: 2 ft.
Dry flowers for winter arrangements
Zone 3*

*Full sun
p. 206*

Perennials 127

Acorus gramineus 'Variegatus'

Variegated Japanese sweet flag
Height: 12 in.
Thrives in shallow water
Zone 6

Part sun to shade
p. 272

Ajuga reptans

Bugleweed, carpet bugle
Height: 4–8 in.
Use as edging, ground cover, or companion plant
Zone 3

Sun to shade
p. 208

128 *Perennials*

Allium schoenoprasum

Chives
Height: 12 in.
Tasty pot plant;
handsome with
other herbs
Zone 3

Full or part sun
p. 210

Artemisia 'Powis Castle'

Height: 2–3 ft.
Handsome
specimen or foil for
other plants
Zone 6

Sun to shade
p. 214

Perennials 129

Astilbe × *arendsii* **hybrids**

*Height: 2–3 ft.
Summer and fall interest from foliage, flowers, and seed heads
Zone 2*

*Part sun to shade
p. 215*

| *Athyrium goeringianum* 'Pictum' | Japanese painted fern Height: 12–18 in. A beautiful and popular deciduous fern Zone 3 | Shade p. 263 |

130 Perennials

Bergenia cordifolia — Heartleaf bergenia
Height: 12–18 in.
Striking foliage plant for partly shaded patio
Zone 3
Part shade
p. 221

Calamintha nepeta
Height: 12–24 in.
Fragrant leaves; favorite of bees
Zone 5
Sun or part shade
p. 228

Perennials 131

Campanula poscharskyana

*Serbian bellflower
Height: 6–9 in.
Trailing stems
dangle from
hanging baskets
Zone 3*

*Full or part sun
p. 232*

Carex morrowii 'Aureo-variegata'

*Variegated
Japanese sedge
Height: 6–8 in.
Mix with ferns and
hostas or in shady
window box
Zone 6 or 5*

*Part sun to shade
p. 272*

132 Perennials

Ceratostigma plumbaginoides

Dwarf plumbago
Height: 12 in.
Fall bloom and leaf colors; good under trees
Zone 5

Full or part sun
p. 236

Chrysanthemum × morifolium

Florist's chrysanthemum
Height: 6 in.–6 ft.
Longtime favorite for fall flowers
Hardiness depends on cultivar

Full sun or light shade
p. 239

Chrysanthemum pacificum

Height: 1–1½ ft.
Grown primarily for handsome foliage
Zone 7

Full sun
p. 240

Coreopsis verticillata

Thread-leaved coreopsis
Height: 2–3 ft.
Airy foliage and flowers look good in hanging basket
Zone 3

Full sun
p. 247

Delosperma cooperi

Purple ice plant
Height: 2–4 in.
Sun-loving, trouble-free succulent
Zone 6 or 5

Full sun
p. 255

Dianthus × *allwoodii* hybrids

Cottage pinks
Height: 8–16 in.
Charming flowers have intoxicating fragrance
Zone 4

Full sun
p. 256

Perennials 135

**Dianthus
deltoides**

Maiden pink
Height: 8 in.
Blooms abundantly
in early summer
Zone 3

Full sun or part
shade
p. 258

**Eupatorium
coelestinum**

Hardy ageratum
Height: 18–24 in.
Blooms for 4–6
weeks in late
summer and fall
Zone 6

Full or part sun
p. 260

Festuca ovina* var. *glauca	*Blue fescue* *Height: 6–12 in.* *Small clumping grass for planters or window boxes* *Zone 4*	*Full sun* *p. 273*

Hamelia patens	*Firebush, hummingbird bush* *Height: 2–3 ft.* *Showy centerpiece for mixed pot* *Zone 8*	*Full or part sun* *p. 275*

Helleborus orientalis

*Lenten rose
Height: 18–24 in.
Grow for foliage as well as flowers
Zone 5*

*Part sun to shade
p. 278*

***Hemerocallis* hybrids**

*Hybrid daylilies
Height: 1–6 ft.
Thousands of cultivars; 'Stella d'Oro' shown here
Zone 4*

*Full sun
p. 279*

138 Perennials

Heuchera hybrids

*Coralbells, alumroot
Height: 12 in. (foliage) to 18 in. (flowers)
H. sanguinea 'Snowstorm' shown here
Zone 4*

*Full sun or part shade
p. 281*

Hosta species and cultivars

*Hostas, plantain lilies, funkias
Height: 6 in.–3 ft. (foliage)
A wide range of cultivars and sizes
Zone 4*

*Part or full shade
p. 284*

Perennials 139

Lamium maculatum

Spotted dead nettle
Height: under 6 in.
Handsome but invasive; 'Beacon Silver' shown here
Zone 4

Sun to shade
p. 301

Lavandula angustifolia

English lavender
Height: 1½ ft.
Fragrant flowers; grow as annual; 'Nana' shown here
Zone 5

Full sun
p. 305

140 Perennials

Liriope muscari Lilyturf Part sun
Height: 1–2 ft. p. 310
Shown here with
deep purple
verbena flowers
Zone 5

Lysimachia Moneywort, Part sun to shade
nummularia creeping Jennie p. 315
Height: 2–3 in.
Hanging-basket or
edging plant
Zone 3

Perennials 141

Melissa officinalis

Lemon balm
Height: 2 ft.
Leaves have lovely
aroma and flavor
Zone 5

Part sun
p. 318

| *Mentha suaveolens* | Pineapple mint Height: 1 ft. or more Most ornamental mint is 'Variegata', shown here Zone 5 | Sun to shade p. 319 |

142 Perennials

Nephrolepis exaltata

*Sword fern
Height: to 5 ft.
Handsome in hanging basket or on stand
Zone 9*

*Shade
p. 264*

***Phalaris arundinacea* 'Picta'**

*Ribbon grass
Height: 2–4 ft.
Trouble-free ornamental; good foil for flowers
Zone 4*

*Sun to shade
p. 273*

Perennials 143

Phormium tenax

New Zealand flax
Height: to 9 ft.
For a tropical look;
'Sundowner' shown
here
Zone 8

Full or part sun
p. 274

Primula × polyantha

Polyanthus
primrose
Height: 8 in.
Early spring
flowers in
numerous pure,
clear colors
Zone 3

Part sun to shade
p. 342

Salvia greggii

Cherry sage, autumn sage
Height: 3 ft.
Colorful scented flowers from spring to fall
Zone 9 or 8

Full or part sun
p. 358

Salvia officinalis

Garden sage
Height: 2 ft.
Grow as seasoning or to make tea
Zone 5

Full sun
p. 359

Saxifraga stolonifera

Strawberry geranium
Height: 6 in.
Use in hanging basket or mixed container
Zone 7

Part or full shade
p. 361

Sedum 'Autumn Joy'

Height: 1½–2 ft.
Attractive foliage, flowers, and seed heads, spring to fall
Zone 3

Full or part sun
p. 363

146 Perennials

Sempervivum tectorum

Hen-and-chickens
Height: 4 in.
(foliage)
A whimsical plant
essential in a
container garden
Zone 4

Full or part sun
p. 363

Thymus × citriodorus

Lemon thyme
Height: to 12 in.
Lemony fragrance;
'Argenteus' shown
here
Zone 4

Full sun
p. 372

Perennials 147

Vinca major

Large periwinkle
Height: 6 in.
Good trailer for
hanging baskets,
window boxes;
'Variegata' shown
here
Zone 7

Sun to shade
p. 380

| ***Yucca filamentosa*** | Adam's-needle
Height: 2–3 ft.
(foliage); 5–6 ft.
(flowers)
Tough, long-lived
plant flowers in
June
Zone 5 | Full or part sun
p. 383 |

Bulbs

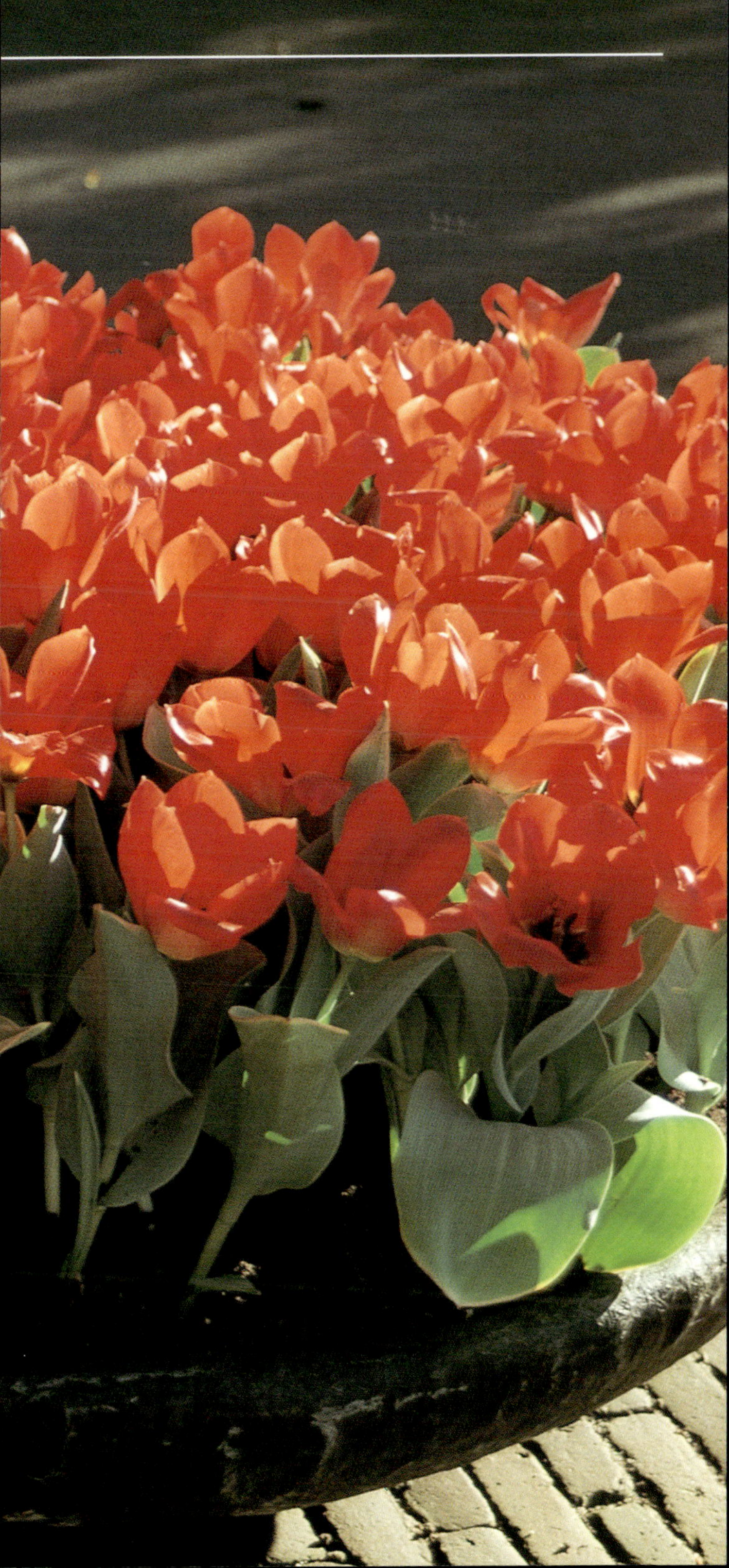

150 *Bulbs*

Agapanthus orientalis

Lily-of-the-Nile
Height: to 5 ft.
Beautiful flowers
are long-lasting
Zone 8

Part or full sun
p. 206

Begonia Tuberhybrida hybrids

Tuberous begonias
Height: to 2 ft.
Upright and
pendulous types are
superb in
containers
All zones

Part sun to shade
p. 219

Bulbs 151

Caladium × *hortulanum*

Caladium
Height: 1–3 ft.
Handsome foliage for shady patio; 'Candidum' shown here
All zones

Part sun to shade
p. 227

Canna hybrids

Height: 2–6 ft.
Striking patio plants; 'The President' shown here
Zone 8

Full or part sun
p. 232

Clivia miniata

Clivia, kaffir lily
Height: to 2 ft.
Familiar houseplant does well outdoors, too
Zone 9

Sun to shade
p. 245

Crocosmia 'Lucifer'

Crocosmia, montbretia
Height: 3 ft.
Handsome foliage and flowers
Zone 5

Full or part sun
p. 249

Bulbs 153

Crocus vernus
*Dutch crocus,
common crocus
Height: 4–8 in.
Lovely in spring;
'Little Dorritt'
shown here
Zone 5*

*Full or part sun
p. 250*

Cyclamen persicum
*Florist's cyclamen
Height: 6–12 in.
Fall to spring
bloom in warm-
winter climates
Zone 9*

*Part sun to shade
p. 251*

154　*Bulbs*

Gloriosa superba　Gloriosa lily
Height: 4–6 ft.
Aptly named;
attracts
hummingbirds
Grown as annual;
all zones

Full or part sun
p. 270

Hyacinthus orientalis

Hyacinth
Height: 6–10 in.
Group with early
spring bulbs; bees
love it
Zone 5

Full or part sun
p. 286

Iris reticulata

Reticulated iris
Height: 4 in.
(flowers); 18 in.
(foliage)
Early spring bloom
Zone 3

Full sun
p. 294

Lilium
Asiatic hybrids

Height: 2–6 ft.
Striking flowers
from May through
June; 'Dreamland'
shown here
Zone 4

Full or part sun
p. 309

156 Bulbs

Lilium
Oriental hybrids

*Height: 3–6 ft.
Last lilies to flower
in summer;
'Stargazer' shown
here
Zone 5*

*Full or part sun
p. 310*

| **Muscari armeniacum** | *Grape hyacinth Height: 6–8 in. Early-spring-flowering perennial Zone 4* | *Full or part sun p. 320* |

Bulbs 157

Narcissus
daffodils

Height: 6–20 in.
As welcome in
containers as in the
ground
Zone 4

Full or part sun
p. 323

Oxalis spp.

Height: 6–10 in.
Valued for foliage
and flowers, alone
or with other
moisture lovers
Zone 7

Full or part sun
p. 330

158 Bulbs

Ranunculus asiaticus

Persian buttercup
Height: 18 in.
Floriferous perennial; 'Tecolote Hybrids' shown here
Zone 8

Full sun
p. 347

Tulbaghia violacea

Society garlic
Height: 1–2 ft.
Repeat bloomer with evergreen leaves
Zone 9

Full sun
p. 375

Bulbs 159

Tulipa **garden tulips**

Height: 6–24 in.
Many sizes and
colors available to
welcome spring
Zone 4

Full sun
p. 375

Zantedeschia albomaculata

Calla lily
Height: 24 in.
Often grown as
annual; flowers
good for cutting
Zone 8

Part sun
p. 385

Vines

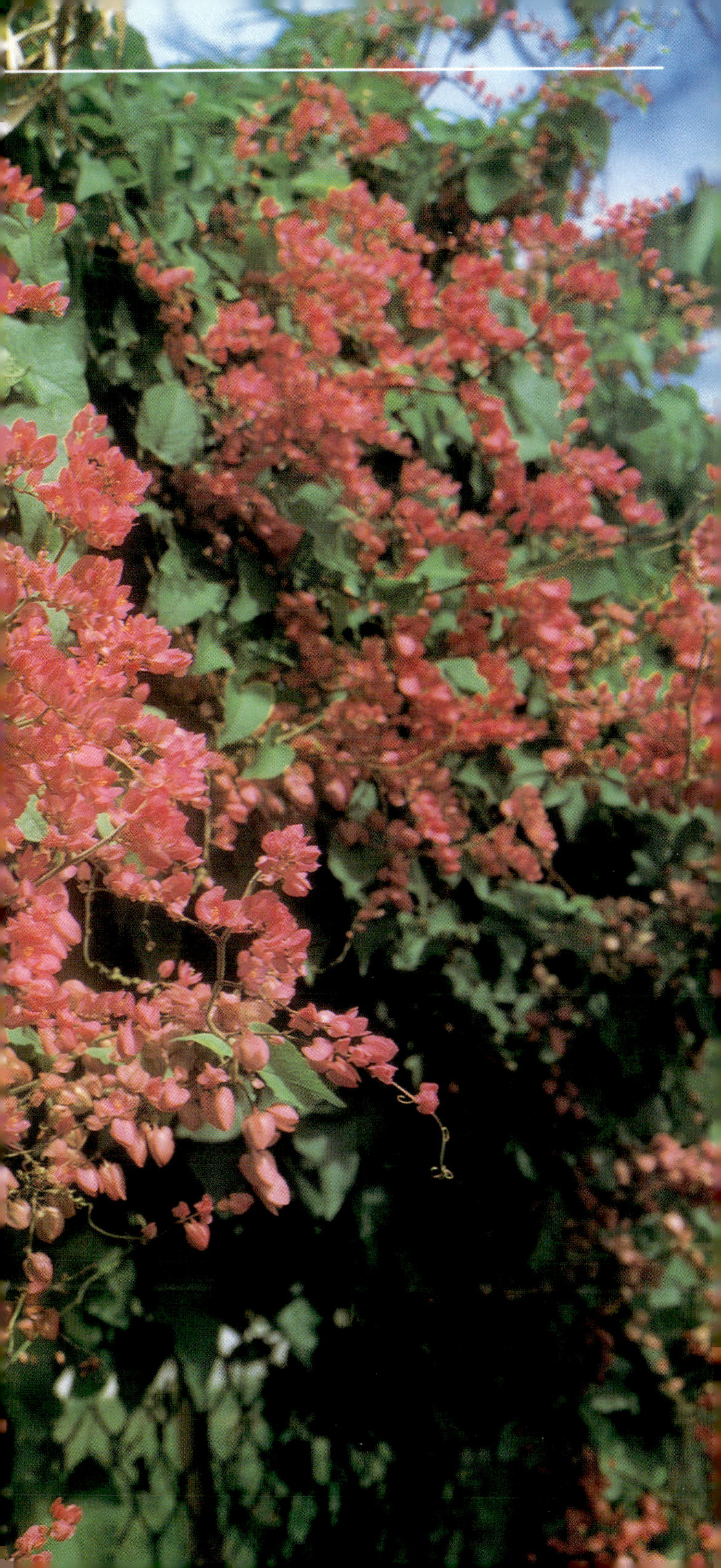

162　Vines

**Antigonon
leptopus**

Coral vine, queen's-
wreath
Height: 6–10 ft.
Grows quickly to
cover lightweight
trellis
Zone 8

Full sun
p. 211

**Bougainvillea
hybrids**

Height: to 20 ft.
Types for hanging
baskets or patio
tubs
Zone 10 or 9

Full sun or light
shade
p. 222

Vines 163

Clematis large-flowered hybrids

*Height: to 15 ft.
Lovely on trellis or draped over shrub or tree
Zone 5*

*Full or part sun
p. 243*

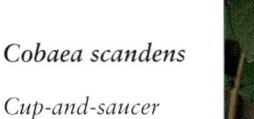

Cobaea scandens

*Cup-and-saucer vine
Height: 8–12 ft.
Evergreen perennial grown as annual; thrives in long, hot, humid summers
Zone 9*

*Full sun
p. 245*

164 Vines

**Euonymus
fortunei selections**

*Winter creeper
Height: varies
Good as ground
cover under tree or
shrub
Zone 5*

*Sun to shade
p. 259*

Ficus pumila

*Creeping fig
Height: to 25 ft. or
more
Good for hanging
basket or topiary,
as shown here
Zone 7*

*Full or part sun
p. 267*

Vines 165

Gelsemium sempervirens
Carolina jessamine
Height: 5–6 ft.
Profuse early-spring flowers are fragrant
Zone 8

Full sun
p. 268

Hedera helix
English ivy
Height: 6 in.–6 ft.
Hanging pots, standards, topiary; 'Rochester' shown here
Zone 6 or 5

Sun to shade
p. 276

Ipomoea purpurea

*Morning glory
Height: to 15 ft.
Excellent screen for patio or deck
Annual; all zones*

*Full sun
p. 293*

Jasminum nitidum

*Star jasmine
Height: to 12 ft.
Evergreen with lovely scented summer flowers
Zone 10*

*Full or part sun
p. 296*

Vines 167

Lathyrus odoratus

*Sweet pea
Height: to 6 ft.
Sweet scent; 'Bijou
Mix' shown here
Annual; all zones*

*Full sun or
afternoon shade
p. 304*

Lonicera × heckrottii

*Gold-flame
honeysuckle
Height: 10–20 ft.
Profuse flowers for
weeks
Zone 5 or 4*

*Full or part sun
p. 313*

168 Vines

***Mandevilla × amabilis* 'Alice du Pont'**

*Height: 10 ft. or more
Flowers continuously until frost
Zone 10*

*Full sun or afternoon shade
p. 317*

Passiflora × alatocaerulea

*Passionvine, passionflower
Height: 10–12 ft.
Quick cover for sunny patio
Zone 8 or 7*

*Full sun
p. 332*

Thunbergia alata

Black-eyed Susan vine
Height: 3–8 ft.
Grow on trellis, over shrub, or in hanging basket; grown as annual
All zones

Full or part sun
p. 371

Trachelospermum jasminoides

Confederate jasmine, star jasmine
Height: to 5 ft.
Fragrant flowers; evergreen foliage
Zone 8

Full or part sun
p. 373

Deciduous Trees and Shrubs

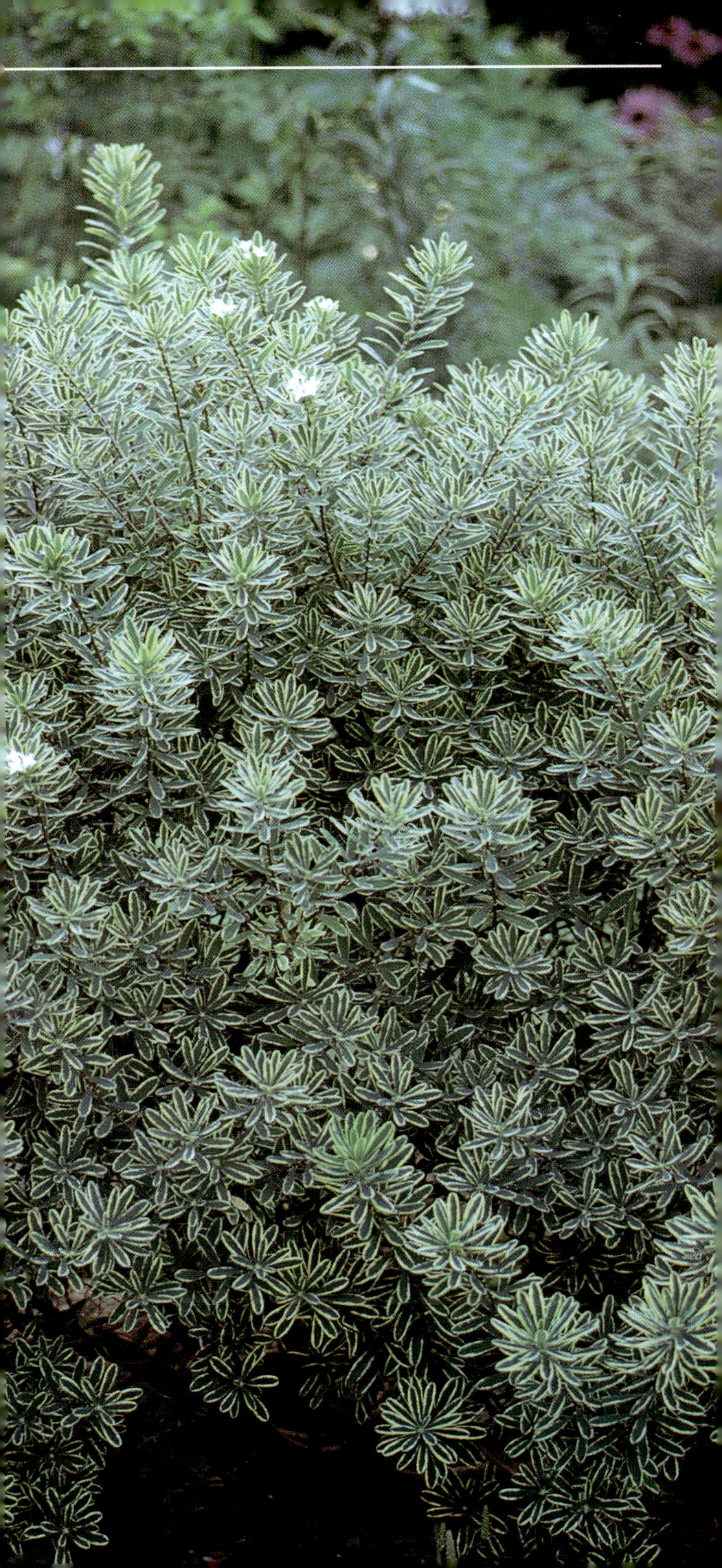

172 Deciduous Trees and Shrubs

Acer palmatum

*Japanese maple
Height: to 10 ft.
Colorful fall
foliage; good
bonsai subject
Zone 6 or 5*

*Sun to shade
p. 204*

Berberis thunbergii

*Japanese barberry
Height: to 6 ft.
Handsome patio or
entry shrub;
colorful foliage
Zone 4*

*Full sun
p. 220*

Deciduous Trees and Shrubs 173

Buddleia davidii	Butterfly bush, summer lilac Height: to 10 ft. but usually less Fragrant flowers from midsummer to fall Zone 5	Full sun p. 224

Caryopteris × clandonensis	Bluebeard, blue spirea Height: 2–3 ft. Autumn flowers; 'Blue Mist' shown here Zone 6 or 5	Full sun p. 234

174 Deciduous Trees and Shrubs

Corylus avellana 'Contorta'
Harry Lauder's walking stick
Height: 7–8 ft.
Prized for its curious, twisted branching
Zone 4
Full or part sun
p. 248

Cytisus × praecox 'Warminster'
Warminster broom
Height: 3–4 ft.
Showy flowers and unusual but interesting bare twigs
Zone 5
Full sun
p. 252

Daphne ×
burkwoodii

Height: 3–4 ft.
Delicious
fragrance; 'Carol
Mackie' shown
here
Zone 4

Full sun or part
shade
p. 254

Ficus carica

Common fig
Height: 5–6 ft.
Distinctive shrub or
tree; delicious fruit
Zone 8 or 7

Full sun
p. 266

Hydrangea macrophylla

Hydrangea
Height: 4–8 ft.
Handsome flowers and foliage; 'Pink Supreme' shown here
Zone 6

Full or part sun
p. 287

Lagerstroemia indica

Crape myrtle
Height: to 25 ft.
All-season interest; 'Natchez' shown here
Zone 7

Full or part sun
p. 300

Deciduous Trees and Shrubs 177

Malus **hybrid crab apples**
Height: 8–10 ft. Spring flowers; 'Donald Wyman' shown here
Zone 4
Full or part sun
p. 316

Potentilla fruticosa
Bush cinquefoil Height: 2–3 ft. Blooms all summer; 'Abbotswood' shown here
Zone 2
Full sun
p. 342

178 Deciduous Trees and Shrubs

Punica granatum

Pomegranate
Height: to 5 ft.
(trained)
Long-blooming;
handsome fruit;
'Nana' shown here
Zone 8

Full sun
p. 345

Rhododendron deciduous species azaleas	Height: to 6 ft. (one shown) Fragrant flowers, fall color; R. schlippenbachii shown here Zone 5 (one shown)	Part sun to shade p. 350

Deciduous Trees and Shrubs 179

Rosa miniature roses

Height: 15 in. (one shown) Hanging baskets, window boxes; hardy

Full sun p. 354

Rosa standard roses

Height: varies 'Cherish' (left) and 'Sunflair' (right) shown here

Full sun p. 355

180 Deciduous Trees and Shrubs

Sambucus racemosa 'Plumosa Aurea'

Red elderberry
Height: 3–6 ft.
Handsome foliage;
spring flowers;
summer fruits
Zone 4

Full or part sun
p. 360

Spiraea japonica

Japanese spirea
Height: 2–3 ft.
Informal plant with
good foliage and
flowers
Zone 3

Full or part sun
p. 365

***Viburnum carlesii* 'Compactum'**

*Korean spice viburnum
Height: 3 ft.
Blooms as leaves expand, usually in April
Zone 4*

*Full or part sun
p. 378*

Vitex agnus-castus

*Chaste tree, pepperbush
Height: 3–6 ft.
Midsummer-to-fall flowers attract butterflies
Zone 7*

*Full sun
p. 382*

Evergreen Trees and Shrubs

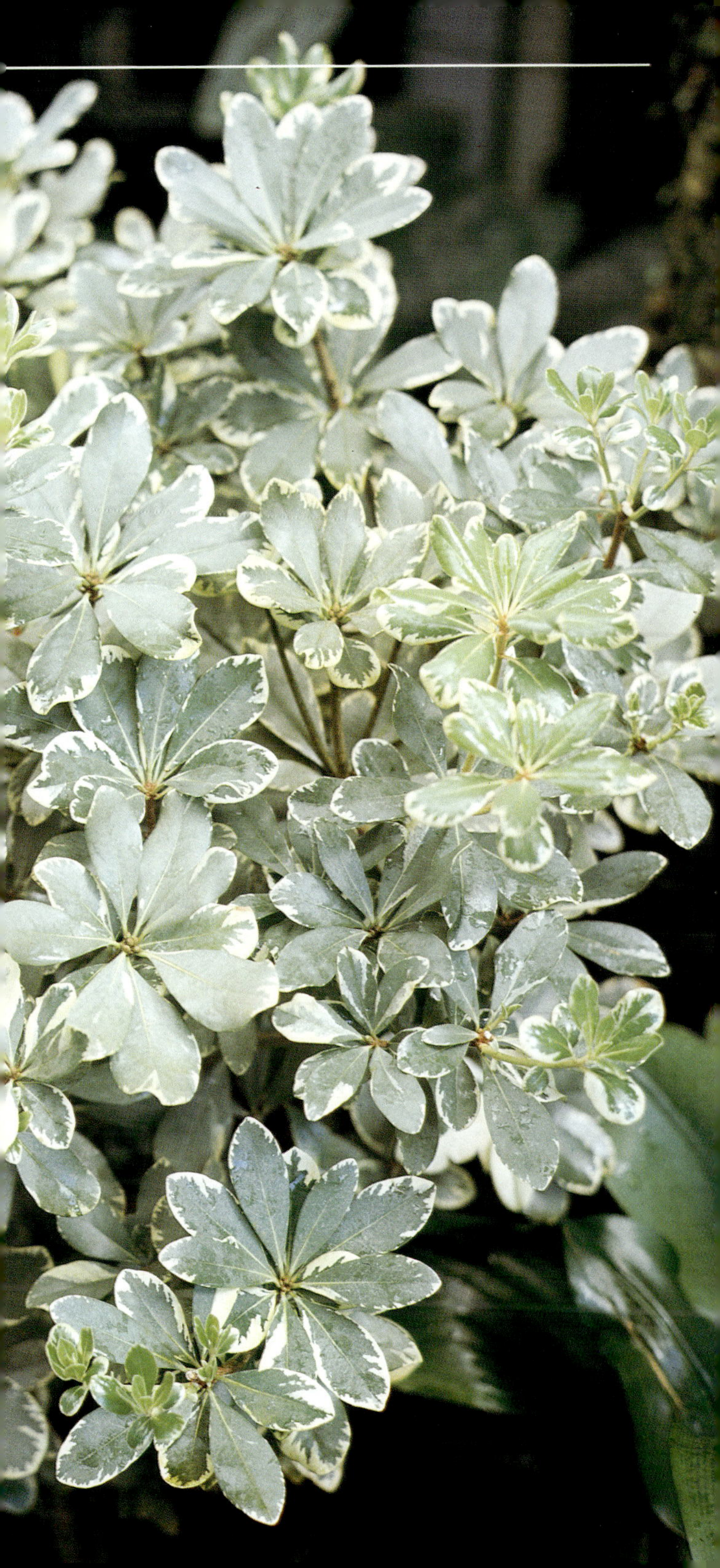

184　*Evergreen Trees and Shrubs*

Agave attenuata　　Agave　　　　　　　Full sun or part
　　　　　　　　　　Height: 5 ft.　　　　shade
　　　　　　　　　　A natural　　　　　　p. 208
　　　　　　　　　　sculpture; flowers
　　　　　　　　　　after many years
　　　　　　　　　　Zone 9

Arbutus unedo　　Strawberry tree　　　Full or part sun
　　　　　　　　　　Height: 6 ft.　　　　p. 212
　　　　　　　　　　Foliage, flowers,
　　　　　　　　　　bark, and form are
　　　　　　　　　　all attractive
　　　　　　　　　　Zone 8

Evergreen Trees and Shrubs 185

Buxus microphylla
Littleleaf box
Height: to 4 ft.
B. m. *var.* koreana
'Wintergreen'
shown here
Zone 5

Full or part sun
p. 226

Callistemon citrinus
Lemon bottlebrush
Height: 4–5 ft.
Attracts hummingbirds
Zone 9

Full sun
p. 229

186　*Evergreen Trees and Shrubs*

Camellia japonica

Camellia
Height: 5 ft.
A must for mild climates; C. j. 'Eugene Lize' shown here
Zone 8 or 7

Part sun to shade
p. 230

Chamaecyparis obtusa and its cultivars

Hinoki cypress
Height: 2–6 ft. (dwarf forms)
Cultivars offer variety of foliage colors
Zone 5

Full or part sun
p. 237

Evergreen Trees and Shrubs 187

Chamaecyparis pisifera cultivars

Sawara cypress
Height: 1–8 ft.
'Filifera Aurea Nana' shown here
Zone 5

Full or part sun
p. 238

Citrus

Height: varies
Includes oranges, lemons (shown here), grapefruits, limes, and others
Zone 9

Full sun
p. 242

188 *Evergreen Trees and Shrubs*

Fatsia japonica *Height: 6–10 ft.*
Handsome
entryway, patio, or
courtyard plant
Zone 7

Part sun to shade
p. 262

Feijoa sellowiana

Pineapple guava
Height: 5–6 ft.
Flowers as well as
fruit are edible
Zone 8

Full sun
p. 263

Evergreen Trees and Shrubs 189

Ilex cornuta

*Chinese holly
Height: usually under 10 ft.
Mounded shrubs thrive in hot weather
Zone 7*

*Full or part sun
p. 289*

Ilex crenata

*Japanese holly
Height: usually under 4 ft.
Grows slowly to form low dense mound
Zone 5*

*Full or part sun
p. 290*

190   *Evergreen Trees and Shrubs*

***Juniperus
chinensis* cultivars**

*Height: varies
Upright forms;
'Pfitzerana' shown
here
Zone 5 or 4*

*Full or part sun
p. 297*

***Juniperus
horizontalis*
cultivars**

*Creeping junipers
Height: under 2 ft.
Low forms; 'Blue
Chip' shown here
Zone 2*

*Full sun
p. 298*

Evergreen Trees and Shrubs 191

Laurus nobilis
Sweet bay
Height: 6 ft.
Can prune to
formal shape;
leaves used as herb
Zone 8

Full sun
p. 305

Leucophyllum frutescens
Texas sage, purple sage
Height: 6–8 ft.
Good foil for
colorful annuals
Zone 8

Full sun
p. 307

192 *Evergreen Trees and Shrubs*

Myrtus communis Myrtle Full sun
Height: 3–4 ft. p. 321
Excellent for
topiary or as patio
focal point
Zone 8

Nandina domestica Heavenly bamboo Sun to shade
Height: 4–5 ft. p. 322
Handsome in
silhouette; thrives
indoors and out
Zone 7 or 6

Evergreen Trees and Shrubs 193

Nerium oleander

Oleander
Height: 6 ft.
Shrub that can be
trained as standard
(shown here)
Zone 8

Full sun
p. 326

Osmanthus fragrans

Sweet olive
Height: 6 ft.
Flowers have
powerful, sweet
fragrance
Zone 9

Full or part sun
p. 329

194 *Evergreen Trees and Shrubs*

Phyllostachys nigra

Black bamboo
Height: 6–8 ft.
Handsome plant
for Japanese flavor
Zone 7

Full or part sun
p. 216

***Picea glauca* 'Conica'**

Dwarf Alberta
spruce
Height: to 10 ft.
Very slow-growing;
use for formal
touch
Zone 3

Full or part sun
p. 336

Evergreen Trees and Shrubs   195

Picea pungens Blue spruce Full sun
Height: varies with p. 337
cultivar
Several dwarf
forms are good for
containers
Zone 3

Pinus mugo Mugo pine Full or part sun
Height: varies with p. 338
cultivar
Fine specimen
plant; look for
dwarf varieties
Zone 3

196 Evergreen Trees and Shrubs

Pinus thunbergiana

*Japanese black pine
Height: varies
Striking branch patterns; good bonsai specimen
Zone 5*

*Full sun
p. 338*

Pittosporum tobira

Height: 3–4 ft.
Durable shrub for difficult spot; 'Variegata' shown here
Zone 8

Part sun to shade
p. 340

Evergreen Trees and Shrubs 197

Prunus laurocerasus

Cherry laurel, English laurel
Height: to 6 ft. (compact forms)
Tidy plant; flowers a bonus; 'Otto Luyken' shown
Zone 7

Sun to shade
p. 344

***Pyracantha* species and hybrid cultivars**

Height: varies
Spring flowers; fiery berries; P. coccinea shown here
Zone 6 (one shown)

Full sun or part shade
p. 346

198 *Evergreen Trees and Shrubs*

Rhaphiolepis indica

Indian hawthorn
Height: 3 ft.
Attractive foliage
and spring flowers
Zone 7

Full sun
p. 348

Rhododendron evergreen azaleas

Height: to 3 ft.
(one shown)
Year-round appeal;
'Gumpo Pink'
shown here
Zone 7 (one
shown)

Part sun to shade
p. 351

Evergreen Trees and Shrubs 199

Rhododendrons Height: 3 ft. (one shown)
Rhododendron yakusimanum *shown here*
Zone 5 (one shown)

Part sun to shade
p. 352

Rosmarinus officinalis

Rosemary
Height: 2–3 ft.
Culinary herb with attractive flowers; 'Arp' shown here
Zone 8

Full sun
p. 356

200 *Evergreen Trees and Shrubs*

***Taxus* cultivars**

Yews
Height: varies
A variety of forms from low and spreading to columnar; T. × media shown here
Zone: varies

Sun to shade
p. 367

| ***Thuja occidentalis*** | *American arborvitae, eastern white cedar*
Height: 2–10 ft.
Year-round interest; good for formal displays
Zone 3 | *Full sun*
p. 370 |

Thuja orientalis **cultivars**

*Oriental arborvitae
Height: varies
Best arborvitae for the South; 'Aurea Nana' shown here
Zone 6*

*Full or part sun
p. 369*

Encyclopedia of Plants

The plants described in this section are organized alphabetically by genus. A short description of the genus is followed by individual entries for featured species and cultivars. These entries pack a lot of information into a small space. We hope they will be easy to follow. Here are a few comments to help you make best use of them.

Names. Plant taxonomists are continually reclassifying plants and renaming the groupings to which the plants are assigned, making any book outdated almost before it appears. We have tried to use widely accepted names and classifications here, even if they are not the most recent versions. For example, we have retained the family name Compositae, rather than the newer Asteraceae, because readers are more likely to be familiar with the older term. Where appropriate, synonymous botanical names are also listed.

How to grow. We often indicate a plant's preference for potting soil as "soilless commercial mix" or "loam-based commercial soil mix" but realize that many gardeners will make their own. Our recommendation should guide you on the type of mix that would be best to make. If you're uncertain about a plant's preference, consult a knowledgeable staff person at your local nursery.

We have also provided information on starting some of the plants from seed, but if you purchase seeds, follow the detailed instructions many suppliers provide.

Acanthus

A-kan´thus. Bear's-breeches
Acanthaceae. Acanthus family

Description
Perennial herbs or shrubs with large toothed leaves and erect spikes of showy flowers. About 30 species, most native to dry climates around the Mediterranean.

n *mollis* p. 126
Bear's-breeches, artist's acanthus
Perennial. Zone 6
Height: 1½–2 ft. Spread: 3–4 ft.
Forms a lush clump of handsome glossy leaves, 2–3 ft. long, deeply lobed, and toothed with small soft spines. Admired by artists, these leaves inspired the design of Corinthian columns. Dozens of whitish, lilac, or rose flowers with green or purplish bracts crowd robust spikes, up to 6 ft. tall, from late spring to early summer. Dramatic as an accent in light shade under a tree. 'Latifolius' has especially large leaves and is more frost-hardy. 'Oakleaf' has deep green, oak-leaf-shaped leaves.

How to Grow
Sun to shade; tolerates heat but not desert heat in sun. Loam-based commercial soil mix; 8–12-in. pot. Ordinary watering. Fertilize only to maintain good color. Easy to propagate by dividing rhizome. Goes dormant after blooming; in mild areas, remove flower spike and water during the summer to maintain leaves. In cold climates, overwinter in basement.

Acer

Ay´sir. Maple
Aceraceae. Maple family

Description
Most are deciduous trees or shrubs with palmately lobed or compound leaves, often turning brilliant colors in fall. Valued as specimen and shade trees, particularly where the soil is rich and moist. More than 110 species, native to the north temperate zone.

n *palmatum* p. 172
Japanese maple
Deciduous shrub. Zone 6 or 5
Height: to 10 ft. Spread: often wider than tall

These mounding shrubs or small trees are popular for their graceful form, attractive foliage, and fall color. Most have overlapping tiers of arching branches that form a wide, rounded crown. The foliage is outstanding in summer and fall, and the bark and branching are attractive in winter. Hundreds of cultivars vary in leaf shape and color, overall habit and size, and hardiness. Long-lived plants, they can be maintained at any size, from tiny bonsai to 10-ft. mounds in boxes or large pots. 'Bloodgood' has deeply lobed leaves that are dark reddish purple all season, and it produces red fruits in fall. 'Oshi Beni' has a spreading habit, and the leaves are brightly colored in both spring and fall. 'Sango Kaku' has bright coral-red bark on the younger twigs and brilliant fall color. The Dissectum group ('Dissectum' or var. *dissectum*) includes many forms with very deeply cut leaves in shades of green, red, bronze, or purple as well as variegated.

A. japonicum 'Aconitifolium' and *A. j.* 'Aureum' (a.k.a. *A. shirasawanum* 'Aureum') are also excellent container plants; leaves are soft green in summer and bright red in fall. 'Aconitifolium' has deeply divided, lacy or feathery leaves that make a vivid display of crimson to violet in fall.

How to Grow
Sun to shade. (Green-leaved types can take full sun. Red- and purple-leaved forms need part sun to develop their color but tend to "bronze" in full sun. Variegated or extra-lacy types need afternoon shade to prevent leaf scorch.) Loam-based commercial soil mix. Tolerates heat (but not drying winds) if soil is kept moist. Ordinary watering. Alkaline or salt-laden water will create leaf burn; leach salts by occasional drenching, or add acidifying agent. Light, frequent feeding helps avoid salt burn. When plant reaches desired size, root-prune and add fresh soil to keep it in same size pot. If there's danger of roots freezing during winter, store in basement or bury pot in garden and mulch heavily.

Achillea
A-kil-lee´a. Yarrow
Compositae. Daisy family

Description
Perennials with pungent gray or green leaves, often finely divided, and flat clusters of small flowers. About 80 species, native to the north temperate zone. Hybridization has produced many excellent garden varieties.

■ **'Moonshine'** *p. 126*
Yarrow
Perennial. Zone 3
Height: 2 ft. Spread: 18 in.
Even without flowers, the basal mound of soft gray, finely dissected leaves would deserve a prominent place in container gardens, but the pure lemon yellow flowers, borne in 2-in. clusters on 2-ft. stalks, harmonize with most other perennials and continue from June to August if deadheaded. Grow in its own pot or with herbs or annuals and perennials that like similar care. *A. taygetea,* a parent of this hybrid, has greener foliage and pale sulphur flowers and can bloom from late May to October.

Yarrows make good cut flowers and bloom for a long season, although the colors fade rapidly from bright to dusty shades. Flowers can be dried for winter arrangements. *A. tomentosa,* woolly yarrow, is a small plant (up to 12 in. high and 18 in. wide) with abundant yellow flowers and deeply cut leaves. *A. clavennae,* silvery yarrow, is also small, with silky silver-gray leaves and white flowers. Larger yarrows require big pots and are less suited for container growing.

How to Grow
Full sun. Soilless commercial mix in a clay pot; use a 12-in. pot for a single specimen. Tolerates dry heat but gets foliar diseases in hot, humid, rainy areas. Doesn't tolerate overwatering. Divide in spring every 2–3 years. Overwinter dormant plant in clay pot in cold but frost-free spot. Keep soil on the dry side.

Agapanthus
Ag-a-pan´thus
Amaryllidaceae. Amaryllis family

Description
Evergreen or deciduous perennials with firm straplike leaves, thick roots and rhizomes, and large round umbels of blue, violet, or white flowers. Only 9 species, native to South Africa, and many named hybrid cultivars.

■ ***orientalis*** *p. 150 Pictured opposite*
Lily-of-the-Nile
Tender perennial. Zone 8
Height: to 5 ft. Spread: 2 ft.
Beautiful spheres of blue flowers on tall slender stems rise above substantial clumps of broad, arching, evergreen leaves.

Stalks bear as many as 100 individual flowers and last much of the summer in the container or as cut flowers. The large cultivars and species make commanding specimens by pools and on terraces; smaller types are easily tucked into groupings of other sun lovers. 'Alba' has white flowers. *A.* 'Peter Pan' is an evergreen dwarf cultivar with foliage clumps to 12 in. tall and blue flowers on 12–18-in. stalks. The 'Headbourne' hybrids are more cold-hardy and reach 2½ ft. *A. africanus* is similar, with many horticultural varieties.

How to Grow
Part or full sun; tolerates heat. Loam-based commercial soil mix. Use a plastic pot or wooden container—expanding roots will break a clay pot. Ordinary watering, but tolerates drought and recovers from drying out. Feed through the summer to encourage bloom; remove faded stalks. Does well when pot-bound, but you can divide when very crowded. In cold climates, overwinter in basement; keep barely moist or stop watering. Resume watering a month before last frost and move to a sunny window.

Agave
Uh-gav′ee. Century plant
Agavaceae. Agave family

Description
Large succulents with thick, often spiny leaves. Many form a squat rosette, but some have short woody trunks. Tall flower stalks like candelabras develop quickly; after flowering, the old leaves die but new shoots grow from the base. About 300 species, native from the southern United States through South America.

■ *attenuata* p. 184
Agave
Large succulent. Zone 9
Height: 5 ft. Spread: 5 ft.
Makes a statuesque rosette of fleshy, pale jade leaves, a natural sculpture for dry landscapes or seaside gardens. One plant in a large container is enough for most settings. Safe near patios and pools because it has no spines. After many years, it suddenly produces a long-lasting spike of greenish yellow flowers that shoots up 12–14 ft., then bends over almost to the ground. After bloom, the parent rosette dies but the "pups" carry on.

Octopus agave, *A. vilmoriniana* (a.k.a. *A. mayonensis*), features curling, twisting leaves, which make the plant a magnificent and unusual specimen in a pot or tub. *A. parryi* is smaller, to 3 ft. wide, and looks like a giant blue-gray artichoke with dark spines along the leaf edges and tips. *A. deserti* rosettes are just 2 ft. wide, with narrower, gray-green, spiny leaves. *A. victoriae-reginae* has a rosette of dark green leaves just a foot wide; slow-growing, it lives many years before flowering.

How to Grow
Full sun or part shade. Loam-based commercial soil mix (you might add sand to weigh down the container to keep plant from tipping). Tolerates dryness. Protect from severe frost. Confining to container will slow plants' growth, making them unlikely to reach flowering size. Eventually they may outgrow your space. Susceptible to mealybugs and scale.

Ajuga
A-joo′ga. Bugleweed
Labiatae. Mint family

Description
Perennial ground covers with semievergreen foliage and spikes of blue or violet flowers in spring. Most stay close to the ground and spread by runners. About 50 species, native to the Old World.

■ *reptans* p. 127 *Pictured opposite*
Bugleweed, carpet bugle
Perennial. Zone 3
Height: 4–8 in. Spread: 8 in. and beyond
Excellent as an edging or ground cover in large containers with shrubs and trees or, for instance, dwarf spring bulbs

such as crocus and scilla. Runner will trail down the sides of a pot. The smooth, shiny, wavy-margined leaves are green, purple, bronze, or variegated in gray, white, cream, or pink and provide color interest for a long season. Short spikes of blue, purple, or white flowers top the foliage for a few weeks in late spring. 'Burgundy Glow' has wonderful variegations of cream, pink, and green. 'Royalty' has dark purple leaves that are crimped and puckered. 'Silver Beauty' or 'Variegata' is gray-green and creamy white. 'Bronze Beauty' has large bronze-purple leaves, and 'Catlin's Giant' has especially large bronze-green leaves. 'Metallica Crispa' has smaller, puckered, spinachlike leaves and is very slow to spread. A more upright, less invasive plant is *A. pyramidalis*.

How to Grow
Sun to shade. Loam-based commercial soil mix. Ordinary watering; slow-release fertilizers work well. Use an 8-in. pot for a single specimen; 3 plants to a 12-in. pot. As companion plants, space small-leaved cultivars 6 in. apart; give larger ones 8 in. or more. *A. reptans* is invasive; prune runners to keep in bounds. No pests or diseases.

Allium
Al′li-um
Amaryllidaceae. Amaryllis family

Description
Bulb-forming perennials with flat or hollow leaves and round clusters of small flowers. Many, including onion and garlic, have pungent leaves and bulbs, but the flowers may smell quite sweet. About 700 species, all native to the Northern Hemisphere.

■ *schoenoprasum* p. 128
Chives
Perennial herb. Zone 3
Height: 12 in. Spread: 18 in.
Plant a few clumps of chives in a pot in a handy spot where you can snip the fresh onion-flavored leaves from spring to fall. (Chop and freeze for winter use, or pot up a plant to keep on the windowsill.) The lavender flowers in 1-in.-wide heads on stiff stalks last a month in late spring; they also make good cut flowers, can be dried for winter bouquets, and look pretty (but taste chaffy) in salads. Combine with other herbs in a large pot or half-barrel; try it in the top of a strawberry jar, with thyme and savory in the pockets below. It is also pretty with dark opal basil and garden sage.

How to Grow
Full or part sun; tolerates heat. Loam-based commercial soil mix. Easy from seed started indoors or out in spring. Divide an old clump in early spring into dozens of new starts. Shear after flowering to tidy up plant and to promote new growth. Overwinter on windowsill or in cold frame. Long lived and trouble-free.

Aloysia
A-loyz´ee-a
Verbenaceae. Verbena family

Description
Deciduous or evergreen shrubs with fragrant leaves. About 30 species, native to Central and South America.

■ *triphylla* p. 100
(*Lippia citriodora*)
Lemon verbena
Tender woody herb. Zone 8
Height: 3–4 ft. Spread: to 2 ft.
The whorls of 3 or 4 thin, papery leaves have a wonderfully intense lemon fragrance; use them in iced drinks, apple jelly, and potpourri. Grown as an annual in cold climates; in mild climates is semievergreen. Bears open clusters of tiny lilac or white flowers in summer. A slender-twigged shrub with a loose, open habit—plant thyme, marjoram, savory, and other low herbs at its feet. You can pinch repeatedly to make it denser.

How to Grow
Full sun; tolerates heat. Loam-based commercial soil mix.

Best in a clay pot; 12-in. by 12-in. pot at maturity. Damaged by standing water. Feed sparingly and cut off faded blooms. In cold climates, can overwinter in a bright, cool, dry place. May lose all its leaves, but continue to water sparingly, and look for new growth in spring.

Antigonon

An-tig′o-non
Polygonaceae. Rhubarb family

Description
Deciduous or evergreen, fast-growing vines with generous clusters of bright flowers throughout summer and fall. Only 2 or 3 species, native to Mexico and Central America.

■ *leptopus* p. 162
Coral vine, queen's-wreath
Deciduous vine. Zone 8
Height: 6–10 ft.
An easy, healthy vine that grows quickly and climbs by tendrils to cover its support with a mass of heart-shaped leaves up to 4 in. long. After the first good rain in late summer or fall, it's covered with a frilly cloud of rosy pink flowers. Can frame a porch or arbor like an edging of fine lace. 'Album' has white flowers.

How to Grow
Full sun; tolerates heat but not drought. Loam-based commercial soil mix; prefers heavy soil, so you could mix in garden soil. Must have a trellis, which can be lightweight. Brittle stems are easily damaged by wind, so place in a protected location. Easy from seed. Plant in spring so that it has all season to develop tubers. Dies back with first frost. Cut back and overwinter tubers indoors; decrease watering while plant is dormant. Prone to aphids and red spider mites.

Antirrhinum

An-ti-ry′num
Scrophulariaceae. Foxglove family

Description
Perennials or annuals with upright leafy stems and colorful 2-lipped flowers. About 40 species, native to the New and Old World.

■ *majus* p. 100
Snapdragon
Perennial grown as an annual. All zones
Height: 6–36 in. Spread: 8–18 in.
A popular annual with velvety flowers in a wide range of colors and forms, from the traditional "snapping" shape loved by children to broader, more open shapes like penstemons or azaleas. There are dwarf varieties, such as 'Floral Carpet' and 'Tahiti', which are good for smaller containers or combinations. Taller ones, such as 'Rockets' and 'Wedding Bells', make excellent focal points for large pots. Combine with petunias, nicotiana, and Iceland poppies. They tolerate frost, providing southern and western gardeners with a long show. For the best selection, order seeds and grow your own plants.

How to Grow
Full or part sun. Loam-based commercial soil mix. Sow seeds in shallow flats to germinate and grow at 60° F. Pinch seedlings to promote branching. In mild-winter areas, set out plants in early fall for winter or spring bloom. In colder regions, plant in early spring for spring or summer bloom. Cut back after blooming, and the plants will often bloom again. Watch for brown spots on the leaves, the symptom of rust infection. Avoid overhead watering, which is conducive to rust. Destroy infected plants. Rust can harbor on other garden plants, so you might want to grow snaps every other year to avoid rust outbreaks.

Arbutus
Ar-bew'tus
Ericaceae. Heath family

Description
Evergreen trees or shrubs with leathery leaves, conspicuous red bark, small pink or white flowers, and orange berries. About 14 species, native to western North America and Europe.

■ *unedo* p. 184
Strawberry tree
Evergreen tree. Zone 8
Height: 6 ft. Spread: 4 ft.
An upright shrub or small tree with a rounded crown, reddish twigs, and shiny, leathery, evergreen leaves. Drooping clusters of small white to pinkish flowers appear in October, blooming alongside the pebbly-textured, bright red, spherical

fruits. Flaking bark is also attractive. Ideal for small or urban gardens along the West Coast; nice in combination with lavenders, rock roses, and other Mediterranean shrubs and perennials. 'Compacta' is a shrubby form, to 5 ft. tall, that flowers and fruits almost continuously. 'Elfin King' is even smaller and is picturesquely contorted.

How to Grow
Full or part sun. Loam-based commercial soil mix; avoid alkaline soil if you mix your own. Planted in a 10–12-in. pot, it won't need a larger pot for a long time. Recovers from drying out. Can be pruned to shape at any time. Overwinter indoors.

Arctotis
Ark-toe´tis
Compositae. Daisy family

Description
Perennials or annuals with a basal rosette of rough or hairy lobed leaves and daisylike flowers on long stalks. About 50 species, native to southern Africa.

■ **garden hybrids** *p. 101*
African daisies
Annuals. All zones
Height: 12–18 in. Spread: 12 in.
Easy annuals for warm, sunny spots. Plants flower profusely both summer and winter (in warm climates). Long-stemmed daisies are 3 in. wide, in shades of bright white, pink, coral, red, yellow, or orange, usually with dark "eyes." Common cultivars are the pink 'Wine' and pale orange 'Flame'; their colors vary with light levels. Plants form a tidy, low clump of rough gray-green leaves, 6 in. long, with toothed or lobed edges. They look cheerful along the edge of a large container, and they make good cut flowers, too. *A. stoechadifolia* var. *grandis* grows taller and has silvery white daisies with deep blue eyes.

How to Grow
Full or part sun; tolerate heat. Loam-based commercial soil mix. Plants prefer clay pots (work well in urns and window boxes, too). Do best when tightly potted; don't repot often. They recover from drying out. Feed sparsely. Pinch frequently to promote bushiness, and deadhead regularly to prolong flowering. Overwinter on sunny windowsill.

Artemisia

Ar-te-miss'ee-a
Compositae. Daisy family

Description

Evergreen or deciduous shrubs or perennials. Most have aromatic foliage, often silver or gray. Flowers are small, rarely conspicuous. About 300 species, native to dry regions in the Old and New World.

■ 'Powis Castle' *p. 128*
Perennial. Zone 6
Height: 2–3 ft. Spread: 2–4 ft.
Forms a generous mound of silvery filigree foliage that is striking at dusk or under patio lights. A handsome foil to bolder plants, such as agapanthus, phormium, and citrus. *A. absinthium* 'Lambrook Silver', wormwood, is a somewhat smaller shrubby perennial hardy to zone 5. Stems rising above a foaming mass of silvery, finely divided, and strongly aromatic leaves are topped with panicles of tiny yellow flowers in summer. Trim back by at least a third in spring and again in midsummer to prevent floppiness. *A. a.* 'Valerie Finnis' has wider leaves and a bolder look.

How to Grow

Sun to shade; tolerates heat. Loam-based commercial soil mix. Start with a 1-gal. pot from the nursery and move up gradually, repotting in spring. Trim back old shoots to force new growth in spring. (Trim 'Lambrook Silver' again in midsummer to prevent floppiness.) In cold climates, overwinter indoors or in a cold frame. Easily propagated by cuttings taken in midsummer. ('Valerie Finnis' can be divided.)

Asparagus

As-pair'a-gus
Liliaceae. Lily family

Description

Perennials, sometimes woody or thorny, with thick or tuberous roots. Stems branch repeatedly to make a fluffy mass of green, but the true leaves are inconspicuous dry scales. The starry flowers, often fragrant, are followed by plump colored berries. About 100 species, native to the Old World, including the vegetable asparagus.

■ *densiflorus* p. 101
Ornamental asparagus, asparagus fern
Tender perennial grown as an annual. Zone 9
Height: 2 ft. or more. Spread: 3 ft. or more
Forms a clump of slender, sometimes prickly stems clothed with thousands of thin flat branchlets that look like evergreen needles or leaves. Dotted with fragrant, starry white flowers in late spring. Combines well with almost all other plants. 'Sprengeri' has arching or drooping stems (up to 6 ft. long) with bright green or yellow-green needles in bunches of 3. 'Myers' has stiffly erect stems (to 2 ft. or more) with dark green needles and looks like a bouquet of fluffy green foxtails. Both are excellent for containers. 'Sprengeri' drapes gracefully from a hanging basket, window box, or raised bed. 'Myers' is an unusual and effective companion for impatiens, coleus, or caladiums.

How to Grow
Full or part sun; tolerates heat. Loam-based commercial soil mix. Stores water in fleshy tubercles on roots and can withstand dry periods but looks better with generous moisture. Fertilize potted specimens frequently from spring to fall. Tops may freeze, but plants resprout from base. Divide old clumps in spring. Trouble-free.

Astilbe
As-till´bee
Saxifragaceae. Saxifrage family

Description
Perennials with a mound of simple or compound leaves and upright plumes of tiny pink, red, or white flowers. About 14 species, 2 from the Appalachians and the rest from eastern Asia. Most of the cultivars are hybrids.

■ × *arendsii* hybrids p. 129
Perennials. Zone 2
Height: 2–3 ft. Spread: 2–3 ft.
Because of their handsome ferny foliage and delicate sprays of flowers, astilbes make charming additions to container groupings. The foliage is deep green to bronze, and the flowers come in shades of white, pale to dark pink, and deep purplish and carmine reds, opening between June and September; spent flowers turn reddish brown and remain attractive for months. Astilbes are best seen by themselves as a focal point or in mixed containers with other moisture-loving

plants such as coleus, wishbone flower, and impatiens. Several plants can be grouped in a large pot for greater visual impact.

How to Grow
Part sun to shade. Best with a soil mix of garden loam, organic matter, and peat moss. Mature plants need at least a gallon-sized pot at maturity. Plants need constant moisture. Fertilize with formula for acid-loving plants. Protect from hot afternoon sun. (Astilbes do best in cool summers and are poor choices for hot, semiarid areas.) Divide crowded clumps in spring. In winter, store the dormant clumps in their pots in a cold frame or trench in the garden.

■ **selected cultivars of astilbes**
'Bressingham Beauty': pure pink, late midseason, 36 in.
'Bridal Veil': pure white, midseason, 36 in.
'Cattleya': orchid pink, late, 42 in.
'Deutschland': white, early, 18 in.
'Fanal': deep red, early midseason, 30 in.
'Glow' ('Glut'): dark red, late, 36 in.
'Peach Blossom': salmon pink, early midseason, 24 in.
'Red Sentinel': deep purplish red, midseason, 20 in.
'Rheinland': carmine-pink, early, 24 in.
'Sprite': pale pink, midseason, 10 in.
'White Gloria': creamy white, midseason, 24 in.

BAMBOOS

Description
Bamboos make handsome container plants. Single specimens throw nice shadows and rustle appealingly in the wind. A group of tubbed plants can make a screen against wind or shade a window. Containers are the only way many people can reasonably grow invasive running bamboos. Below is a selection of interesting bamboos you can grow in containers.

■ *Phyllostachys nigra* p. 194 *Pictured opposite*
Black bamboo
Bamboo. Zone 7
Height: 6–8 ft. Spread: 3–5 ft.
Black bamboo has shiny black culms (as the woody upright stems are called) 1 in. thick and narrow dark green leaves 1–4 in. long. Lovely in a Japanese-style garden but best in shade where summers are hot. Yellow-groove bamboo, *P. aureosulcata* (zone 6), is the hardiest of the running (grove-making) bamboos. The culms are rich green with yellow grooves

that run vertically from node to node. They grow up to 1½ in. thick. The narrow lance-shaped leaves are papery thin and light green.

How to Grow
Full or part sun; tolerates heat but not desert wind. Loam-based commercial soil mix. Can be grown indefinitely in 6–8-in. pots but is at its best in large pots or tubs. The more water you provide, the bigger the plant grows. Feed to maintain color and vigor. Pot divisions in spring, container-grown plants anytime. Maintenance is simple: remove the oldest, tattered culms at ground level.

In zone 6 or warmer, these bamboos should overwinter with little damage to foliage or culms. Zone 5 gardeners can grow these species like herbaceous perennials. Culms may freeze to the ground, but rhizomes are hardy to –20° F if protected with a layer of snow or mulch. Can overwinter indoors, but leaves are likely to drop.

■ other bamboos
Sasa palmata (zone 7) is a vigorous, running bamboo with slender erect stems up to 6 ft. high. Papery thin, bright green leaves, 12–16 in. long and 2–4 in. wide, are clustered at the tips of the stems and branches. Needs little care—just cut old or shabby stems to the ground in spring. *S. veitchii* (zone 7) is a much shorter running bamboo, reaching 2–3 ft. Its broad, papery, bright green leaves turn creamy white around the edges in fall. Indispensable for a Japanese-garden effect.

Another short running bamboo is *Arundinaria viridistriata* (a.k.a. *Pleioblastus viridistriatus* and many other names). Much hardier (zone 4), its new leaves are vibrant gold with bright green stripes. *A. variegata,* 1–3 ft. in height, is similar but has white-striped leaves.

The clumping bamboo *Bambusa multiplex* 'Alphonse Karr' (zone 8) makes a tall, graceful fountain of arching stems topped by clouds of feathery green foliage. Stems are vertically striped bright yellow and green. The hardy clumping bamboos *Fargesia nitida* and *F. murielae* (zone 4) are compact and graceful. (They may be offered under the genus *Semiarundinaria*.)

Begonia
Bee-go´nee-a
Begoniaceae. Begonia family

Description
Tender perennials or shrubs, often categorized as having tuberous, rhizomatous, or fibrous roots. Leaves exhibit a tremendous variety of sizes, shapes, colors, and textures. Many kinds of begonias have abundant, brilliant, waxy flowers. About 900 to 1,000 species, native to tropical climates, with more than 10,000 recorded hybrids and cultivars.

■ × *semperflorens-cultorum* *p. 102*
Wax begonia
Tender perennial grown as an annual. All zones
Height: 6–12 in. Spread: 6–12 in.
A favorite for containers, these compact, leafy plants are covered with flowers for months on end. The fleshy stems branch repeatedly, making bushy mounds. The green, green-and-white, reddish purple, or bronze leaves always look fresh and shiny. Look closely and you'll see that the red, pink, or white blossoms occur in separate clusters of male flowers (slightly larger, with a tuft of yellow stamens) and female flowers (smaller, with a winged ovary behind the petals).

All begonias are excellent for window boxes and patio planters. They are invaluable in mixed containers of shade lovers such as coleus, ferns, and caladiums. The bronze- or purple-leaved forms are darkest if grown in sun; use them with ageratum or dusty-miller as edging in large containers and planters. Dozens of strains are listed in every seed catalog and available at local nurseries every spring.

How to Grow
Sun to shade; tolerates heat. Loam-based commercial soil mix. Can be crowded into mixed pots. Tolerates occasional dryness but can't take soggy conditions. Will burn badly in full sun if not watered regularly. Feed every 2 weeks. Cuttings root easily, and seeds, though tiny, germinate and grow

quickly. Place on a sunny windowsill after frost for a few weeks' bonus. If you keep plants to the following spring, cut back hard and fertilize. Prone to mildew.

■ **Tuberhybrida hybrids** *p. 150*
Tuberous begonias
Tender perennials grown for summer display. All zones
Height: to 2 ft. Spread: to 2 ft.
A triumph in the art and science of plant breeding, tuberous begonias produce huge flowers, which are single, semidouble, or double, with plain or frilled petals, 2–8 in. wide, in every color except blue. Large bowls filled with begonias are stunning. The pendulous types are perhaps the most spectacular of all plants for baskets and raised planters—combine with other trailers such as vinca vine, lobelia, and asparagus vine. Most upright types need staking but reward you with blossoms of incredible lushness. (The 'Non-Stop' hybrids don't need staking and are particularly floriferous.) Impatiens, browallia, and torenia are good companions for upright types. For the widest selection, order tubers from specialty nursery catalogs.

How to Grow
Part sun to shade. Add peat moss to increase moisture retention of a loam-based commercial soil mix. Start tubers in flats or small pots indoors, several weeks before last frost, and pot them up when shoots are 3 in. tall. Put 1 tuber per 8-in. pot, 3 in a 14-in. pot. Brittle stems are damaged by winds. Feed every 2 weeks throughout the summer. In fall, let tops dry out and die down, then lift tubers, pack them in wood shavings or peat moss, and store them in a cool, dry place. Sprinkle occasionally with water to avoid desiccation.

Berberis
Ber´ber-iss. Barberry
Berberidaceae. Barberry family

Description
Evergreen or deciduous shrubs, usually spiny, with bright yellow wood. Some have abundant yellow flowers and persistent red, yellow, or black berries. About 450 species, native to Eurasia and Africa.

■ *thunbergii* p. 172
Japanese barberry
Deciduous shrub. Zone 4
Height: to 6 ft. Spread: to 6 ft.
Long a staple for hedges, the newer cultivars of this tough, reliable shrub offer a compact habit and richly colored foliage. All have dense thorny stems, small teardrop-shaped leaves, and bright red berries in fall. For best color, grow in full sun. The compact cultivars grow naturally round without pruning and are easy but handsome sentinels either side of an entryway. Purple-leaved forms combine well with most pink- or blue-flowered perennials and also with magenta flowers and silver foliage.

'Atropurpurea Nana', also called 'Crimson Pygmy', has deep crimson coloring and a very compact, rounded shape (2 ft. high by 5 ft. wide). 'Kobold' is equally compact, with bright green leaves. 'Gold Ring' has yellow-edged leaves; 'Aurea' has bright yellow leaves; 'Bonanza Gold' is compact, with bright gold leaves. The new foliage of 'Rosy Glow' is marbled with pink and white, which contrasts beautifully with older, dark purple leaves.

How to Grow
Full sun. Soilless commercial mix. Start in a 12–14-in. pot; eventually could be planted in a tub. Feed with slow-release

fertilizer in spring. Very hardy to cold but weakened by extremely hot summers. Remove dead stems and prune to shape after flowering. Overwinter outdoors, or store in cold location.

Bergenia
Ber-jean´ee-a
Saxifragaceae. Saxifrage family

Description
Perennials, often evergreen, forming large clumps of substantial leaves with clusters of small flowers on upright stalks. Fewer than 10 species, native to eastern Asia, and many hybrids.

■ *cordifolia* p. 130
Heartleaf bergenia
Perennial. Zone 3
Height: 12–18 in. Spread: 12–24 in.
This hardy and vigorous perennial forms a clump of large, thick, cabbagelike leaves, waxy and green in summer, turning rich glossy red in fall as the temperature starts to drop. In mild climates the foliage stays pretty all winter. Nodding clusters of pink flowers rise barely above the leaves in spring. Makes a nice contrast with the divided foliage of ferns or astilbes. Many nurseries now carry hybrid cultivars selected for outstanding winter foliage or prettier flowers on taller stalks. These include 'Bressingham White', 'Rotblum', 'Silver Light' ('Silberlicht'), and 'Sunningdale'.

How to Grow
Part shade. Loam-based commercial soil mix. Large pot (12-in.) will minimize winter freeze-thaw damage. Divide crowded plantings in spring or fall. In zone 5 and north, overwinter in cool greenhouse or cold frame. In some areas leaves attract many pests, including aphids, slugs, snails, caterpillars, rabbits, chipmunks, and squirrels.

Bougainvillea
Boo-gan-vil´ee-a
Nyctaginaceae. Four-o'clock family

Description
Evergreen woody vines, often spiny, sometimes shrublike. The actual flowers are small, but the bright-colored papery bracts

make a show that lasts for months. About 14 species, from Central and South America, and many hybrid cultivars.

■ hybrids *p. 162*
Woody vines. Zone 10 or 9
Height: to 20 ft.
Although hardy in only the mildest regions of the United States, bougainvilleas are increasingly popular as container plants to grow outdoors in summer and bring indoors for winter protection. Stems are tough and thorny, and if pruned hard they're sturdy enough to stand upright like a shrub. Where hardy, the vines can climb a building or wall. The plain green leaves are evergreen without cold but drop at the slightest frost. The masses of papery floral bracts keep their bright colors for months. Blooms form on new growth, so the plants recover quickly from frost damage or pruning.

There are dozens of cultivars in colors ranging from red, orange, pink, and purple to yellow and white, including double-flowered and variegated-leaf forms. Some are dwarfs that can live in the same pot for years. 'Barbara Karst' is a vigorous plant with red flowers; for hanging baskets, try 'Raspberry Ice' (a.k.a. 'Hawaii'), a hardy, shrubby, spreading plant with colorful leaves and red flowers; 'Crimson Lake' (a.k.a. 'Mrs. Butt') is good for hot climates; 'Texas Dawn' has pink flowers. 'San Diego Red' can be trained as a standard; 'La Jolla' is shrubby, good for tubs and large pots; 'Brilliant Variegated' has gray-green and silver leaves and is good for hanging baskets.

How to Grow
Full sun in most areas; light shade in the hottest desert regions. Loam-based commercial soil mix; good drainage is im-

portant. Plants tolerate occasional drying out, which seems to promote more abundant flowering. Be very careful not to disrupt the brittle roots when repotting. Young plants are very tender, but older plants can survive a light frost. Prune away damaged wood in spring, and new growth will soon replace it. Prune heavily in spring to maintain shape. Protect shrubby forms from wind by providing a strong stake. In cold climates, bring pots into a cool, bright room for the winter, and water just enough to keep the leaves from wilting.

Brassica
Brass'i-ka
Cruciferae. Mustard family

Description
A diverse group of annuals, biennials, and perennials, including cabbage, Chinese cabbage, kale, broccoli, cauliflower, mustard, turnips, canola, and some ornamentals. About 30 species, native to the Old World, and thousands of varieties and cultivars.

■ *oleracea* p. 102
Flowering kale, flowering cabbage
Annual. All zones
Height: 12 in. Spread: 18 in.
Cheerful and easy as the centerpiece of a container planting, flowering kale looks like a giant crepe-paper flower, but the crinkly-textured rosette is actually made of brightly colored leaves. The bright pink, rose, lavender, purple, white, and/or green leaves stay crisp and colorful for months. Grows and looks best in fall and isn't damaged by frost until temperatures go below 20° F. Newer strains are much slower to bolt, and they maintain color and form longer. Excellent with pansies and spring bulbs; effective color combinations with tulips and hyacinths. Also provides winter interest in warm climates.

How to Grow
Full or part sun. Loam-based commercial soil mix, free-draining and on the light side for good root penetration. Sow seeds in summer, or buy plants to set out in early fall. Break up root balls when planting in final container. Spring-started plants are liable to bolt in hot weather; you can remove flower stalks to maintain form. Feed monthly; slow-release fertilizer is ideal. Subject to all the pests that attack cabbage, but these usually don't do much damage late in the season.

Browallia

Bro-all′ee-a. Bush violet
Solanaceae. Nightshade family

Description
A few species of annual or perennial herbs, native to tropical America, that are grown in the greenhouse or outdoors for their pretty flowers.

■ *speciosa* p. 103
Bush violet
Perennial shrub grown as an annual. Zone 10
Height: 12–24 in. Spread: 12–18 in.
A small bushy plant with oval veined leaves, bush violet is a perfect companion for begonias and impatiens in a shady or partly shady spot. Plants are wonderful as trailing specimens in hanging baskets. The showy flowers bloom for a long time, and their cool blue color is especially welcome during summer heat. Will bloom in winter in mild climates.

How to Grow
Part sun to shade. Loam-based commercial soil mix amended with organic matter to increase water retention, particularly in hanging baskets. Buy plants or start seeds indoors 8–10 weeks before last frost. Plant several to a 10-in. pot, or combine in a mixed container. Pinch to promote bushiness. Needs constant moisture—is easily damaged by drying out. Trouble-free.

Buddleia

Bud′lee-a. Butterfly bush
Loganiaceae. Buddleia family

Description
Deciduous or evergreen shrubs or small trees with clusters or spikes of small flowers, often fragrant and quite popular with butterflies. About 100 species, native to tropical and subtropical regions in the Old and New World.

■ *davidii* p. 173 *Pictured opposite*
Butterfly bush, summer lilac
Deciduous or semievergreen shrub. Zone 5
Height: to 10 ft. but usually less. Spread: to 10 ft.
A trouble-free shrub with long clusters of fragrant flowers at the tip of every arching branch. Blooms on new wood from midsummer to fall. Set one close to a window or on a patio

where you can watch all the butterflies (and bees, too) come hover around the blossoms. Attractive in combination with colorful annuals.

The many cultivars differ mostly in flower color, which includes pink, white, violet, lilac, and rich purple. Whatever the petal color, most forms have a bright orange eye in the center of the flower. Particularly valuable for containers is the 'Nanho' series, compact or dwarf plants with white, blue, or purple flowers. *B. d.* 'Harlequin' has white variegated foliage, purple-red flowers, and a restrained growth habit. 'Lochinch' is a hybrid between *B. davidii* and *B. fallowiana* with silvery gray leaves on especially vigorous stems and lovely lavender-blue flowers. *B. crispa* (zone 7) has woolly white, deciduous leaves and shorter clusters of lilac flowers. *B. alternifolia,* the hardiest butterfly bush, offers dense clusters of mildly fragrant lilac-purple flowers covering the previous year's stems in early summer. 'Argentea' is the prettiest form, with silky silvery leaves that sparkle in the sun.

How to Grow
Full sun. Loam-based commercial soil mix; good drainage is essential. Tolerates dryness. Repot every 1–2 years. Prune buddleias in containers to the ground in late winter to force a fountain of fresh shoots. They can grow 5 ft. tall in a season. (Prune *B. alternifolia* after it flowers.) Generally pest-free, but spider mites may attack plants in hot, dry areas.

Buxus
Bucks´us. Boxwood
Buxaceae. Box family

Description
Evergreen shrubs or trees with a dense, branching, rounded

habit and smooth leathery leaves. Flowers are inconspicuous. About 30 species, native to the Old and New World.

■ *microphylla* p. 185
Littleleaf box
Evergreen shrub. Zone 5
Height: to 4 ft. Spread: to 4 ft.
The dense branching and closely set, glossy, fine-textured foliage make this an ideal shrub for containers, and it can be sheared into formal shapes or topiary. Boxwood adds an air of elegance to outdoor sitting areas, entryways, and shady corners. Usually grown as a specimen, it can be incorporated in mixed planters, too.

There are two main varieties and many cultivars, which differ in habit, mature size, winter foliage color, and hardiness. Var. *japonica* is the most robust, with an open, spreading habit. It tolerates heat. Var. *koreana* grows slower and shorter. It's quite hardy, but it can turn an ugly yellowish brown in winter. Cultivars with a compact habit and good green color even in cold winters include 'Compacta' (slow-growing), 'Green Beauty' (upright), 'Winter Beauty', 'Winter Gem', and 'Wintergreen'.

A series of new hybrids between *B. microphylla* var. *koreana* and *B. sempervirens* combine the hardiness of Korean box with the green winter color of common box; they are very good for containers. 'Green Velvet' grows naturally round without any pruning; 'Green Mound' and 'Green Gem' are similar. 'Chicagoland Green' is faster-growing and finer-textured. *B. sempervirens* 'Suffruticosa' is a compact, slow-growing form of common box that forms a low billowing mound. Leaves and flowers are fragrant.

How to Grow
Full or part sun. Loam-based commercial soil mix; must be well drained. Start in a 12–14-in. pot; at maturity may need a 20–22-in. pot or tub. Boxwoods have shallow roots that need special attention. Water regularly; a mulch may help keep them from drying out, but leave an open space around the trunk to prevent stem rot. Feed with slow-release fertilizer and occasional soluble fertilizer supplement during active growth. Prune to shape after new growth emerges in spring. Overwinter out of strong winds; keep soil on the dry side. Subject to several pests, including leafminers, spider mites, and nematodes.

Caladium
Ka-lay′dee-um
Araceae. Arum family

Description
Tender perennials with basal tubers sprouting clumps of large, often colorful leaves. About 7 species, native to tropical South America.

■ × *hortulanum* *p. 151*
(*C. bicolor*)
Caladium
Tender perennial grown as an annual. All zones
Height: 1–3 ft. Spread: 2 ft.
Plant tubers in spring and enjoy the brightly colored foliage until frost. The large (to 12 in. long) arrowhead-shaped leaves have a delicate papery texture and come in solid, mottled, or spotted patterns of crimson, rose, pink, pale green, and translucent white. The bold variegated foliage of 'Candidum' lights up a shady area. Caladiums are lovely mixed with ferns, impatiens, begonias, and coleus or with houseplants, such as spider plant, summering outdoors on a partly shaded patio.

How to Grow
Part sun to shade. Amend commercial loam-based soil mix with peat moss to increase moisture retention. Plant 1 tuber per 8-in. pot; 3 for a 14-in. pot. Position tubers bumpy side up in pots indoors and put them in a warm place for a few weeks to develop roots, then move them outdoors when night temperatures reach 55° F. Place in a spot protected from wind. Needs constant water when in active growth. Feed with high-nitrogen fertilizer. Stop watering and let leaves die down (or freeze down) in fall, then dig tubers and let them dry for a week in a warm place before burying them in a box of vermiculite or sawdust. Store at 50°–60° F for the winter.

Calamintha
Kal-a-minth′a
Labiatae. Mint family

Description
Perennials, sometimes woody at the base, with scented leaves and small clusters of pale flowers. Only 7 species, native to Eurasia.

- ***nepeta*** *p. 130*
(sometimes listed as *C. nepetoides*)
Perennial. Zone 5
Height: 12–24 in. Spread: 18 in.
One of the most charming plants introduced to gardeners in recent years. Makes a mound of gracefully arranged gray-green foliage topped with a hazy cloud of tiny white or lilac flowers for weeks in summer and fall. Bees love it. The shiny leaves provide a pleasant mint scent when brushed against; place near a patio or entryway so you can enjoy the fragrance. The long, leafy sprays make a great filler in fresh flower arrangements. Combine it with *Heuchera* 'Palace Purple', *Berberis* 'Crimson Pygmy', *Ajuga* 'Tricolor', or Oriental lilies. Shop at herb nurseries to find other calamints, including the lovely white-splotched *C. grandiflora* 'Variegata', which has pink flowers. All are pretty and fragrant.

How to Grow
Full sun or afternoon shade; tolerates heat. Loam-based commercial soil mix. One plant per 10-in. pot. Feed with slow-release fertilizer. Cut back long stems in fall; overwinter in cold frame or unheated garage. Repot every 3–4 years. Easy to grow from seed or from cuttings of basal shoots. Has no pests or diseases.

Calendula
Ka-len´dew-la
Compositae. Daisy family

Description
Annuals or perennials with slightly hairy leaves and long-stemmed daisylike blossoms. About 20 species, most native to the Mediterranean region.

- ***officinalis*** *p. 103*
Pot marigold
Annual. All zones
Height: to 2 ft. Spread: 8–12 in.
Bright and cheerful blossoms on long stalks top this easy-to-grow annual. Traditionally called pot marigold in England, the flowers are edible and can be used fresh or dried to add color and a mild flavor to salads, soups, or rice. Flower colors range from pale cream to yellow, gold, and bright orange. Plants make good cool-season companions for pansies, forget-me-nots, snapdragons, and ornamental kale in autumn. There are compact strains; the taller ones make good cut flowers.

How to Grow
Full or part sun. Loam-based commercial soil mix. Tolerates some frost, so set out early. Easily stressed by drought. Does best in cool weather. Grow for summer bloom in the North, for fall to spring bloom where winters are mild. Deadhead to prolong blooming. Cut back and fertilize in midsummer to encourage fall bloom. Attacked by pests if stressed by heat; otherwise trouble-free.

Callistemon
Kal-i-stee´mon. Bottlebrush
Myrtaceae. Myrtle family

Description
Evergreen shrubs or trees with leafy stems and distinctive bottlebrush-like spikes of red or yellow flowers. About 20 species, native to Australia.

■ *citrinus* *p. 185*
Lemon bottlebrush
Evergreen shrub. Zone 9
Height: 4–5 ft. Spread: 4–5 ft. (Dwarf forms)
A mounded shrub with arching branches that can be trained as a small tree. The bright red flowers make 6-in. "bottlebrushes" near the ends of the branches; flushes of bloom appear sporadically in all seasons and attract hummingbirds. Interesting woody seed capsules persist on the stems for years. The slender lemon-scented leaves are silky and pink at first, turning dark green and firm as they mature. *C. viminalis,* weeping bottlebrush, has an upright trunk and slender branches that hang straight down. Bright red 8-in. bottlebrushes dangle in the breeze. The species is too tall for containers, but 'Captain Cook' is a dwarf (to 6 ft.) variety, and 'Little John' reaches only 3 ft.

How to Grow
Full sun. Loam-based commercial soil mix. Tolerates heat and recovers from drying out. Plant *C. citrinus* in a deep, 10–16-in. pot; an 8–10-in. pot will do for dwarf forms. May need iron supplement if water contains sodium or calcium. To train a tree, provide a stake and remove lower branches until a head is formed. Prune just behind spent blooms to limit size. Move indoors over winter in cold climates.

Camellia
Ka-mee′lee-a. Camellia
Theaceae. Tea family

Description
Evergreen shrubs or trees with leathery leaves. Many have showy waxlike flowers in fall, winter, or spring. About 80 species, native to eastern Asia, and thousands of cultivars.

The evergreen foliage is attractive all year, but the flowers are the real attraction. Unfortunately, it's difficult to get camellias to flower in areas with long, cold winters. If you live in zone 7 or colder, you'll need a cool greenhouse to ensure flowering.

■ **japonica** *p. 186*
Evergreen shrub. Zone 8 or 7
Height: 5 ft. Spread: 3–4 ft.
These camellias are handsome evergreen shrubs that grow well in containers for a patio or entryway. They can be trained into standards or espaliers. The oval, dark green leaves are glossy and leathery. Plump round flower buds at the ends of the branches open into showy single or double flowers in white, shades of pink, or red. Flowers are usually scentless, but they have exquisite petals and make lovely corsages.

There are thousands of cultivars, each blooming for a long season, starting in fall, winter, or early spring. Most gardeners choose formal double blooms such as the white 'Alba Plena' and 'Purity' or the red 'Glen 40' and 'Pope Pius IX'. Fanciers prefer the newer, larger, less formal types such as the rose-red 'Giulio Nuccio' or the pink 'Mrs. D. W. Davis'. 'Elegans' has large, pink, anemone-type flowers on an arching, mounded, tiered shrub; 'C. M. Wilson' (pale pink) and 'Shiro Chan' (white) are similar.

C. reticulata is grown chiefly for its spectacular flowers, which can reach 9 in. across in some varieties. Flowers are round with fluted petals, pink to deep purplish red, often marked with white. The plant tends to be open and lanky, not particularly handsome out of bloom. Move its container to a featured spot for the midwinter to early-spring bloom. Growers outside California and possibly the Gulf Coast will need a cool greenhouse to ensure flowers. Cultivars have different flower colors, shapes, and sizes. New hybrids of *C. reticulata* and *C. japonica* are handsome shrubs with exquisite flowers but are very tender to cold.

C. sasanqua cultivars tend to be smaller, neater, more easily shaped shrubs, with smaller leaves and single or double flowers in shades of white, pink, or red, borne profusely over a long period from autumn into winter. Some have a light fragrance. They tolerate full sun or considerable shade and are fine container plants, spilling nicely over edges or trained on a trellis. 'Jean May' is compact and upright, with double pink flowers. 'Mine-No-Yuki' ('White Doves') has double white flowers on limber shoots that are easily trained to climb or to trail. 'Yuletide' has single deep red flowers in midwinter on a compact upright shrub.

Cultivars of *C. hiemalis,* often grouped with *C. sasanqua,* are small (2–3 ft. tall by 5–6 ft. wide) spreading shrubs with tiered or layered branches. They're especially lovely trailing from a planter, hanging basket, large window box, or urn. 'Shishi Gashira' is low and compact, with semidouble, bright rose flowers. 'Showanosakae' grows faster and is more open and willowy, with light pink flowers.

The Ackerman hybrids were developed by crossing the hardiest camellia, *C. oleifera,* with other species. These new plants have a dense habit, small evergreen leaves, and pretty single or double flowers up to 4 in. wide. Grown in the ground, sheltered from dry winter winds, they're hardy in zone 6, possibly zone 5; container gardeners in those zones might give them a try, too.

How to Grow

Part sun to shade. Needs well-drained, acidic potting soil amended with plenty of peat or organic matter. Use an acid-type fertilizer after bloom. Keep soil moist and cool; mulch helps. With root pruning, can grow in a 12-in. pot; a 2-ft. box or tub allows plants to grow larger. Repot just before, during, or after bloom. Pinch runaway shoots; cut back to dormant growth buds (slight swellings on stems) to encourage bushy growth. In marginal areas, overwinter in cool (40° F) greenhouse. Control petal blight by destroying affected flowers and changing mulch each year. Fungal leafspot and scale insects also cause problems.

Campanula
Kam-pan´you-la. Bellflower
Campanulaceae. Bellflower family

Description

A popular and diverse group of perennials, biennials, and annuals, varying in size and form but most with showy blue, violet, pink, or white flowers. About 300 species, most native to the north temperate zone.

■ *poscharskyana* p. 131
Serbian bellflower
Perennial. Zone 3
Height: 6–9 in. Spread: 12 in. or more
Long trailing stems spread rapidly from a central mound to dangle from a hanging basket or other container. Plants are covered with loose clusters of starry lavender-blue or white flowers in spring. Combines well with bolder plants, such as vinca vine, marigolds, or dusty-miller. Tolerates dryness and grows fast. *C. portenschlagiana,* the Dalmatian bellflower (zone 4), offers a tight mound of shiny green, ivylike leaves that is attractive even without flowers. Long trailing stems emerge from this mound, carrying clusters of marvelous violet-blue (or white) flowers like little bells or cups.

How to Grow
Full or part sun. Loam-based commercial soil mix; must be well drained. Fertilize regularly, deadhead, and trim stems as needed. Easy to grow from cuttings or divisions. Overwinter in cold frame or cool greenhouse.

Canna
Kan′na
Cannaceae. Canna family

Description
Tender perennials with thick starchy rhizomes, leafy upright stems topped with large showy flowers, and seeds like shiny beads. About 25 species, native to the New World tropics.

■ hybrids *p. 151*
(*C.* × *generalis*)
Tender perennials. Zone 8
Height: 2–6 ft. Spread: 2–3 ft.

The bold leaves and brilliant flowers add a tropical touch to patio plantings. Easy to grow in large containers, cannas have big flowers in bright red, orange, salmon, pink, yellow, or white and bloom from early summer to fall. Plants make a clump of erect stems, each with several broad leaves in shades of green, reddish green, bronze, or variegated. Place nasturtiums, grasses, or cascading petunias at their feet for added drama.

There are many cultivars, differing in flower color, leaf color, and stature. The 'Pfitzer Dwarfs' (2–4 ft.) come in crimson, pink, coral, and yellow. 'The President' (3 ft.) has bright red flowers and deep green leaves. 'Wyoming' (4 ft.) has orange flowers and bronze leaves. 'Striped Beauty' (3–4 ft.) has yellow flowers and cream-striped green leaves.

How to Grow

Full or part sun; tolerate heat. Loam-based commercial soil mix. Large pot—at least 12 in. by 14 in. Plant one clump per pot. Plants prefer steady moisture but tolerate some dryness. Remove faded flowers for neatness and prolonged bloom. Leaf caterpillars are the only pest.

In zone 8 or warmer, plant rhizomes in spring and divide every few years. In zone 7 or colder, start rhizomes in pots indoors, a month before last frost, and put them in a warm place to start growing roots. Move them outdoors when night temperatures are above 50° F. When frost kills tops in fall, dig up rhizomes and dry them for a few days before storing them in a box of damp peat moss for the winter. Divide rhizomes in spring before repotting.

Capsicum
Kap´sigh-kum
Solanaceae. Nightshade family

Description

Shrubby perennial herbs that are grown for their attractive fruits, which include edible hot and sweet peppers, as well as just for ornament. About 20 species, native to tropical America.

■ *annuum*   p. 104   Pictured on p. 234
Ornamental pepper
Perennial grown as an annual. All zones
Height: 8–14 in. Spread: 8–12 in.
Ornamental peppers, with their dark green oval leaves, small white flowers, and showy fruits, can strike a note of surprise

in mixed containers. The conical fruits, which turn from green and yellow to red late in the season, are produced in prominent clusters and are especially effective combined with bronze foliage plants such as perilla, 'Blackie' sweet potato, or bronze coleus. Cultivars include 'Fiesta', 'Holiday Cheer', 'Holiday Time', 'Aurora', 'Maya', 'Candlelight', and 'Jigsaw'.

How to Grow
Full sun; tolerates heat. Loam-based commercial soil mix. Put 1 plant per 6-in. pot or add to mixed container. Start seeds indoors 6–8 weeks before last frost; set outside after night temperatures rise above 55° F. Needs constant moisture. Bring inside when frost threatens for a few more weeks of show. Red spider mites can be a problem during dry weather.

Caryopteris
Kare-ee-yop´ter-is. Bluebeard
Verbenaceae. Verbena family

Description
Deciduous shrubs or perennials with simple leaves and abundant clusters of tiny blue, violet, or white flowers. About 6 species, native to eastern Asia, and a few hybrids.

■ × *clandonensis* p. 173
Bluebeard, blue spirea
Deciduous shrub. Zone 6 or 5
Height: 2–3 ft. Spread: 2–3 ft.
A small shrub that combines very well with perennials (it's often sold as a perennial). New spring shoots have neatly spaced pairs of downy gray leaves. Fluffy clusters of lavender-blue flowers tip each shoot in August and September—a

welcome splash of color at that time of year—and attract butterflies. Combines well with lespedeza, *Sedum* 'Autumn Joy', and late-blooming roses. Also looks good with silver-foliage plants, buddleias, *Coreopsis* 'Moonbeam', and ornamental grasses. 'Blue Mist' has an informal rounded shape and pale flowers. 'Dark Knight' is upright, with dark violet blossoms. 'Longwood Blue' has abundant sky blue flowers. 'Worcester Gold' offers yellow leaves.

How to Grow
Full sun; tolerates heat. Loam-based commercial soil mix plus added grit to improve drainage. Recovers from drying out. One plant per 14–16-in. pot. Feed with slow-release fertilizer in spring; supplement during summer with soluble fertilizer. Cut back drastically to a woody base in spring to promote shapely new growth. Overwinter dormant plant in unheated garage; keep soil dry. Pest-free.

Catharanthus
Kath-a-ran´thus
Apocynaceae. Dogbane family

Description
Perennials or annuals with simple opposite leaves and white or rosy flowers with 5 broad petals. About 8 species, most native to Madagascar.

■ *roseus* p. 104
(*Vinca rosea*)
Madagascar periwinkle
Perennial grown as an annual. All zones
Height: 1–2 ft. Spread: 1 ft. or more
Beautiful on its own or with almost any plant in its color range—*Cosmos* 'Sonata', gomphrena, and *Salvia farinacea*. Grows quickly from seed to make a mounding bushy plant of glossy green foliage covered with cheerful 5-petaled flowers in shades of white, pink, or rose, often with a contrasting eye. Thrives in hot weather, dry or humid, and keeps blooming after other annuals have given up. Many cultivars are available from seed catalogs or local garden centers.

How to Grow
Full or part sun. Loam-based commercial soil mix. Transplant seedlings carefully (they can be shocked by rough handling), about 5 in. apart after danger of frost is past. Needs regular watering but rots if overwatered. Pest-free.

Celosia

Sel-lo´see-a
Amaranthaceae. Amaranth family

Description

Annuals or perennials with strong upright stems, thin leaves, and dense heads or plumes of tiny, chaffy, brightly colored flowers. About 50 species, native to tropical climates.

■ *argentea* p. 105
Cockscomb
Annual. All zones
Height: to 2 ft. Spread: 1 ft.

A heat-loving annual that's colorful in all parts, with particularly brilliant red, orange, gold, salmon, or pink flower heads. The individual flowers are tiny, but they're crowded into dense fluffy plumes in var. *plumosa* or into odd wavy crests in var. *cristata*. Both dwarf and taller forms are commonly available and can be worked into an exciting combination of mixed annuals. Try with *Zinnia angustifolia, Cosmos sulphureus*, nasturtiums, and big spikes of red or blue salvias. Gardeners who disdain big masses of bright colors should check the specialty seed catalogs; there are other celosias with graceful slender spikes of pale flowers.

How to Grow

Full sun; thrives in heat (performs poorly in cool climates). Loam-based commercial soil mix. Recovers from drying out. Wait until nights are warm before transplanting seedlings into pots outside. Space close together if you want single-stemmed flower heads; allow more space and pinch out tips for branched plants with many smaller heads. Flowers can be cut and dried.

Ceratostigma

Ser-rat-o-stig´ma
Plumbaginaceae. Plumbago family

Description

Shrubs or woody perennials with simple leaves and dense heads of blue flowers. About 8 species, native to Africa and Asia.

■ *plumbaginoides* p. 132
Dwarf plumbago
Perennial. Zone 5
Height: 12 in. Spread: 12 in. or more

A spreading perennial with clear blue flowers, 1/2 in. wide and borne in dense heads. Bloom continues from the heat of summer through fall. Leaves are smooth and plain, dark green in summer and reddish purple in fall. Makes a good companion for spring bulbs, as it leafs out in late spring and then fills in the gaps when the bulb foliage dies down. Also lovely when its fall colors complement autumn foliage and ripe red berries. Try in window boxes or as a ground cover to a large specimen tree or topiary.

How to Grow
Full or part sun; tolerates heat if partly shaded. Loam-based commercial soil mix. Put 1 plant per 10-in. pot; 3 plants in a 14-in. pot. Cut old stems to the ground in spring. Rooted stolons can be transplanted in spring or fall. Space 8 in. apart for a ground cover. Divide in spring; discard woody old crowns, save vigorous young shoots. Goes dormant in winter even in the mildest climates. Overwinter in unheated garage; keep soil on the dry side.

Chamaecyparis
Kam-ee-sip'ar-is. False cypress
Cupressaceae. Cypress family

Description
Evergreen conifers with needlelike juvenile foliage and scaly adult foliage. Wild trees grow huge and yield important timber, but hundreds of dwarf forms are better suited for gardens and containers. About 7 species, native to North America and eastern Asia.

■ *obtusa* **and its cultivars** *p. 186*
Hinoki cypress
Conifers. Zone 5
Height: 2–6 ft. Spread: 1–3 ft. (Dwarf forms)
The Hinoki cypress's rich emerald green color and the soft texture of the flattened sprays of tiny rounded scales are appealing. The dwarf forms make excellent patio plants. There are hundreds of cultivars, differing in foliage color and texture, rate of growth, mature size, and habit. 'Nana Gracilis' (slowly growing to 6 ft. and eventually reaching 10–12 ft.) has shiny dark green foliage arranged in dense curving sprays; it's one of the most popular of all dwarf conifers. 'Nana' and 'Kosteri' are even more dwarf, reaching only 3 ft. after decades. 'Crippsii' (to 30 ft.) has broad sprays of golden fo-

liage. 'Coralliformis' or 'Torulosa' (to 10 ft.) has bright green foliage compressed into slender cordlike strands.

How to Grow

Full or part sun. Loam-based commercial soil mix. Smallest forms can fit in 6-in. pots; larger in pots or boxes up to 16 in. Keep soil moist. Underpotting will restrict growth, as will root pruning. Feed bonsai and plants in small pots frequently; larger plants can be fed in early spring and early summer, or use a slow-release fertilizer. Repot only when plant shows signs of stress—roots on surface of soil, drying out too quickly, poor color. Protect from winter sun and wind, which can discolor or scorch the foliage. Keep root mass from freezing solid. Spider mites may be a problem in hot, dry weather; hose them off.

■ *pisifera* cultivars *p. 187*
Sawara cypress
Conifers. Zone 5
Height: 1–8 ft. Spread: 1–5 ft.
Smallest and slowest-growing cultivars make handsome bonsai; larger cultivars add unusual foliage texture and color to patios and decks. 'Boulevard' or 'Cyano-Viridis' makes an irregular cone, slowly reaching 10 ft. or more, and has especially soft and fluffy foliage, silver-blue in summer, tinged purple in winter. 'Boulevard' retains dead brown foliage and needs pruning for tidiness and to reveal the branch structure as it ages. 'Filifera Aurea Nana' has long, threadlike, golden foliage on a small dense plant. 'Nana' makes a very small (2-ft.), flat-topped, dark green bun.

How to Grow
Like *C. obtusa*.

Chrysanthemum
Kri-san´thee-mum
Compositae. Daisy family

Description
Gardeners and taxonomists have different visions of the genus *Chrysanthemum*. To gardeners, it's a group of easy-to-grow annuals, perennials, and subshrubs with daisylike blossoms that are cheerful in the garden and long lasting as cut flowers. Their foliage often has a pungent fragrance. The plants gardeners grow belong to just a few species, but there are thousands of cultivars.

Taxonomists used to lump between 100 and 200 species, including many of no interest to gardeners, into the genus *Chrysanthemum*, but it was a motley grouping that invited revision. There have been various attempts to regroup the species into several smaller genera, which explains why some of the Latin names listed below have synonyms. Fortunately, the common names are much less confusing and generally reliable for distinguishing one plant from another.

■ × *morifolium* p. 132
(*Dendranthema* × *grandiflorum*)
Florist's chrysanthemum, hardy garden chrysanthemum
Perennial. Hardiness depends on cultivar
Height: 6 in.–6 ft. Spread: 1–5 ft. or more
Popular for their brightly colored, long-lasting flowers in fall, chrysanthemums are easy to grow in containers and raised planters. Inexpensive plants are available in bloom at almost any time of year—great for party decorations. Plants can be trained as standards, bonsai, or cascades. There's an endless array of cultivars, colored white, yellow, bronze, orange, pink, red, or purple, sometimes with two or more colors in the same flower. Some have tall erect flower stalks, good for cutting. Others form low spreading mounds. Blossoms may be single (like daisies), double (flat in back but rounded and fluffy in front), pompom (ball-shaped), button (less than 1 in. wide and rounded), or fancy forms with "petals" shaped like spoons or quills. There are plenty of good garden varieties hardy even in zone 6 or 5. *C. frutescens* has largish, light yellow daisies and is a first-rate container plant in mild-winter climates. *C. nipponicum,* a great shrubby Shasta daisy, is worth hunting for.

Chrysanthemums need short days (actually long nights) to flower. They begin to form flower buds as the nights get longer in late summer and fall. Early bloomers need fewer hours of darkness to begin budding; some start blooming as early as late August, so they avoid hard frosts in northern gardens. Late bloomers need more hours of darkness to initiate buds. They get frozen in cold northern gardens, but they start late and continue past Christmas in California and the South. In mild climates, mums may keep blooming or bloom again in spring, since nights are long all winter.

How to Grow

Full sun or light shade part of the day. Soilless or loam-based commercial soil mix; should drain well. Pot individual plants in 4–6-in. pots, depending on your needs. Space 6–8 in. apart in window boxes or big pots. Keep moist—water stress causes plants to lose lower leaves. Frequent light feeding. Pinch tips back hard two or three times to shape low growers into dense bushy mounds. Stake tall forms if you want straight stems, and remove side buds if you want just one big flower per stalk. After flowering, cut stalks back to 6-in. stubs and store in an unheated garage or a cold frame over winter. In spring, divide clump into separate rooted shoots or root tip cuttings. Several strains of hardy chrysanthemums can be raised easily from seed and will blossom the first year from an early spring sowing. Watch for and control aphids and spider mites.

■ *multicaule* p. 105
(*Coleostephus myconis*)
Annual. All zones
Height: 6–8 in. Spread: 8–10 in.
Daisylike flowers rise about 1 ft. above a low mat of fleshy, smooth, narrow foliage. Bright yellow flowers up to 2$\frac{1}{2}$ in. across have wide rays. Single plants are not impressive, but they are attractive when mixed in large containers with annuals, such as stocks, snapdragons, and larkspur, and with perennials. In window boxes, try them with petunias, lantana, mimulus, nierembergia, and lobelia. Happiest in cool weather. In warm climates, plants may live a second year. *C. paludosum* (*Leucanthemum paludosum*) is similar in size but has white, yellow-centered daisies, resembling miniature Shasta daisies.

How to Grow

Full sun. Loam-based commercial soil mix; must be well drained. Easy from seed started indoors 8–10 weeks before last frost. Keep moist and feed lightly.

■ *pacificum* p. 133
Perennial. Zone 7
Height: 1–1$\frac{1}{2}$ ft. Spread: 4 ft.
Grown primarily for its foliage—the small scalloped leaves

are gray-green edged with white. It forms a low, spreading mound. Blooms too late for northern gardens but bears clusters of little gold buttons in the South. Try as a trailing plant.

How to Grow
Full sun; tolerates heat. Soilless or loam-based commercial soil mix; must be well drained. If you don't want it to sprawl, pinch several times to encourage more compact habit. Old plants get woody at the base and are hard to divide. Start new plants by rooting tip cuttings in spring.

■ *parthenium* p. 106 *Pictured above*
(*Matricaria capensis, Tanacetum parthenium*)
Feverfew
Perennial herb grown as an annual. Zone 5
Height: 1–3 ft. Spread: 1–2 ft.
Carefree and easy to grow, with pungently aromatic ferny foliage and masses of $1/2$-in. daisies off and on all summer and fall. Pretty in a pot all by itself or as a companion to verbenas, petunias, lilies, or salvias. 'Aureum', with golden yellow foliage, is lovely with purple, yellow, and orange flowers at its feet or with variegated leaves of ribbon grass or flowering maple. Cut flowers are very long lasting in water. There are double forms, both white and yellow.

How to Grow
Full or part sun. Loam-based commercial soil mix. Seedlings grow quickly; use a 10-in. by 10-in. pot for small nursery-grown plants. Cut back after flowering to encourage repeat bloom. Attacked by aphids but has few other pests. Can overwinter in cold frame or cool greenhouse.

Citrus
Sit´rus
Rutaceae. Citrus family

Description
Evergreen trees or shrubs, usually spiny, with glossy simple leaves, richly fragrant white or pale pink flowers, and aromatic juicy fruit. This genus includes oranges, lemons, grapefruits, limes, and other citrus fruits; all are notably handsome plants. About 16 species, native to southern and southeastern Asia.

■ **cultivars** *p. 187*
Where the climate allows (minimum temperatures above 20°–28° F), all citrus fruits give 4-season beauty with shiny, leathery, bright green leaves; powerfully fragrant blossoms; and showy, tasty fruit. Most citrus are available on dwarfing rootstock; such plants are best for containers. They bear full-size fruit on half-size plants and make excellent shrubs in containers.

The 'Eureka' lemon is tasty and ripens in coolish summers. Where hardy, it is seldom out of fruit. 'Lisbon' lemon is somewhat more heat-tolerant. 'Improved Meyer' is hardier to cold and tends to be a smaller plant, with rounded, orange-yellow, less-acid fruit. 'Ponderosa' lemon bears huge fruits early in its life and is widely available. Other good choices include the 'Bearss' seedless lime, 'Minneola' tangelo, 'Dancy' tangerine, 'Marsh' seedless and 'Ruby' grapefruits, 'Valencia' and 'Washington' navel oranges, and 'Owari Satsuma' mandarin. Kumquats and 'Chinotto' orange are extremely attractive in leaf and fruit and are in good scale as container plants.

Calamondin (× *Citrofortunella mitis*) is an attractive, columnar container plant. Tiny orange fruits are often grown for ornament, though they are a standby in Filipino cooking.

A few nurseries in the South and the Pacific Northwest are

experimenting with citrus supposed to be hardy in zone 8, but these are not yet widely available. Gardeners in cold climates can maintain a dwarf citrus tree for years in a 12-in. pot, taking it outdoors for the summer and overwintering it in a cool sunroom or greenhouse, or even a bright window.

How to Grow
Full sun. Soilless or loam-based commercial soil mix. Will grow in 6–8-in. pots but are bigger and better in 12-in. or larger pots. Root-prune to control size. Feed frequently during growing season; may need supplemental iron and trace elements. Little pruning is required. Subject to many pests and diseases, but few concern home gardeners. Watch for spider mites, scale, snails, and fruitworms. Overwinter on a sun porch or in a cool greenhouse at temperatures above 25°–28° F.

Clematis
Klem´a-tis
Ranunculaceae. Buttercup family

Description
Most clematis are deciduous vines, but some are evergreen vines and a few are deciduous perennials or semishrubs. In climbing types, the leaf petiole wraps like a bent elbow around a wire or other support. Most have wide flat flowers with 4 to many sepals (in clematis, what look like petals are actually sepals); some have smaller, nodding, urn-shaped flowers. In fall, watch for fluffy clusters of feathery-tailed seeds. About 250 species, nearly all native to the north temperate zone, and hundreds of hybrid cultivars. The large-flowered hybrids are perhaps the most popular of all garden vines.

■ **large-flowered hybrids** *p. 163   Pictured on p. 244*
Deciduous vines. Zone 5
Height: to 15 ft.
Outstanding in bloom, hybrid clematis have flat blossoms 3–8 in. wide, with 4–8 or more large sepals in shades from white and pink to rich red, purple, and blue. Most clematis have similar foliage (dark green and leathery) and habit (slender stems that look weak but climb vigorously). Use by themselves or to provide height in a mixed container. A single plant trained up a lightpost or trellis by your entryway or draped over a taller shrub (such as a standard rose) will make a brilliant mass of color for weeks. No more gorgeous hardy vine exists. If space is limited, the early-blooming hybrids are best.

There are hundreds of cultivars, grouped according to their parent species and differing in flower color and season of bloom. Local nurseries usually stock only a limited number, so you'll need to search mail-order suppliers if you want to explore the world of clematis. Fortunately, all clematis are beautiful, and many people will be perfectly happy with what is locally available. Some favorites include 'Duchess of Edinburgh' (larger double white flowers); 'Sieboldii' (white with purple center); 'Kermesina' (deep red); 'Comptesse de Bouchard' (soft rosy pink with rounded sepals); 'General Sikorski' (medium blue with puckered edges); 'The President' (deep violet-purple with pointed sepals); 'Polish Spirit' (rich purple-blue); 'Guernsey Cream' (creamy yellow); and 'Silver Moon' (silver-mauve).

How to Grow

Full or part sun. Loam-based commercial soil mix; must drain well. Keep soil moist. Feed with slow-release or soluble fertilizer; stop fertilizing after late summer. Pot should be at least 1 ft. wide by 18 in. deep. Wood, stone, or clay pots are ideal; raise off ground on bricks to enhance drainage and aeration. Overwinter in frost-free spot.

Pruning is important, but the timing depends on whether plants bloom on new or old shoots. If you're not certain which type your plant is when you purchase it, observe its growth and flowering the first year to find out. Those that bloom on new growth should be pruned hard, cut back to within 8 in. in earliest spring when the leaf buds begin to expand. Provide support immediately for the new shoots, which are brittle and break easily in the wind. Those that bloom on old shoots in spring and on new shoots in summer are pruned later. Remove only dead or damaged shoots in very early spring; do the main pruning-back immediately after bloom in spring.

Clivia
Kly′vee-a. Kaffir lily
Amaryllidaceae. Amaryllis family

Description
A small number of South African species of perennial herbs, one of which is widely grown as a houseplant. They have fleshy roots, and the base of the stem is bulblike.

■ *miniata* p. 152
Clivia, kaffir lily
Bulb. Zone 9
Height: to 2 ft. Spread: to 3 ft.
A handsome evergreen perennial, clivia has a thick rootstock that produces broad, dark green, strap-shaped leaves. In late winter or early spring, dense, rounded clusters of lilylike flowers rise on stout 2-ft. stems. Flower color varies from deep reddish orange to (rarely) yellow. Hardy outdoors only in the mildest climates, clivia is an excellent container plant, thriving and blooming best when its roots nearly fill the container. It will flower in fairly heavy shade indoors, under house overhangs, or under trees. Use it to adorn an entry or a shaded corner of the patio.

How to Grow
Sun to shade. Loam-based commercial soil mix, well drained and enriched with organic matter. Young plants will bloom in 6-in. pots. Repot only when plant threatens to push itself out of its container; a 12-in. pot will hold a mature clump for many years. Keep soil moist; can survive an occasional dry spell. Immediately after flowering and through the summer, give plenty of water, light, and liquid fertilizer. In fall, move to cool spot (50° F) indoors and let soil almost dry out. In late winter, when flower spikes begin to elongate, provide more light, water, and heat.

Cobaea
Koh-bay′ah
Polemoniaceae. Phlox family

Description
A small group of shrubby climbing plants native to tropical America, one species (below) commonly grown for ornament.

■ *scandens* p. 163
Cup-and-saucer vine

Evergreen perennial grown as an annual. Zone 9
Height: 8–12 ft.
From late summer until frost, cup-and-saucer vine supplies many prominent 3-in.-wide flowers, which open as yellow-green bells and age to a purple saucer of wide, flaring tepals. Compound leaves have 4–6 oval leaflets; climbs by tendrils. You can grow it on its own or combine it on a shady trellis with morning glory, canary creeper, or other vines. *C. s.* var. *alba* has green flowers that turn white.

How to Grow
Full sun. Thrives in long, humid, hot summers; doesn't do well in cool areas. Loam-based commercial soil mix. Start seeds in peat pots 6–8 weeks before last frost; move to container outdoors when night temperatures stay above 50° F. Needs constant moisture.

Coleus
Ko´lee-us
Labiatae. Mint family

Description
Perennials or annuals, usually succulent, with square stems, opposite leaves, and small white or pale lavender flowers. About 150 species, native to the Old World tropics.

■ *blumei* hybrids *p. 106*
(*Solenostemon scutellarioides*)
Coleus
Tender perennial grown as an annual. All zones
Height: 1–2 ft. Spread: 1–2 ft.
Their glowing foliage colors make coleus good leafy companions in large mixed pots with pink geraniums, lobelia, and vinca vine. Can be worked into any combination to highlight flowers that share the colors of the coleus foliage. Try coleus with wax and tuberous begonias, impatiens, caladiums, wishbone flower, and browallia in lightly shaded containers. Especially beautiful when seen backlit. There are hundreds of cultivars and seed strains. Some are more compact; some are multicolored; some have fringed or ruffled leaves. Leaf colors include green, chartreuse, yellow, cream, pink, salmon, orange, and red. The spikes of tiny blue flowers aren't unattractive, but they detract from the leaves.

How to Grow
Part sun or filtered shade; tolerate heat. Loam-based com-

mercial soil mix. Start seeds indoors 8 weeks before last frost, or buy plants at local nurseries. Set outside when night temperatures stay above 50° F. To encourage compact, bushy plants, pinch tips and remove flower buds as they form. Can be crowded into a pot. Keep soil moist and feed often with high-nitrogen liquid fertilizer. Overwinter on a sunny windowsill or take cuttings and root them in a glass of water to save favorite plants from year to year. Watch for and control slugs, whiteflies, and mealybugs.

Coreopsis
Ko-ree-op´sis
Compositae. Daisy family

Description
Perennials or annuals, most with abundant displays of yellow daisylike blossoms. More than 100 species, native to the New World and Africa.

■ *verticillata* p. 133
Thread-leaved coreopsis
Perennial. Zone 3
Height: 2–3 ft. Spread: 2–3 ft.
Valued for its deeply divided, fine, feathery foliage and pale golden yellow blossoms, 1–2 in. wide, borne for 4–6 weeks in midsummer. Flowers go well with warm colors and blues. 'Golden Showers' has large, bright lemon yellow flowers. 'Moonbeam' forms a dense clump with pale yellow flowers. Both are good for hanging baskets as well as pots. 'Zagreb' is compact (about 1 ft. tall), with darker yellow flowers; it

makes a good pot plant. *C. rosea* (zone 4) has similar delicate foliage and 1-in. pale pink flowers; try it in a hanging basket.

How to Grow
Full sun; tolerates heat. ('Moonbeam' tolerates light shade.) Soilless or loam-based commercial soil mix; needs good drainage and will recover from drying out. Divide and repot every 3 years to maintain vigor. There are too many flowers to deadhead individually, but you can trim off the top of the plant to encourage a second bloom. Poor drainage and waterlogging lead to mildew and other problems.

Corylus
Kor´i-lus. Hazelnut, filbert
Betulaceae. Birch family

Description
Deciduous shrubs or trees with drooping catkins in spring, toothed leaves that make a dense crown in summer, and edible nuts in fall. About 10 species, native to the north temperate zone.

■ *avellana* 'Contorta' *p. 174*
Harry Lauder's walking stick
Deciduous shrub. Zone 4
Height: 7–8 ft. Spread: 5–6 ft.
Most interesting in winter, this is a curiosity with contorted branches that twist into irregular spirals. The bark is shiny brown. Male catkins up to 3 in. long dangle conspicuously in late winter and early spring. Leaves are coarse and dull. Most effective as a specimen or combined with dwarf conifers, winter-hardy cacti, and succulents or with perennials with appealing foliage, such as lamb's-ears. Cut branches are excellent for floral arrangements.

How to Grow
Full or part sun. Loam-based commercial soil mix; must be well drained. Plant in a large pot or tub, where it will stay for years. These plants are almost always propagated by grafting, but the understock inevitably suckers vigorously, making corrective pruning an annual ritual. Cut all straight shoots back to the base. You can prune to shape at any time, though spring is best. Subject to various blights and diseases.

Cosmos
Kos′mos
Compositae. Daisy family

Description
Perennials or annuals with slender branching stems, finely divided opposite leaves, and bright daisylike blossoms on long stalks. About 26 species, native to the southwestern United States and Mexico.

■ *sulphureus* p. 107
Yellow cosmos
Annual. All zones
Height: to 3 ft. Spread: to 2 ft.
Smaller and brighter than common cosmos. The rough stems branch repeatedly and make a bushy plant with no pinching. The daisylike flowers are bright yellow, orange, or reddish orange. Blooms nonstop for months if deadheaded regularly. Combine with foliage accents or other bright colors—burgundy fountain grass, Dahlberg daisies, red dahlias, Chinese basil—or contrast with soft-colored foliage such as gray artemisias or blue fescue. 'Diablo', 'Bright Lights', and 'Sunny Red' are popular strains; 'Dwarf Klondike' and 'Sunny' strains are small ($1\frac{1}{2}$ ft. tall). *C. bipinnatus* 'Sonata' strain has 3-in. flowers on a compact 2-ft. plant. Comes in mixed shades or separately in pink or white.

How to Grow
Full sun. Loam-based commercial soil mix with coarse sand to improve drainage. Recovers from drying out. Sow seeds indoors 6 weeks before last frost. Transplant seedlings into display pots carefully—they don't like the disturbance—or sow directly in display pots.

Crocosmia
Kro-kos′mee-a
Iridaceae. Iris family

Description
Perennials with small corms, slender irislike leaves, and long stalks of very bright flowers. About 10 species, native to South Africa, with a few hybrids and cultivars.

■ 'Lucifer' p. 152
Crocosmia, montbretia
Perennial. Zone 5

Height: 3 ft. Spread: 1 ft.
Makes wonderful long sprays of clear bright red, long-lasting flowers in summer, excellent as cut flowers. The color absolutely gleams on a sunny day. Also makes a handsome fan of slender ribbed leaves. Excellent vertical accent in a container grouping of brilliant flowers. At its feet, plant annuals such as ageratum, nicotiana (smaller kinds), zinnias, Swan River daisies, and dwarf dahlias. Underground corms multiply rapidly to form showy clumps. Other crocosmias (usually called montbretia) are old-fashioned favorites with yellow, orange, red, or bicolor flowers.

How to Grow
Full or part sun. Loam-based commercial soil mix; add coarse sand for better drainage. In spring, plant 3 or 4 corms about 4 in. deep in a large clay pot, 12 in. high and wide. Feed regularly throughout the summer. Divide after several years when clump gets crowded. Overwinter in cold frame or cold basement, or lift bulbs in fall and store indoors like gladioli. Nearly trouble-free; if stressed by drought, spider mites can be a problem.

Crocus
Kro′kus
Iridaceae. Iris family

Description
Perennials with small corms, grassy leaves, and bright white, yellow, blue, or purple flowers on short stems in spring or fall. About 80 species, native from the Mediterranean region to China.

■ *vernus* p. 153
Dutch crocus, common crocus
Perennial. Zone 5
Height: 4–8 in. Spread: 6 in.
These are the most commonly grown crocuses, and a cheerful pot of them provides welcome late-winter or early-spring bloom. Flowers withstand frost, and they open in the sun and close at night or on cloudy days. The large-flowered (2–4 in. long by 1–3 in. wide) cultivars are hybrids of this species. 'Peter Pan' is white, 'Pickwick' is lilac with darker stripes, 'Remembrance' is purple, and 'Yellow Mammoth' is just like its name.

Golden bunch crocus (*C. ancyrensis* 'Golden Bunch', zone 3) produces cheery clusters of small bright golden flowers, as many as 10 blossoms to a corm. Golden crocuses (*C. chrysanthus*, zone 4) are smaller and more delicate than the common Dutch crocuses, with masses of honey-scented flowers in early spring. There are many cultivars with flowers in shades of yellow, white, blue, or purple, including some with striped or bicolor petals. 'Blue Pearl', 'Cream Beauty', 'Ladykiller', and 'Snow Bunting' belong to this species. All are easy to force for early display on the patio or as a greeting by the front door.

Autumn crocus (*C. speciosus*, zone 5) flowers during fall foliage season. Petals are blue, lavender, purple, or white, sometimes with dark veins. They are easy to grow in pots. Plant as soon as bulbs are available in late summer for a spectacular late addition to the patio container garden.

How to Grow
Full or part sun. Loam-based commercial soil mix; for better drainage, add coarse sand. Plant 1 in. deep in shallow pots or wooden boxes; position corms almost touching for best display. Chill for 8–12 weeks. Keep soil moist while chilling and during bloom. Fertilize as new shoots show and again after flowering to restore energy. Allow leaves to ripen naturally after flowering, then dry corms and pot again in fall.

Cyclamen
Sick′la-men, sy′kla-men
Primulaceae. Primrose family

Description
Perennials with a tuft of waxy-textured rounded leaves that sprout from flattish tubers. Long-lasting white, pink, or magenta flowers have thrown-back petals and nod above the foliage on long stalks. Only 17 species, native from central Europe to the Middle East.

■ *persicum* p. 153
Florist's cyclamen
Perennial. Zone 9
Height: 6–12 in. Spread: 6–14 in.
Florist's cyclamen blooms from late fall to early spring in the warm-winter climates where it grows well in pots. On the West Coast and in the South, cyclamens make beautiful accent plants in partly shaded spots on patios and balconies. Eye-catching clumps of silver-mottled, heart-shaped leaves are topped by graceful flowers with upright petals in pink, red, magenta, or white, marked with a darker "eye" that faces

downward. Best grown in a pot by themselves and grouped with primroses, ranunculus, and other cool-season plants. Dwarf strains are available, including some that are fragrant.

How to Grow
Part sun to shade. Loam-based commercial soil mix amended with coarse sand so it is moisture-retentive and well drained. Place tubers just below soil surface, 1 to a 6-in. pot, 3 to a 12-in. pot. Prefers to be slightly moist during active growth but is stressed by drought and doesn't like wet feet. Fertilize regularly to ensure continued bloom. Remove faded flowers and leaves. In summer, after corms go dormant, store pots on their side in a cool, dark place and don't water until they show signs of sprouting. Undisturbed plants will gradually multiply. When repotting is necessary, do it as they resprout in autumn. Relatively pest-free; spider mites bother stressed plants.

Cytisus
Sigh′ti-sus. Broom
Leguminosae. Pea family

Description
Bushy shrubs with prolific displays of pealike flowers. Some are deciduous, some evergreen, some nearly leafless with bright green twigs. More than 30 species, native to the Mediterranean region, and several hybrids.

■ × *praecox* 'Warminster' *p. 174*
Warminster broom
Deciduous shrub. Zone 5
Height: 3–4 ft. Spread: 2–4 ft.
Very showy in spring when the branches are covered with masses of creamy white or pale yellow flowers, $1/2$ in. wide, that resemble pea blossoms. The flowers last a long time but have a faintly unpleasant smell. Short narrow leaves appear in spring but drop quickly. Most of the year the bush is a compact mound of wiry gray-green twigs. Although deciduous, it has year-round interest and makes an interesting contrast to broad-leaved evergreens. A useful plant for tough conditions of wind and casual treatment. Other cultivars differ mostly in flower color. 'Allgold' has bright yellow flowers. 'Hollandia' has two-tone flowers, pinkish red and white.

'Moonlight', a low, mounding form of the related species *C. scoparius*, has very pale yellow or cream flowers.

How to Grow
Full sun. Loam-based commercial soil mix; must be very rich but drain quickly. Plant 1 or 2 in an 8–10-in. pot. Prune after flowering to prevent leggy growth and to remove unsightly seedpods. Start pruning while plants are young; cutting back into old wood is not successful. Keep soil from freezing in winter. Generally pest-free.

Dahlia
Dahl'ya
Compositae. Daisy family

Description
Tender perennials with tuberous roots, pinnate leaves, and composite flowers on long stalks. Once grown for the edible tubers; now hundreds of hybrid cultivars are prized for their colorful flowers. About 28 species, native from Mexico to Colombia.

■ **hybrids** *p. 107*
(*D. hortensis*)
Dahlias
Perennials grown as annuals. All zones
Height: 1–6 ft. Spread: 1–3 ft.
Remarkable for their bright blossoms that come in all colors but blue, dahlias add pizzazz to a container garden from midsummer on, when other plants may be past their prime. The innumerable cultivars are grouped according to the size and shape of their blossoms, which can be as small and round as golf balls, as big and flat as dinner plates, or any combination in between. Many have twisted, curled, or quill-like florets. Bloom continues until frost.

Dahlias have opposite, pinnately compound leaves on sturdy upright stalks ranging from 1 ft. to 6 ft. tall. Dwarf varieties ('Piccolo', 'Rigoletto') or patio types ('Park Princess') are particularly useful for containers. Large "dinner-plate" dahlias are rarely grown in containers because of their size. If you want to give them a try, plant in large pots (14 in. by 14 in. minimum), water frequently, and provide sturdy stakes.

It's easy to grow dahlias from seed. They bloom the first summer and form tubers that you can save if you choose. For fancier flowers, buy tubers of named cultivars. Local nurseries sell a small assortment of dormant tubers in spring. Mail-order specialty nurseries offer a much wider selection.

How to Grow

Full sun; tolerate heat. Loam-based commercial soil mix; add peat moss for moisture retention and coarse sand to improve drainage. Plant tubers about 6 in. below the rim of a deep pot, cover with 1 in. of soil, then add soil as shoots grow. Plants need constant moisture; do not tolerate drought. Fertilize heavily for best flower production. Pinch tips for bushy plants with many smaller blossoms; remove side shoots and buds to produce fewer, larger blossoms. Dig tubers in fall, and store in a cool, dark place surrounded by peat moss or wood shavings. Sprinkle occasionally with water to avoid desiccation; use fungicide if they show signs of rot. Separate the tubers carefully in spring, and replant the ones with the most vigorous buds and shoots. Bothered by spider mites and grasshoppers.

Daphne
Daf′nee
Thymelaeaceae. Daphne family

Description

Deciduous or evergreen shrubs with simple alternate leaves and small 4-lobed flowers that are usually very fragrant. All parts, particularly the bright-colored fruits, are poisonous. About 50 species, native to Europe and Asia.

■ × *burkwoodii* p. 175
(*D. caucasica* × *D. cneorum*)
Semievergreen shrub. Zone 4
Height: 3–4 ft. Spread: 3–4 ft.
Forms a dense, compact, mounded shrub with neat, small, oval leaves. A profusion of small, starry, pale pink flowers covers the plant for several weeks in late spring. They are deliciously fragrant, and one plant perfumes the entire garden. 'Carol Mackie' has striking foliage; the leaves are green edged with gold. 'Somerset' has green leaves and a more upright growth habit. Place one where you'll pass it often.

Winter daphne (*D. odora,* zone 7) is a lovely shrub for mild climates, with perhaps the sweetest fragrance of all daphnes. Forms a perfect symmetrical mound covered with glossy leaves up to 3 in. long. Decorative clusters of buds tip each branch in fall and winter, opening from reddish purple to white in very early spring. Lovely near the front door or along a path, where you can appreciate the fragrance daily. 'Aureo-Marginata' has cream-edged leaves.

How to Grow

Full sun in cool climates, part shade where summers are hot. Loam-based commercial soil mix amended with organic matter and coarse sand to improve drainage. Tolerates hot weather. Buy container-grown plant and repot in display pot; roots resent disturbance. Repotting is not needed for many years. Needs no pruning beyond the removal of damaged shoots. Slow-growing but free of pests or diseases if drainage is good.

Delosperma
De-lo-sper′ma
Aizoaceae. Carpetweed family

Description

Mostly tender succulent herbs or shrubs with densely branched, spreading habits and small but numerous bright-colored flowers over a long season. About 130 species, native to South Africa and Madagascar.

■ *cooperi* p. 134
Purple ice plant
Succulent perennial. Zone 6 or 5
Height: 2–4 in. Spread: 12 in. or more
Brilliant flowers are dazzling on a sunny patio. Narrow succulent leaves are sprinkled with bright magenta, daisylike flowers from June until frost. Probably best grown in an ornamental pot by itself and placed with pots of other sun-loving succulents and annuals, such as portulaca, hen-and-chicks, agaves, and aloes. Does well in arid and semiarid areas. Will tumble over the sides of a pot. *D*. 'Alba', a dwarf, has white flowers and is less hardy. The foliage of *D. nubigena*, hardy ice plant, is bright green in summer, turning red in winter. Yellow daisylike blooms are produced in late spring and summer.

How to Grow

Full sun; tolerates heat. Loam-based commercial soil mix with coarse sand added for good drainage. Flattish bowls and pans of terra cotta are good containers. Can survive drying out and general negligence once established. Cuttings root easily. In cold climates, overwinter in cold frame or cool greenhouse.

Dianthus
Dy-an′thus. Pink
Caryophyllaceae. Pink family

Description
Low-growing annuals, biennials, or perennials. The opposite leaves are often as slender as blades of grass, thickening at the base where they join the stem. Flowers are borne singly or on branched stalks. They have 5 to many petals, sometimes with fringed edges, in shades of pink, rose, or white, sometimes red, purplish, or yellow. Many have a very sweet or spicy fragrance. About 300 species, most from Europe and Asia.

■ × *allwoodii* hybrids *p. 134*
Cottage pinks, border carnations, Allwood pinks
Perennials. Zone 4
Height: 8–16 in. Spread: 12 in.
A large and popular group of hybrids, worth growing for their flowers, foliage, and above all their enchanting fragrance. Slender blue-green-gray leaves form closely packed tufts or mats, evergreen in mild climates, handsome until deep winter in colder zones. The clove-scented flowers are single or double, 1½–2 in. wide, in shades of dark red, rose, pink, or white. Bloom continues from late spring through summer, sometimes lasting 2 full months. Excellent combined with silver-foliage plants, such as artemisias, lavenders, and lamb's-ears.

'Aqua' (pure white), 'Doris' (salmon with a dark eye), 'Ian' (scarlet), and other named cultivars have lovely flowers but are not as hardy and rarely survive zone 5 winters. The 'Alpinus' strain, easily raised from seed, is very hardy (zone 3). It forms tight mounds of blue-gray foliage, topped with very fragrant single flowers in many shades. The *D. × allwoodii* hybrids result from crossing *D. caryophyllus* and *D. plumarius*.

Cottage pinks (*D. plumarius,* zone 4) are old-fashioned pinks that are easy to grow and have lovely fringed flowers with a delicious spicy fragrance. They form looser mounds of foliage and grow more slowly than do the Allwood hybrids and will tolerate more moisture, too. They combine well with lavender, catmint, Shirley poppies, feverfew, and roses. There are many seed strains and named cultivars, with flowers in shades of red, pink, or white.

How to Grow
Full sun. Loam-based commercial soil mix amended with organic matter and lime and with coarse sand to improve drainage. Use 1 plant per 10-in. pot. Place pots where air can circulate freely. Use twiggy sticks to support flower stalks of tall forms. Shear off faded flowers to prolong blooming or to encourage repeat blooming. Divide and replant after 2–3 years. Cuttings root easily. Overwinter in cold frame or other cold location.

■ *chinensis* **hybrids** *p. 108*
China pinks
Annuals. All zones
Height: 6–9 in. Spread: 8 in.
China pinks provide a bright splash of summer color in pots by themselves or in a window box with ivy, *Artemisia stellerana*, and pink geraniums. Easy from seed and quick to flower, most have stiff upright stems that branch repeatedly, topped with flat clusters of several small single or double flowers in shades of red, pink, white, or bicolors. They are usually scentless, but they provide months of color.

Carnations (*D. caryophyllus*) are tender perennials usually purchased as seedlings and grown for a season. The species includes the classic florist's carnations, fussy, long-stemmed cutting types that are grown mostly in greenhouses. The types known as hardy or border carnations, such as 'Dwarf Fragrance', with spicy 2-in. flowers on 12-in. plants, and 'Black and White Minstrels', with deep maroon and white flowers, make a better choice for containers.

How to Grow
Full sun. Soilless commercial mix amended with lime. Start seeds indoors, and set plants out about the time of last frost. Plant 1 in a 6-in. pot, 3 in a 10-in. pot. They start flowering in as little as 10 weeks from seed. Locate pots where air circulates to avoid fungal problems. Deadheading keeps plants looking neater and prolongs flowering.

Border carnations bloom 4–6 months after starting seeds. All of these, even the dwarfs, need staking. Subject to aphids, spider mites, and thrips; also to fungal and viral infections, particularly in humid climates.

■ *deltoides* p. 135
Maiden pink
Perennial. Zone 3
Height: 8 in. Spread: 18 in.

An easy plant that provides a carpet of small blooms in early summer. Use in color-schemed groupings or spilling over the edge of a window box or planter. Flowers are scentless, single, ¾ in. wide, and red, rose, or white, often with dark marks in the center, rising over a low mat of grassy green leaves. Shear faded flowers to encourage repeat blooming. Look for named cultivars, some available from seed, which are selected for flower size and color. All self-sow prolifically. Start maiden pinks once, and you'll never be without them.

Cheddar pink (*D. gratianopolitanus*, zone 4) is smaller, with marvelous bluish foliage in a tightly packed mat and lovely flowers with a heavenly fragrance. Try it with low silvery artemisias, balloon flower, and catmint. 'Bath's Pink' is a new cultivar with single, soft pink flowers. 'Tiny Rubies' is an old favorite. It makes a very compact mat of foliage, covered with hundreds of small, double, deep pink flowers on 4-in. stems. In spring, cut back all straggly growth, reducing the plant to one-third its former size; cut off all flower stalks when blooms fade.

How to Grow
Full sun or part shade. Soilless mix or loam-based mix amended with coarse sand to improve drainage. Recovers from drying out. May die in cold, wet winters or hot, humid summers. Overwinter dormant plants in cold frame or unheated garage.

Euonymus
You-on'i-mus
Celastraceae. Spindletree family

Description
Deciduous or evergreen shrubs, creeping vines, or small trees. Most have simple opposite leaves and inconspicuous flowers. Bright-colored red, orange, or pink fruits open in fall to reveal even brighter seeds, attractive to birds but poisonous to humans. More than 170 species, native mostly to Asia.

■ *fortunei* selections *p. 164*
Winter creeper
Evergreen vines or shrubs. Zone 5
Height: varies. Spread: varies
This species has contributed many attractive hardy evergreen vines and shrubs. Several of the most popular forms are described below. The vining forms make good ground covers for large specimen trees or shrubs, or they can climb a wall, fence, chimney, or tree. The shrubby upright forms combine well with conifers or other evergreens. Forms with colored leaves inject light into shady spots or mix well with flowering plants. Sprawling "juvenile" plants rarely flower; upright "adult" forms do. The actual flowers are inconspicuous, but the pea-sized fruits are startlingly colorful: the pinkish red hulls open to reveal bright orange seeds and hang on through winter. Here's a sampling of cultivars:

'Coloratus' spreads to make a good ground cover, 1 ft. tall and several feet wide. Leaves are 1–2 in. long, dark green in summer and purple-maroon in winter.

'Emerald Gaiety' is a compact shrub, usually under 2 ft. tall and wide. 'Emerald 'n' Gold' is similar, but its dark green leaves are edged with gold in summer, purplish-green and pink in winter.

'Gracilis', also sold as 'Silver Edge', is a trailing ground cover, usually just a few inches tall and spreading up to 2 ft. wide. The relatively thin green leaves are edged with white or cream in summer, turning pink in winter.

'Kewensis' is a dainty plant with tiny leaves only $1/4$ in. long. It hugs the ground like a rug and makes a charming ground cover for small spaces. It also climbs nicely, but the leaves get larger as it goes higher. Climbing specimens occasionally flower and fruit.

'Sarcoxie' is a shrubby form, growing about 4–6 ft. tall. It has thick, glossy, dark green leaves and often flowers and fruits.

'Silver Queen' is a shrubby, spreading form; its leaves have white margins.

E. f. var. *radicans* is tough and versatile, with thick, glossy, dark green leaves 1 in. long. It can grow as a shrubby bush, sprawl over the ground, or climb 40 ft. up a wall or tree. *E. f.* 'Variegatus' is equally versatile, with variably green-and-white, all-green, or all-white leaves.

E. f. var. *vegetus* is usually a shrub about 4–5 ft. tall and wide, but it sometimes takes off as a vine and climbs up to 40 ft. The broadly elliptical leaves, 1–2 in. long, are thick and glossy. This is the hardiest of evergreen vines and is very useful as an evergreen shrub. It regularly flowers, so put it where you can enjoy the colorful fruits all winter, displayed against the rich green foliage.

How to Grow
Sun to shade; tolerate heat. Soilless commercial mix for good drainage. Use 1 plant to a 20–22-in. pot. Don't overwater; feed with slow-release fertilizer and occasional soluble supplements. Plants require no special care; can be pruned to shape. Subject to leafspot and powdery mildew, especially in humid conditions or where air circulation is poor. Euonymus is unusually susceptible to scale insects, and severe infestations can be fatal. Check often, and spray with horticultural oil if needed. Stem or tip cuttings root easily in summer if planted in a shady spot and covered with a glass jar.

Eupatorium
You-pa-toe´ree-um
Compositae. Daisy family

Description
Perennials with opposite or whorled leaves on upright stalks topped with showy clusters of many small flower heads. Many species have been divided out of this formerly large genus. Remaining are about 40 species, native to the eastern United States and Eurasia.

■ *coelestinum* p. 135
(now *Conoclinium coelestinum*)
Hardy ageratum
Perennial. Zone 6
Height: 18–24 in. Spread: 2 ft. or more
Branched clusters of fluffy, powder blue flowers enliven the garden for 4–6 weeks in late summer and fall. The lush, light

green foliage is attractive throughout the growing season. 'Alba' has white flowers. Grow as a specimen, since its vigorous nature may crowd out other plants.

How to Grow
Full or part sun; tolerates heat. Loam-based commercial soil mix. Use 1 plant per 12-in. pot. Feed with slow-release fertilizer. Remove spent flowers to limit self-seeding. Divide every 2–3 years in spring when new shoots emerge. Overwinter dormant plant in unheated garage or cold frame.

Exacum
Ecks′a-kum
Gentianaceae. Gentian family

Description
About 20 species of herbs or subshrubs from the Old World tropics.

■ *affine* p. 108
Persian violet, tiddlywinks
Biennial grown as an annual. All zones
Height: 1–1½ ft. Spread: 1 ft.
A handsome plant that always looks impeccable—ideal for a window box and short enough not to block the view. Little mounds of shiny green leaves are smothered in blossoms for a long period. Flowers are periwinkle purple with bright yellow stamens. Tolerates a diversity of weather conditions.

How to Grow
Full sun. Loam-based commercial soil mix. Don't overpot—prefers a shallow, 4–5-in. pot at maturity, or group several in a window box. Too much water weakens stems. Feed once a month. Self-branching; staking sometimes helps older plants keep nicely massed together. Overwinter on a sunny windowsill, or start again from seed in spring.

Fatsia
Fat′si-a
Araliaceae. Aralia family

Description
An evergreen shrub with large, glossy, palmately lobed leaves. Only 1 species, native to Japan.

■ *japonica* p. 188
Evergreen shrub. Zone 7
Height: 6–10 ft. Spread: 6–10 ft.
An upright shrub with big, coarse, glossy, palmately compound leaves, often 12 in. wide and long. Sometimes makes rounded clusters of tiny white flowers on branched stalks, followed by small dark fruits. Valued for its boldness, which goes well with modern architecture, or can be combined with gingers, bananas, palms, and other large-leaved plants for a tropical effect. Excellent focal point for entrance, patio, or courtyard. Crossed with *Hedera hibernica*, it produced the hybrid × *Fatshedera lizei*, which has big ivylike leaves on mostly unbranched stems that don't quite stand alone but look good trained against a wall. Both *Fatsia* and × *Fatshedera* grow well in containers and are often used as houseplants.

How to Grow
Part sun to shade; protect from hot afternoon sun. Loam-based commercial soil mix enriched with organic matter. Needs large container. Keep soil moist, but it will recover from drying out. Can prune hard in spring—be bold. Difficult to shape by pruning; tends to grow as it chooses. Subject to spider mites and other pests, especially if grown as a houseplant, but usually not serious problems.

Feijoa
Fee-jo´a
Myrtaceae. Myrtle family

Description
Evergreen shrubs with opposite oblong leaves, ornamental flowers, and edible fruits. Only 2 species, native to South America.

■ *sellowiana* p. 188
(*Acca sellowiana*)
Pineapple guava
Evergreen shrub. Zone 8
Height: 5–6 ft. Spread: 5–6 ft.
Attractive and useful, this densely branched shrub has healthy oval leaves, dark green above and gray below, and showy edible flowers, 1$\frac{1}{2}$ in. wide, with waxy white petals and lots of bright red stamens. The round fruits, like small gray-green eggs, are very fragrant and tasty. It flowers in early summer; fruit ripens in fall. Grows well in containers, and a single specimen makes a good patio plant. If you want to eat the fruit, look for 'Coolidge', 'Nazemetz', or 'Pineapple Gem'—all are self-pollinating and have good flavor.

How to Grow
Full sun. Soilless or loam-based commercial soil mix. Will bear fruit in pots as small as 10 in. but performs better in larger containers. Root-prune to maintain container size. Tolerates some drying out but will drop fruit. Pinch to fatten branches and control sprawl. Overwinter indoors.

FERNS

Description
Ferns from a number of genera are excellent container plants. Some are hardy enough to overwinter outdoors in cold-winter areas; those that aren't often make effective houseplants after the weather turns cold.

■ *Athyrium goeringianum* 'Pictum' p. 129
(*A. nipponicum* 'Pictum')
Japanese painted fern
Deciduous fern. Zone 3
Height: 12–18 in. Spread: 18 in.
This is America's most beautiful and most popular garden fern. The triangular fronds are tricolored in burgundy, silver-gray, and green. Place in a shady spot with pots of black mondo grass, *Heuchera* 'Palace Purple', blue-leaved hostas, or deep pink primulas. *A. otophorum*, 18–24 in. tall, is another colorful fern, maturing from pale silver and greenish gold to dark green and red.

How to Grow
Shade. Soilless commercial mix amended with humus. Use 1 plant per 8–10-in. pot. Place crown on top of soil and cover

with mulch. Needs constant moisture. Old fronds make an excellent mulch, or you can remove them after all danger of frost is past. You can divide mature plants in early spring or late fall. Protect roots from freezing in winter.

■ *Nephrolepis exaltata* p. 142
Sword fern
Evergreen fern. Zone 9
Height: to 5 ft. Spread: forms patch
A common and easy-to-grow container fern. Bright green fronds arch and droop nicely over the edge of a hanging pot or fern stand. *N. cordifolia*, often sold as *N. exaltata,* is similar but grows only 2–3 ft. tall. It can be a ground cover in large planters and will tolerate sun if humidity is high.

How to Grow
Shade. Soilless commercial mix. Mature plant needs an 8-in. or larger pot. Requires constant moisture, but don't overwater. Divide when crowded. Doesn't tolerate frost; overwinter indoors as a houseplant.

■ other ferns
For hanging baskets, try hare's-foot fern (*Polypodium aureum*), which offers 3–5-ft. blue-green fronds that droop attractively. Squirrel's-foot fern (*Davallia trichomanoides*) has shorter, finer fronds; bear's-foot fern (*Humata tyermannii*) is similar but slower-growing. All are tender and must winter indoors.

Tender tree ferns make good container plants when young—a 5–6 ft. plant can survive in a 16-in. pot. Hawaiian tree fern (*Cibotium glaucum*, a.k.a. *C. chamissoi*) has light green, feathery fronds. Australian tree fern (*Cyathea cooperi*, a.k.a. *Alsophila australis*) is a fast-growing plant with delicately cut fronds. The hardiest (to 20° F) is the Tasmanian tree fern (*Dicksonia antarctica*), a slow-growing plant with long arching fronds.

Southern maidenhair fern (*Adiantum capillus-veneris*, zone 8) is a dainty plant, just 6–12 in. tall, that thrives in warm sheltered areas with high humidity. Lacy, soft green fronds fan out from shiny black stipes. Bring it in for the winter in cold climates—it makes a lovely houseplant. American maidenhair fern (*A. pedatum*, zone 3) is a larger plant whose fan-shaped fronds on thin wiry stems retain a delicate appearance. Maidenhair ferns (pictured opposite) do better if a little lime is available; add oyster shell or limestone pebbles to the pot.

Holly fern (*Cyrtomium falcatum*, zone 9) forms an arching clump 2–3 ft. high and wide of leathery, glossy, dark green fronds. Hardy only in mild climates, it can winter indoors in cold regions. The toothed leaflets, up to 4 in. long, look somewhat like English holly leaves. Best in sheltered sites, though it tolerates hot, dry air better than some ferns do.

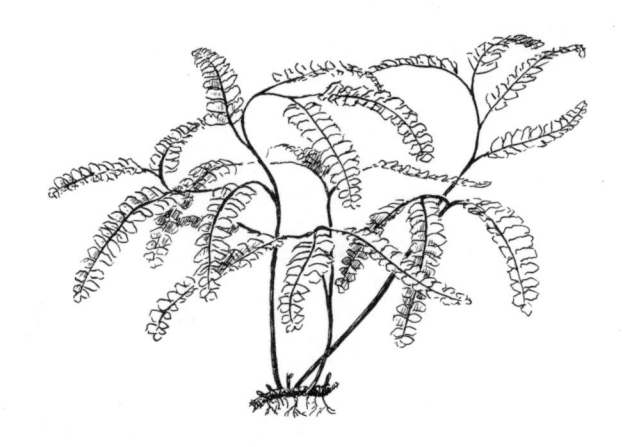

Leatherleaf fern (*Rumohra adiantiformis,* a.k.a. *Aspidium capense,* zone 9) is a tough fern for warm-winter climates. It makes clumps of firm, leathery, finely divided, dark green fronds up to 3 ft. long. It combines well with calla lilies, tuberous begonias, and caladiums. Bird's-nest fern (*Asplenium nidus*) features undivided green fronds up to 4 ft. long. Huge plants can grow in 6–8-in. pots.

The genus *Polystichum* supplies a number of smallish ferns that make good container plants. Christmas fern (*P. acrostichoides,* zone 3) features leathery evergreen fronds that are glossy green and up to 5 in. wide and 2–3 ft. long. *P. braunii,* or Braun's holly fern, has the same erect grace but needs constant moisture and deep shade. *P. tsus-simense,* or rock fern, is similar but smaller. It makes a compact rosette of stiff, leathery, shiny, blackish green fronds. Western sword fern (*P. munitum,* zone 4) is an easy-to-grow West Coast native that forms erect clumps of large sword-shaped fronds with a leathery texture and dark green color. Tassel fern (*P. polyblepharum,* zone 4), a lovely easy-to-grow Japanese fern, forms a mounded rosette of stiff, glossy green foliage. Don't let it dry out. Soft shield fern (*P. setiferum,* zone 5) produces narrow lance-shaped fronds that spread like a starfish. The fronds have a soft velvety texture, feathery appearance, and dark green color. There are many cultivars, each with uniquely lovely foliage. After you've grown one, you'll want to try them all.

Ficus

Fy′kus. Fig
Moraceae. Mulberry family

Description
Trees, shrubs, or clinging vines, nearly all with thick evergreen leaves. All figs have sticky milky sap and bear flowers and seeds inside a fleshy receptacle—the fig. About 800 species, from tropical and warm climates worldwide.

■ *carica* p. 175
Common fig
Deciduous tree. Zone 8 or 7
Height: 5–6 ft. Spread: 2–3 ft.

A distinctive shrub or tree, often multitrunked, with large, coarse, lobed leaves on thick stems. Makes a bold, interesting specimen. The tiny flowers develop into sweet, tasty figs. One crop is borne in early summer, on the previous year's wood; the main crop forms on new wood and ripens in fall. Cultivars differ in fruit size, flavor, color, and tolerance of heat and cold. 'Kadota' and 'Mission' have large sweet fruits and are popular in California. 'Brown Turkey', an old favorite with dark purple-brown fruits, is hardier (zone 7 or 6) than most figs. Figs do especially well if placed against the south wall of a building, where reflected heat helps ripen the fruit. Gardeners in cold zones can grow a fig tree in a large tub or planter if it can be rolled out on the patio for summer and wintered in a garage or basement that stays near freezing temperatures.

How to Grow
Full sun. Loam-based commercial soil mix. Pot or tub should be as large as you can lift or otherwise move. Recovers from drying out; don't overwater. Prune to control size and shape, removing weak or crossed limbs. Pinching early in season promotes branching, but eliminates early fruit crop. Protect

fruit from birds. North of zone 8, store above freezing. Plants—tub and all—can be buried under soil and straw, or left upright and wrapped in old blankets and straw. Watch out for the milky sap—it stains hands and clothing.

■ *pumila* p. 164
(*F. repens*)
Creeping fig
Evergreen vine. Zone 7
Height: to 25 ft. or more
An evergreen vine that clings tenaciously to stone, brick, wood, or metal walls, spreading and branching to make a vertical carpet of foliage. Trails nicely over the edges of pots or hanging baskets; try combining it with other plants, such as verbena. Young plants have slender stems and "juvenile" foliage: thin, papery, heart-shaped leaves $1/2$–1 in. long. Older plants that have climbed partway up a wall develop stout branches of "adult" foliage: thick, leathery, oval leaves 2–4 in. long. 'Minima' has small leaves and grows slowly. 'Variegata' has small leaves blotched with white.

How to Grow
Full or part sun; scorches brown or yellow in hot afternoon sun or winter sun. Loam-based commercial soil mix amended with coarse sand to improve drainage. Doesn't recover well from drying out. Keep constantly moist; thrives in high humidity. Don't hesitate to prune in spring before new growth begins if vine gets too big or if you don't like coarseness of adult foliage. Usually recovers from frost injury that kills tops of shoots. Subject to spider mites.

Fuchsia
Few´sha
Onagraceae. Evening primrose family

Description
Most are tender evergreen shrubs or small trees with simple leaves and showy flowers that dangle like earrings from the stems. About 100 species, most native to Central and South America.

■ **hybrids** p. 109
(*F.* × *hybrida*)
Hybrid fuchsias
Tender shrubs grown as annuals. All zones
Height: varies. Spread: varies

Where summers are cool and foggy along the Pacific coast, fuchsias make splendid flowering shrubs. In most parts of the United States, they are grown as annuals in hanging baskets or planter boxes. The growth habit ranges from 6-in. mounds to 6-ft.-tall standards to 2–3-ft. trailers. Plump round buds open into dangling flowers with 4 flared-back sepals (usually white, red, or pink), 4 to many rounded petals (white, pink, red, or purple), and prominent protruding stamens and pistil. There are hundreds of cultivars, with flowers $1/2$–4 in. wide, single or double, solid-color or two-tone. The blossoms are scentless but attract hummingbirds, and they open continuously from early summer to fall. Most fuchsias are killed by a hard frost, but there is a hardy fuchsia sold as *F. magellanica* or *F.* 'Riccartonii'. It dies to the ground but recovers in zone 7, bearing red-purple flowers on upright stems that reach 3 ft. or more in a season.

How to Grow
Part sun to shade. Soilless or loam-based commercial soil mix amended with plenty of organic matter and coarse sand for rapid drainage. Won't tolerate hot sun or dry air. You can grow them as annuals in pots as small as 4–6 in. Large plants grown as perennials, including standards, require a 12–14-in. pot. Keep moist. Early in season pinch tips often to promote branching. Cut perennials back to main framework branches in early spring. Fertilize lightly every 2 weeks. Watch for spider mites, whiteflies, and aphids. Hosing foliage frequently helps discourage pests. Fuchsia mites are a scourge in California, deforming new growth. Control is difficult—consult knowledgeable nursery staff. Overwinter in frost-free cellar; in Northwest, mulch heavily in cold frame.

Gelsemium
Jel-see′mee-um
Loganiaceae. Buddleia family

Description
Woody evergreen vines with fragrant yellow funnel-shaped flowers, most abundant in late winter. All parts of the plant are poisonous. Only 2 or 3 species, 1 or 2 from eastern North America and the other from eastern Asia.

■ *sempervirens* p. 165
Carolina jessamine, yellow jasmine
Evergreen vine. Zone 8
Height: 5–6 ft. Spread: 1 to 6 ft.

A versatile vine, it climbs well on fences, trellises, lampposts, and mailboxes or can serve as a ground cover. A profusion of fragrant yellow blossoms, about 1 in. long and clustered, open first in very early spring, sometimes continuing off and on for several weeks. The slender leaves are dark green in summer, often purplish in winter. 'Pride of Augusta' has double flowers.

How to Grow
Full sun; tolerates heat. Loam-based commercial soil mix. Best in a deep pot 10 in. wide or larger. Cut back hard after flowering to control size, then pinch tips during subsequent growth to encourage branching. Overwinter in greenhouse, conservatory, or cool sun porch.

Gerbera
Jer´ber-ra, ger´ber-ra
Compositae. Daisy family

Description
Perennials with a basal rosette of oblong lobed leaves and large daisylike blossoms on solitary stalks. About 35 species, most native to Africa or Asia.

■ *jamesonii* p. 109
Gerbera daisy, Transvaal daisy
Perennial grown as an annual. Zone 9
Height: to 18 in. Spread: to 18 in.
The most aristocratic and shapely daisy, a good container plant and an excellent cut flower with nice long stalks. (Long-stemmed varieties may be harder to find at nurseries—grow them from seed.) The yellow-eyed daisies, to 5–6 in. wide, have cream, yellow, orange, pink, or red rays. They bloom

most in summer and fall, off and on in winter and spring. Individual blossoms last a week or more. Makes a basal rosette of narrow lobed leaves, to 10 in. long, smooth green above and woolly gray below.

How to Grow
Full sun or afternoon shade. Soilless or loam-based commercial soil mix. Pots 6–8 in. wide accommodate largest plants. When planting, be careful not to bury crown, and don't let soil wash in and cover crown later. Regular watering and frequent fertilizing. If grown as a perennial, divide older plants in early spring, keeping several crowns per division. Seeds are expensive, but seedlings may bloom the first year. Overwinter indoors as a houseplant, giving it bright light and cool (60° F) nights. Snails and slugs eat leaves outdoors; aphids, whiteflies, and spider mites attack them indoors.

Gloriosa
Glo-ree-oh′sa
Liliaceae. Lily family

Description
Tuberous-rooted climbing vines with showy flowers. Various forms are now grouped into 1 species, native to tropical Asia and Africa.

■ *superba* p. 154
Gloriosa lily
Grown as an annual. All zones
Height: 4–6 ft. Spread: depends on support
Aptly named, this is a glorious, superb plant. Greenish yellow buds open into brilliant crimson flowers with dramatic, flared-back tepals, aging to a rich dark red. Hummingbirds fight over these flowers, visiting many times a day. Each tuber produces 1 or more brittle, branching stalks with shiny leaves tapering into tendrils that reach for support, curling around any nearby wire, string, or twig. Scarlet sage (*Salvia coccinea*) makes a good filler around the base of the stalks.

How to Grow
Full or part sun. Loam-based commercial soil mix amended with organic matter to retain moisture. For maximum show, plant several tubers 3 in. deep in a 12-in. by 12-in. pot; set out after danger of frost is past. Provide support in or next to pot—a trellis, strings, or brushy sticks. Keep moist and protect from hot, drying winds. Fertilize before and during

bloom. New shoots are very vulnerable to slugs and snails. Vines will turn yellow about 2 months after flowering, or when frost strikes. Carefully dig tubers, remove soil and old stalks and roots, and pack them in dry peat moss or crumpled paper. Store in cool room over winter.

Gomphrena
Gom-free′na
Amaranthaceae. Amaranth family

Description
Annuals or perennials with simple leaves and small flowers clustered in dense chaffy heads. About 100 species, native to southeastern Asia, Australia, and Central America.

■ *globosa*   p. 110
Globe amaranth
Annual. All zones
Height: 8–16 in. Spread: 6–12 in.
Provides bright color all summer with minimal care, thriving in hot dry weather, and very popular for dried arrangements. The marble-sized flower heads look like stiff, papery clover blossoms. Comes in many shades of purple, pink, red, orange, or white. Some seed strains are mixed; others are available in separate colors. Use to set off ornamental grasses and other foliage plants, or combine with taller spiky plants, such as mealy-cup sage or 'Indigo Spires'. 'Buddy' is compact (6–8 in. high), with brilliant magenta-purple blossoms.

How to Grow
Full sun; tolerates heat but is very tender to cold. Loam-based commercial soil mix. Sow seeds indoors 6 weeks before last frost; space transplants 5 in. apart—they'll fill in quickly when weather heats up. Put outside when night temperatures are reliably above 50° F. Recovers from drying out. Cut flowers for drying before they fade.

GRASSES

Description
Grasses from a number of genera are excellent container plants. We have selected five as entries, but there are many more, some of which we discuss briefly below under "other grasses."

***Acorus gramineus* 'Variegatus'** *p. 127*
Variegated Japanese sweet flag
Grasslike perennial. Zone 6
Height: 12 in. Spread: 12 in.
Forms a low tuft of slender white-striped leaves that brightens any shady spot. Foliage contrasts with larger-leaved plants. Looks natural near a pool or fountain; it thrives in a shallow tray of water. Spreads rather slowly. 'Ogon' is similar, with yellow instead of white stripes. *A. calamus* 'Variegatus' is a larger plant, up to 3 ft. tall; its leaves have similar variegation and a spicy fragrance.

How to Grow
Part sun to shade. Loam-based commercial soil mix. Start in a small pot; move up a size each spring. Keep moist. No maintenance required. North of zone 6, bring it indoors to enjoy over winter.

■ ***Carex morrowii* 'Aureo-variegata'** *p. 131*
Variegated Japanese sedge
Perennial "grass." Zone 6 or 5
Height: 6–8 in. Spread: 18 in.
One of the classiest variegated plants, this is a must for gardeners who shy away from the unkempt appearance of some grasses. It forms a neat, low, evergreen tuft of leaves striped bright yellow and green. Use it to brighten a dark shady area or a shady window box, or as a ground cover in larger pots under taller plants. Looks great with ferns and hostas. Flowers are inconspicuous.

How to Grow
Part sun to shade. Loam-based commercial soil mix. Use 1 plant to a 10-in. pot. Keep moist. Feed with slow-release fer-

tilizer in spring. Needs minimal maintenance; simply prune away any damaged foliage in spring. Overwinter in cold frame.

■ *Festuca ovina* var. *glauca* p. 136
Blue fescue
Clumping grass. Zone 4
Height: 6–12 in. Spread: 8–10 in.
A small clumping grass, ideal for small courtyard gardens, permanent raised planters, or window boxes, where its diminutive habit can be appreciated. Blue combines well with many other colors, and while blue flowers come and go, this plant's blue foliage remains through the growing season and into winter (it's "everblue" in mild climates). Combines well with hardy geraniums; pink, blue, and white pansies; 'Azure Pearls' and 'Salmon Pearls' petunias; *Lobelia erinus* cultivars; *Artemisia stellerana* 'Silverado'; ageratum; and *Sedum* 'Vera Jameson'. Narrow spikes of flowers appear sporadically in summer; leave them if you like, but removing them focuses the plant's energy on foliage production.

Seedling plants are commonly sold but vary considerably in blueness. The best bright blue forms, such as 'Elijah's Blue' and 'Sea Urchin', must be propagated by division. *F. amethystina,* the large blue fescue (18–24 in. or more), makes bigger, showier clumps, but the foliage is equally delicate and blue. It tolerates heat better than regular blue fescue does.

How to Grow
Full sun. Soilless commercial mix. Put 1 plant in an 8-in. pot, or space 8–10 in. apart in a planter. Allow soil to become slightly dry between waterings. Cut back once a year, in fall or spring. Clumps can (and should) go years without division. Overwinter in cold frame; keep soil dry.

■ *Phalaris arundinacea* 'Picta' p. 142
Ribbon grass
Perennial grass. Zone 4
Height: 2–4 ft. Spread: invasive
One of the first grasses grown as an ornamental, this plant is noted for its variegated foliage and fortitude. The upright stems hold leaves 4–10 in. long, bright green with lengthwise white stripes. One clump can lighten a dark corner or provide a foil for clashing colors. The pinkish white flowers in midsummer are not particularly ornamental. Invasiveness is a problem in large permanent planters. You can control its spread by planting in a bottomless container. Can also be grown as an aquatic, and it won't spread from a container surrounded by water! Best grown by itself in a pot and placed

among other pots for vertical accent. Goes well with hen-and-chicks, coleus, and other variegated plants.

How to Grow
Sun to shade. Loam-based commercial soil mix amended with peat moss to increase water retention. A small division will fill a 12-in. pot by midsummer. Needs constant moisture. In most areas, foliage is pretty in spring and early summer but turns brown by August. Cut it back to 6 in. and it will sprout fresh new growth. Doesn't need fertilizer unless it goes brown after it is cut back. Easily propagated by division.

■ *Phormium tenax* p. 143
New Zealand flax
Perennial used like an ornamental grass. Zone 8
Height: 2–9 ft. Spread: 2–9 ft.

A dramatic plant that adds a tropical look to any container garden. The sword-shaped leaves, up to 9 ft. long and 5 in. wide, grow in fans, like irises, and make crowded clumps. New cultivars offer a variety of foliage colors—bronzy, purplish, reddish, and striped with cream or yellow. The dull reddish brown flowers are trumpet-shaped, 2 in. long, and borne in branched clusters atop tall naked stalks in summer. (Rarely blooms in the North.) Compact 2–5-ft. cultivars fit into smaller areas. (The species seldom exceeds 5 ft. when grown in containers.) Plant wandering Jew or thyme at the feet of large specimens for contrast.

How to Grow
Full or part sun; tolerates heat. Loam-based commercial soil mix. For best results, start with a 1-gal. specimen and move up to larger containers as it grows; can stand to be potbound. Recovers from drying out. Needs no care beyond removal of dead or damaged leaves and old flower stalks. Can be divided, but you'll need several helpers to tackle a large specimen. Overwinter in greenhouse or on sun porch.

■ other grasses
Clumping grass (*Hakonechloa macra* 'Aureola', zone 5) forms a soft graceful mound of ribbonlike leaves, green tinted with gold, buff, and bronze. Use as an accent or focal point in a group of pots. Part sun to shade; keep moist. Cut back hard once a year.

Blue oat grass (*Helictotrichon sempervirens*, a.k.a. *Avena sempervirens*, zone 4) makes a tufted mound of slender blue leaves up to 18 in. long, lovely from spring to fall and sometimes on through winter. Full sun, well-drained mix. Cut back once a year to 4 in.

Fountain grass (*Pennisetum alopecuroides*, zone 5), a vibrant flowing fountain of 3-ft. leaves, is dark green in summer and warm apricot, almond, or orange in fall. From August to October it bears many fluffy flower spikes, 6–8 in. long, shading from reddish purple to coppery tan. Full sun; takes lots of water; cut back in early winter. 'Hameln' is more compact, with foliage 18–24 in. tall and flower stalks to 30 in. 'Little Bunny' is extremely dwarf, growing only 8–10 in. high. *P. orientale* is a similar plant hardy only to zone 7. It's more compact, forming upright clumps of gray-green foliage 1–2 ft. tall, topped with long, fluffy, arching spikes of pinkish purple flowers. Grow as an annual in northern climates.

Grown as an annual north of zone 8, crimson fountain grass (*Pennisetum setaceum*) makes an arching or mounded 2-ft.-high clump of fine-textured rusty green foliage. Fluffy nodding spikes of rose or purple-tinted flowers are 6–12 in. long, borne from June through fall. Nice with pink flowering tobacco, which accents the pink tints of the grass flowers. 'Purpureum' (also called 'Atropurpureum') has purple leaves and deep crimson flowers. 'Burgundy Giant' is larger in all its parts.

Bowles' golden grass (*Milium effusum* 'Aureum') provides clumps of arching green-gold leaves reaching 2 ft. or so in height. Looks good with spring bulbs in part sun or shade.

Try hare's-tail grass (*Lagurus ovatus*), a 12–18-in.-tall annual, for the children. Soft seed heads that look like little bunny tails appear about 4 months after the seeds are sown. Would go well with annuals in a window box.

Hamelia
Ha-mee'lee-a
Rubiaceae. Madder family

Description
Deciduous shrubs with showy red or yellow flowers. About 16 species, native to Central America.

■ *patens* p. 136
Firebush, hummingbird bush
Woody-based perennial. Zone 8
Height: 2–3 ft. Spread: 2–3 ft.
A showy centerpiece for a mixed pot, perhaps with compact nicotianas, tassel flower, heliotrope, and sweet potato vine. Thrives in hot weather, blooming nonstop from early summer to frost. The red to red-orange flowers are tubular, about 2 in. long, dropping quickly but constantly replaced by new

buds. The simple opposite leaves are dark green with a red midrib and turn red-orange in fall. Place it near the patio where you can watch the hummingbirds come and go.

How to Grow
Full or part sun; tolerates heat. Loam-based commercial soil mix. Shouldn't get too dry; feed regularly through summer. Shear to control shape and height and to promote perpetual bloom. Cut back to the ground after fall frost. Spider mites may need control. Overwinter in greenhouse or on sun porch in the North.

Hedera
Hed′er-a. Ivy
Araliaceae. Aralia family

Description
Woody evergreens with different juvenile and adult appearance. Juvenile shoots are clinging vines with lobed leaves. Adult growth is upright and bushy with elliptical leaves and bears umbels of greenish flowers followed by dark blue-black berries. Only 4 or 5 species, most native to the Mediterranean region, but hundreds of distinct forms have been propagated and named.

■ *helix* p. 165
English ivy
Evergreen woody vine. Zone 6 or 5
Height: 6 in.–6 ft.
Easy to grow and to train, English ivy provides year-round good looks. There are hundreds of cultivars, varying in leaf shape and size, coloring and variegation, vigor, and hardiness. Use the fine-leaved or variegated forms in hanging pots, window boxes, or trained as standards or topiaries. There are compact, bushy forms, too.

Most cultivars are juvenile forms with lobed leaves and rooting stems. 'Needlepoint' grows slowly and has close-set small leaves with pointed lobes. 'Glacier' has pale foliage splotched with white and gray, usually turning pinkish in winter. 'Goldheart' has dark green leaves with big yellow spots in the center.

How to Grow
Full sun (in coldest areas) to shade; tolerates heat. Soilless or loam-based commercial soil mix. Most kinds are happy forever in 4-in. pots; those trained as standards or pyramids may

need bigger pots. Set plants deeply, removing a few lower leaves and covering that part of the stem, to encourage deep rooting. Feed lightly and often; water freely when plant is growing rapidly. Pinch to promote bushiness. Once established, prune as needed to control spread. Train on a wire frame for topiary; stake and thin out lower growth to make a standard. Requires little water in winter; bring indoors in cold areas. Be patient if top dies in winter; plant may come back from roots.

Heliotropium
Hel-ee-oh-trop´ee-um
Boraginaceae. Borage family

Description
Several hundred species of herbs and shrubs found in temperate and tropical regions worldwide. Cultivated varieties were Victorian favorites.

■ *arborescens* *p. 110*
Heliotrope
Evergreen shrub grown as an annual. Zone 10
Height: 12–36 in. Spread: 10–24 in.
This rather bushy shrub produces tight flat clusters of tiny lavender or purple flowers prized for their sweet "cherry pie" scent. The simple wrinkled leaves are dark green, often tinged with purple. The attractive flowers are useful in mixed pots or as specimens, positioned near outdoor living areas where their fragrance can best be enjoyed. They bloom profusely when weather warms, from late June until frost, or spring to autumn in mild-winter climates. Not all seedlings are very fragrant. 'Marina', a dwarf to 10 in. tall with uniform violet-purple flowers over very dark leaves, is handsome but not noted for scent. 'Iowa' or unimproved species types (often with lilac or violet flowers) have a better chance of producing scented seedlings. When you get a good one, save the seed.

How to Grow
Full sun. Loam-based commercial soil mix amended with peat moss. If grown as a perennial, can reach 3 ft. or larger, so will need a 1-gal. pot eventually. Needs constant moisture (performs well in high humidity). Easy from seed and cuttings (summer or fall). Overwinter on sun porch, in greenhouse, under lights, or in bright window. Ease back on water and fertilizer; will drop leaves. Spider mites and whiteflies may cause problems.

Helleborus
Hell-e-bore´us. Hellebore
Ranunculaceae. Buttercup family

Description
Low, spreading perennials with thick rhizomes and roots that are quite poisonous. Leaves are mostly basal, palmately lobed. Flowers are showy in winter or spring. About 20 species, native to Europe and Asia.

■ *orientalis* *p. 137*
Lenten rose
Perennial. Zone 5
Height: 18–24 in. Spread: 24 in. or more
The easiest and most widely adapted of all hellebores, providing year-round interest in flowers and foliage. Clusters of several nodding cup-shaped flowers, 2–3 in. wide, open in early spring. Flowers come in many shades of pink, plum, white, or chartreuse speckled with maroon; float some flowers in a shallow bowl where you can observe their markings. Forms a glossy mound of long-stalked evergreen leaves, sometimes 1 ft. wide, divided into 5–11 coarse-toothed leaflets. (Due to extensive breeding within the *H. orientalis* group of plants, some horticulturists suggest referring to them as *H.* × *hybridus*.)

Don't confuse Lenten rose with the so-called Christmas rose, *H. niger* (zone 4), which has fine-toothed dark evergreen leaves and saucer-shaped clear white flowers up to 4 in. wide. It is more temperamental than other hellebores and blooms in early spring, if at all. Corsican hellebore (*H. argutifolius*, zone 7) is a bushy plant with handsome gray-green leaves and flowers of less interest.

How to Grow
Part sun to shade. Loam-based commercial soil mix amended with plenty of organic matter and coarse sand to improve drainage. Ordinary watering okay. One plant per pot. *H. orientalis* is easy to grow from seed; others aren't. *H. niger* resents being disturbed; repot sparingly and carefully. Hellebores reestablish slowly if moved or divided. Remove old leaves in spring before flowering; shiny new ones will soon take their place. Remove old stems from *H. argutifolius* in late spring.

Hemerocallis
Hem-mer-o-kal′lis. Daylily
Liliaceae. Lily family

Description
Perennials with funnel- or bell-shaped flowers held on a branched stalk above a clump of narrow arching leaves. About 15 species, most native to China or Japan, and many hybrids. There are thousands of named cultivars.

■ **hybrids** *p. 137*
Hybrid daylilies
Perennials. Zone 4
Height: 1–6 ft. Spread: 15 in.–2 ft. or more
Wonderful plants for sunny containers, easy to grow throughout the United States. Each flower lasts only a day, but new buds open over a period of weeks. Flowers range from 2 in. to 7 in. wide, in shades of cream, yellow, orange, salmon, pink, rose, brick red, purplish red, lavender, or green. Some are bicolors, and many have contrasting midribs or throats. All (except the doubles) have 3 petals and 3 sepals, which may be similar or different in shape and color. Modern hybrids offer a variety of flower forms, ranging from the traditional lilylike shape to round flat flowers with wide ruffled petals, spiderlike flowers with long slender petals, and double flowers with a puff of extra petals. A few kinds have a slight sweet fragrance. Many of the newer cultivars are tetraploid plants with unusual vigor; their flowers have more substance and are borne abundantly on thick sturdy stalks.

Most cultivars have one major burst of flowering and are classified as early-, mid-, or late-season bloomers. Some rebloom later in the year, and a few bloom almost continuously. By planting several kinds, you can have nonstop bloom from May or June through late September.

Daylily plants are long lived and form dense clumps or

spreading patches of long slender leaves. Kinds with evergreen foliage do best in mild-winter regions. The deciduous types are more reliable where winters are cold. Usually the mound of foliage is about 1–2 ft. tall. The flower stalks, called scapes, range from 1 ft. to 6 ft. tall, depending on variety.

Most nurseries sell potted daylily plants, but for the widest selection and best prices, buy from mail-order specialists. Their catalogs list hundreds of varieties, labeled according to flower color and form, scape height, and season of bloom.

How to Grow

Full sun; light afternoon shade where summers are hot. Soilless or loam-based commercial soil mix amended with organic matter and coarse sand to improve drainage. Don't bury plant's crown, which can rot due to constant watering in the container. Don't let soil dry out completely. Remove spent flowers and flower stems. Rarely touched by insects or diseases, daylilies require very little maintenance. Some multiply fast enough to be divided every few years; others can grow undisturbed for decades. Divide crowded plants in spring or fall and repot. In areas with very low winter temperatures, store in frost-free location.

■ popular daylily cultivars

'Black-eyed Stella': Golden yellow flowers, 3 in. wide with a dramatic red eye, on 20-in. scapes; prolific rebloomer.

'Condilla': Deep gold double blossoms, nicely rounded, $4\frac{1}{2}$ in. wide, on 20-in. scapes. Early to midseason.

'Ed Murray': Dark red flowers with a yellow throat and rim, $4\frac{1}{2}$ in. wide, on 30-in. scapes. Midseason.

'Eenie Weenie': A true dwarf, just 10 in. tall, with prolific light yellow flowers, 3 in. wide, in midseason.

'Hyperion': Light yellow flowers, 6 in. wide, on 42-in. scapes; lovely fragrance. One of the oldest and most widely planted cultivars. Midseason.

'Joan Senior': Nearly white 6-in. flowers on 25-in. scapes. Early to midseason; sometimes reblooms.

'Mary Todd': Yellow flowers, 6 in. wide, on 26-in. scapes. One of the first tetraploids, and still a winner. Early.

'Pardon Me': Bright red flowers with a greenish yellow eye on 18-in.-tall scapes at midseason; reblooms.

'Ruby Throat': Brilliant red, slightly ruffled flowers with a green throat, 6 in. wide, on 25-in. scapes. Midseason.

'Siloam Double Classic': Fragrant, double salmon-pink flowers, 5 in. wide, on 16–18-in. scapes. Early to midseason; repeats once established.

'Stella d'Oro': Gold flowers, 3 in. wide, on 12-in. scapes. Blooms continually from early summer through fall (pictured opposite). 'Happy Returns' is similar, with yellow flowers.

Heuchera
Hew′ker-a. Alumroot
Saxifragaceae. Saxifrage family

Description
Perennials with thick rhizomes, a tuft of rounded or lobed basal leaves, and many tiny cup-shaped flowers on slender stalks. About 55 species, native to North America.

■ **hybrids** *p. 138 Pictured on p. 282*
(*H.* × *brizoides* or *H. sanguinea*)
Coralbells, alumroot
Perennials. Zone 4
Height: 12 in. (foliage) to 18 in. (flowers). Spread: 12–18 in.
Coralbells is a good old-fashioned perennial, worth growing for both its foliage and its flowers. Mix it with annuals, such as pansies, and perennials, such as dwarf hostas or variegated Japanese Solomon's-seal. Makes a compact mound of thick, leathery, almost evergreen leaves, which may be round or kidney-shaped, toothed or lobed, crimped or ruffled. The wiry leafless stalks hold tiny pink, red, or creamy white flowers well above the foliage, forming an airy cloud of bloom.

The following hybrids may be listed under *H.* × *brizoides* or *H. sanguinea*, a red-flowered species native to the Southwest. Their parentage is uncertain, but they're all excellent plants for most parts of the United States. 'Coral Cloud' has salmon-pink flowers. 'Chatterbox' and 'Tattletale' are pink. 'June Bride' and 'White Cloud' are white. 'Pluie de Feu' ('Rain of Fire') is bright red, and 'Mount St. Helens' is dark red.

H. micrantha 'Palace Purple' is a recent introduction grown for its semievergreen mound of shiny lobed and toothed leaves, up to 4 in. wide, on tall stalks. Foliage color ranges from deep purplish red to bronze or brownish, varying among plants and generally prettier if shaded from midsummer sun. Combines well with any silver-gray perennial and also with blues or whites. Also noteworthy are new cultivars such as *H. americana* 'Pewter Veil', which has purple foliage with silver veining; *H.* 'Chocolate Ruffles', whose deep purple leaves are deeply cut and ruffled; and *H.* 'Bressingham Bronze', which produces large, shiny, purple-bronze leaves that are blood red on the underside. These are excellent specimen plants for a pot or tub.

How to Grow

Full sun where summers aren't too hot; part shade otherwise. Loam-based commercial soil mix amended with organic matter to increase water retention; neutral to slightly alkaline pH is ideal. Clay or wooden containers help by allowing freer movement of air. Position crown level with soil surface. When watering, try to keep crown from remaining too moist. Remove entire stalks of faded flowers to prolong bloom. If you overwinter outside, mulch to prevent frost heaving—plants tend to shove up out of the soil and must be reset. Keep soil on the dry side over winter. Divide every few years in early spring.

Hibiscus
Hy-bis′kus. Mallow
Malvaceae. Mallow family

Description
A diverse group of annuals, perennials, shrubs, and trees, most with showy bell-shaped flowers. Many are grown as ornamentals; others provide food, tea, medicine, or fibers. About 200 species, native to the Old and New World.

■ *rosa-sinensis* p. 111
Rose-of-China
Perennial shrub often grown as an annual. Zone 10
Height: 3–4 ft. Spread: 3–4 ft.
Striking flowers and glossy evergreen foliage make this a landscape standby in warm climates, while gardeners in cold climates buy plants each year, treating them as annuals. Saucer-shaped flowers range from 3 to 7 in. in diameter and from white through cream to yellow and orange, palest pink to deep red; some are multicolored. Plants flower in summer, or all year if overwintered in a greenhouse. Use to decorate a poolside, deck, or patio; grouping several plants in boxes makes a flowering screen or hedge.

How to Grow
Full or part sun. Loam-based commercial soil mix. Young plants will bloom in 6–8-in. pots; the size of containers for mature plants is determined by your strength and available space. Water heavily while in growth and bloom; feed twice a month to maintain flower production. Pinch tips to encourage branching. Overwinter in greenhouse. Cut out some of the oldest wood every spring to limit size and to encourage healthy new flowering wood.

Hosta
Hoss′ta. Plantain lily
Liliaceae. Lily family

Description
Perennials that make neat clumps of broad-bladed leaves. The small lilylike flowers are usually violet, blue, or white, sometimes very fragrant. Plants spread slowly by underground rhizomes. About 40 species, native to China, Korea, and Japan, and many hybrids and thousands of cultivars.

■ **species and cultivars** *p. 138*
Hostas, plantain lilies, funkias
Perennials. Zone 4
Height: 6 in. to 3 ft. (foliage). Spread: most wider than tall

Hostas are the preeminent perennials for shady gardens coast to coast, and they are as valuable and versatile in containers as in the ground. They are very easy to grow and thrive with almost no maintenance, forming larger, more beautiful clumps every year. Tufts of long-stalked, wide-bladed leaves rise directly from short underground stems. Older plants have dozens of these tufts crowded closely together. Single plants mature into mounded specimens.

Hostas are valued chiefly for their leaves, which can be slender, lance-shaped, heart-shaped, or rounded. Texture can be smooth, crinkled, or ruffled. Colors include light to dark green, blue-green, blue-gray, and gold. There are many white- or gold-variegated forms. Generally, the blue-leaved forms grow and look best in full shade, but the gold-leaved forms need part sun to brighten their color.

Most hostas have lavender or purplish flowers borne on erect stems about twice the height of the foliage. The tubular 6-lobed flowers can be horizontal or drooping. Some gardeners think that hosta flowers detract from the impact of the foliage and remove them. Others let them develop. *H. plantaginea* and its cultivars are exceptional for having large white flowers that are showy and wonderfully fragrant.

Plant sizes range from doll-sized to jumbo, and all can make handsome container plants. Small hostas are under 8 in. tall and look best when several are grouped together. Medium hostas grow up to 12 in. high and 18 in. wide and are good for edging paths or beds. Medium-large hostas grow up to 18 in. tall and 2–3 ft. wide; they can be grouped or placed alone as specimens. Large hostas, which grow over 2 ft. tall and make clumps several feet wide, are excellent as sentinels either side of a shaded entryway, or marking the corners of a deck or patio or the turnings of a shady path.

How to Grow

Part or full shade. Soilless or loam-based commercial soil mix amended with organic matter and coarse sand to improve drainage. Pot size varies (from 4 to 12 in. or so) with plant size. Hostas are most luxuriant if soil is constantly moist; a generous layer of mulch helps retain soil moisture. Where slugs and snails are common pests, hostas are their favorite food, and black vine weevils are a problem in the South.

Hostas rarely need division; they can live for years in one pot. If you want to multiply your stock, knock a big plant out of its pot in spring when leaves first emerge. Cut or pull clump into smaller clusters, each with several shoots and plenty of roots. If necessary, hostas can be transplanted or divided later in the growing season. Just be sure to keep them well watered afterward. Overwinter outside or in garage or cold frame.

■ selected hostas

'Blue Cadet': Medium. Makes a sturdy clump of blue-gray foliage, with small heart-shaped leaves.

fortunei 'Francee': Medium-large. A fast-growing variegated ground cover. Leaves are forest green edged in bright white. Tolerates almost full sun. *H. f.* 'Hyacinthina' is medium-large. Makes rounded mounds of gray-green leaves edged with a white hairline. Spreads vigorously.

'Ginko Craig': Medium. The lance-shaped leaves are green with white edges. *H. tardiflora*, a similar edging hosta with dark green lance-shaped leaves, blooms very late in fall.

'Gold Standard': Medium-large. Grows fast, making broad mounds of big heart-shaped leaves, gold edged with green. Tolerates part sun.

'Hadspen Blue': Medium. The extremely blue leaves have rich texture and substance.

'Krossa Regal': Medium-large. Shaped like a vase, with leaves flowing outward at the top. The large heart-shaped leaves are powdery blue-gray. The light orchid flowers are borne on 6-ft. stalks. Makes a distinctive specimen.

plantaginea: Large. Called August lily for its deliciously fragrant, trumpet-shaped white flowers in August. The smooth leaves are light green, shiny, and deeply veined. The cultivar 'Grandiflora' has slightly larger flowers. 'Aphrodite', recently introduced from China, has fragrant double white flowers. 'Honeybells' has light green leaves and fragrant pale violet or lavender flowers. 'Royal Standard' is a vigorous hybrid with rich green leaves and fragrant white flowers; it adapts well to shade or sun. All of these fragrant hostas are lovely in the garden and make long-lasting cut flowers that will perfume a room.

sieboldiana 'Elegans': Large. The rounded leaves have rich substance and a seersucker texture, with a lovely blue-gray color in shade, blue-green in sun. *H. s.* 'Frances Williams' is large; the rounded, cupped leaves have heavy substance and a seersucker texture, with a blue-green center and irregular green-gold margins. One of the most popular hostas nationwide, it makes quite a specimen. Tolerates sun and dry soil better than many hostas do. *H. sieboldiana* itself has rich green leaves.

sieboldii 'Kabitan': Medium. An edger that almost hugs the ground. The narrow leaves are gold with ruffled dark green edges. Spreads by rhizomes.

'Sum and Substance': Large. A spectacular plant that makes huge mounds of glossy, heavy-textured foliage. Leaves can be 2 ft. wide. Color is chartreuse in shade, bright gold in half-day sun. Very reliable. Pest-resistant.

ventricosa 'Aureo-Marginata': Medium-large. The rich green leaves with irregular creamy or white margins have wavy edges and twisted tips.

venusta: Small. The leaves are only 1–2 in. wide, and mature clumps are 4 in. high by 8 in. wide. *H. v.* 'Variegata' is similar, but its leaves have cream centers and two-tone green edges. Both are tiny and look precious in pots.

'Wide Brim': Medium-large. The blue-green leaves have irregular creamy margins that darken to gold. Vigorous.

Hyacinthus
Hy-a-sin'thus. Hyacinth
Liliaceae. Lily family

Description
Bulb-forming perennials with a few strap-shaped leaves and a stubby stalk of sweet-scented flowers in spring. Only 3 or 4 species, native to the Mediterranean region.

■ *orientalis* p. 154
Hyacinth
Bulbous perennial. Zone 5
Height: 6–10 in. Spread: 6 in.
Popular for its intense fragrance and sturdy cheerful appearance. Blooms last for about 2 weeks in early spring. Each bulb makes one spike with dozens of single or double flowers

in pink, blue, lavender, rose, yellow, or white; bees love them. Leaves appear with the flowers and remain for 2–3 months. Combine with Spanish bluebells, grape hyacinths, daffodils, early tulips, and other spring bulbs, as well as cold-tolerant annuals such as pansies, forget-me-nots, and primroses.

How to Grow
Full or part sun. Loam-based commercial soil mix. Plant tips slightly below soil level and close together (almost touching) in fall. Provide 12–14 weeks of chilling. Bulbs may rot if soil is wet. Feed before, during, and after bloom. You can set bulbs in garden later, but for best display, buy new bulbs each fall.

Hydrangea
Hy-dran´jee-a
Saxifragaceae. Saxifrage family

Description
Deciduous or evergreen shrubs with opposite rounded leaves and bushy clusters of white, pink, or blue flowers. More than 20 species, native to North and South America and eastern Asia.

■ *macrophylla* p. 176
Hydrangea
Deciduous shrub. Zone 6
Height: 4–8 ft. Spread: 6–10 ft.
An excellent shrub for large pots on the patio or flanking an entry. Showy rounded clusters of white, pink, red, or blue flowers bloom in summer and fall. Its many thick, erect, unbranched stems reach their full height in a single season. The big opposite leaves have a thick texture and shiny green color; fresh healthy foliage is handsome by itself. Use an annual such as Madagascar periwinkle to lighten its bold effect.

Hundreds of cultivars compose two groups. 'Pia' (a dwarf 2 ft. high), 'Nikko Blue', and other hortensia types have domed clusters of flowers that are all sterile, with conspicuous papery petallike sepals. 'Mariesii' and other lacecap types have flatter clusters with small fertile flowers in the middle and a lacy ring of sterile flowers around the edge. 'Mariesii Variegata' has lovely green-and-white leaves and blue flowers; it grows slowly and stays 2–3 ft. tall. 'Forever Pink' grows 3 ft. tall and as wide and offers early flowers and excellent foliage.

Flower color varies with soil pH. Acidic conditions (pH below 5.5) improve blue coloring. Neutral to alkaline conditions (pH of 6.5 or higher) favor the pink and red colors.

Hardiness varies among cultivars. Most produce flowers on the previous year's shoots, and they fail to bloom if a cold winter kills the shoots to the ground, even though the roots will survive and produce a vigorous crop of new shoots. Flowering is reliable only where winters are mild in the Deep South or Pacific coastal regions. In colder climates plants must be overwintered in a cool garage or basement.

For reliable bloom where winters are cold, plant *H. arborescens* 'Annabelle' or 'Grandiflora'. Both have big clusters of sterile flowers, borne on new shoots that grow 3–5 ft. tall in a season (they'll need space). Treat them like herbaceous perennials, cutting all stems to the ground each winter. Their flowers start out as green buds, lighten to creamy white as they expand, and darken to tan as they age.

How to Grow

Full or part sun; tolerates heat. Loam-based commercial soil mix amended with plenty of organic matter and coarse sand for improved drainage. Use aluminum sulfate to acidify soil for blue flowers and lime to produce red flowers. Needs constant moisture; easily dries out, so monitor soil moisture closely. Blooms on previous season's growth. While plant is dormant, remove stems that have already flowered. Further thinning will promote larger flower clusters. Hydrangeas are long lived and trouble-free.

Ilex

Eye′lecks. Holly
Aquifoliaceae. Holly family

Description

Mostly evergreen (some deciduous) trees or shrubs, usually with thick leathery leaves, sometimes spiny, and round red, gold, or black fruits. About 400 species, native worldwide, and many hybrids and cultivars. The species and cultivars discussed here provide a "formal" look to patios, courtyards, and entryways.

Hollies produce male and female flowers on separate plants; you need both sexes for good berry production. Hybrids can be pollinated by either parent; what's most important is that the flowers must be open at the same time. Usually one male will suffice to pollinate 10–20 females. They don't need to be placed side by side, as bees will carry the pollen several hundred yards. If there's already a suitable male holly in your neighborhood, you don't need another.

■ *cornuta* p. 189
Chinese holly
Evergreen shrub. Zone 7
Height: usually under 10 ft. Spread: to 10 ft.
Chinese hollies, which thrive in hot weather, are popular landscape plants in the South and Southwest. Most make irregular mounded shrubs; their evergreen leaves feel like plastic and have a shiny, rich green color. Berries are very big, bright red, and long lasting, but plants need a long hot summer for berries to develop.

The typical Chinese holly has nearly rectangular leaves, 2–3 in. long, with sharp spines at the corners and tip. It makes a large upright shrub. 'Dwarf Burford' has small (1½-in.), almost spineless leaves that cup downward; bears small berries; and grows slowly, reaching about 10 ft. 'Carissa' has spineless leaves, does not produce berries, and stays under 4 ft. tall. 'Rotunda' has stout spines on the leaves and no berries; it grows to 4 ft. tall and makes a formidable burglar-proof barrier planting under windows.

Topal hollies (*I.* × *attenuata*, zone 7) are a group of hybrid American hollies, selected and grown mainly in the southeastern states. Most are upright, slender, pyramidal trees with narrow evergreen leaves and red berries. They tolerate full sun, part sun, or shade. They're suitable for containers if you prune them, perhaps as topiary, from an early age.

How to Grow
Full or part sun; tolerates heat. Loam-based commercial soil mix amended with coarse sand to improve drainage; slightly acidic pH is ideal. Clay pots or wooden tubs. Withstands drought and being root-bound (if well fed). Fertilize in late winter. Prune if necessary prior to new growth appearing in spring. Quite susceptible to scale; treat with dormant oil spray. In cold climates, move indoors and keep drier during winter.

n *crenata* p. 189
Japanese holly
Evergreen shrub. Zone 5
Height: usually under 4 ft.; can reach 20 ft. Spread: varies
Most forms grow slowly into low dense mounds. The thick, leathery, dark green leaves are small ovals ($1/4$ to $3/4$ in. long) with tiny marginal teeth. The small, inconspicuous berries are black. Japanese hollies are often used as a trouble-free substitute for boxwood in small gardens. Cultivars vary in size, habit, and hardiness. 'Helleri' is compact and bushy, usually under 4 ft. 'Compacta', 'Convexa', 'Glory', and 'Hetzii' reach about 6 ft. 'Golden Gem' has gold foliage if grown in the sun. 'Convexa', 'Glory', and 'Northern Beauty' are undamaged by winter lows in zone 5.

Yaupon holly (*I. vomitoria*, zone 7) is a southeastern native with small, narrow, dark green leaves and huge crops of small, juicy-looking red berries. It's easily trained as a small tree suitable for large containers, with picturesque crooked trunks and limbs. Dwarf cultivars make compact mounds of foliage and can be sheared into any desired shape. 'Nana' makes a dense twiggy hemisphere, 3–5 ft. high and wide, covered with tiny leaves but few berries; 'Stokes Dwarf' is even smaller. 'Pendula' has an upright trunk and weeping branches. Tougher and easier than *I. crenata* but not as hardy.

How to Grow

Full or part sun. Loam-based commercial soil mix amended with organic matter and coarse sand for improved drainage. Wooden containers are best; stands crowded conditions if well fed and watered. Don't allow to dry out. Needs minimal care or pruning. Grows naturally into a compact dense shrub. Subject to spider mites in hot, dry conditions but otherwise trouble-free. Overwinter in frost-free location.

n **other hollies**
Lusterleaf holly (*I. latifolia*, zone 7) has surprisingly large and luxuriant leaves, up to 8 in. long; small yellowish fragrant flowers; and generous clusters of large red berries. Grows strongly upright, nearly columnar, with a dense crown. A wonderful contrast to fine-textured companions such as nandina or bamboo; large plants make sentries by an entryway or gate.

I. 'Nellie R. Stevens' (*I. aquifolium* 5 *I. cornuta*, zone 7) is a tough, durable hybrid holly that makes a handsome pyramidal tree, and it can be trained as a topiary in this form. Fast-growing and trouble-free. The dark green evergreen leaves are waxy-textured, 1–2 in. long, with just a few spines.

Can be pollinated by a male Chinese holly (*I. cornuta*) and bears a heavy crop of bright red berries.

I. 'China Girl' (zone 5) has a round habit that can be trained into a topiary. Tolerant of high humidity and lower temperatures, it has light green leaves. The female produces a heavy crop of berries.

Impatiens
Im-pay'shens. Balsam, jewelweed, touch-me-not
Balsaminaceae. Balsam family

Description
Annuals or perennials, most with succulent stems, 5-parted flowers, and fruit capsules that burst open to eject the seeds. About 850 species, many native to Africa and Asia.

n **New Guinea hybrids** *p. 111*
Patient Lucy
Perennials grown as annuals. All zones
Height: 2–3 ft. Spread: 3–4 ft.
The sparkling, plentiful flowers are the main attraction here, though the dense mound of upright foliage is good-looking, too. Open-faced blossoms about 2 in. wide appear year-round (in mild climates) but are particularly heavy in fall and winter. There are many worthwhile selections, in white, lavender, pink, red, purple, and other colors except yellow. The long, slender, shiny leaves have a marked midrib and are usually bronze, reddish, or green but sometimes yellow. Plant one in a large (8–12-in.) container or several in a massive window box.

How to Grow
Part sun. Soilless or loam-based commercial soil mix. Plants need constant moisture (dry out too quickly in clay pots). Feed every 2 weeks during summer, once a month when overwintering indoors. Usually self-branching, but an initial pinching helps establish bushy habit. Overwinter in a south or west window for blossoms through the winter; nighttime temperatures should be above 55° F. Prone to cyclamen mite and aphids.

n ***wallerana*** *p. 112 Pictured on p. 292*
Impatiens
Perennial grown as an annual. All zones
Height: to 2 ft. Spread: to 2 ft.
One of the best annuals for containers in the shade, popular

in all parts of the United States. The succulent light green stems branch repeatedly, making a bushy mound without needing to be pruned or pinched. The thin leaves look good in shade but wilt quickly in hot sun. Flowers are 1–2 in. wide in shades of red, orange, pink, purple, or white, sometimes striped or two-tone. (Red-flowered types attract hummingbirds.) Some forms have double flowers like little roses. Attractive as a specimen in a pot, hanging basket (dwarf types), or window box. Combines well with begonias, ferns, hostas, astilbes, caladiums, coleus, lilies, and hydrangeas.

How to Grow
Shade. Soilless or loam-based commercial soil mix amended with coarse sand to improve drainage. Never allow soil to dry out, but plants bloom better if soil is slightly dry, but not dry enough to wilt foliage. Fertilize every 2 weeks with liquid fertilizer. Easy from seed sown indoors 10 weeks before last frost. Don't cover seeds (they need light to germinate); put them in a warm place (70°–75° F). Before first frost, root a few cuttings in water and pot them up for winter houseplants.

Ipomoea
Ip-po-mee′a. Morning glory
Convolvulaceae. Morning glory family

Description
A diverse group of annuals, perennials, vines, and shrubs, all with 5-lobed funnel-shaped flowers. Includes the sweet potato (*I. batatas*) and other food and medicinal plants, several or-

namentals, and some weeds. About 500 species, most native to warm or tropical climates worldwide.

■ *purpurea* p. 166
(*I. tricolor*)
Morning glory
Annual vine. All zones
Height: to 15 ft.
Morning glory is a nostalgic addition to a patio or balcony, climbing quickly to cloak a lattice trellis or railing with a screen of heart-shaped leaves. The funnel-shaped flowers, up to 5 in. wide, open in the morning and last just one day. Flowers can be blue, lavender, pink, red, or white, often with contrasting markings like 5-pointed stars. The moonflower, sold either as *I. alba* or as *Calonyction aculeatum*, is a vigorous vine that needs a sturdy support. Its large white flowers open at dusk and are sweetly fragrant. Cypress vine (*I. quamoclit*) has finely divided leaves and scarlet flowers. The cardinal climber (*I.* × *multifida*) has larger flowers. *I. coccinea*, the red star vine, is a native of tropical America. All of the preceding must have a trellis, tepee of sticks, fence, or deck railing; without support they simply try to climb back into the pot, rather than trailing. *I. batatas* 'Blackie', grown for its striking dark foliage, is best as a trailing plant in pots, hanging baskets, or window boxes.

How to Grow
Full sun; tolerates heat. Loam-based commercial soil mix. Can tolerate some dryness but becomes more susceptible to spider mites if too dry. Soak seeds overnight before planting. Seedlings transplant poorly, so start seeds in peat pots or directly in display pot. Set outside after danger of frost is past. Provide support immediately.

Iris
Eye´ris
Iridaceae. Iris family

Description
Perennials that form either rhizomes or bulbs, with flat sword-shaped or linear leaves. The characteristic flowers have 3 inner segments (the standards) and 3 outer segments (the falls). Although it's easy to recognize an iris as an iris, there's wonderful diversity within the genus. About 300 species, most native to the north temperate zone, and some hybrids and many cultivars.

■ *reticulata* p. 155
Reticulated iris, violet-scented iris
Perennial. Zone 3
Height: 4 in. (flowers); 18 in. (foliage). Spread: 2–3 in.
These irises grow from little bulbs that have a netlike (reticulated) covering. They are inexpensive, so plant lots of them close together. The short-stalked flowers open in early spring, along with crocuses, snowdrops, and hellebores. They have a delicious grapelike scent. Individual blossoms are fleeting, but a large group lasts a few weeks. The smooth 4-sided leaves elongate after the flowers fade, disappear by summer. 'Harmony' is dark sky blue with yellow spots on the falls; 'Cantab' is pale blue with orange spots; 'J. S. Dijt' is reddish purple.

How to Grow
Full sun. Loam-based commercial soil mix. Tolerates hot, dry summers (dormant then). In fall, plant bulbs 1 in. deep and 2 in. apart in shallow container. In warm climates, keep cool over winter. In cold climates, mulch containers in cold frame or store in cold basement or shed. To force early bloom, bring into the house in late winter and place in a cool spot. Or leave them outside and wait for later bloom. Feed after they bloom, then let plants dry out. Remove yellowed leaves and store in pots or peat moss until fall. Trouble-free.

■ other irises
Many irises can be grown in containers. To decide which are worth the effort, consider how long the flowers last and how attractive the foliage will be after the flowers have gone. Irises can also be selected according to their soil preference. Some require wet soil or will even grow immersed in water; try

these in containerized bog or water gardens. Others do best when the soil is dry during their period of summer dormancy. Plant rhizomatous irises during their summer or winter dormancy; plant bulbous irises in the fall and overwinter outdoors. The following are some of the irises that merit consideration for container growing.

I. cristata, dwarf crested iris (zone 3; pictured opposite), whose lavender, blue, purple, or white flowers open just above ground level in early spring, makes a handsome ground cover for a permanent planter or in a large pot with a tree. *I. tectorum,* Japanese roof iris, also has lovely crested flowers, as well as attractive upright evergreen foliage 1 ft. or more tall; look for the variegated cultivar. *I. pallida* is a large plant with fragrant lavender-blue flowers; 'Variegata' has variegated leaves. Dutch, Spanish, and English irises, collectively called Xiphium hybrids, have big bright flowers in a wide range of colors on tall erect stalks. Excellent for cutting. Plant in huge pots, but otherwise treat like *I. reticulata.*

Siberian iris, *I. sibirica* (zone 4), forms large fountainlike clumps of arching dark green leaves. Flowers are delicate and come in shades of purple, blue, or white. Grown in pots 8 in. or larger or in planters, these irises may take several years to produce an impressive clump.

The following irises thrive in submerged pots during spring, summer, and fall but are best lifted out of the water during the winter and kept just moist. They'll also grow if not submerged but in soil kept continually moist. Try *I. ensata,* Japanese iris (zone 4; pictured below), a large plant with huge (8–10 in. wide) flat blossoms, often mottled or delicately patterned, in shades of white, violet, blue, or purple. *I. laevigata* also has spectacular large flowers in shades of white or purple. *I. pseudacorus,* yellow flag iris (zone 3), offers clear yellow flowers for 2–3 weeks in late spring; the leaves grow quite tall and look like cattails in summer. *I. versicolor* (pictured above), the native blue flag, is shorter but looks similar and blooms at the same time.

Jasminum

Jas′mi-num. Jasmine
Oleaceae. Olive family

Description

Deciduous or evergreen shrubs or vines with white, yellow, or pink flowers, often sweetly fragrant. About 450 species, almost all native to the Old World tropics.

■ *nitidum* p. 166
Star jasmine
Evergreen vine. Zone 10
Height: to 12 ft.
The shiny, deep green leaves of this rambling vine are speckled purple buds that open into fragrant white starlike blossoms. The vine doesn't twine, so it must be tied to its support—a trellis or tepee of bamboo stakes. Flowers mainly in summer, but sometimes in spring and fall. Place near an outdoor seating area or a doorway to take full advantage of the scent.

J. mesnyi grows a few feet shorter, producing large unscented yellow flowers in spring and summer. Summer jasmine (*J. officinale*) is a strong twining vine that can grow to 15 ft. if you let it. The sweetly scented flowers are less than 1 in. wide, blooming from summer into fall. A deciduous vine, it can be stored over the winter in a cold room (40°–45° F). Chinese jasmine (*J. polyanthum*) is evergreen. Fragrant white flowers emerge from pinkish buds in late winter and spring. Overwinter like summer jasmine.

How to Grow
Full or part sun. Soilless commercial mix in, ultimately, a 16–18-in. pot. (Pot up each spring.) Feed with slow-release fertilizer in spring, adding soluble feed every month through growing season. Prune to shape and keep in bounds; prune hard after flowering. Overwinter *J. nitidum* and *J. mesnyi* indoors in temperatures of at least 50°–55° F.

Juniperus
Jew-nip′er-us. Juniper
Cupressaceae. Cypress family

Description
Evergreen conifers, including low, spreading shrubs and upright trees. Leaves are needlelike or scalelike. Female cones are berrylike. Wood, foliage, and fruits are often very fragrant. About 50 species, native to the Old and New World.

UPRIGHT FORMS

■ *chinensis* cultivars *p. 190*
(now *J. × media*)
Conifers. Zone 5 or 4
Height: varies. Spread: varies
Planted in containers, the upright cultivars of this tough evergreen are useful as accents in a formal setting, on their own, flanking an entrance, or as a focal point in a group of containers. Most have needlelike juvenile foliage and scalelike adult foliage, often mixed on the same plant; the foliage has a pleasant sweet fragrance when crushed. Fruits are pea-sized blue balls. The following cultivars are especially common.

'Mint Julep' is a compact plant with many trunks that reach out in all directions at a 45° angle. It has pretty dark green foliage year-round. 'Pfitzerana' branches at a lower angle; it may get too large for container growing after a number of years. There are compact, gold, and blue forms of Pfitzer juniper. 'San Jose' juniper grows slowly and stays low, under 2 ft. tall and wide, with needlelike green foliage. 'Torulosa' or 'Kaizuka', commonly called Hollywood juniper, has irregular branching that makes an interesting asymmetric profile, and its foliage is dense, scalelike, and bright green. It, too, may eventually outgrow container culture.

How to Grow

Full or part sun. Loam-based commercial soil mix. Plants tolerate heat but not poor drainage. Feed with a slow-release fertilizer in spring. Can be pruned to shape. Subject to bagworms and spider mites. If overwintered outdoors, keep plants well watered and protected from strong winds.

■ other upright junipers

Rocky Mountain junipers (*J. scopulorum* cultivars, zone 4) vary in habit; most have dense foliage and make good specimens or screens. The blue or blue-green foliage holds its color in winter and has a very pleasing aroma when crushed. 'Blue Heaven', 'Gray Gleam', 'Pathfinder', and 'Wichita Blue' grow slowly into upright pyramids of blue-green or blue-gray foliage.

Several southwestern native junipers are tough trees for dry, sunny climates. *J. flaccida*, or weeping juniper, has an erect trunk with elegant weeping branches and fine-textured blue-green foliage. *J. deppeana*, or alligator juniper, has rich blue foliage and checkered bark that resembles alligator hide. *J. communis* 'Compressa' (pictured above) is a slow-growing, columnar plant well suited for a trough garden. *J. virginiana* 'Grey Owl' has soft gray-blue foliage in a spreading form up to 4 ft. high.

LOW FORMS

■ *horizontalis* cultivars p. 190 *Pictured opposite*
Creeping junipers
Conifers. Zone 2
Height: under 2 ft. Spread: 4–6 ft. or more

These tough plants should live for years in containers. Use on sunny patios, placing pots in front of taller plants, in formal arrangements, or trailing over the edge of a large planter. There are hundreds of cultivars, varying in foliage texture (dense or loose, needlelike or scalelike), foliage color (bright green to blue in summer, turning purple or bronze in winter), and habit (ground-hugging or mounded). Some of the most common are 'Bar Harbor', with flat matted foliage, blue-gray in summer and blue-purple in winter; 'Blue Chip', mounding higher, with a good silver-blue color most of the year; and 'Wiltonii' or 'Blue Rug', flat and trailing with silvery blue foliage.

How to Grow
Full sun. Loam-based commercial soil mix amended with coarse sand to improve drainage. Put 1 plant in a 20–22-in. pot. Feed with slow-release fertilizer in spring. Prune to shape. (Sometimes they are grafted to form a standard so foliage cascades.) Native to Canada and the northern United States; quite hardy to cold but less tolerant of heat and humidity. Older plants sometimes get bald in the middle, and the only solution is to replace them. Subject to spider mites and juniper blight. Overwinter outdoors; keep well watered.

■ other low junipers
Shore juniper (*J. conferta,* zone 6) stays low and spreads wide. Fine needles have a soft texture and range in color from grayish to green to blue-green, depending on cultivar. 'Blue Pacific' has bright blue-gray foliage and usually stays under 1 ft. 'Emerald Sea' has pretty green foliage, spreads to 8 ft., and is hardier (zone 5).

J. squamata 'Blue Star' (zone 4) is 2–3 ft. tall with a wider spread. Unusual for its densely needled texture, irregular mounded shape, and bright blue color, this small shrub makes a colorful specimen and can be used to good effect with other plants. It has a distinctly sparkly appearance. 'Blue Carpet' has similar foliage but stays low and spreads as a ground cover.

J. scopulorum 'Blue Creeper' is a spreader that grows 2 ft. tall and 6–8 ft. wide, with bright blue color all year. *J. sabina* 'Broadmoor' spreads very wide while remaining under 1 ft. in height. Foliage is soft and bright green. *J. procumbens* 'Nana' has very tight, slightly bluish foliage that takes a purple cast in winter. *J. horizontalis* 'Mother Lode' features bright golden foliage in summer, turning yellow-orange in fall and plum-tinged in winter.

Lagerstroemia
Lay-ger-stree′mee-a. Crape myrtle
Lythraceae. Loosestrife family

Description
Deciduous or evergreen shrubs or trees with showy clusters of red, purple, or white flowers. About 55 species, native to tropical Asia and Australia.

■ *indica* p. 176
Crape myrtle
Deciduous tree or shrub. Zone 7
Height: to 25 ft. Spread: to 10 ft.
Crape myrtle is handsome in several seasons and is a versatile container plant grown in hanging baskets as well as large concrete structures. It has spectacular blooms from summer until frost. The small flowers in large clusters have a texture like crepe paper and come in many shades of pink, rosy red, purple, or white. Leaves are smooth ovals, 2–4 in. long, sometimes turning red, orange, or purplish in fall. Gray-tan outer bark flakes off the handsome muscular-looking trunks to reveal smooth mahogany inner bark. Cultivars vary in

flower color and ultimate size; dwarfs only 3–5 ft. tall, such as the 'Petites' series, are well suited to containers. Plants of the strain called 'Crape Myrtlettes' flower within months of the seeds being sown and make nice hanging baskets; they'll grow to 3–4 ft. at maturity.

L. fauriei, with pretty bark but less-showy flowers, is hardier (zone 6) and quite resistant to powdery mildew. It has been crossed with *L. indica* to produce a series of new hybrid cultivars, recently released by the National Arboretum, that are notably healthy and hardy. Most have Native American names, such as 'Acoma', 'Hopi', and 'Sioux'; 'Natchez' has especially showy bark, pure white flowers, and good fall color.

How to Grow

Full or part sun. Loam-based commercial soil mix amended with coarse sand to improve drainage. Thrives in hot weather and recovers from dryness. Blooms on new growth; if shoots freeze back in a severe winter, it will recover the same year. Prune hard in spring to control growth and to encourage larger flowers. Remove suckers to expose and feature the trunks. Older cultivars were subject to powdery mildew and other foliar fungal diseases, but new ones are resistant. Aphids may infest new growth but don't cause serious or lasting damage.

Lamium
Lay′mee-um. Dead nettle
Labiatae. Mint family

Description

Low-growing, creeping, and spreading annuals or perennials with 4-sided stems, opposite leaves, and attractive 2-lipped flowers. Many species are weedy. About 40 species, native to northern Africa and Eurasia.

■ *maculatum* *p. 139 Pictured on p. 302*
Spotted dead nettle
Perennial. Zone 4
Height: under 6 in. Spread: invasive
While not a great neighbor in a mixed container (it's too invasive), it is wonderful in its own container. The toothed leaves are heart-shaped or oval, to 2 in. long, on upright or trailing stems; they're quite handsome spilling over the sides of a pot. The silver-leaved forms are prettiest. Foliage is evergreen where winters are mild. Short spikes of 1-in. tubular

flowers are showy and appear from spring through summer. 'Beacon Silver' has green-edged silvery leaves and pink flowers; 'White Nancy' has similar leaves and white flowers.

How to Grow

Sun to shade (growth is denser in sunny spots). Soilless or loam-based commercial soil mix—not fussy. One plant will quickly fill a container of any size. Looks best in shallow pot that will be viewed from above. Prefers constant moisture; recovers from drying out but may become patchy or leggy in rainy season. Shear if it gets shabby in midsummer; new growth will soon develop. Overwinter in a garage—it can survive freezing—or take a few cuttings and start a new pot inside. Aphids may cause problems.

Lantana

Lan-ta′na
Verbenaceae. Verbena family

Description

Perennials or shrubs, often with prickly stems and rough leaves, that bear rounded clusters of small bright flowers and black berries. About 150 species, most native to tropical America.

■ *camara* p. 112
Common lantana
Semievergreen shrub. Zone 8 or 7
Height: 2–4 ft. Spread: 2–6 ft.
A low shrub that spreads into a wide mound, providing a summer-long display of bright flowers on tough, heat-resistant plants. It grows well in anything from patio half-barrels to hanging baskets. (It's sometimes trained as a standard—

it can have a 3-ft.-wide head on a trunk 5 ft. tall.) Round 1–2-in. clusters of papery-textured 4-lobed flowers come in shades of creamy white, yellow, gold, pink, orange, or red. Individual flowers are often two-tone, and the flowers within a cluster frequently shade from one color to another, such as yellow to pink. The effect is bright and cheerful. The dark green leaves feel scratchy and smell pungent; they drop off when temperatures fall below freezing.

How to Grow
Full sun; tolerates heat. Loam-based commercial soil mix. Grown as an annual, it will thrive in a 6–8-in. pot; as a standard or shrub, use a 12–16-in. pot. Feed lightly. Pinch frequently to keep plant bushy. Tolerates salt along the coasts. Overwinter indoors or in greenhouse. If left outside in milder climates, it may freeze back in cold winters but will recover from base. Prune hard in spring to remove damaged wood; shape as desired. Subject to aphids, spider mites, and whiteflies.

■ *montevidensis* p. 113
Trailing lantana
Semievergreen shrub. Zone 7
Height: 6–18 in. Spread: to 3 ft.
One of the few good hanging-basket plants for hot, dry, windy locations, trailing lantana has sprawling stems and lavender blossoms that bloom throughout the growing season. (A white variety is also available.) It cascades from planter boxes or makes a good ground cover, and it's somewhat more cold-hardy than common lantana. Most lantana cultivars are hybrids between this species and *L. camara*.

How to Grow
Like *L. camara*.

Lathyrus
La′thi-russ
Leguminosae. Pea family

Description
Annuals or perennials with winged stems, pinnately compound leaves, and showy flowers. Many are vines that climb by tendrils. About 150 species, most native to temperate climates in the Old and New World.

■ *odoratus* p. 167
Sweet pea
Annual. All zones
Height: to 6 ft. Spread: 6–12 in.
An old-fashioned favorite, beloved for the penetrating sweetness of its lovely flowers, which have wavy or frilled petals in clear shades of red, pink, purple, or white. They make excellent cut flowers. The vines grow quickly. Place a pot at the base of a trellis or fence, or provide a trellis in the pot—an old-fashioned method is to insert bamboo sticks around the edge of the pot, tying their top ends together. Dwarf varieties stand alone without support. Not all kinds are fragrant; be sure the catalog description or seed packet indicates sweetness. Annual sweet peas do best in cool weather and wither in hot summers. Warn children that sweet peas are not like garden peas, and their seeds are not edible.

How to Grow
Full sun or afternoon shade. Loam-based commercial soil mix amended with plenty of organic matter. Sweet peas don't transplant well, so seed directly in display pot or start in peat pots. You can start them very early, mid-March in the North, earlier in the South. Thin to 4–6 in. apart in pot. Provide constant moisture and fertilize regularly. Pick flowers regularly to prolong bloom.

Laurus
Law′rus. Laurel
Lauraceae. Laurel family

Description
Evergreen trees with aromatic leaves, long used as a flavoring. A garland of laurel leaves symbolized honorable achievement in ancient Greece; today we speak of "resting on one's laurels." Only 2 species, native to the Mediterranean region and adjacent Atlantic islands.

■ *nobilis* p. 191
Sweet bay
Evergreen tree or shrub used as an herb. Zone 8
Height: 6 ft. Spread: 3 ft. (sheared pyramid)
A dense evergreen with year-round unchanging good looks. Can be trained as a formal specimen. The pointed oval leaves are stiff, leathery, dark green, and pleasantly fragrant when crushed. They are used in soups, stews, and sauces. Tight clusters of small greenish yellow flowers are inconspicuous in early spring, but shiny black fruits are sometimes noticed in fall. 'Saratoga', which may be a hybrid between *L. nobilis* and *L. azorica*, has rounder leaves with a milder aroma and is immune to psyllids.

How to Grow
Full sun; tolerates heat. Loam-based commercial soil mix. Looks best in large formal-looking pots or boxes 14–16 in. wide (at plant's maturity). Recovers from drying out. Feed lightly through spring and early summer. Shape with pruning shears by snipping individual leaves or small twigs, not with hedge shears, which will mutilate foliage. Can be trained into lollipop standards or formal cones, balls, or pyramids. Bring indoors when temperatures reach mid- to low teens. Use horticultural oil spray to control scale and psyllids.

Lavandula
La-van'dew-la. Lavender
Labiatae. Mint family

Description
Perennials or shrubs, mostly evergreen in mild climates, with very fragrant foliage and flowers. About 20 species, native to the Mediterranean region and surrounding areas.

■ *angustifolia* p. 139 Pictured on p. 306
(*L. officinalis, L. vera*)
English lavender, common lavender
Evergreen subshrub, considered an herb. Zone 5
Height: 1½ ft. Spread: 1 ft.
Prized for the legendary fragrance of its small lavender-purple flowers, which form crowded spikes on slender stalks in early summer. The habit is bushy, with many erect stems. The closely spaced leaves are stiff and slender, 1–2 in. long, with a fuzzy gray surface. Evergreen only in mild climates; it discolors and then freezes back where winters are cold. Excel-

lent container plant for sunny, dry locations. Pot on its own because of its preference for drying out between waterings.

Herb nurseries offer dozens of cultivars. 'Hidcote' has dark purple flowers, 'Jean Davis' has pale pink, and 'Munstead' has lavender-blue. *L. × intermedia,* sometimes called lavandin, is a hardy, vigorous, hybrid lavender. It flowers later than English lavender and has the sweetest, most intense fragrance. Several other lavenders delight gardeners in mild climates. *L. stoechas,* or Spanish lavender, has a jaunty topknot of dark purple bracts atop broad compact flower spikes. It makes a compact mound of slender gray leaves with a pleasant fragrance and is hardy in zone 8 and worth trying in zone 7. *L. dentata,* or French lavender, has soft, gray-green, sawtoothed leaves that feel sticky and smell resinous. It's hardy only to zone 9, where it blooms almost year-round.

How to Grow
Full sun. Loam-based commercial soil mix amended with coarse sand to increase drainage and with lime. Prefers a clay pot and crowded conditions; no larger than a 6-in. pot for a single plant. Pinch early to encourage full, dense habit. Allow to dry out between waterings. Feed frugally. In containers, is best treated as an annual and grown from seed each year. Pest-free; if foliage dies back, remove entire stem.

Leucophyllum
Loo-ko-fill'um
Scrophulariaceae. Foxglove family

Description
Small shrubs with silvery foliage and rosy to purplish 5-petaled flowers. Native to dry, sunny sites in Texas and Mexico.

■ *frutescens* p. 191
Texas sage, purple sage, ceniza
Evergreen shrub. Zone 8
Height: 6–8 ft. Spread: 4–6 ft.

A compact, slow-growing plant, good for drier inland and coastal areas; its silvery foliage is a handsome foil for brightly colored annuals. Makes a bushy mound that branches readily if pruned, with silver-gray, densely hairy, oval leaves clustered at the tips of the branches. ('Silver Cloud' has very pronounced silvery foliage.) Bell-shaped flowers, to 1 in. wide, appear in flushes, usually just after a rain. Easy and attractive. There are several cultivars and hybrids offering white flowers. 'Green Cloud' has green foliage; 'Compactum' is smaller and denser than the species and has purple flowers. *L. candidum* is also shorter and bushy (2–3 ft. tall), with lots of rich violet-purple flowers.

How to Grow

Full sun. Loam-based commercial soil mix amended with coarse sand to improve drainage—roots rot when too wet. Clay or wooden containers are best. Native to hot, dry regions of west Texas; thrives in summer sun and needs little care. Prune to size in early spring. Doesn't do well in cool or humid conditions. Overwinter indoors in colder regions.

Lilium

Lil′ee-um. Lily
Liliaceae. Lily family

Description

Lilies are perennial plants with scaly bulbs and leafy, upright, unbranched stalks. The showy flowers have 6 petals and sepals that all look similar; technically these should be called tepals, but gardeners call them all petals. There are about 100 species, nearly all native to the north temperate zone. Many of the species can be grown in containers; however, in recent decades breeders have produced a wonderful assortment of hybrid lilies with excellent color, fragrance, form, and vigor. The hybrids are generally more adaptable and easier to grow, and often more rewarding, than the species.

Lily flowers are big—up to several inches wide. They come in bright and pastel shades of red, orange, pink, salmon, peach, gold, yellow, or white; some are decorated with darker spots or freckles or raised bumps called papillae. Some are scentless, but others are intensely fragrant, with a penetrating sweetness that fills the entire garden. All lilies make excellent cut flowers. Most bloom in summer. The hybrids are described as early, midseason, or late, which roughly corresponds to June, July, and August.

Lily plants range in height from 1 ft. to 8 ft. The stems look silly when they first emerge in spring, with tufts of leaves crowded together like a topknot. As the stems elongate, the glossy bladelike leaves get spaced out into scattered or whorled arrangements. Lilies don't have much foliage in proportion to the flowers.

With so many options in stem height, flower color, and season of bloom, you can choose lilies to combine with any of your other favorite container plants. Lilies grow particularly well in containers, where it's easy to provide ideal soil and watering. If you plant different pots or tubs with early, midseason, and late varieties, you can have flowers on the patio all summer.

How to Grow

Most lilies are fully hardy in zone 4 or 5; in fact, they need at least 6–12 weeks of cold weather to rest and form new flower buds.

Lilies grow best in full sun or afternoon shade. Too much shade makes lily stems stretch for the light, and they get too weak to hold up their flowers. (Tall varieties often need staking anyway.) Lilies also tolerate summer heat if given thick mulch, regular deep watering, and afternoon shade. Use top-quality peat-based potting soil amended with coarse sand to improve drainage. To keep the soil cool in summer, underplant with spreading annuals such as sweet alyssum or lobelia. (Most shallow-rooted annuals make ideal companions.)

Lily bulbs never go completely dormant, and they must not be allowed to dry out. Mail-order specialists usually ship the bulbs in late fall (sometimes in spring), packed in damp peat moss and wrapped in plastic. Pot them as soon as possible after they arrive. If you must delay planting, store the bulbs in the refrigerator or a cool but not freezing garage or basement. The bagged bulbs sold at garden centers are often weakened by storage in warm, dry conditions and don't grow as well as freshly dug or refrigerated bulbs. If you want to shop locally, look for healthy container-grown lilies, which can be repotted anytime from spring to fall.

Plant the bulbs 2–3 times as deep as their diameter. Space the bulbs about 4–6 in. apart, and plant groups of 3 or 5 for the best show. Lilies can be left in the pots in autumn if they are stored in a cold frame, cellar, or trench in the garden. If not, remove them from the pots and store in slightly moist peat moss or wood shavings in a dark, cool spot indoors.

Lilies have few insect pests, although aphids sometimes attack the buds. Much more serious is a mosaic virus that the aphids spread. It causes yellow streaks or mottling on the leaves, disfigures the buds and flowers, and weakens the plants. (The same virus also infects tulips, causing streaked or mottled blooms.) There is no cure for this virus. Remove and destroy any plants that show symptoms. Various fungal diseases attack lily leaves and bulbs under conditions of wet soil or high temperatures and humidity; these diseases are more easily prevented (by placing pots where they will enjoy good air circulation) than cured.

■ **Asiatic hybrids** *p. 155*
Perennials. Zone 4
Height: usually 3–4 ft. but can be 2–6 ft. Spread: 1 ft.
This is the biggest group of hybrids and includes genes from about 20 Asian species that have been crossed repeatedly. The flowers are typically 4–6 in. wide and face up, out, or down. Colors include white, yellow, orange, pink, lavender, and red. Most of these hybrids are not fragrant, but they begin the lily season, blooming from late May through June. They are easy to grow and multiply quickly. Specialists offer hundreds of cultivars, and more are introduced each year. 'Doeskin' has many Turk's-cap flowers of peach champagne on 3–4-ft. stems. 'Pink Floyd' bears upward-facing pale pink blossoms on 3-ft. stems.

The "brushmark" Asiatics have made a big splash; the inner petals are painted with a deep, contrasting dark stroke. 'Rodeo' has pale peach flowers with bronze brushmarks; 'Bull's Eye' is yellow with deep red marks; 'Sugarpie Suzie' is dusty pink with deep bronze brushmarks. All grow 3–4 ft. tall and carry upward-facing flowers.

Oriental hybrids *p. 156*
Perennials. Zone 5
Height: usually 3–6 ft.; some shorter. Spread: 12–18 in.
The last lilies to flower in late summer, these generally have flat flowers, 6–8 in. or more wide, with recurved petals. Most face out or down, but some new Oriental hybrids have upward-facing flowers. Almost all are fragrant, some extremely so. Colors include white, many shades of pink, and red; often with yellow stripes or throats. There are scores of cultivars; after you've grown one, you'll want to try several more. 'Casablanca' has pure white unspotted flowers up to 10 in. wide on 4-ft. stems. The 'Imperial' strain has 8-in. flowers on 5–6-ft. stems in shades of crimson, gold, pink, or white. 'Le Rêve' has pure pink flowers of heavy substance on sturdy 3-ft. stems. 'Stargazer', one of the best for pots, has upward-facing flowers, crimson edged with white and marked with dark spots, on 2–3-ft. stalks.

Liriope
Li-rie′oh-pee. Lilyturf
Liliaceae. Lily family

Description
Evergreen perennials forming tufts or spreading mats of grassy foliage. Only 5 species, native to southeastern Asia.

■ *muscari* *p. 140* *Pictured opposite*
Lilyturf
Perennial. Zone 5
Height: 1–2 ft. Spread: to 1 ft.
Forms grasslike clumps or mats of leathery evergreen leaves, up to $1/2$ in. wide and 12–24 in. long. Very useful as an edging or ground cover in planters; the arching foliage contrasts well with upright formal companions, such as yuccas. Green-leaved varieties combine with flowering companions; silver-leaved ones look good on their own. Makes numerous slender spikes, 12–18 in. tall, of small lavender or white flowers in summer, followed by shiny, round, blue-black berries. 'Majestic' (violet flowers) and 'Big Blue' (blue flowers) are large plants (2 ft. tall) with dark green leaves. 'Silvery Sunproof' (15–18 in.) has leaves edged with stripes that lighten from gold to creamy white, and violet flowers. 'Monroe's White' has pure white flowers held well above the dark green leaves. 'John Burch' has broad, bold yellow, variegated leaves and crested blue-lavender flowers.

L. spicata, or creeping lilyturf, can be shorter. It spreads quickly by underground runners, making a grassy mat of narrow, soft dark green leaves. 'Silver Dragon' is compact (6–8 in. tall), with white-striped leaves. The green-leaved form is somewhat hardier than *L. muscari*.

How to Grow
Part sun; tolerates full shade, but most cultivars don't bloom as well, and variegated forms may turn green in shade. Loam-based commercial soil mix amended with coarse sand for improved drainage. Firm soil around transplants. Needs constant water to become established; tolerates short dry spells after first summer. After several years, divide crowded clumps any time during growing season. Cut shabby old foliage in late winter prior to appearance of new growth. No serious pests or problems.

Lobelia
Lo-bee′lee-a
Campanulaceae. Bellflower family

Description
A diverse genus of annuals, perennials, shrubs, and even some trees. All have simple alternate leaves, and their flowers, usually 2-lipped, are held upside down on pedicels that twist 180°. Flowers are often small but brilliant, in shades of red, purple, blue, yellow, or white. About 365 species, most native to tropical and warm climates.

■ *erinus* p. 113
Edging lobelia
Annual. All zones
Height: 4–8 in. Spread: to 12 in.
Blooms throughout summer and fall, with tiny irregular

flowers in all shades from light to dark blue, and also white and wine red. The trailing types are excellent for window boxes, patio containers, and hanging baskets. The upright types are bushy and compact, good for edging planters. Traditionally combined with red geraniums and white petunias for patriotic displays; also with silver-foliage plants such as dusty-miller. Several strains are available from seed catalogs or sold as small transplants in spring.

How to Grow
Full sun or part shade. Soilless commercial mix provides light, freely draining medium it prefers. Clay pots aerate roots best. Doesn't like hot summers but can succeed if it is established before hot weather begins, shaded from afternoon sun, and regularly watered. Start seeds indoors 10–12 weeks before last frost. Sow on soil surface; seeds are tiny and need light to germinate. Set plants in display containers after danger of frost is past. Space 6–9 in. apart; don't crowd (trailers especially). Never allow to dry out, but excessive watering causes molds and rotting. Feed monthly. Shear back partway in midsummer to rejuvenate plants if flowering slows. Pest-free.

Lobularia
Lob-you-lay′ree-a
Cruciferae. Mustard family

Description
Annuals or perennials with slender sprawling stems, narrow leaves, and many small flowers over a long season. Very similar to and often merged with *Alyssum*. Only 5 species, native to the Mediterranean region.

■ *maritima* p. 114 *Pictured opposite*
Sweet alyssum
Annual. All zones
Height: to 6 in. Spread: 12 in.
Indispensable for containers, this easy, adaptable annual blooms from late spring until hard frost. Forms a spreading mound or mat of branching stems with tiny leaves and masses of 4-petaled flowers in shades of white, pink, rose, or purple. Some (but not all) have a sweet honeylike fragrance. The froth of blossoms looks lovely cascading over the side of a pot of mixed annuals, as well as from hanging baskets and window boxes. Wonderful under potted roses or shrubs. Several strains are available from seed, and all nurseries sell the seedlings in spring.

How to Grow
Full sun; tolerates heat. Loam-based commercial soil mix. Start seeds indoors 6 weeks before last frost or sow direct. Shear back halfway when plants get tatty in midsummer, and they will be renewed. Pest-free.

Lonicera
Lon-iss´er-a. Honeysuckle
Caprifoliaceae. Honeysuckle family

Description
Shrubs or woody vines, usually deciduous or semievergreen, with simple opposite leaves. Small or large flowers, often sweetly fragrant, are borne in pairs or whorls, followed by soft berries. About 180 species, native to the Northern Hemisphere.

■ × *heckrottii* p. 167 *Pictured on p. 314*
Gold-flame honeysuckle, everblooming honeysuckle
Semievergreen vine. Zone 5 or 4
Height: 10–20 ft.
A lovely vine with smooth, firm, blue-green leaves, opposite on lower parts of the stem but joined together into rounded disks near the top. Foliage is evergreen where winters are mild, hangs on late even in cold climates. Slender 1-in. flowers are borne in clusters, blooming most heavily in spring and continuing sporadically until frost. The flowers are carmine outside and yellow inside, fading to pink as they age. Train it on a trellis to screen an unwanted view from the patio or to frame a doorway. Alternatively, use it as a focal point in a group of pots or as a ground cover in a large planter. Doesn't set berries, so it doesn't spread.

Japanese honeysuckle, *L. japonica* (zone 4), is a vigorous vine famous for its sweetly fragrant white flowers and invasive growth, which is much more controllable in a container. It blooms most heavily in late spring and early summer but continues off and on for months. 'Halliana', or Hall's honeysuckle, is the most vigorous and most commonly grown form and has white flowers that turn yellow as they age. 'Purpurea' is a vigorous form with dark purple-green leaves and flowers that are white inside, purple outside. 'Aureo-reticulata', the gold-net honeysuckle, has leaves veined with yellow and is less vigorous.

L. sempervirens, trumpet honeysuckle (zone 4), one of the easiest and most rewarding vines, is effective on a mailbox, fence, or trellis or scrambling into a tree. Tubular orange-red flowers with yellow throats bloom heavily for a month or so in early summer, then intermittently through fall. Growth is restrained, not aggressive like that of Japanese honeysuckle.

How to Grow

Full or part sun; tolerates shade but doesn't bloom much. Loam-based commercial soil mix amended with coarse sand to improve drainage. Start in a large pot (12–14 in.); could eventually be moved to a half-barrel. Tolerates hot weather; give it water if it wilts. Feed with slow-release fertilizer in spring; supplement with soluble fertilizer while flower buds are developing. Cut back hard in late winter. Store dormant plant in unheated garage over winter. Subject to aphids and various other pests and diseases, which can disfigure foliage and flowers, but usually recovers with little permanent damage.

Lysimachia
Li-si-mack´ee-a. Loosestrife
Primulaceae. Primrose family

Description
Annuals, perennials, or a few shrubs with simple leaves. Flowers are usually yellow or white, often with 5 petals. About 150 species, native worldwide.

■ *nummularia* p. 140 *Pictured above*
Moneywort, creeping Jennie
Perennial. Zone 3
Height: 2–3 in. Spread: 1 ft. or more
An attractive trailing plant for containers in part or full shade. The shiny, round, coin-sized ($3/4$–1 in. wide) leaves fit side by side on stems that tumble out of a pot or hanging basket. Especially pretty as a carpet for impatiens, coleus, or begonias. Bright yellow flowers match the leaves in size and shape. Blooms in summer. 'Aurea' is the same plant with citron yellow foliage; it is very effective with the blue flowers of browallia.

How to Grow
Part sun to shade. Loam-based commercial soil mix. Can be crowded at the edge of a pot; will root in bare spots. Needs constant moisture. Divide in spring or fall. Winter outdoors, or root cuttings indoors. Pest-free.

Malus

Mal′lus. Apple, crab apple
Rosaceae. Rose family

Description
Deciduous trees with white or pink 5-petaled blossoms in spring, blooming as the leaves unfold, and plump fleshy fruits. The difference between apples and crab apples is the size of their fruits; apples are more than 2 in. wide, crab apples are less than 2 in. wide. There are about 25 species in the genus, all native to the north temperate zone. Nearly all the apples grown for fruit and the crab apples grown as ornamentals are hybrids of uncertain parentage, so they're referred to simply by the cultivar name.

■ **hybrid crab apples** *p. 177 Pictured below*
Deciduous trees. Zone 4
Height: 8–10 ft. Spread: 6–10 ft.
Crab apple trees make a puffy cloud of bloom in spring, with 1–2-in. flowers in shades of white, pale to rosy pink, or purplish red. The display lasts for 1–3 weeks, depending on the weather. The leaves start expanding as the flowers open. New leaves are often reddish, turning dark green or reddish purple all summer and sometimes yellowing in fall. The trees grow at a moderate or fast rate. Mature size and shape varies among cultivars. Some trees are rounded; others spread wider than tall; some make upright ovals; and a few have erect trunks and weeping limbs.

Fruit size, shape, and color also vary. Smaller fruits tend to stay firm longer and hang on the tree until winter, when they gradually soften and are eaten by birds.

Modern selections show much more disease resistance than old favorites do. 'Weeping Candied Apple' has irregular weeping branches carrying leaves with a reddish cast and pink flowers. The small, dark red fruits stay on the tree until spring. Several weeping varieties are lovely. 'Red Swan' has disease-free foliage, white flowers, and shiny red fruits. 'Coral Cascade' has disease-resistant foliage, soft pink to white flowers, and coral fruits. 'Red Jade' has long, graceful, weeping branches; light pink buds opening to white flowers; and dark red fruits.

How to Grow
Full or part sun. Good garden loam amended with peat moss to improve moisture retention and with coarse sand for good drainage. Plants prefer acidic pH. Need plenty of room; can remain in tub or large pot for many years. Never allow plant to dry out. Feed annually with slow-release fertilizer in spring. Prune before growth begins in spring. Prune young trees to establish shape, to encourage wide branch angles, and to remove crossed or weak branches. Mature trees need pruning only to remove damaged limbs, water sprouts (vigorous limbs that grow straight up), and suckers that arise from rootstock. May be attacked by aphids, borers, Japanese beetles, scale, spider mites, and tent caterpillars. Crab apples grow well in most of the United States except the coastal Southeast or desert Southwest. Grow where hardy unless you're willing to shift a heavy container indoors.

Mandevilla
Man-de-vil′la
Apocynaceae. Dogbane family

Description
Tender evergreen vines or shrubs with milky sap, showy funnel-shaped flowers that open to 3-in. morning-glory-shaped trumpets, and pairs of long slender pods. More than 110 species, native to tropical America.

■ × *amabilis* 'Alice du Pont'   *p. 168*
Evergreen vine. Zone 10
Height: 10 ft. or more
Despite its tenderness, this vine is widely available and commonly grown as a summer patio plant. It thrives in pots or hanging baskets and blooms from the day you bring it home until killed by frost. It climbs by twining and will cover a trellis in a few months. Pinch tips to encourage branching. Pairs of large oval leaves make a dark green background for the clusters of lovely trumpet-shaped, clear pink flowers, 2–4 in. wide, with deep throats and 5 rounded petals. Individual flowers last for days. *M. sanderi* 'Red Riding Hood' has

smaller, shiny, leathery leaves and 2-in. dark pink flowers with gold throats. Makes a fine hanging-basket plant. *M. laxa,* or Chilean jasmine, is a deciduous vine that dies to the ground but grows back in zone 8. It has long slender leaves and 2-in. pure white flowers that smell like gardenias. *M. boliviensis* has long thin leaves, shiny and pale green; waxy white flowers with yellow throats bloom year-round.

How to Grow
Full sun or afternoon shade. Loam-based commercial soil mix. Can grow all summer in a 12-in. pot, but larger pots reduce frequency of repotting. Space no closer than one every 2–3 ft. in large box. Feed once every 3 weeks. Stop feeding, reduce watering, and cut stems back partway to overwinter indoors in a sunny window, or buy new plants each year. Where grown outdoors, trim back old, frozen, or tangled shoots in late winter. Prone to mealybugs.

Melissa
Me-lis′sa. Balm
Labiatae. Mint family

Description
Perennials with square stems; toothed, pale green, opposite leaves; and small flowers borne in long clusters. Only 3 species, native to Europe and Asia.

■ *officinalis* p. 141
Lemon balm
Perennial herb. Zone 5
Height: 2 ft. Spread: 2 ft.
Very easy to grow, with a wonderful lemony aroma and flavor. Invasive in the ground or when grown with others in

a window box or planter, it minds its manners on its own in a pot and makes a bushy mound if pruned repeatedly. The upright stems have opposite leaves with distinct veins and toothed edges. Ordinary plants are bright green. There's also a yellow-variegated form, but it's unstable; a golden form has best color when kept in low light. The crushed leaves are good in hot or iced tea.

How to Grow
Part sun. Loam-based commercial soil mix. Best in a small container (6 in. maximum); tends to look weedy if given too much room. Don't overwater (no drip irrigation). Propagate by dividing clumps in spring. Pinch when young to encourage branching, then shear 2–3 times during the season to renew foliage; don't shear if you like the white flowers. Will stay green over winter and can be left outdoors to resprout in spring. Prone to whiteflies.

Mentha
Men'tha. Mint
Labiatae. Mint family

Description
Perennials with square stems, opposite leaves that have a penetrating fragrance, and small flowers in dense heads or spikes. About 25 species, native to the Old World, and a great many hybrids.

■ *suaveolens* *p. 141*
Pineapple mint
Perennial herb. Zone 5
Height: 1 ft. or more. Spread: to 3 ft.
The white-variegated form of pineapple mint is the most ornamental of all mints and has bright green-and-white leaves about 1 in. long. Less vigorous and invasive than spearmint, it's safer to include in large planters, but use a bottomless 12-in. pot to confine it. Shear during the season to renew the foliage and to discourage flowering (the flowers aren't very decorative). The flavor is mild, but the leaves make a pretty, edible garnish for beverages or salads.

Spearmint (*M. spicata*) is taller and vigorously invasive. The toothed leaves are usually dark green and can be smooth or hairy, veined or wrinkled. Stems are topped with long slender spikes of tiny pale lilac flowers. *M. × piperita*, or peppermint, is a hybrid of spearmint and water mint, *M. aquat-*

ica, with a sharp penetrating fragrance. Its leaves are usually not hairy, but they can be wrinkled and may be green, purplish, or variegated with white.

Pennyroyal, *M. pulegium* (zone 6), is a low-growing mint with a strong penetrating fragrance, used to repel fleas and mosquitoes—not recommended for culinary or medicinal use. The leafy stems branch repeatedly and spread into a dense flat mat of dark green leaves, but it isn't invasive. *M. requienii,* or Corsican mint, is much daintier, with tiny bright green leaves and a cool, lingering, crème-de-menthe fragrance. It makes a mosslike ground cover and must have sun.

Nurseries sell many forms of spearmint and peppermint under a variety of names and offer a number of other mints also. Smelling the leaves is the best way to distinguish between them. Don't even think about growing mints from seed—what you get won't be worth the effort. Selected plants, propagated by cuttings, have much better fragrance.

How to Grow
Sun to shade. Loam-based commercial soil mix. One plant per large pot. Prune hard every few months to rejuvenate. Recovers from drying out. Feed twice a month. Overwinters outdoors, in a cellar, or on a child's bedroom windowsill.

Muscari
Mus-kay′ree. Grape hyacinth
Liliaceae. Lily family

Description
Perennials with small bulbs, grassy leaves, and little round flowers in slender clusters at the top of leafless stalks. About 60 species, native from Europe to Asia.

■ *armeniacum* p. 156
Grape hyacinth
Perennial. Zone 4
Height: 6–8 in. Spread: 6 in.
These charming little plants with fragrant violet or blue blossoms in early spring make vibrant additions to the patio. They are especially appealing set at the feet of daffodils, tulips, and hyacinths. Each bulb produces 1–3 stalks topped with 20–40 closely packed, drooping, urn-shaped flowers. Bulb specialists offer several related species and cultivars, some with clear blue or white flowers. All are easy and long lived.

How to Grow
Full or part sun. Loam-based commercial soil mix. Use pots 8 in. wide or larger. Plant in fall, 1 in. deep, almost touching adjacent bulbs. Chill between 30° and 40° F for 10–16 weeks in garage or cellar. Move when shoots are 2 in. or more tall. Water and feed until plants go dormant in summer, then store pots, unwatered, or transplant into the garden. If you keep them in the pot, top-dress every 1–2 years with compost or organic fertilizer. Divide when clumps get crowded.

Myrtus
Mir′tus. Myrtle
Myrtaceae. Myrtle family

Description
Evergreen shrubs or small trees with opposite leaves and fragrant flowers. Only 2 species, native to the Mediterranean region.

■ *communis* p. 192
Myrtle
Evergreen shrub. Zone 8
Height: 3–4 ft. Spread: 3 ft.
This tough, slow-growing, drought-resistant shrub is excellent for topiary and makes a fine little container shrub for a patio or deck. It is often underplanted with a creeper, such as violets. Myrtle has a rounded habit and dense foliage (it looks like privet), which can be sheared. The species can grow to a 20-ft. tree, but dwarfs, such as 'Microphylla', 'Compacta', and 'Compacta Variegata', stay under 3 ft. and have dense foliage. The leathery, stiff, bright green leaves are oval with pointed tips, 2 in. long. They release a strong but pleasant fragrance when crushed. Sweet-scented white flowers like small powderpuffs open over a long season in summer, followed by dark blue berries.

How to Grow
Full sun; tolerates heat. Loam-based commercial soil mix amended with coarse sand for drainage, which is a must. Prefers being tightly potted in a clay pot. Mature plants can be moved up (slowly) to a 12-in. pot. Don't let soil dry completely; causes dieback. Water sparsely in winter. Feed once a month during growing season. Stake if you're training as topiary. Overwinter in sunny location that is cool at night. Problem-free.

Nandina

Nan-dee´na. Heavenly bamboo
Berberidaceae. Barberry family

Description
An evergreen shrub with big clusters of small white flowers and bright red berries. Only 1 species, native to eastern Asia.

■ *domestica* p. 192
Nandina, heavenly bamboo
Evergreen shrub. Zone 7 or 6
Height: 4–5 ft. Spread: 2 ft.
Easy, versatile, and attractive. Forms a clump of erect, unbranched, bamboolike stems with horizontal tiers of lacy foliage in subtle colors. Nandinas fit into narrow spaces and are good for entryway plantings. They look great in silhouette—backlight them at night. The compound leaves are divided into many smooth oval leaflets, 1–2 in. long. At first they are pastel pink or coppery, then turn light to dark green in summer and rich crimson or purple in fall and winter. Loose clusters of creamy white flowers open in early summer. Heavy sprays of shiny red berries last from fall to spring. Single plants fruit lightly or not at all, so plant several if you want berries.

There are many cultivars. Various low-growing forms are called 'Nana' or 'Compacta'; some are nicer than others. 'Harbour Dwarf' is highly recommended; it stays under 2 ft. tall, spreads by suckers, and turns bronzy orange or red in winter. 'San Gabriel' forms a 1–2-ft. mound of extremely narrow, almost needlelike leaves. 'Umpqua Chief' and 'Moyers Red' are vigorous growers that stay about 5–6 ft. tall and have bright red winter color. 'Alba' has white berries.

How to Grow
Sun to shade; needs some sun to develop bright foliage color; tolerates heat. Soilless or loam-based commercial soil mix. Will do well for years in a 12–14-in. pot or box. Repot when plant appears seriously root-bound. Recovers from drying out. Prune older stems to soil level to encourage low, dense, new growth; or prune all stems back to soil level if plant becomes too dense. Tops may freeze in zone 7 or 6; cut back to live wood in spring. Thrives over winter in bright room. No common pests or diseases.

Narcissus
Nar-sis´sus
Amaryllidaceae. Amaryllis family

Description
Long-lived bulbous perennials with flat or rushlike leaves and showy yellow or white flowers. There are about 27 species, nearly all native to Europe, and thousands of hybrids and cultivars.

■ **daffodils, jonquils, and narcissus** *p. 157*
Perennials. Zone 4, except where noted
Height: 6–20 in. Spread: 4–8 in.
The genus *Narcissus* includes all the various plants called daffodils, jonquils, and narcissus. They are lovely container plants for all sorts of situations—patios, decks, entryways, in pots by themselves, as companions for annuals. Potted in autumn, chilled for 12–16 weeks, and placed on the patio in spring, daffodils can provide several months of enjoyment as potted bulbs come into flower.

Daffodils grow well throughout the United States and thrive in many types of containers. Plant them in deep pots to accommodate their large bulbs and extensive roots. Interplant them with cool-season annuals such as stock, primroses, ranunculus, pansies, schizanthus, and dusty-miller. They can also be combined in grouped pots with grape hyacinths, hyacinths, and tulips.

Enthusiasts group *Narcissus* into 12 divisions, based on flower form. The flowers have 2 parts: a round central cup, or corona; and a flat ring of 6 petallike segments, collectively called the perianth. Flowers are borne on leafless stalks, singly or in small clusters. Many kinds are fragrant. All make excellent cut flowers.

How to Grow

Full or part sun. Loam-based commercial soil mix amended with coarse sand to improve drainage. Plant bulbs in fall, positioning the tips just below the soil surface. For best display, plant as many as will fit in the pot, just barely touching each other. Keep moist but not too wet. Move them to a protected area such as a porch or garage when temperatures drop below freezing. Set outside in early spring.

Resist the urge to trim off the leaves after the flowers have faded. Let them mature and die back naturally; they feed the bulb and provide for the following year's flowers. If you need the pot, plant the bulbs in a corner of the garden where they can replenish themselves.

If you leave bulbs in the same container for a few years, you may need to divide large clumps just as you would in the garden. Dig clumps when the leaves start to yellow, shake the soil off the roots, separate the bulbs, and replant them promptly. If you wait until the leaves die down completely, separate the bulbs and spread them to dry in a shady place, then remove the withered leaves and roots. Store the bulbs in mesh bags in a cool, dry shed or cellar with good air circulation until it's time to repot them in fall.

Daffodils are trouble-free plants. Few pests or diseases attack them. Mice, voles, gophers, rabbits, and deer avoid them. Take note and warn children that daffodil bulbs, leaves, and flowers are poisonous if eaten.

■ recommended daffodils

Heights are approximate and will vary under different growing conditions. All zone 4, except where noted. (Plants from divisions 3, 11, and 12 are usually not available. Species daffodils, division 10, are not included, because they tend to be rare, small, and expensive.)

Trumpet daffodils, division 1: The trumpet-shaped corona

is as long as the perianth segments. Flowers are 3–4 in. wide, borne singly. 'Dutch Master', 'Golden Harvest', and 'Unsurpassable' are yellow. 'Mount Hood' opens pale yellow and fades to white. 14–18 in. tall. Early to midspring.

Long-cup daffodils, division 2: This is the most popular group, with by far the most cultivars to choose from. The cup is more than one-third as long as, but less than equal to, the perianth segments. Flowers are up to 4½ in. wide, borne singly. 'Carlton' is all-yellow, with a long corona. 'Ice Follies' has a broad cup that opens yellow and fades to white and a white perianth. 'Binkie' is reversed, with white cup and yellow perianth. 'Salome' has a long salmon-pink corona and a white perianth. 14–18 in. tall. Early to midspring.

Double daffodils, division 4: These have a tuft or mound of extra petals, in addition to or instead of a cup. Flowers are 1–4 in. wide, borne singly or clustered. 'Cheerfulness', sweetly fragrant, has small white flowers with pale yellow centers. 'Golden Ducat' is all-yellow. 'Tahiti' is yellow marked with red-orange. 12–16 in. tall. Mid- to late spring.

Triandrus hybrids, division 5: Flowers have a flared-back perianth and droop from the top of the stalk in groups of 2 or more. 'Hawera' is a miniature, 8 in. tall, with 1-in. flowers. 'Thalia' has white flowers 2 in. wide on 16-in. stalks. Mid- to late spring.

Cyclamineus hybrids, division 6: These have long tubular coronas and distinctly turned-back perianth segments. Flowers are about 2 in. wide, borne singly. 'February Gold' and 'Peeping Tom' are yellow. 'February Silver' is white with a yellow corona. All are short (under 8 in.). Very early spring.

Jonquilla hybrids, division 7: The sweetly fragrant flowers are ½–1 in. wide, with small cups, borne in clusters of 1–3. The narrow leaves are dark green. Stems are round or rushlike, not flat. 'Suzy' has a yellow perianth and an orange cup. 'Trevithian' is golden yellow. The species *N. jonquilla* has clear yellow flowers. Up to 16 in. tall. Mid- to late spring.

Tazetta hybrids, division 8: Flowers are almost flat, ½–1¼ in. wide, in clusters of 3–20. Stems are stout; leaves are broad. 'Geranium' is white with a red-orange cup, grows 14 in. tall, blooms in late spring, is hardy to zone 5, and is very fragrant. Because 'Paperwhite' types don't require any cold treatment, they are especially easy to grow in southern or West Coast patio gardens. They aren't usually appropriate for outdoor containers in northern areas.

Poeticus hybrids, division 9: 'Actaea' is the most common member of this group. Called pheasant's-eye narcissus, it has a pure white perianth and a small yellow cup with a thin red line around the edge. Very sweet-scented. 18 in. tall. Blooms at the end of the season.

Nerium

Neer′i-um. Oleander
Apocynaceae. Dogbane family

Description
Evergreen shrubs with leafy stems and big clusters of showy 5-lobed flowers. All parts are extremely poisonous. Only 2 species, native from the Mediterranean region to Japan.

■ *oleander* p. 193
Oleander
Evergreen shrub. Zone 8
Height: 6 ft. Spread: 3 ft.
Very tough but also very showy. Blooms throughout the heat of summer, with clusters of 2–3-in. single or double flowers in white, creamy yellow, pink, salmon, rose, or red. (Double flowers don't drop clean when faded.) A few kinds are fragrant. Forms a big mound of slender leafy stems, erect or sometimes arching under the weight of the flowers. The long narrow leaves are smooth and leathery, dark green above and pale below. Use as a single tubbed specimen, or line up several to edge a deck or patio. Oleanders are easily trained as standards and espalier. They thrive indoors and out—in the past they were favored conservatory plants. 'Petite Pink' and 'Petite Salmon' are compact, 3–4 ft. tall. 'Algiers' (red), 'Casablanca' (white), and 'Tangier' (pink) are intermediate size, 6–8 ft. tall. There are many other cultivars, differing in size, flower color, and hardiness (some are hardy to zone 9).

How to Grow
Full sun. Loam-based commercial soil mix. Will bloom in a 6–8-in. pot, but to attain any size, it should have a 12–16-in. pot, or larger. Recovers from drying out. Damaged by hard frost but usually recovers. Prune in winter, cutting some of the stems to the ground. Flowers on new growth. Overwinter indoors. Fast-growing. Attractive to scale insects and aphids. A bacterial disease causes galls; prune out injured wood.

Nicotiana

Ni-ko-she-ay′na. Tobacco
Solanaceae. Nightshade family

Description
Annuals, perennials, or a few shrubs, usually with sticky, smelly leaves. All have tubular 5-lobed flowers and make

small, round, dry pods loaded with thousands of tiny seeds. *N. tabacum* leaves are dried for smoking tobacco. *N. rustica,* much higher in nicotine, is used as an insecticide. About 70 species, native to the Old and New World.

■ *alata* p. 114
(*N. affinis*)
Flowering tobacco
Annual. All zones
Height: 1–3 ft. Spread: 1 ft.
Blooms reliably all summer long in shades of white, pink, rose, lavender, red, crimson, or chartreuse. Flowers are like 1-in. stars with long tubular throats, borne on erect branching stalks. Older cultivars open in the late afternoon or evening; new strains stay open all day. Some kinds are sweetly fragrant, especially in the evening. The basal leaves are large and have sticky hairs. Plants tolerate cool temperatures and so are good for high-altitude gardens.

Flowering tobacco combines well with other annuals or perennials. The 'Nikki' series (16 in.) is very floriferous but has little fragrance. The 'Starship' and 'Domino' series are slightly more compact (about 1 ft.); the 'Merlin' series is dwarf, only 8 in. tall. These series all make ideal companions for lilies, petunias, salvia, and spike dracaena. Of the larger kinds, the species is sweetly scented and grows to 3 ft., and its white flowers are also fragrant in the evening. 'Sensation Mixed' (2–3 ft.) has fragrant blooms that stay open all day. 'Fragrant Cloud' (3 ft.) has large white flowers that are very fragrant in the evening.

Woodland tobacco, *N. sylvestris,* is a large (to 6 ft. high and 3 ft. wide), dramatic plant with tall branching stalks topped with loose drooping clusters of white flowers. Try it in a large patio planter or whiskey barrel, where you can enjoy the intense night fragrance of the flowers.

How to Grow

Full or part sun; tolerates heat. Loam-based commercial soil mix. Seeds are small, like those of petunias. Sow indoors at 70° F 6–8 weeks before last frost. Pinch when potting plants to encourage bushy growth. Feed in midsummer when heat is highest. Cut off spent flower stalks to reduce seeding and to renew bloom. Attacked by tomato hornworms and whiteflies.

Ocimum

Oh´si-mum. Basil
Labiatae. Mint family

Description

Annuals, perennials, or shrubs, most with very fragrant foliage, used for flavoring, fragrance, and medicine. About 150 species, native to warm and tropical regions, especially Africa.

■ *basilicum* p. 115
Sweet basil, common basil
Annual herb. All zones
Height: to 2 ft. Spread: 1 ft.
As indispensable as tomatoes for summer cuisine, basil is a bushy herb with shiny, wonderfully fragrant leaves. Grows as well in pots as in the garden if provided ample moisture and sunshine. Plant in window boxes or pots of herbs near the kitchen door for a quick pinch. The erect stems are woody at the base and branch repeatedly. The opposite leaves are 1/2–4 in. long, depending on the cultivar. Narrow spikes of small white or purplish flowers form at the top of the stems in summer, but most gardeners pinch them off. Regular sweet basil has excellent flavor. Many special cultivars are available from

seed. 'Cinnamon' has a sweet spicy fragrance. 'Purple Ruffles' and 'Opal' are rather bland, but they have pretty dark purple foliage that combines well with pink-, red-, or orange-flowering annuals or perennials. 'Spicy Globe' makes a 6-in. ball of tiny tasty leaves.

How to Grow
Full or part sun; tolerates heat. Loam-based commercial soil mix. Use 1 plant per 8–10-in. pot; can crowd with other annuals in larger pots. Keep moist. Prefers hot weather. Easy from seed, started indoors 8 weeks before last frost or sown direct. Pinch for bushiness. Attacked by Japanese beetles in the Northeast.

Osmanthus
Oz-man'thus
Oleaceae. Olive family

Description
Evergreen shrubs or trees with tough leathery leaves, sometimes spiny-toothed, and small but very fragrant flowers. About 15 species, most native to eastern Asia.

■ *fragrans* p. 193
Sweet olive
Evergreen shrub. Zone 9
Height: 6 ft. Spread: 3–4 ft.
A bulky shrub—dense, erect, and eventually treelike—grown primarily for its unforgettable sweet, fruity fragrance. The clusters of tiny white flowers are powerful enough to perfume a large patio in spring and summer and sporadically through the year. The pointed oval leaves, to 4 in. long, are thick and leathery. Use as a single specimen, pruned to control its size. 'Aurantiacus' is similar but has pale orange flowers that are even more fragrant; it blooms heavily from September to November. *O. × fortunei* is a hybrid between *O. fragrans* and *O. heterophyllus*. It is hardy to zone 7 and has fragrant flowers in autumn and spiny-edged hollylike leaves. It grows slowly to about 6 ft. tall.

Holly-leaf osmanthus, *O. heterophyllus* (a.k.a. *O. aquifolium,* zone 7 or 6), is a slow-growing shrub, excellent for containers. The leathery, thick, dark green leaves resemble English holly (*Ilex aquifolium*). The tiny white flowers are sweetly fragrant, blooming mostly in autumn. 'Gulftide' is especially compact and dense. 'Variegatus' has leaves bordered with creamy white.

How to Grow
Full or part sun. Loam-based commercial soil mix. Best in a large tub, pot, or box, but with top pruning, root pruning, and occasional fresh soil, it can be kept in a 10–12-in. pot. Overwinter indoors. Pest-free.

Oxalis
Oks-al´iss
Oxalidaceae. Wood-sorrel family

Description
Hundreds of species, many grown for their late-winter and early-spring flowers.

n **species oxalis** *p. 157*
Oxalis
Tender bulbs. Zone 7
Height: 6–10 in. Spread: 6–10 in.
Clumps of striking 4-petaled leaves, some with dark markings or a deep bronze color, are spangled with airy sprays of tiny 5-petaled flowers on leafless stems held above the foliage. Lovely in a small pot as a specimen, oxalis can also be planted at the base of larger plants such as 'Gartenmeister' fuchsia, cannas, roses, spike plants, and calla lilies. Very easy and rewarding to grow. *O. acetosella* (European wood sorrel) has white flowers with purple veins; may be sold as "shamrock." *O. deppei* 'Iron Cross' has green leaves, the inner third of which are colored deep maroon, and coral-pink flowers. *O. crassipes* offers pink or white flowers over a tight mound of round-lobed foliage. *O. purpurea* var. *bowiei* has shell pink flowers over pale green leaves; blooms in fall and winter in zones 9–10 and in fall farther north.

How to Grow
Full or part sun; tolerate heat. Loam-based commercial soil mix. Plant several tubers in a 6-in. pot, or one each in 2¼-in. pots. Start them indoors 6 weeks before last frost, and keep at 60° F or warmer for good sprouting. Keep moist. Remove spent flower stalks. Let plants go dormant in fall or early winter, then store tubers in pots, or remove from pots and store in peat moss or wood chips in cool, dark place. Divide tubers in spring if necessary.

Papaver
Pa-pay´ver. Poppy
Papaveraceae. Poppy family

Description
Annuals or perennials with showy flowers borne singly on long stalks, lobed or dissected basal leaves, and milky sap. About 50 species, native to the Old and New World.

n *nudicaule* p. 115
Iceland poppy
Perennial grown as an annual. Zone 2
Height: 1–2 ft. Spread: 8–14 in.
A beautiful series of garden flowers developed from an Arctic wildflower. The mildly fragrant, cup-shaped flowers have a mass of golden stamens nested in 4 or 8 crinkled silky petals. Colors include shades of yellow, orange, pink, red, and white. The light gray-green basal leaves are lobed or jagged along the edges. Both leaves and flower stalks are covered with whiskery hairs. Usually raised from seed in mixed colors. 'Champagne Bubbles' and 'Sparkling Bubbles' are popular strains. Beautiful with a carpet of lobelia in window boxes and even hanging baskets. Other good companions include petunias and dusty-miller, which provide interest after the poppies stop blooming.

How to Grow
Full sun. Loam-based commercial soil mix. Iceland poppies can't take summer heat and are grown as winter annuals in the South and in California. Set out small potted plants in fall for bloom the following spring, and discard after bloom. Northern gardeners can sow the tiny seeds indoors 8–10 weeks before last frost or buy small plants in spring for bloom in early summer. (Iceland poppies do well through the summer in cool mountain areas.) Take care not to damage roots when transplanting, or start seeds in peat pots. Don't let them dry out. In all areas, deadheading helps prolong bloom.

Passiflora
Pas-si-flo´ra. Passionflower
Passifloraceae. Passionflower family

Description
Mostly evergreen vines that climb by tendrils. The large round flowers are fascinating and complex and sometimes

very fragrant. Some kinds are valued for their sweet fruits. About 350 species, most native to tropical America.

■ × *alatocaerulea* p. 168
Passionvine, passionflower
Semievergreen vine. Zone 8 or 7
Height: 10–12 ft. (quickly). Spread: equally broad

A rambunctious vine with unbelievably intricate flowers, 3–4 in. wide, in shades of purple or white. Very fragrant and blooms all summer. The vine climbs or scrambles over fences, trellises, or shrubs, clinging by tendrils. Good for quick shade on an arbor or for hiding an ugly view. Leaves are 3-lobed, 3–4 in. long. Evergreen and aggressive where winters are mild. Dies back to the ground after hard freezes but blooms on new growth the next year.

The hybrid *P.* 'Incense' is hardy to zone 5 in a protected site against a building foundation or wall. It has violet flowers, 5 in. wide, with a lacy corolla and an intensely sweet fragrance. *P. incarnata,* the hardy native maypop, is a deciduous vine with sweet lavender-colored flowers 3 in. wide and egg-sized fruits with yellow rind and sweet pulp. A number of other species are worth trying, including *P. caerulea,* blue passionflower, which has smaller leaves, flowers, and fruit; and *P. edulis,* passion fruit, which produces delicious, fragrant, 3-in.-long fruits. *P. vitifolia* has big cardinal red flowers against grapelike foliage and blooms very easily in containers. *P.* 'Jeanette' has amethyst blossoms with curly filaments and blooms profusely even where light levels are low.

How to Grow
Full sun. Loam-based commercial soil mix. Needs generous room for roots. Use 1 plant per large pot; space every 2–3 ft. in planter. Don't let it dry out. Feed weekly. Prune to encourage branching, and provide support for tendrils to grasp. Allow plenty of space—this vine gets big fast. In winter, cut back and move indoors in sunny spot, or grow as annual from root cuttings. Various caterpillars eat the leaves but do no serious harm; watch for whiteflies and red spider mites.

Pelargonium
Pel-ar-go'nee-um. Geranium
Geraniaceae. Geranium family

Description
Perennials, shrubs, and some annuals. Some are succulent. True geraniums (*Geranium* spp.) have "regular" flowers—

radially symmetrical, with all petals the same. These have "irregular" flowers—with a top and bottom, like a face. Many species have leaves with a distinctive shape, marking, or fragrance. About 280 species, most native to South Africa, and hundreds of hybrid cultivars.

■ × *hortorum* p. 116
Common geranium, zonal geranium
Tender perennial grown as an annual. All zones
Height: 6–48 in. Spread: same
One of the best and easiest flowering plants for pots, window boxes, and planters. Makes big spherical clusters of 1-in.-wide flowers in many shades of red, pink, salmon, or white. Particularly handsome with white-flowered companions—sweet alyssum, petunias, verbena—and grasses. Each cluster is long-lasting, and the plants bloom almost continuously. The circular to kidney-shaped leaves have scalloped or toothed edges and a soft hairy surface. Most have a band or zone of a darker color; some kinds have distinct variegation. Stems are fleshy and erect. Old-fashioned geraniums used to get tall and straggly by late summer. These have been superseded by new compact strains that stay just 1–1½ ft. tall.

Martha Washington geranium, *P.* × *domesticum,* has the showiest flowers of any geranium, often likened to azaleas but borne in loose round clusters on long stalks. There are many cultivars, and most are strikingly marked.

How to Grow
Full sun; tolerates heat. Soilless or loam-based commercial soil mix that drains well. Use a 4–12-in. pot. Feed biweekly with a dilute fertilizer solution. Plants are compact when you buy them but may get straggly later unless you keep pruning and pinching the tips. Root tip cuttings in late summer to overwinter indoors on a sunny windowsill, or cut back to

stubs and store in a cool cellar with just enough sprinkling to prevent dehydration. (In zone 9, geraniums are hardy outdoors.) Whiteflies, aphids, and tobacco budworm are common pests. The new compact strains are grown from seed, sown indoors in late winter for bloom 15–20 weeks later.

■ *peltatum* p. 116
Ivy geranium
Tender perennial grown as an annual. All zones
Height: 1 ft. Spread: 3–4 ft.
This is the best geranium for hanging baskets, raised planters, and window boxes. The stems trail like vines. The bright green 5-lobed leaves are thick and glossy. The star-shaped flowers are red, pink, purplish, white, or bicolor, in small clusters on long stalks. It is extremely tolerant of seaside winds.

How to Grow
Like *P.* × *hortorum*. Pinching is very important to keep plants from becoming stringy.

■ scented geraniums p. 117 *Pictured below*
Tender perennials grown as annual herbs. All zones
Height: varies. Spread: 1½–2 ft.
This group includes dozens of species and hybrids grown for their attractive and strongly scented foliage. Their delicate white, pink, or lavender flowers are pretty, too, blooming in winter or spring. Most grow well year-round in containers, outdoors from spring to fall and moved to a sunny windowsill in winter. Place them near a path, bench, or patio where you can stroke the foliage to release the lovely fragrances. A plant from a 4-in. pot in spring can make a big mound by fall. The leaves are used in potpourri and perfumery, as garnishes, and to flavor jellies and cakes.

P. crispum, the lemon-scented geranium, has erect stems that reach 3 ft. tall, small round leaves with crinkled margins, and a rich lemony fragrance. There are several cultivars, including some variegated ones. *P. graveolens,* the rose geranium, is a bushy 2–3-ft. plant with branching stems and softly pleated, toothed, deeply lobed leaves. There are several cultivars and hybrids with different flowery and fruity scents. *P. tomentosum,* the peppermint geranium, spreads wider than tall and has large round-lobed leaves covered with soft furry hairs. The fragrance is intensely minty.

How to Grow
Like *P.* × *hortorum.* Can stand crowded pots if well fed and watered. Overwinter well on windowsill or in sunroom.

Petunia
Pe-too´nee-a
Solanaceae. Nightshade family

Description
Annuals or perennials with sticky hairy stems and leaves and showy, sometimes fragrant, funnel-shaped flowers. About 35 species, native to warm and tropical regions in Latin America.

■ × *hybrida* p. 117
Common garden petunia
Tender perennial grown as an annual. All zones
Height: 1–3 ft. Spread: 1–3 ft.
One of the most popular plants for containers and hanging baskets, easy and colorful. Blooms profusely for months. The round flowers are single or double, in shades of red, rose, pink, purple, violet-blue, pale yellow, white, or striped combinations. Some kinds are very sweetly fragrant, especially at night. All have straggly stems and small oval leaves covered with sticky hairs. Old-fashioned "balcony" petunias are sweetly scented and best for cascading effects. *P. integrifolia* has smaller profuse flowers on long stems; they are deep pink with a dark eye.

Scores of cultivars are available from seed, in solid and mixed colors. Most fall into one of two groups. The Grandiflora types are larger plants with flowers 4–5 in. wide and are subject to botrytis, which disfigures the leaves and flowers. The Multiflora types are more compact, with flowers 2–3 in. wide, and are resistant to botrytis—a big advantage in humid climates.

How to Grow
Full or part sun; tolerates hot and cool weather. Loam-based commercial soil mix. Start tiny seeds indoors 8 weeks before last frost. Use 1–3 plants in a 12-in. hanging basket. Fertilize monthly. Frequent deadheading prolongs bloom, and frequent pinching makes plants bushier. Sheer back in midsummer and fertilize heavily if flower production has slowed. Generally problem-free but can be damaged by air pollution or attacked by tobacco budworm, aphids, and leaf viruses.

Picea
Py-see´a. Spruce
Pinaceae. Pine family

Description
Evergreen coniferous trees with drooping cones and stiff needles that make a distinct pattern of bumps where they attach to the twigs. Widely harvested for paper pulp and timber (the resonant wood is used for stringed instruments); grown for Christmas trees and as ornamentals. About 34 species, native to cool regions of the Northern Hemisphere. Spruces grow very well in the Northeast and Northwest and are the best conifers for the Upper Midwest. They don't, however, do well in the hot summers of the South and Southwest.

■ *glauca* 'Conica' *p. 194*
Dwarf Alberta spruce
Conifer. Zone 3
Height: to 10 ft. Spread: 3 ft.
Native across Canada, the species withstands heat, wind, and dryness but needs cold winters. More common than the species is 'Conica'. It looks like a cone upholstered with slightly prickly fake fur—the pale green needles are only $1/4$–$1/2$ in. long and densely crowded on the twigs—and it takes decades to reach 10 ft. tall. An even smaller form, 'Gnome', grows to only about 1 ft. 'Densata', often called Black Hills spruce, is a conical form that grows about 6 in. a year, with dense, dark blue-green needles. In containers, these small spruces are typically used in pairs to flank an entrance. Their hardiness makes them particularly valuable for cold-winter areas.

How to Grow
Full or part sun. Loam-based commercial soil mix amended with organic matter for increased moisture retention. Wooden or clay containers will help prevent excessive heating of soil.

Protect root zone with a layer of mulch; roots are too shallow for underplanting. Don't allow to dry out. Shapes itself naturally and doesn't need much, if any, pruning. Protect shallow roots from winter cold. Various insect pests are usually minor; red spider mites can be serious problem.

■ *pungens* p. 195
Blue spruce, Colorado spruce
Conifer. Zone 3
Height: varies with cultivar. Spread: same
A symbol of the Colorado Rockies, where its erect pyramidal shape echoes the mountain peaks. Popular in other regions for its colored foliage and rigid posture. Young trees are especially neat and formal, with tiers of horizontal branches. Older specimens often lose their lower limbs and may get straggly and irregular. The needles are very stiff and sharply pointed, about 1 in. long. "Blueness" varies among seedlings; some trees are pale silvery blue, others a drab gray-green. Grafted cultivars cost more than seedlings but have reliably blue color. 'Hoopsii' is one of the best cultivars, with beautiful bright blue needles and rapid dense growth. 'Fat Albert' grows slowly into a compact chubby cone with good blue color. 'Blue Spreader' is a dwarf form with creeping branches, good for trailing over the edge of a stone planter. 'Globosa' and 'R. H. Montgomery' are both compact and globular.

The dwarf cultivars of Norway spruce, *P. abies*, with conical, mounded, spreading, or weeping habits, make good container plants. They're slow-growing but tough. 'Pendula', for example, can be used as a "ground cover" in a planter; to maintain its low form, snip off vertical shoots.

How to Grow
Like *P. glauca* but prefers full sun.

Pinus

Py'nus. Pine
Pinaceae. Pine family

Description
Evergreen coniferous trees with needlelike leaves, almost always borne in clusters of 2–5. The main trunk is strongly upright. Each year's growth makes a new whorl of branches on the main trunk and the side limbs. The woody cones may be small or large; a few kinds have edible seeds. More than 90 species, native to both temperate and tropical climates in the Old and New World.

Most pines are propagated by seed, and plants within a species may vary in habit, vigor, hardiness, and needle color. There are only a few vegetatively propagated cultivars. Several Old World species are planted throughout the United States, but our various native pines are also very common and are versatile, reliable, popular trees.

■ *mugo* p. 195
Mugo pine
Conifer. Zone 3
Height: varies by cultivar. Spread: same
More like a shrub than a tree, this pine is broad and bushy. Most of the plants sold are labeled as dwarfs (sometimes listed as *P. mugo* var. *mugo*), but some are more compact than others. True dwarfs are excellent for grouping in a planter or as specimens in individual tubs. Larger forms make good screens. All have dense, dark green foliage. The stout needles are crowded on the stems, 2 in. long, in groups of 2. The oval cones are 1–2 in. long. 'Gnome' forms a dense, globular, dark green mound; 'Mops' is an excellent dark-needled, compact form, 3 ft. tall and wide at maturity. *P. mugo* var. *pumilio* is a prostrate form that can spread 8–10 ft. wide; it's good for raised planters.

How to Grow

Full or part sun. Loam-based commercial soil mix amended with organic matter and coarse sand to improve drainage. Hardy to cold but can't take extreme heat. Grows for a long time in a container. Prune in spring to maintain shape. Feed with slow-release fertilizer. Very prone to scale insect infestation. Good for coastal gardens; not damaged by salt spray.

■ *thunbergiana* p. 196
(*P. thunbergii*)
Japanese black pine
Conifer. Zone 5
Height: varies by cultivar and pruning. Spread: same
Fast-growing, adaptable, and picturesque, this is a good tree for planters—young trees can be pruned or sheared for dense, rounded growth. Older specimens in planters or large containers can be trained as bonsai or grown larger, pruned to showcase the crooked trunk and irregular spreading crown. Needles are stiff, dark green, about 3 in. long, in groups of 2. Cones are 2–3 in. long. Indispensable for Japanese-style gardens. 'Thunderhead' is a dwarf form with a broad habit, dark green needles, and distinct white "candles" (new growth) in spring; 'Oculus-draconis' offers needles banded with yellow.

How to Grow
Like *P. mugo*. Full sun. You can root-prune to reduce its vigor. Recovers from drying out. To maintain required size and shape, prune new candles when they are fully grown, reducing them as much as three-quarters of their length. Feed older plants with slow-release granular fertilizer in spring. Protect from low winter temperatures (wrap container in burlap, for example). In recent years, many trees in the Northeast have died from blue canker stain disease. No cure is known.

■ other pines
Bristlecone pine (*P. aristata*, zone 5) is a native of the American West. It grows very slowly but lives indefinitely—some old-timers are judged to be more than 4,000 years old. It makes a picturesque specimen or bonsai. The irregular crooked limbs are covered with stout needles 1–1$\frac{1}{2}$ in. long, dark green with white specks of resin, in groups of 5.

Lace-bark pine (*P. bungeana*, zone 5) is valued for its handsome bark, which flakes off in large patches like a sycamore's. Grows very slowly.

Tanyosho pine (*P. densiflora* 'Umbraculifera', zone 4) makes a distinct umbrella-shaped crown with many close-set branches. Grows slowly and makes a handsome container specimen at all ages. Can't take hot, dry winds. The dwarf variety 'Pendula' has sprawling branches and looks handsome hanging over a raised planter.

Japanese white pine (*P. parviflora*, zone 4) is frequently used in containers or trained as a bonsai tree.

Dwarf white pine (*P. strobus* 'Nana', zone 4) is a dwarf form of one of the most ornamental pine species. Soft-textured, with an attractive form, it grows slowly to 3–7 ft. and twice as wide. Prefers rich, moist, organic soil. Is damaged or killed by salt and by air pollution. Susceptible to blister rust and white pine weevil.

Scotch pine (*P. sylvestris*, zone 3) is widely planted for Christmas trees. Older trees become quite picturesque, with open branching and an irregular rounded crown. 'Nana' and 'Watereri' are dwarf forms suitable for containers, as is 'French Blue', which has a mounded compact habit and attractive blue-green foliage.

Pittosporum
Pit-o-spo´rum
Pittosporaceae. Pittosporum family

Description
Evergreen shrubs or trees with shiny leathery leaves and attractive, often fragrant flowers. Some have valuable timber. About 200 species, native to warm and tropical climates in the Old World.

■ *tobira* p. 196
Evergreen shrub. Zone 8
Height: 3–4 ft. Spread: 3–4 ft.
A durable shrub that makes an irregular but dense mound of foliage. Large, thick, glossy dark green leaves with rounded tips are clustered at the tips of the branches. Best for containers are the smaller varieties, such as 'Variegata', with gray-green leaves mottled with white, and 'Wheeler's Dwarf', with small dark green leaves. All bear clusters of small,

creamy white, intensely aromatic flowers in late winter and spring. Berries colored and shaped like olives follow. Tough and adaptable, these shrubs are good for shady spots and locations with low humidity.

How to Grow
Part sun to shade; tolerates heat. Loam-based commercial soil mix; prefers heavy soil. Looks best in a 6–10-in. pot; plant is top-heavy, so use a heavy pot. Tolerates drying out. Feed once a month during active growth. Dwarf varieties are self-branching. Can prune by heading back individual branches, but leaves are too big for clipping with hedge shears. Overwinter indoors in sunny, cool spot (endures temperatures to 35° F). Subject to scale and aphids.

Portulaca
Por-tew-la′ka. Moss rose, purslane
Portulaceae. Purslane family

Description
Low-growing annuals with plump succulent leaves on trailing stems. Some have showy flowers. About 40 species, nearly all from warm and tropical climates.

■ *grandiflora* p. 118
Moss rose
Annual. All zones
Height: under 1 ft. Spread: 1 ft.
A favorite annual for hot, dry sites. Blooms from early summer until frost. The trailing stems are covered with plump cylindrical leaves and waxy round flowers, 1 in. wide, single or double, in shades of yellow, orange, red, pink, or white. Old-fashioned types closed by late afternoon and didn't open at all on cloudy days, but new strains keep longer hours. Excellent for containers on sunny patios; especially pretty cascading from terra-cotta bowls on railings or ledges. Good companion for succulents, cacti, or yuccas.

How to Grow
Full sun; tolerates heat. Loam-based commercial soil mix. Flat pots are fine for this shallow-rooting plant; space 3–4 in. apart for immediate effect. Buy plants in spring or direct-sow seeds about the time of last frost. Seeds are tiny, but seedlings grow fast. Water regularly until plants are established. Shear halfway back and fertilize in midsummer to promote fresh growth and to renew flowering.

Potentilla

Po-ten-til′la. Cinquefoil
Rosaceae. Rose family

Description

Annuals, perennials, or shrubs with stiff or wiry stems, compound leaves, and 5-petaled flowers. About 500 species, native to the north temperate zone.

■ *fruticosa* p. 177
Bush cinquefoil
Deciduous shrub. Zone 2
Height: 2–3 ft. Spread: 3–4 ft.
One of the few shrubs that bloom all summer, with 1-in. flowers in shades of yellow or white. Makes a plump round specimen or a flowering accent among other containers. The palmately compound leaves have 3–7 slender leaflets and are covered with silky hairs. The habit is bushy and dense because the stems branch repeatedly. Hard to beat for ease of care and reliable bloom. 'Abbotswood' has white flowers; 'Goldstar' is deep yellow; 'Katherine Dykes' and 'Primrose Beauty' are pale yellow.

How to Grow

Full sun. Loam-based commercial soil mix. Plant in a short 14–16-in. pot; can move up to a tub eventually. Supplement a slow-release fertilizer with liquid feed during bloom season. Blooms on new wood, so it can be cut to the ground and still flower. This should be done at least every other year in early spring to keep the plant dense and compact. Overwinter dormant plant outdoors or in unheated garage; keep soil on the dry side. Spider mites can be a problem in hot, dry weather.

Primula

Prim′you-la. Primrose
Primulaceae. Primrose family

Description

Low-growing perennials with a rosette of basal leaves and clusters of showy flowers on leafless stalks. About 400 species, native worldwide, mostly in cool climates.

■ × *polyantha* p. 143
Polyanthus primrose
Perennial. Zone 3
Height: 8 in. Spread: 12 in.

These hybrids are the easiest primroses to obtain and to grow and provide color in every conceivable shade. They're among the earliest plants to bloom in spring—and often the latest in fall, as many strains rebloom after a rainy summer (or if they've been watered regularly). Forms a basal rosette of light green leaves, 3–6 in. long, with crinkled edges. Short stalks carry umbels of upward-facing, almost flat flowers 1–2 in. wide. Yellow and orange flowers, solid or two-tone, are fragrant. There are several excellent strains, including 'Barnhaven' hybrids, 'Pacific Giants', 'Regal', and 'Cowichan'. 'Hose-in-Hose' types have double flowers, with 2 layers of petals. Where winters are mild and summers are very hot, polyanthus primroses are used as winter annuals that provide color in containers from fall through spring.

How to Grow

Part sun in spring, shade in summer. Soilless or loam-based commercial soil mix amended with plenty of organic matter. Plant singly in 6-in. pots or many together in larger pots. Can survive short dry spells but does better with constant moisture. Feed lightly but often during bloom season. Divide crowded clumps in late summer, early fall, or winter. Where winters are severe, put in cold frame and mulch to insulate. Foliage may be attacked by aphids, flea beetles, spider mites (where summers are hot), slugs, and snails.

■ **other primroses**

Common primrose (*P. vulgaris* or *P. acaulis*, zone 5) is an English wildflower, beloved by generations of gardeners for its simple charm. The fragrant flowers, 1–1½ in. wide, are pale yellow with a deeper yellow eye, borne singly on thin fuzzy stalks. Excellent with dainty wildflowers and early spring bulbs. Strains in extended colors with bigger flowers can be grown like *P.* × *polyantha*. *P. juliae* and its hybrids resemble miniature *P.* × *polyantha* or *P. acaulis* types. They're lovely planted en masse in a large container.

Japanese or candelabra primrose (*P. japonica*, zone 5) offers tiers of rosy red, pink, magenta, or white flowers stacked one above another on stalks 1–2 ft. tall. Blooms for 2 weeks or more in May or June. Needs moist soil during the growing season—if the soil dries out, it dies. Can thrive in soil that is constantly moist. *P. malacoides* looks like a small-scale candelabra primrose, with superimposed tiers of white, pink, or reddish lavender. Usually grown as a winter annual in mild-winter climates, it's effective massed in large pots.

P. auricula hybrids are often grown by fanciers as "collector's items" potted singly in 4–6-in. pots. Flowers are marked by rings and collars of green, black, gray, or white on red, yellow, blue, or green grounds. *P. obconica* and *P. sinensis* are grown in mild-winter climates as winter-spring annuals and as houseplants elsewhere.

Prunus

Proo'nus
Rosaceae. Rose family

Description

A valuable group of deciduous or evergreen trees or shrubs. All have alternate simple leaves, pink or white flowers, and fleshy fruits with one hard seed or pit. This genus includes cherries, prunes, plums, peaches, and apricots. Many species are grown as ornamentals, and some are used for timber. About 400 species, most native to the Northern Hemisphere.

■ *laurocerasus* p. 197
Cherry laurel, English laurel
Evergreen shrub or small tree. Zone 7
Height: to 6 ft. (compact forms). Spread: varies
Low-spreading cultivars of this otherwise upright tree make good container plants. Leaves are thick and glossy, 4–6 in. long and 2 in. wide. Upright 3–5-in. clusters of very sweet-scented small white flowers are a bonus, standing out like exclamation points against the foliage in midspring. 'Otto Luyken', 'Schipkaensis', and 'Zabeliana' are low-spreading cultivars that stay under 4–6 ft. and spread wider than tall. They flower profusely even in the shade. 'Schipkaensis' and 'Zabeliana' have narrow leaves and are hardy on protected sites in zone 6. Use these tidy plants as a dark green background for other plants or as specimens on their own.

How to Grow
Sun to shade. Loam-based commercial soil mix. Start plant in a 20–22-in. pot; could move up eventually to a whiskey barrel. Needs little care. Prune to shape, but don't shear, which chops the big leaves and looks quite messy. Water well before cold weather; keep out of strong winds. In harsh climates, store in unheated garage. Insects occasionally chew the foliage but do no serious damage.

Punica
Pew′ni-ka. Pomegranate
Punicaceae. Pomegranate family

Description
Deciduous shrubs or small trees with showy flowers and large fruits with juicy pulp. Only 2 species, native to Eurasia.

■ *granatum* p. 178
Pomegranate
Deciduous shrub. Zone 8
Height: to 5 ft. (trained). Spread: to 3–5 ft.
An old favorite for hot climates, where it blooms all summer. Flowers are bright orange-red, 1–2 in. wide; double forms resemble carnations. The round fruits, 3–5 in. wide, have a leathery red rind and are stuffed with sweet juicy seeds. The narrow pointed leaves are glossy bright green in summer, yellow in fall. In containers it's usually trained as a multi-branched shrub. Use as a specimen or accent in a potted herb garden. 'Wonderful' has the most delicious fruits. 'Nana' is a dwarf form, 1$\frac{1}{2}$–3 ft. tall, that can live in a pot for years. It has near-evergreen foliage, single orange-red flowers, and small dry fruits. Other cultivars have pretty salmon-pink, yellow, white, or two-tone flowers.

How to Grow
Full sun. Loam-based commercial soil mix. Start in a 10–12-in. pot; can move up to a tub eventually. Supplement slow-release fertilizer with liquid feed during active growth. Train young plants as desired. Prune in spring, removing tangled inner branches and cutting back long shoots. Flowers on new wood. Store in unheated garage over winter; keep soil on the dry side. No serious pests or diseases.

Pyracantha
Py-ra-kan´tha. Firethorn
Rosaceae. Rose family

Description
Evergreen thorny shrubs with simple leaves, round clusters of white flowers, and red or orange berries. The berries are very showy from fall to spring. Birds don't eat them until other food sources have been depleted. Closely related to *Cotoneaster* and *Crataegus*. Only 6 species, native to southeastern Europe and Asia.

■ **species and hybrid cultivars** *p. 197*
While not in the first line of container plants, pyracanthas offer a bold, solid effect in large containers and planters, with evergreen leaves, attractive flowers in spring, and fiery berries in fall. They look good in combination with colorful annuals. *P. coccinea,* scarlet firethorn (zone 6), is a fast-growing shrub valued for its profuse crops of berries; it requires persistent pruning to keep in bounds. 'Lalandei' is one of the most common cultivars. *P. koidzumii,* firethorn (zone 7), is similar to scarlet firethorn. 'Santa Cruz' is a low prostrate shrub with bright red berries.

Many pyracantha cultivars are hybrids of uncertain parentage. All are semievergreen shrubs with glossy foliage, clusters of white flowers in spring, and bright berries. They differ in size, habit, vigor, hardiness, and fruit color. 'Gnome' (zone 6) is compact and dense, usually under 6 ft. tall, with orange berries; susceptible to scab. 'Red Elf' (zone 7) forms a dwarf compact mound and has bright red fruits; susceptible to fire blight. 'Tiny Tim' (zone 7) grows to 3 ft. and has red berries, small leaves, and sparse or no thorns. 'Ruby Mound' (zone 7) has a low, mounding habit, growing 3 ft. tall and 5 ft.

wide. Taller varieties, such as 'Mohave', can be grown in a large concrete container and trained against a wall or trellis.

How to Grow
Need full sun for maximum fruit production but grow fine in part shade. Loam-based commercial soil mix amended with coarse sand for drainage. Avoid disturbing roots when transplanting. Recovers from drying out. Prune hard in early spring to restrict to container size and to train to shape. Overwinter in unheated garage. Subject to fire blight, which makes the shoots die back from the tips; scab, which makes hard dark spots on the berries and leaves; and various insect pests. Look for new pest- and disease-resistant varieties.

Ranunculus
Ra-nung'kew-lus
Ranunculaceae. Buttercup family

Description
A diverse group of about 250 species; several of those with tuberous (sold as bulbs) and fibrous roots are grown in the garden. Flowers are usually yellow. Children learn if they like butter by holding *R. acris* beneath their chins.

■ *asiaticus* *p. 158*
Persian buttercup
Perennial tuber. Zone 8
Height: 18 in. Spread: 18 in.
An extremely floriferous plant that makes an excellent cut flower. Pots in bloom justify the description "a riot of color." Plants grow from tubers that resemble clustered claws. Stems with fresh green foliage carry many full-petaled double flowers in cream, yellow, orange, pink, or white; many are bicolored or have picotee edges. The dwarf 'Bloomingdale' strain grows 8–10 in. tall. Easy to grow in mild-winter climates, Persian buttercups are more difficult where winters are cold and summers hot. An enormously popular plant in the 18th century, but only a small number of named varieties are available today.

How to Grow
Full sun. Loam-based commercial soil mix amended with coarse sand for improved drainage. In mild-winter climates, plant tubers in late fall for early spring bloom; in cold-winter, hot-summer climates, start tubers indoors and set out after last frost. (Plants need considerable time to bloom, and

an early onset of hot weather ends flowering.) Set tubers closely in containers and cover with 1–2 in. of soil. Keep soil moist. After bloom, let foliage ripen, then dry out pots, lift tubers, and store for the next planting cycle.

Rhaphiolepis
Ra-fee-ol′e-pis, ra-fee-o-leep′is
Rosaceae. Rose family

Description
Evergreen shrubs with thick leathery leaves and small but showy flowers. About 14 species, native to eastern Asia.

■ *indica* p. 198
Indian hawthorn
Evergreen shrub. Zone 7
Height: 3 ft. Spread: 3 ft.
A mounding shrub with thick, glossy, dark green leaves and abundant clusters of pink or white flowers for several weeks in spring. Individual flowers are only ½ in. wide, but clusters can be 4–6 in. wide. Small blue berries ripen in late summer. Oval leaves with pointed tips are clustered at the ends of the branches; new growth is bronzy red. In containers this shrub is rather formal-looking, good for flanking a sunny entry, lining a path, or marking the edges of a deck or terrace. *R. umbellata* is a similar species with rounded leaves and fragrant white flowers ¾ in. wide. Several cultivars that are often listed under *R. indica* may be hybrids between the two species. Pink-flowered cultivars include 'Ballerina', 'Charisma' (double flowers), and 'Enchantress'. 'Clara' and 'Snow White' have white flowers.

How to Grow
Needs full sun for maximum flowering. Soilless or loam-based commercial soil mix. A mature plant is comfortable in a 12-in. pot; root-prune to maintain pot size. Pinch young plant to establish good form. Prune after flowering to shape as desired. Overwinter indoors or in greenhouse. Has only minor pest and disease problems.

Rhododendron
Roe-doe-den´dron. Rhododendron and azalea
Ericaceae. Heath family

Description
This complex and fascinating genus offers container gardeners a variety of evergreen or deciduous shrubs with spectacular flowers in spring or summer. There are about 800 species, most native to the north temperate zone, and thousands of hybrids and cultivars. All have simple alternate leaves, sometimes glossy but often dotted or covered with tiny hairs or scales on the bottom or on both surfaces. The flowers have 5 or more petals or lobes and are borne in round clusters called trusses. The seedpods are small dry capsules. Plant size ranges from tiny shrublets and low creepers to large trees; smaller plants are best for containers.

Although gardeners consider azaleas a separate group of plants, botanists include them with rhododendrons. The distinction isn't clear-cut. In general, azaleas have smaller leaves, often deciduous, and funnel-shaped flowers with 5 stamens; rhododendrons have larger, evergreen leaves and bell-shaped flowers with 10 stamens. But there are many exceptions, including evergreen azaleas, deciduous rhododendrons, and rhododendrons with small leaves. Plants in this genus often defy categorization; there is considerable variation within some species, and natural or man-made hybrids blur the boundaries between species.

Container growing allows gardeners to grow these handsome plants in regions of the country where in-ground cultivation is difficult due to conditions of soil and climate (the Great Plains, Rocky Mountains, and arid Southwest). Elsewhere, it allows gardeners to grow even more of them or to experiment with species and varieties not suitable for their conditions.

Wherever rhododendrons and/or azaleas are grown, local nurseries stock an assortment of the most popular types, usually in 1–5-gal. containers. For a wider selection, contact mail-order specialists. These plants ship well, so don't hesitate to order from a catalog.

How to Grow

Most rhododendrons and azaleas do best in light shade. Too much shade leads to lanky growth and sparse flowering. Some kinds tolerate full summer sun in cool climates, but hot summer sun can bleach or burn leaves.

The potting soil can be commercial soilless or loam-based, or homemade. It should be free of clay and lime, contain much humus, and be slightly to fairly acidic. Good drainage is very important. Repot as plants grow; the largest will eventually need 16–24-in. boxes. Plants are easy to repot at any time of year, even when in full bloom. Keep soil constantly but not overly moist; they also appreciate atmospheric humidity. Apply diluted acid-type fertilizer following the manufacturer's directions.

Remove faded flowers promptly to prevent seed formation, which wastes the plant's energy. Prune, if necessary, just after flowering. Overwinter indoors if necessary. Outdoors, protect from winter sun and wind, which desiccate evergreen leaves and cause as much damage as do cold temperatures; avoid this by wrapping the plants with burlap for the winter. Mulch around the pots to maintain uniform soil temperature.

Various insect and disease problems can damage or kill plants, especially those already stressed by poor soil or indifferent care. Ask your Cooperative Extension agent or local nursery to identify which problems might occur in your area.

- **deciduous species azaleas** *p. 178*

This diverse group includes many of the parent species used in breeding hybrid azaleas. They offer hardiness, ease of care, disease-resistant foliage with good fall color, extra-early and extra-late bloom, a wide range of flower colors, and sweet fragrance. Among the best of these is *R. schlippenbachii*, the royal azalea, an Asian species that grows to about 6 ft. and is hardy to zone 5. Its large fragrant flowers, clear pink with reddish brown spots inside, open in early spring. The wide rounded leaves are clustered at the ends of the twigs and develop good fall color.

Local nurseries may not carry many (if any) deciduous species azaleas, so you may need to comb mail-order catalogs to find them. Hybrid cultivars, on the other hand, are grown and sold by the thousands. Hybrids, such as the Mollis, Exbury, and Knap Hill kinds, offer showier flowers in red, orange, yellow, pink, or white, and many have attractive fall foliage color as well. Northern Lights hybrids are hardy to zone 3.

■ evergreen azaleas *p. 198*

Evergreen azaleas are very popular for their masses of bright flowers in spring, and their foliage is neat and attractive all year. Most of the cultivars are hybrids developed by individuals or institutions with particular breeding goals, such as increased cold-hardiness or compact habit. Most bloom between mid-April and mid-June, with flowers in shades of pink, rose, red, or white. A few are lavender, salmon, or orange. Many have double flowers with one layer of petals inside the other, called "hose-in-hose." Few of the evergreen azaleas are fragrant, and none offer the intoxicating sweetness found in the deciduous types. Plant habits range from prostrate spreaders that hug the ground and trail over walls, to compact rounded shrubs with branches in layered tiers, to upright growers with erect stems.

The flowers can be very large, up to 5 in. wide. Some of the largest, loveliest flowers are the Belgian Indicas, often grown in greenhouses and sold by florists. These are grown in pots and hanging baskets indoors and out in California. Potted specimens can be maintained for years (overwinter them indoors in cold climates). The Southern Indicas were developed from the Belgian Indicas and have flowers nearly as large, but the plants are hardier, suitable for zone 9 or 8. They make substantial container plants as shrubs, standard trees, or espaliers. Most are vigorous upright shrubs that bloom in April or May. 'Fielder's White' (white), 'Formosa' (rosy purple), 'George Lindley Taber' (light pink), and 'Pride of Mobile' (pink) are popular cultivars.

Gumpo azaleas also have large flowers, on low, spreading plants with small leaves. 'Gumpo Pink', 'Gumpo Rose', and 'Gumpo White' are popular cultivars that flower in June. Used primarily in bonsai, they are hardy to zone 7.

Other hybrids have masses of smaller flowers. The Kurume hybrids are compact and bushy, usually 3–4 ft. tall, with small glossy leaves. They are literally covered with bloom in April or May and are hardy to zone 7. Popular cultivars include 'Coral Bells' (pink), 'Hino Crimson' (bright red), 'Hinodegiri' (cerise), 'Snow' (white), and 'Ward's Ruby' (dark red). Display them prominently when they're in bloom, and move them to more out-of-the-way shady areas at other times.

Breeders have been working on hardy evergreen azaleas. The Glen Dale hybrids have flowers like the Southern Indicas but were bred in Maryland for hardiness in zone 7 or 6. They bloom from May to July. Many have flowers marked with a second-color blotch or stripe, and sometimes whole branches will have flowers that contrast with the rest of the plant. The Girard hybrids, from Ohio, offer a wide range of bright-colored single and double flowers and bloom reliably in zone 6. Their foliage often turns dark reddish purple in winter.

Compact or spreading azaleas are ideal for trailing over the edge of tallish 8–12-in. pots. The Robin Hill hybrids have exceptionally large flat flowers in soft pastel shades, on compact, low, spreading plants, hardy to zone 7. The North Tisbury hybrids are prostrate or trailing plants that have large flowers in June and are hardy to zone 6.

■ rhododendrons *p. 199*

A rhododendron in full bloom makes a colorful display unequaled by other shrubs. The large flowers come in nearly all colors and last about 2 weeks, longer in cool, cloudy weather. Even if they didn't bloom, many rhododendrons have outstanding foliage that provides year-round interest. Leaves come in several shades of green and can be large or small, thick or thin, glossy or furry, flat or curled. Plant sizes range from compact dwarfs to giants that can hide a two-story house. This group is a collector's dream come true: there are hundreds of species and thousands of cultivars, each with unique flowers and foliage.

Hybrids of two native species valued for their hardiness, *R. catawbiense* and *R. carolinianum*, called 'Ironclads', are widely grown in pots in colder regions (zone 5). Some Asian species bloom very early, with forsythias. *R. dauricum,* from the mountains of Korea and Japan, is hardy but semievergreen in zone 6 or 5. It grows slowly to about 5 ft. tall. There are lavender, pink, and white forms. *R. mucronulatum,* from Korea and China, is hardy but deciduous in zone 5. It grows upright to about 6 ft. The species has scentless rosy purple flowers; 'Cornell Pink' has clear pink flowers. *R. moupinense,* from China, is one of the best species for early bloom. Evergreen and hardy to zone 7, it's a low spreading plant, under 2 ft. tall, with small leaves. The fragrant flowers are white or pink with red marks.

R. yakusimanum and its cultivars and related hybrids are among the best where weather is cold (and elsewhere for that matter). This Japanese species is hardy to zone 5 and makes a dense, compact, rounded plant about 3 ft. tall. Tender new leaves are covered with soft white fur; mature leaves are shiny dark green on top with golden brown felt below. Pink buds open to snow-white flowers in May, and even young plants bloom heavily. 'Ken Janeck' and 'Mist Maiden' are especially vigorous and attractive cultivars.

Rosa
Ro′za. Rose
Rosaceae. Rose family

Description
Roses are the most popular of all flowers and have been grown in gardens since the days of the ancient Egyptians, Romans, and Chinese. There are about 100 species and literally thousands of cultivars. All are deciduous or evergreen shrubs with thorny stems, compound leaves, and an upright, climbing, or trailing habit. Wild rose flowers have 5 petals and many stamens. Garden roses often have many petals. Rose fruits, called hips, have a fleshy hull with several hairy seeds inside.

Everyone loves roses, but some gardeners hesitate to grow them, fearing that the plants will require too much special care. This isn't true. Many roses are easy, reliable, and trouble-free. Growers today offer both heirloom varieties and new introductions that are hardy, vigorous, and disease-resistant and require no spraying and little pruning.

Roses are excellent container plants; having them right up on the deck or patio brings the flowers that much closer to admire and smell. They can be displayed on their own or with other container plants. Standard roses add a formal touch; miniatures are increasingly popular and are much hardier than most other roses. Below we comment on the categories of roses that are frequently grown in containers.

How to Grow
Roses require at least half a day of full sun (preferably morning) and bloom best in full sun. Use a loam-based commercial soil mix amended with lots of organic matter and coarse sand for drainage. Never let them dry out, and avoid wetting the leaves when watering. Feed every 7–10 days with soluble fertilizer.

Roses need careful pruning to establish the shape of the

bush, to remove old or damaged shoots, and to promote vigorous growth and abundant flowering. When and how to prune varies among the different groups; for more information, consult *Taylor's Guide to Roses*. In general, prune before the plant begins growth in spring, and prune plants in containers harder than you would those in the ground.

Overwinter as necessary in a frost-free location. Outdoors in marginal areas, apply a thick mulch for insulation. Roses are subject to several pests and diseases, but the occurrence and severity of different problems vary from rose to rose and from place to place. The best policy is to choose disease-resistant varieties, place them in favorable sites, and provide the best possible care.

■ **miniature roses** *p. 179*
Miniature roses are short plants—usually about 12 in. tall but ranging from 6 to 18 in.—with thin canes, closely spaced small leaves, and perfect little buds and flowers. There are dozens of cultivars in all colors. 'Red Cascade', for example, offers abundant 1-in.-diameter flowers on vigorous cascading canes, excellent for hanging baskets or window boxes. 'Rise 'n Shine' is a more upright plant to 15 in. tall with clear yellow flowers. Miniature roses are most familiar as pot plants for a cool sunny windowsill in winter, but many kinds are fully hardy outdoors. They are excellent in patio containers.

■ **floribundas and polyanthas**
Floribundas are bushy plants that are usually hardier and more disease-resistant than most hybrid tea roses. Floribundas have well-formed flowers in a wide range of colors, borne in small to large clusters. They bloom prolifically, repeating or continuing throughout the season. Consider the smaller roses in this group for pots or troughs. 'Angel Face' grows to

3 ft. tall and bears small clusters of very fragrant, double, mauve flowers 3½–4 in. wide. 'Iceberg' grows 4 ft. tall with clusters of fragrant, double, pure white flowers 3 in. wide that resemble hybrid tea roses. 'European' is 2–3 ft. tall with prolific clusters of bright red flowers. 'Allgold' is disease-resistant, grows 2½ ft. tall, and has unfading yellow flowers.

Polyanthas are neat little shrubs that start blooming late in the season but continue until frost. Most are hardy and carefree. Flowers are small but generously produced, in large clusters. 'Cecile Brunner' grows 2½–3 ft. tall and has clusters of double light pink flowers that resemble miniature hybrid tea roses. There's also a fine climbing 'Cecile Brunner', but neither form is reliably cold-hardy. 'The Fairy' is very hardy and healthy and blooms continuously with clusters of very double pink flowers 1–1½ in. wide. It grows 2 ft. tall and 3 ft. wide and is also grown as a standard.

■ shrub roses

This is a catchall group, including both favorites and new introductions. The flowers come in many forms, but the plants share several desirable attributes: vigor, adaptability, healthy foliage, good habit, and ease of care. These are the best candidates for gardeners who want to enjoy roses without going to much trouble.

'Wife of Bath' is a repeat bloomer that grows 3 ft. tall and 2 ft. wide and provides fragrant, rose-pink, cupped flowers. 'Gruss an Aachen' bears a heavy crop of pearl pink, cupped flowers on a bush 3 ft. tall and as wide. For large containers, try 'Bonica', a dense rounded bush about 4–5 ft. tall and wide with clusters of small, scentless, double, soft pink flowers that bloom nonstop all season. 'Carefree Beauty' grows 4 ft. tall and has clusters of fragrant, semidouble, medium pink flowers all summer. 'Sea Foam' is a low, spreading bush, under 2 ft. tall, that will spill over a large planter. It has glossy dark green leaves and clusters of lightly scented, pure white flowers.

■ standards *p. 179*

Most of the various classes of roses can be grown as standards, bud-grafted onto the top of a 2–4-ft.-tall woody stem. Creating standards can be a tricky business, so you're more likely to buy one. Provide a sturdy support and enough weight in soil and pot to keep the top-heavy plant from tipping over. Prune according to the type of plant budded on top, trying to keep the growth symmetrical.

Good varieties for taller standards, budded at 3–4 ft., include 'Iceberg', 'European', 'The Fairy', and 'Bonica' (all described previously). 'Françoise Austin' has white flowers and a nice pendulous habit; 'Linda Campbell' has huge clusters of red flowers and is disease-resistant. Shorter standards for smaller pots are often referred to as patio roses.

Rosmarinus
Ros-ma-ry′nus. Rosemary
Labiatae. Mint family

Description
Evergreen shrubs with slender opposite leaves and small 2-lipped flowers. Only 2 species, native to the Mediterranean region.

■ *officinalis* p. 199
Rosemary
Evergreen shrub used as an herb. Zone 8
Height: 2–3 ft. Spread: 2 ft.
A favorite culinary herb most often grown for culinary use, but its flowers can be impressive, too. The gray-green needle-like leaves, $1/2$–$1\frac{1}{2}$ in. long, are very aromatic. Small light blue, lilac, or white flowers form on old wood and last for weeks in winter and spring ('Huntington Blue' has lovely, deep blue flowers). Makes a bushy, upright, or spreading shrub that can be trained and pruned into formal shapes. Useful as a specimen or in a patio grouping with creeping herbs, such as thyme. 'Arp' is the most cold-hardy cultivar, surviving on protected sites in zone 6. Upright growers, such as 'Blue Spire', 'Collingwood Ingram', and 'Tuscan Blue', can be trained as topiary. 'Huntington Blue', 'Lockwood de Forest', and 'Prostratus' are prostrate forms with sinuous branches that look good draping over the sides of a pot. 'Blue Boy' is a miniature that blossoms through the winter, as does 'Pinkie'.

How to Grow
Full sun; tolerates heat. Loam-based commercial soil mix; add lime to make it slightly alkaline. Mature plants do nicely in 6–12-in. pots. Has deep roots, so a deep pot is useful, though you'll still have to root-prune. Suffers from overwatering and from drying out. Feed once every 3 weeks in spring and summer. Pinch growing tips to promote full, bushy growth. Overwinter indoors in cool (40° F and up at night), sunny room. Prone to mildew.

Salvia
Sal'vee-a. Sage
Labiatae. Mint family

Description
Annuals, perennials, or shrubs with square stems, opposite simple leaves, and 2-lipped flowers. About 900 species, native worldwide. A few species have aromatic foliage that is used for seasoning, potpourri, or home remedies. Several species are grown for their bright-colored flowers.

■ *elegans* p. 118
(*S. rutilans*)
Pineapple sage
Tender perennial grown as an annual. Zone 9
Height: 4–5 ft. Spread: 3–4 ft.
Grows bushy and upright, making a shrub-sized plant in a single season. Provides a strong focal point in a large container with herbs such as basil or colorful flowers; especially appealing with late-blooming Oriental lilies like 'Casablanca'. The rich green leaves have a strong pineapple fragrance and flavor. Use them in fruit salad or for iced or hot tea. Bears 8-in. spikes of slender red flowers from late summer until frost. Hummingbirds love it. Overwinter on a sunny windowsill indoors. Herb specialists have other salvias with fruit-scented leaves.

How to Grow
Full sun; tolerates heat. Loam-based commercial soil mix. Needs a 12-in. or larger pot. Place outdoors after danger of frost is past. Can be stressed by low water. Pinch once or twice to promote bushiness. Rarely grown from seed. Root a cutting in fall to overwinter indoors, or buy a new plant each spring. Whiteflies and spider mites bother it when plant is stressed.

■ *farinacea* p. 119 Pictured on p. 358
Mealy blue sage
Perennial grown as an annual. Zone 8 or 7
Height: to 2–3 ft. Spread: 1 ft.
Blooms and blooms from late spring to hard frost. Branches near the base and makes many upright stalks with small gray-green leaves on the bottom and crowded spikes of violet-blue flowers on top. The long-stalked flower spikes add height to mixed pots. Looks lovely with pink geraniums and dusty-miller. Cultivars with dark blue, light blue, or white flowers are available from seed catalogs or as bedding plants in spring. *S. guaranitica,* or blue sage, grows 3–5 ft. tall and

wide and has fragrant dark green leaves and dark violet-blue flowers 1–2 in. long late in summer; best grown as a single specimen in a large (14 in. by 14 in.) pot. Both are native to Texas and the Southwest. 'Indigo Spires' is a hybrid between these two species, with smooth gray-green leaves and very dark violet-blue flowers on dozens of crowded spikes that extend 2 ft. above the foliage. It blooms from midsummer until hard frost. In a very large pot it's a wonderful accent to cannas. Hardy to zone 8, it is sterile and must be propagated by cuttings or by division.

How to Grow

Full or part sun; tolerates heat. Loam-based commercial soil mix. Start seeds indoors 8 weeks before last frost. Gets lush with regular watering. Pinch for bushy growth. Keeps blooming even if you don't remove old flower stalks. Overwinter indoors in sunny spot; cut back hard in spring.

■ *greggii* p. 144
Cherry sage, autumn sage
Shrubby perennial. Zone 9 or 8
Height: 3 ft. Spread: 3 ft.
A low bushy plant with colorful flowers from spring to fall. Useful in mixed groupings of containers with other Mediterranean-type plants—*Cistus, Helianthemum,* oreganos, blue fescue. The small crisp leaves are fragrant and semievergreen. The scented flowers are rosy pink, red, salmon, purple, or white, 1 in. long, arranged in loose clusters. Native from Central America into Texas and the Southwest.

Mexican bush sage, *S. leucantha,* is another tender perennial (zone 8 or 7) and forms a large clump of graceful arching stems tipped with long spikes of rosy purple bracts and small white flowers. Thrives in hot, dry weather and blooms nonstop from midsummer to late fall. Seldom sets seed.

How to Grow
Full or part sun. Loam-based commercial soil mix amended with coarse sand for good drainage. Trim off spent flowers to stimulate further bloom. Overwinter indoors; put small plants on a windowsill. Cut back in early spring to keep it bushy.

■ *officinalis* p. 144
Garden sage
Perennial herb. Zone 5
Height: 2 ft. Spread: 2 ft.
The fragrant gray-green leaves of this favorite herb are used for seasoning and to make a therapeutic tea; place a pot near the kitchen. Woody at the base, it is evergreen in mild climates but freezes back where winters are cold. Tall spikes of blue-purple flowers are colorful for weeks in early summer. Variegated cultivars such as 'Tricolor' (white, purple, and green leaves) and 'Icterina' (green and yellow leaves) are hardy only to zone 8 or 7. 'Purpurea' has a purple suffusion in its dark green leaves. 'Compacta' is a smaller plant. Keep your eye out for new salvias, which seem to arrive monthly. Some are spectacular, such as *S. gesneriiflora*, which has arching clusters of scarlet flowers. (It isn't fully hardy outside California.)

How to Grow
Full sun. Loam-based commercial soil mix amended with coarse sand for good drainage. An 8–10-in. pot should accommodate the largest plants. Recovers from drying out. Feed lightly through growing season, especially if you're harvesting leaves. Cut back frozen shoots in late spring, before new growth starts, and remove faded blooms in summer. Divide every few years; plants aren't long lived. Root cuttings to overwinter tender cultivars, or buy new plants in spring.

■ *splendens* p. 119
Salvia
Annual. All zones
Height: 1–3 ft. Spread: 8 in. or more
Popular and widely grown, with stiff erect spikes of bright flowers all summer. Blooms nonstop even without deadheading. Makes a bushy plant with dark green foliage. There are dwarf, medium, and tall strains. Scarlet flowers are by far the most common, but there are also pink, salmon, lavender, purple, and white forms. All attract hummingbirds. The spikes are effective in mixed containers with plants of a rounded or trailing habit, such as petunias, lobelias, and fibrous begonias.

Ornamental grasses will disguise the plant's stiff habit. Dwarf cultivars include 'Scarlet Pygmy' and 'St. John's Fire'.

Two Texas species have equally bright red flowers but are looser, more casual-looking plants. *S. coccinea,* or scarlet sage, grows fast from seed and flowers nonstop from early summer to fall. It reaches 2–3 ft. tall. 'Lady in Red' is a popular cultivar, grown from seed as an annual. There are also pink and white forms. *S. roemeriana,* or cedar sage, forms a rosette of fuzzy rounded leaves and has flowers on spikes 12–18 in. tall in summer. Both species are perennial in zone 8 or 7.

How to Grow
Full or part sun; tolerates heat. Loam-based commercial soil mix. Can be crowded in large containers if well watered. Start seeds indoors 10 weeks before last frost; do not cover, as seeds need light to germinate. Set out after temperatures rise above 50° F (plants are stunted in colder conditions). Needs regular watering. Pinch for bushy growth; feed regularly to ensure continued bloom.

Sambucus
Sam-boo´kus. Elderberry
Caprifoliaceae. Honeysuckle family

Description
About 20 species of shrubs, small trees, and (rarely) herbs, some grown for ornamental purposes, others for their fruit.

■ *racemosa* '**Plumosa Aurea**' *p. 180*
Red elderberry
Deciduous shrub. Zone 4
Height: 3–6 ft. Spread: 3–6 ft.
The cultivars of this species offer a rounded bush of very attractive foliage with 5–6-in. panicles of white flowers in spring and red fruits in summer. 'Plumosa Aurea' has deeply cut, bright yellow foliage; 'Sutherland Gold' has golden yellow foliage. *S. nigra* 'Laciniata' has finely dissected green leaves. The yellow forms brighten up a shady spot or a grouping of containers. The cut-leaf form provides interesting texture and contrast with large-leaved plants.

How to Grow
Full or part sun; yellow leaves may burn in hot afternoon sun. Loam-based commercial soil mix. Mature plant may need a tub or whiskey barrel. Needs constant moisture. Prune to

shape during growing season; cut back hard in late winter to control size of plant and to encourage branching. Overwinter in unheated garage if necessary.

Saxifraga
Sax-i-fra′ga, sax-if′fra-ga
Saxifragaceae. Saxifrage family

Description
Perennials and a few annuals, usually forming a compact rosette of basal leaves. About 300 species, most native to montane or alpine sites.

■ *stolonifera* p. 145
(*S. sarmentosa*)
Strawberry geranium, strawberry begonia
Perennial. Zone 7
Height: 6 in. Spread: 2 ft. or more
A good plant for a hanging basket, a specimen pot, or a mixed container in a mild, shady spot. Forms rosettes of hairy, rounded or heart-shaped leaves, dark green with white veins on top and reddish underneath. Makes graceful loose clusters of small white flowers in early summer. Spreads like a strawberry, making baby plants at the ends of slender runners—use as a ground cover for a large potted tree.

How to Grow
Part or full shade; tolerates heat. Loam-based commercial soil mix. One plant per 8-in. pot. Needs constant moisture. Spreads quickly and can be invasive in planters; prune unwanted runners as needed. Root runners for new plants. Grow as houseplant over winter. Subject to mealybugs.

Sedum
See′dum. Stonecrop
Crassulaceae. Orpine family

Description
Small perennials, sometimes shrubby, with succulent leaves and stems. There are 300 or more species, most from the north temperate zone, and several hybrids and cultivars. Authorities disagree on the taxonomy of this group, so some plants are listed under various Latin names, but the cultivar names go along unchanged.

■ 'Autumn Joy' p. 145

(a hybrid of *S. spectabile* and *S. telephium*)
Perennial. Zone 3
Height: 1½–2 ft. Spread: 1½–2 ft.
An attractive and easy-to-grow perennial with handsome foliage from midspring on and interesting flowers and seed heads for many weeks in late summer and fall. Forms a spreading clump of thick unbranched stems surrounded with plump, succulent, blunt-toothed leaves. The tiny starry flowers form clusters like broccoli, 4–6 in. wide, starting out pink, then deepening to dark salmon and finally rusty red. Combines well with pots of chrysanthemums, ornamental kale, and ornamental grasses, such as *Pennisetum alopecuroides*. S. 'Indian Chief' may be the same plant as 'Autumn Joy'.

S. spectabile, one of the parent species, grows about 18 in. tall and prefers dry soil. It has thick stems; opposite, egg-shaped, pale green leaves; and flat clusters of star-shaped flowers ¼–½ in. wide. 'Brilliant' has deep pink flowers, 'Meteor' is reddish pink, and 'Stardust' is very pale pink or off-white.

How to Grow

An adaptable plant; prefers full sun and well-drained, gritty potting soil (soilless commercial mix will do) but does well even in somewhat moist soil and part shade. Plant 1 per pot or at least 2 ft. apart in large planters. Leave dry stems and seed heads to look at into winter, then cut back and store in cold frame or unheated garage. Divide clumps every third year to keep them from flopping open when they flower. No major pests.

■ other sedums

All of the following sedums make interesting specimens for

low pans or shallow clay pots. They forgive an occasional drying out but resent too much moisture.

S. brevifolium reaches 3 in. tall and has tiny leaves and white flowers. *S. confusum*, a spreading plant 6–12 in. tall, bears yellow flowers in spring. *S. spathulifolium* has rosettes of colorful leaves at the ends of short stems and yellow flowers from spring into summer. *S. s.* 'Cape Blanco' has silvery gray foliage 2–3 in. tall; *S. s.* 'Purpureum' has purple-tinged foliage. All these plants are good for miniature gardens and rock-garden tubs.

The trailing stems of *S. lineare* 'Variegatum' (5–10 in. tall) and *S. morganianum* are shown to good advantage in hanging baskets. The first has white-edged leaves and yellow flowers in late spring. *S. morganianum* is called donkey tail for its stems of fleshy, closely spaced leaves.

S. oxypetalum, a gnarled specimen, offers fragrant red flowers; it is evergreen in mild climates, deciduous in cold. *S. sieboldii* 'Medio-Variegatum' has beautifully arching stems about 12 in. long.

Sempervivum
Sem-per-vy´vum
Crassulaceae. Orpine family

Description
Low-growing perennials that make a dense rosette of succulent leaves and multiply by offsets. About 40 species, native mostly to Europe.

■ *tectorum* *p. 146*
Hen-and-chickens, hens-and-chicks
Perennial. Zone 4
Height: 4 in. (foliage); 12 in. (flower stalks). Spread: 1 ft. or more

These little succulents make friends easily. Even the smallest container garden has room for several clumps. Put them in a hypertufa trough with other succulents; bold rosettes in a shallow pan break up the monotony of standard-size pots. Each "hen" rosette spreads 4–6 in. wide and is closely surrounded by many smaller "chicks." Flat clusters of starry reddish flowers top thick stems that stick up like chimneys. Blooms in midsummer. *S. arachnoideum* is a miniature version with marble-sized rosettes of leaves joined by a cobweb of fine hairs. There are dozens of selections in different sizes and colors.

How to Grow
Full or part sun. Loam-based commercial soil mix. Space 6 in. apart and they'll fill in by midsummer. Recovers from drying out; doesn't need to be fed regularly. Very easy and trouble-free. In harsh climates you may need to store in shady, protected area—snow cover is useful—or in cold frame.

Senecio
Se-nee´see-oh
Compositae. Daisy family

Description
A huge and diverse group of annuals, perennials, vines, and shrubs, including some succulents. Although many species have been reassigned to other groups in recent years, this is still one of the largest plant genera, with more than 1,500 species worldwide.

■ *cineraria* p. 120
(formerly *Centaurea cineraria*)
Dusty-miller
Perennial usually grown as an annual. All zones
Height: to 12 in. Spread: 8 in. or more
Easy and popular, valued for its beautiful silvery gray or white leaves. It combines well with almost any plant and makes a good foil for bright-colored flowers. Use it to tie together a hodgepodge of plants in a grouping of containers. Especially pretty with blue flowers, such as lobelia and Swan River daisy. Leaf size and shape vary among cultivars—some are very deeply cut and lacy, but others are broad and bold. The leaves are evergreen in mild climates. Overwintered plants have small yellow flowers on 2-ft. stalks the second and following years, but these are insignificant compared with the foliage.

How to Grow
Full or part sun. Loam-based commercial soil mix. Doesn't mind being crowded in a pot. Does best with regular watering but tolerates dry spells. Pinch for extra bushiness. Easily propagated by seed or by cuttings. Can overwinter on sunporch or in greenhouse. Subject to fungal infections in wet soil or humid weather but otherwise trouble-free.

Spiraea
Spy-ree'a. Spirea
Rosaceae. Rose family

Description
Deciduous shrubs with simple alternate leaves and clusters of small white or pink flowers. About 70 species, native to the north temperate zone.

■ *japonica* p. 180
Japanese spirea
Deciduous shrub. Zone 3
Height: 2–3 ft. Spread: 2–3 ft. or more
A compact shrub that blooms in summer, after the other spireas. It makes a somewhat informal, airy container plant that stays low and spreads wider than tall. Twiggy and fine-textured, it has small dark green leaves. Combine it with colorful flowers. 'Albiflora' has white flowers. 'Little Princess' and 'Nana' (also called 'Alpina') have pink flowers and are very compact, about 1$\frac{1}{2}$ ft. tall by 2 ft. wide. 'Shibori (also known as 'Shirobana') has a mixture of dark rosy pink, pale pink, and white flowers, all at the same time, and grows 2–3 ft. tall. 'Goldmound' has pink flowers and golden yellow leaves that don't burn in the South.

S. × *bumalda* cultivars (zone 3; now grouped with *S. japonica*) form low, twiggy, fine-textured mounds that need little pruning. The round flat clusters of dainty little flowers last for several weeks in summer. The following cultivars are the most popular. 'Anthony Waterer' has rosy pink flowers and green foliage. 'Coccinea' is similar but has deeper reddish pink flowers. 'Crispa' has light pink flowers and crinkled toothed leaves that darken from pinkish to red to green as they mature. 'Goldflame' has crimson flowers and leaves that are pure gold in summer, touched with red and copper in both spring and fall (summer leaves stay green in the South). 'Lime Mound' has light pink flowers and leaves that change from yellow to lime green to orange-red as the season progresses.

How to Grow
Full or part sun; tolerates heat. Loam-based commercial soil mix; doesn't do well in poorly drained mix. Give plenty of room—tubs or large pots. Due to fast growth, consider as a short-term container subject. Keep moist. Remove spent blooms to prolong flowering. Prune to shape in early spring. Easy to grow. No serious pests or diseases.

Tagetes

Tay-gee´teez, taj´eh-tees. Marigold
Compositae. Daisy family

Description
Annuals or perennials with strong-scented leaves, mostly opposite and usually finely dissected. The composite flowers are most often yellow. About 50 species, 1 from Africa and the rest from Central and South America.

■ *lucida* p. 120
Mexican mint marigold
Perennial herb. Zone 8
Height: to 1 ft. Spread: 6 in.
A good substitute for French tarragon in hot climates. The foliage, stems, and flowers have a rich anise fragrance and flavor and can be used for tea or seasoning. Makes a bushy clump of erect stems, covered with narrow leaves about 1 in. long. May be evergreen in mild winters. The small, single, yellow blossoms in summer and fall are best pinched off before the plant forms seed—otherwise the plant usually perishes. Produces few flowers in northern gardens. Grow with more ornamental fillers such as drapers and trailing plants. Plant several together to keep them from falling over.

How to Grow
Full sun. Loam-based commercial soil mix. Don't overpot; in crowded conditions, well-drained soil is a must. Don't overwater; feed once a month. Pinch regularly or it will become straggly. Harvest leaves whenever you choose. Cut back to the ground in early spring. Doesn't overwinter well indoors, so start from seed or buy a new plant each year. In mild winter climates, let dry out between winter waterings; resume watering if it slips into semidormancy. Often succumbs to damping-off and root rot in winter.

■ *patula* p. 121
French marigold
Annual. All zones
Height: 6–14 in. Spread: 8–14 in.
A relatively compact plant with several dwarf cultivars, this is a favorite to provide bright color in window boxes and in pots near a patio or an entryway. The smooth, aromatic, dark green leaves have many toothed segments. The single or double flower heads, 1–3 in. wide, come in shades of yellow, orange, red, mahogany, or bicolor. Flowers from early summer until frost whether you deadhead it or not. 'Janie' has soft orange flowers; 'Naughty Marietta' is yellow with a dark red

blotch; 'Scarlet Sophie' is deep orange with ruffled petals; 'Suzie Wong' has large single yellow blooms.

African marigold (*T. erecta*) is a big bushy plant with smooth green leaves and large, rounded, double flower heads in shades of yellow, orange, or creamy white. Blooms nonstop from early summer to frost. Many strains are available as seeds or seedlings. The Inca series grows 12–16 in. high with 4-in.-wide flowers in orange, yellow, or gold.

Lemon gem marigold (*T. tenuifolia* 'Lemon Gem', a.k.a. *T. pumila* and *T. signata*) makes a bushy ball of delicate lacy foliage with a lemony fragrance. Blooms profusely until frost. The single blossoms have the charm of wildflowers, in a shade of clear yellow that combines with other colors more easily than does the typical gold of most marigolds. (Look also for 'Golden Gem', with gold flowers, and 'Paprika', with scarlet flowers.) Use it to fill the gaps in a large container planting. Plants have a tendency to split apart in summer storms. *T. filifolia*, Irish lace, another small marigold, is grown for its mound of ferny foliage and bears white flowers in late summer.

How to Grow
Full sun; tolerates heat. Soilless commercial mix. Direct-sow seeds, or start indoors 4–6 weeks before last frost. Use 1 plant per 8-in. pot or 3 in a 12-in. pot. Pinch off tips and first few flowers to promote bushiness. Leggy or top-heavy plants are liable to tip over in summer storms. Deadheading helps improve appearance and prolong bloom. Marigolds are generally pest-free, but Japanese beetles will eat the flowers. Wet soil, humid air, and excessive rain can rot the roots, foliage, and flowers.

Taxus
Tax'us. Yew
Taxaceae. Yew family

Description
Conifers with dense fine-grained timber, flat needlelike leaves, and fleshy red or brown fruits with one hard seed inside. The foliage and seeds contain poisonous compounds. Only 7 species, native to the Old and New World.

■ **cultivars** *p. 200*
Conifers. Hardiness varies
Height: varies. Spread: varies
Yews are among the most popular and versatile evergreens.

Most are slow-growing, with dense, dark green foliage. They tolerate repeated pruning and are often sheared into formal shapes. Needles are flat and narrow, under 1 in. long, with pointed tips. Male plants produce a cloud of pollen in spring. Females bear fruits in fall. The foliage and seeds of all yews contain dangerously poisonous compounds, but birds eat the fruits safely because the seeds are so hard that they pass undigested. Grow yews as specimens in individual containers; the low forms work well in raised planters. A nice effect is achieved by growing a vine such as clematis over an upright yew.

Nearly all the yews grown in this country are cultivars of *T. baccata*, the English yew, or *T. cuspidata*, the Japanese yew, or are hybrids between those species, classified as *T. × media*, the hybrid yew or AngloJap yew. The cultivars differ in cold-hardiness, ultimate size, habit, rate of growth, foliage color, ability to retain good foliage color during cold weather, and berry production (only female clones set fruit). Yews are a long-term investment, so consider all of these attributes when choosing which cultivar to plant.

How to Grow

Sun to shade. Yews tolerate more shade than do other conifers and do well on the north or east side of a building. Loam-based commercial soil mix amended with coarse sand for good drainage, which is vital. Water regularly, though all are somewhat drought-tolerant. Can stay years in one container. Prune or shear in late spring following elongation of new growth. Feed in spring with slow-release fertilizer. Yews are generally trouble-free; treat scale when it occurs with a dormant oil spray.

■ recommended yew cultivars

Cultivars of *T. baccata* have the darkest green—sometimes almost black—foliage but are reliably hardy only to zone 6. 'Adpressa' has short dark green needles, red fruits, and spreading branches and grows wider than tall. 'Repandens' is another spreading form, growing 2–3 ft. tall and several feet wide, good for raised planters. 'Fastigiata', or 'Stricta', often called Irish yew, grows narrowly upright into a dense column of foliage, about one-fourth as wide as it is tall. It makes a fine accent plant for formal entrances.

Most cultivars of *T. cuspidata* are hardy to zone 5. Needles are medium or dark green in summer but may discolor to a dirty tan or brown on exposed sites in winter. 'Nana' is very dense and spreads about twice as wide as it is tall; it has good green winter color. The larger cultivars are good for big planters, especially when pruned to show off their appealing cinnamon-red bark and stem structure.

The most common and popular yews are cultivars of *T.* × *media*. Most are hardy to zone 5. 'Brownii' is a dense, rounded, spreading form that can reach 8 ft. but is easily kept shorter by pruning. 'Hatfield' ('Hatfieldii') grows slowly, makes a broad dense pyramid up to 12 ft., and stays bright green all year. 'Hicksii' is similar to *T. baccata* 'Fastigiata' but hardier. It's narrowly upright and fast-growing, with dark green needles and red fruits. 'Sentinalis' grows slowly to 8 ft. high by 2 ft. wide. 'Greenwave' forms a low mound with arching branches.

Thuja
Thew'ya. Arborvitae
Cupressaceae. Cypress family

Description
Tall evergreen conifers, usually with scalelike foliage arranged in flat fans or sprays. Only 5 species, native to eastern Asia and North America, and hundreds of selected cultivars.

■ *occidentalis* p. 200
American arborvitae, eastern white cedar
Conifer. Zone 3
Height: 2–10 ft. Spread: varies with pruning
A useful evergreen for the Northeast and Upper Midwest, with fewer pest and disease problems than pines, spruces, or firs. Selected cultivars lend themselves to formal container schemes; those with colored foliage are particularly useful. Smaller cultivars look good in raised planters. The rich green foliage is quite fragrant when crushed. The tiny scalelike leaves are arranged in flat sprays that tilt in all directions. Seedling trees and some cultivars are prone to winterburn and turn dingy tan or brown if damaged by cold dry winds or

bright winter sun. Except where noted, the cultivars described below stay rich green all winter. The small woody cones have overlapping scales that open in midwinter. Chickadees, nuthatches, and other birds eat the seeds.

'Aurea' ('Golden') is bright yellow in summer, bronzy in winter, and grows to about 3 ft. tall and wide. 'Hetz Midget' starts out like a basketball, grows only 1–2 in. per year, and eventually matures at 3 ft. tall and wide.

'Rheingold' makes a small cone of foliage in metallic shades of gold, copper, and bronze. It's sometimes seen with prickly (juvenile) rather than scaly (adult) foliage. Usually stays under 5 ft. 'Little Gem' grows slowly to 2 ft. high and twice as wide and has dark green foliage. 'Little Giant', 'Nana', and 'Umbraculifera' are also small plants suitable for container growing.

'Emerald' is a narrow, compact form (10 ft. tall by 4 ft. wide), good for emphasizing an entryway. 'Woodwardii' is a naturally rounded form that grows very slowly to 8 ft. or more. It's subject to winterburn.

How to Grow

Needs sun; gets loose and leggy if grown in shade. Loam-based commercial soil mix amended with organic matter for moisture retention. Prune to maintain size, if necessary. The most common problem is winter storm damage. Heavy wet snows can open up the center and spread the leaders apart or leave them sprawling on the ground. Prevent this by using wire or rot-resistant twine to tie the leaders together in several places. Susceptible to bagworms and spider mites but generally trouble-free. Suffers in hot summers and doesn't do well across the southern United States.

■ *orientalis* cultivars *p. 201*
(called *Platycladus orientalis* by some botanists but few gardeners)
Oriental arborvitae. Zone 6
Height: varies. Spread: varies

The best arborvitae for container gardeners across the southern United States. They're not as cold-hardy, but they tolerate hot dry weather better than does *T. occidentalis*. Plants form a core of upright stems with many horizontal limbs that branch into flat vertical sprays of tiny twigs, densely covered with scaly or prickly foliage. The foliage has only a slight fragrance. Odd fleshy cones have a bumpy surface and might be confused with insect galls. They are blue-green for several months, turning brown when they mature.

'Aurea Nana' ('Golden Ball') is a compact dwarf that makes a rounded cone about 3 ft. tall. The golden foliage turns bronze in winter. 'Juniperoides' is conical, 4–6 ft. tall, with feathery gray-green foliage that turns plum-purple in winter. 'Westmont' makes a very small dense cone, slowly growing to 2–3 ft. Foliage is deep green tipped with yellow, turning bronze in winter. 'Elegantissimus' is also compact, with bright yellow leaves in spring.

How to Grow
Full or part sun. Loam-based commercial soil mix amended with coarse sand to improve drainage. Plants thrive for several years in one container if well fed. Prefer regular watering but recover from drying out. Place in location protected from wind. Prune yearly to shape and to control size. Move to sheltered location to protect against cold; wrap in burlap for short-term protection. Susceptible to bagworms and spider mites. Hose foliage to remove dust and dirt that collect during dry weather or in urban conditions.

Thunbergia
Thun-burr'gee-ah
Acanthaceae. Acanthus family

Description
About 100 species of herbs or shrubs found in the warm regions of Africa, Madagascar, and Asia. Some are erect; others have a vining habit.

■ *alata* p. 169
Black-eyed Susan vine
Tender perennial grown as an annual. All zones
Height: 3–8 ft.
This twining climber has toothed oval leaves and flat, 5-petaled flowers with a dark "eye" and orange-yellow, buff, or apricot petals. From midsummer to frost, the flowers grow on trellises, scamper over large potted shrubs, or dangle from hanging baskets (where they will clamber up the supports). The white blooms of 'Angel Wings' are lightly fragrant. *T. grandiflora*, or sky flower, has trumpet-shaped lavender-blue flowers and is perennial in zone 10.

How to Grow
Full or part sun. Loam-based commercial soil mix. Start seeds indoors in peat pots 6–8 weeks before last frost; transplant in a pot at the base of shrubs or a trellis. Needs constant moisture; best grown where summers are warm and moist—dislikes cool temperatures and arid climates.

Thymus

Thy′mus. Thyme
Labiatae. Mint family

Description
Perennials or small shrubs with very small opposite leaves and clusters of small white, pink, rosy red, or purple flowers. Most are aromatic and can be used as seasoning. About 350 species, native to Europe and Asia.

■ × *citriodorus* p. 146
Lemon thyme
Perennial herb. Zone 4
Height: to 12 in. Spread: spreading
Thyme should be part of any container herb garden, grown in a sunny spot by the kitchen. Lemon thyme makes a low, spreading mound of tiny glossy dark green leaves with a distinct lemony fragrance. Flowers are pale purple. The cultivar 'Aureus' has leaves with yellow edges; 'Argenteus' has silver-edged leaves.

Common thyme (*T. vulgaris*) is a bushy little plant, woody at the base, with many erect wiry stems covered with fragrant semievergreen foliage. The small rounded leaves are gray or gray-green. Masses of tiny lilac flowers attract bees in summer. Use it at the edge of a container. 'Silver Queen' has silvery foliage; 'Aureus' and 'Golden Dwarf' offer yellow variegation. Woolly thyme (*T. pseudolanuginosus*) makes a very flat mat of fuzzy silver-gray foliage; fragrance and flowers are secondary to its woolliness.

Fresh or dried thyme leaves are indispensable for cooking, but fragrance and flavor vary widely among seedlings and cultivars. Raise your own seedlings if you want several plants to edge a planter, but go to the nursery and sniff the leaves to choose a good specimen for a kitchen herb garden.

How to Grow
Full sun. Soilless commercial mix amended with coarse sand to improve drainage. One plant per 8-in. clay pot. Established plants can tolerate considerable dryness but can't take soggy soil, especially in winter. Shear after flowering to reduce self-seeding and to promote new growth. Feed with slow-release fertilizer in spring; add liquid supplement if you harvest leaves. Overwinter in cold frame or unheated garage; water sparingly. Cut back in early spring, removing damaged and old woody stems. No common insect pests, but leaves and roots may rot in wet soil, in humid weather, or if shaded by neighboring plants.

Trachelospermum
Tra-kel-o-sper'mum
Apocynaceae. Dogbane family

Description
Woody vines with twining stems, evergreen leaves, milky sap, and fragrant 5-petaled flowers. About 20 species, all but one native to southeastern Asia.

■ *jasminoides* p. 169
Confederate jasmine, star jasmine
Evergreen vine. Zone 8
Height: to 5 ft. Spread: varies
Very popular in California and the Southwest, this versatile vine is grown for all-year foliage and fragrant white flowers. It can be trained on a stake, on a trellis, or as an espalier, and its stems are stiff and woody enough for it to stand unsupported as a small shrub. The shiny dark green leaves are stiff ovals. Blooms heavily for several weeks in late spring and early summer, with clusters of pinwheel-shaped flowers $1/2$ in. wide, opening white and fading to creamy yellow. They are especially fragrant in the evening.

How to Grow
Full or part sun; tolerates heat. Soilless or loam-based commercial soil mix. Mature plant is happy in an 8–12-in. pot; a bigger pot provides stability for a stake or other support. Tolerates some dryness but needs watering during droughts. Fasten stems to the support until they catch on. Pinch frequently to maintain as a shrub. Prune out old woody stems as needed to renew growth. Overwinter in cool sunny room or in greenhouse. Trouble-free.

Tropaeolum

Tro-pee′oh-lum. Nasturtium
Tropaeolaceae. Nasturtium family

Description
Annuals or perennials with showy red, orange, or yellow flowers. More than 80 species, native to the mountains of Central and South America.

■ *majus* p. 121
Nasturtium
Annual. All zones
Height: 1 ft. Spread: 2 ft. or more
Easy, adaptable, and colorful, nasturtiums are handsome mixed with colorful annuals or vegetables in pots, hanging baskets, and window boxes and striking at the base of cannas or shrubs in tubs. The fleshy stems can climb or sprawl to 2 ft. or more (dwarf kinds remain compact). Leaves are like parasols, with a long stalk attached in the center and a rounded blade up to 6 in. wide. The surface is smooth, almost waxy. Large long-stalked flowers have a spicy fragrance and come in bright shades of yellow, orange, red, mahogany, cream, or bicolor. The flowers are edible and make a colorful garnish or salad item. Seed catalogs list several strains, including one with white-variegated leaves.

How to Grow
Full or part sun. Loam-based commercial soil mix; blooms best in poor soil. Seeds are large enough that children can handle them easily. Nasturtiums do not transplant well. Direct-sow in display pot or hanging basket in early spring, covering $1/2$ in. deep, or start in peat pots. Thin to 6–12 in. apart.

Keep moist. Fertilize sparingly—too much makes leaves at the expense of flowers. Subject to aphids but generally carefree.

Tulbaghia
Tul-baj´ee-a
Amaryllidaceae. Amaryllis family

Description
Small perennials that smell (when bruised) like onions or garlic, with small bulbs, grassy foliage, and umbels of 6-petaled flowers. More than 20 species, native to Africa.

■ *violacea* *p. 158*
Society garlic
Tender perennial. Zone 9
Height: 1–2 ft. Spread: 6–12 in.
A pretty little plant that blooms most in summer but repeats throughout the year. Clusters of starry lilac blooms (white is rare) are held on 1–2-ft. stalks and make good cut flowers. The garlic-scented foliage is evergreen. Leaves are flat and slender, up to 12 in. long. There are variegated forms with white-striped leaves. *T. fragrans* produces fragrant lavender-pink flowers.

How to Grow
Full sun. Loam-based commercial soil mix. Put 1 plant in a 6- or 8-in. pot. Divide (after bloom) when clump fills the pot. Overwinter indoors. Easy and trouble-free.

Tulipa
Too´li-pa. Tulip
Liliaceae. Lily family

Description
Spring-blooming perennials with edible bulbs, broad flat leaves, and showy flowers. About 100 species, most native to Central Asia, and countless hybrids and cultivars.

■ garden tulips *p. 159*
Perennials, often short lived. Zone 4
Height: 6–24 in. Spread: 6–12 in.
A large pot full of tulips welcomes spring with bright flowers. Modern garden tulips are complex hybrids, the result of cen-

turies of deliberate breeding. There are thousands of named forms, divided into several classes based on time of bloom, flower form, and genetic background. As a group, tulips flower over a season of many weeks from early to late spring. Individual flowers last just a week or so. The flowers are held singly on long stiff stalks (good for cutting) and come in all shades of red, orange, yellow, pink, purple, white, bicolor, and multicolor. Some kinds have a pleasant fragrance. Flowers can be single or double, 2–6 in. wide, in various rounded shapes. The petals usually spread wide open on sunny days, closing again at night or during cloudy weather. Each bulb normally makes one flower and a few broad basal leaves. The gray-green leaves are a pleasant backdrop for the flowers, but they aren't very attractive in subsequent weeks as they mature and finally wither.

Some of the most popular classes are the cottage tulips, Darwin tulips, and Darwin hybrids; all have large egg-shaped or cup-shaped flowers on tall stems in late spring. There are early and late classes of double tulips, with peony-like flowers on short stems. The Greigii tulips have leaves striped or mottled with dark reddish purple and large flowers on short stems. Lily-flowered tulips have long slender flowers, narrow in the middle, with pointed petals that flare out at the top. Rembrandt tulips are like Darwins with striped or streaky petals, and Parrot tulips have fringed petals with bright multicolored streaks and splotches; container growing is best for Parrots, whose markings are caused by a virus that can infect other tulips and lilies.

Most species of wild tulips are small plants that bloom earlier than garden tulips. They have the charm of wildflowers and are lovely in an informal container garden. The bulbs are uncommon at local garden centers but are listed in several catalogs.

How to Grow

Full sun. Soilless or loam-based commercial soil mix. Short tulips will thrive in shallow "bulb pans." Tall ones need tall pots for visual scale and to keep them from blowing over. In fall, plant bulbs so they nearly touch, cover with 1 in. or so of soil, then store planted pots in a cool place in the shade. In mild-winter areas, cover pots with mulch to delay top growth until roots have formed. In very mild regions, bulbs must be refrigerated for 6–8 weeks to give them an artificial "winter" or else they will not bloom. (A similar treatment is used to force potted bulbs for indoor bloom.) After flowering, continue watering for the several weeks it takes the foliage to mature. When leaves have faded, turn the bulbs out of the pots and store bulbs in a cool, dry place until fall.

Aphids may infest the leaves and buds; wash them off with soapy water. Fungal infections sometimes disfigure the leaves and flowers; pull and destroy infected plants.

Verbena
Ver-bee´na
Verbenaceae. Verbena family

Description
Annuals, perennials, or shrubs with toothed or dissected foliage and spikes or clusters of small flowers. About 250 species, nearly all native to the New World.

■ × *hybrida* *p. 122*
Garden verbena
Annual. All zones
Height: 6–12 in. Spread: 12 in.
This colorful annual thrives in hot, sunny weather and blooms nonstop all summer. The starry flowers form dense round clusters, 2–3 in. wide, in bright shades of red, pink, purple, or white. Usually forms a sprawling mat of stems, although some kinds are supposed to grow upright. They are ideal mixers in hanging baskets and large containers with petunias, salvias, cockscomb, and catharanthus. The 'Romance' series comes in red, purple, white, and pink on relatively compact plants. 'Imagination' bears small purple flowers on long trailing stems, perfect for spilling over pot sides or in baskets. 'Homestead Purple' makes large, showy purple flowers on long stems and blooms profusely. 'Peaches and Cream' is an apt name for a compact plant with ivory and peach-pink flowers.

How to Grow
Full sun or afternoon shade; tolerates heat. Loam-based commercial soil mix amended with coarse sand to improve drainage. Seeds are difficult to germinate; it's easier to buy transplants, and garden centers have mixed or solid-color packs. Plants can be crowded in mixed pots. Deadhead to prolong bloom. Some gardeners take cuttings of favorites to winter over. Spider mites can be a nuisance during hot weather.

Viburnum

Vy-bur′num
Caprifoliaceae. Honeysuckle family

Description

Deciduous or evergreen shrubs or small trees with simple opposite leaves and showy clusters of 5-petaled flowers, usually white or pink and sometimes very fragrant. About 150 species, native to the Old and New World, and several hybrids.

Viburnums offer considerable attractions to a container garden. The evergreen species have handsome foliage year-round, and the deciduous species offer rich fall color. Several are very showy in bloom, and some have an unforgettable spicy fragrance. Many produce colorful berries that attract birds in fall and winter. Nearly all are upright growers with multiple stems. Some are (or can be kept) bushy and compact; others tend to get leggy. A few spread by suckers and form thickets, and a few mature into small trees. A sampling suitable for container growing is discussed below.

How to Grow

Full or part sun; tolerate heat. Loam-based commercial soil mix. Most require large containers; stone, clay, or wooden containers are best. Never allow to dry out—a thick organic mulch helps keep the roots cool and moist. Feed with slow-release fertilizer. Prune after flowering to control size, although this removes the fruits. Renew established plants by cutting old and weak stems to the ground in early spring. Protect during the winter, particularly the evergreens. Viburnums are generally trouble-free but can be infested with aphids and other pests, or powdery mildew and other foliar diseases. Choose resistant varieties and place where air circulation is good.

■ **deciduous viburnums** *p. 181*

Korean spice viburnum, *V. carlesii* (zone 4), grows 4–5 ft. or more tall and wide and is valued for its extremely fragrant white flowers, which form dome-shaped clusters 2–3 in. wide in April, followed by clusters of black fruit. Leaves are dull green in summer, sometimes turning reddish in fall. 'Compactum', which makes a neat sphere only 3 ft. tall and wide, is the best one for containers. You might try 'Cayuga', a heavy-blooming compact to spreading plant with disease-resistant foliage. These viburnums bloom when it's still too cool to sit outdoors or open a window, so put them where you'll pass them daily during bloom.

Double file viburnum, *V. plicatum* var. *tomentosum* (zone 6, pictured opposite), is one of the most beautiful ornamental shrubs, with true 4-season appeal. Spreads wider than tall, with layer upon layer of horizontal tiered branches. Foliage is rich green in summer, turning deep red-purple in fall. Flowers form flat clusters like 2–4-in. snowflakes, held well above the foliage for about 2 weeks in April or May. The fruit clusters are bright red in July, turning black later if the birds don't eat them first. 'Summer Snowflake' and 'Watanabei' (they may be the same plant) have smaller flowers but continue blooming on new growth all summer. More compact and rounded than other cultivars, they grow about 6 ft. tall and wide. Can't take hot, dry weather. 'Shasta' blooms and fruits heavily.

European cranberry bush, *V. opulus* (zone 3), is an attractive upright shrub with showy flowers in May, shiny red fruits in fall and winter, and fall color ranging from yellow-red to reddish purple. Most are large plants, but 'Compactum' grows 4–6 ft. high and has excellent flowers and fruits. 'Nanum' is a true dwarf, maturing at 18–24 in., with pretty little leaves. It is somewhat shier flowering and fruiting.

V. trilobum, the American cranberry bush, is very similar to European cranberry bush but even hardier, surviving in zone 2. 'Compactum' and other dwarf forms reach about 6 ft. tall and wide. Both *V. opulus* and *V. trilobum* are stressed by hot, dry weather; water before the leaves start to wilt. Stressed plants are more subject to aphids, borers, and diseases. *V. × burkwoodii* 'Eskimo' is compact (4–5 ft. tall and wide), with lustrous, dark green, semievergreen leaves and clusters of pure white flowers in tightly packed "snowballs."

■ **evergreen viburnums**

V. davidii (zone 8) is compact, growing 3 ft. high and wide. The dark blue-green leaves are smooth ellipses, up to 6 in. long, with 3 deep parallel veins. Flat 3-in. clusters of scentless, dull white flowers are followed by extremely pretty blue berries. Plant 2 or more shrubs to increase berry set. Prefers acidic soil.

Laurustinus, *V. tinus* (zone 7), is an erect narrow shrub that responds well to pruning. Leaves are dark green, shiny ovals. Dense clusters of pink buds and white flowers, slightly fragrant, last for weeks in late winter and early spring. Pretty blue berries ripen in summer. 'Eve Price', a compact form with smaller leaves, is best for containers.

Vinca
Ving'ka. Periwinkle
Apocynaceae. Dogbane family

Description
Trailing vinelike perennials with opposite leaves and 5-petaled flowers. Only 7 species, native to the Old World. Closely related to *Catharanthus*.

■ *major* p. 147
Large periwinkle
Perennial. Zone 7
Height: 6 in. Spread: 3 ft. or more
Cultivars of *V. major* are well suited for hanging baskets and window boxes, where their trailing runners can cascade freely. Comfortable in sun or shade, they can be combined with a wide range of plants. The paired oval leaves are smooth and glossy, 1–3 in. long. The short upright stems bear violet-blue flowers with 5 wide petals. Blooms mostly in early spring, but a few flowers may appear in summer or fall. A variegated form with white blotches on the leaves is too often used with geraniums; try it in an all-white color scheme or with other variegated plants. 'Aureomaculata' offers leaves with a chartreuse center and green edges; great for hot color schemes.

Common periwinkle, *Vinca minor* (zone 4), is best used as a ground cover with a large potted tree or topiary. Flowers for several weeks in spring. The more sun, the more flowers; plants in deep shade may not bloom at all. The flowers are usually lavender-blue, but pale blue, darker purple, and white forms are also available. 'Argentea-variegata' has white-edged leaves; those of 'Variegata' are edged with golden yellow.

How to Grow
Sun to shade. Loam-based commercial soil mix. Needs regular watering in full sun. Shaded plants can tolerate short dry spells but will grow slowly. Easy to propagate by division; dig up rooted runners and space them 6 in. apart for a ground cover. Shear or prune long runners to encourage branching and make a denser cover. Pest-free.

Viola
Vy-oh'la. Violet, pansy
Violaceae. Violet family

Description
A diverse group of annuals, perennials, and a few small shrubs. Most have characteristic violet-type flowers, but the leaves and habit are variable. About 500 species, native to the Old and New World. Many of the species are distinguished by minor differences, and they hybridize readily. The identity of some cultivars is uncertain.

■ × *wittrockiana* p. 122
Pansy
Annual or short-lived perennial. All zones
Height: to 12 in. Spread: to 12 in.
Pansies are popular container plants, blooming from fall to spring where winters are mild and from spring to fall where summers are cool. They can be tucked into almost any container in sun or partial shade and are particularly good with spring bulbs, such as hyacinths and daffodils, and ornamental kale in autumn. They have shiny evergreen leaves. Young plants form compact clumps; later the stems stretch and sprawl. The wide (1–4 in.), flat, facelike flowers are loaded with personality and come in a very wide range of colors— red, pink, yellow, white, blue, and mahogany, usually marked with dark blotches. There are dozens of seed strains, selected for flower color and size. Long-stemmed types are good for cutting and last several days in water. Pansies grow quickly from seed and are normally raised as annuals and discarded

when the plants get straggly. Across the South and Southwest, they die out in the heat of summer. In the North, they may overwinter and go on for a few years.

Violas, *V. cornuta,* have solid-colored pansylike flowers, 1–2 in. wide, in shades of white, yellow, apricot, pink, ruby, blue, purple, or near-black. A few cultivars are grown as perennials and propagated by division, but most seed strains are grown and used as annuals, like pansies. Both pansies and violas do very well in window boxes and hanging baskets.

How to Grow
Full sun or afternoon shade. Loam-based commercial soil mix. Start seeds or purchase plants for spring or fall display. Fall-planted seedlings overwinter with no protection even in zone 6 and start blooming earlier than spring transplants. Don't let them dry out; feed regularly. Pinch back and feed when they get straggly. Deadhead or they'll stop blooming. Occasionally infested with aphids or spider mites.

Vitex
Vy′tex
Verbenaceae. Verbena family

Description
Deciduous or evergreen shrubs or trees with opposite compound leaves and clusters of small flowers. Both foliage and flowers can be aromatic. About 250 species, mostly tropical, native to the Old and New World.

■ *agnus-castus* p. 181
Chaste tree, pepperbush
Deciduous shrub or small tree. Zone 7
Height: 3–6 ft. Spread: 3–6 ft.
This late bloomer provides color when most needed. Grows as a multitrunked shrub or small tree with a loose, open, umbrella-shaped crown. Leaves are palmately compound with 3–9 toothed leaflets. Dark green above and gray-green or silvery below, they release a spicy or peppery fragrance when crushed. Clustered 4–10-in. spikes of small lilac or lavender flowers bloom on the new growth from midsummer through fall and attract butterflies. Adaptable and easy to grow, it makes a fine container specimen that can also be trained as a standard. Combine with buddleias, *Sedum* 'Autumn Joy', or dwarf plumbago. Selections with white or pink flowers are also available. *V. negundo* var. *heterophylla,* the cut-leaved chaste tree, has less attractive flowers but handsome finely di-

vided, feathery, gray-green foliage that turns bronze or purplish in fall. The top dies back, but the roots are hardy to zone 5. Grow it like a buddleia, cutting the stems to the ground each spring. It recovers fast and starts blooming by midsummer.

How to Grow
Full sun; thrives in hot weather. Loam-based commercial soil mix. Start in a 20-in. pot; can eventually be moved to a tub. Recovers from drying out. Prune in spring to control size. Store in unheated garage over winter. Trouble-free.

Yucca
Yuk´a
Agavaceae. Agave family

Description
Woody perennials with short or medium-height trunks; stiff, swordlike, fibrous leaves; erect branched stalks of large flowers, usually white; and large woody or fleshy fruits. About 40 species, native to North America.

■ *filamentosa* p. 147
Adam's-needle
Grasslike perennial. Zone 5
Height: 2–3 ft. (foliage); 5–6 ft. (flowers). Spread: 5–6 ft.
Yuccas make excellent focal points in a container garden or highlights for entrances (positioned so that the pointed leaves will do no harm). An asset in the winter landscape, they provide a bold form year-round. Adam's-needle, a southeastern native, is the most commonly offered yucca. It spreads slowly

to make a wide patch with many rosettes of sword-shaped leaves 2–3 ft. long. The evergreen leaves have sharp tips and curly fibers along the edges. The tall branched stalks of large white flowers are very showy in June. Gather the woody pods in fall for dried arrangements. 'Golden Sword' and other variegated forms have pretty gold or cream stripes on the leaves. Plants sold as *Y. filamentosa* may actually be *Y. flaccida* or *Y. smalliana;* it's hard to distinguish these similar-looking plants. *Y.* 'Bright Eyes', which grows only 18 in. tall, is ideal for container gardeners without a lot of space.

Yuccas aren't restricted to dry climates or xeriscape gardens. They combine well with perennials or grasses in many climates. Try underplanting a specimen with trailing plants—a handsome contrast to the yucca's formal spiky form.

How to Grow

Full or part sun. Loam-based commercial soil mix amended with coarse sand for improved drainage. Tolerates winter cold, summer heat, and wind. Tolerates being root-bound and lasts many years in the same pot. Established plants form offsets at the base that can be removed and transplanted. Only care required is the removal of old flower stalks and dead leaves. Move to shelter or unheated garage in bad northern winters.

■ other yuccas

The following yuccas are suitable for containers, keeping in mind that the larger the plant, the larger the container that is required.

Y. elata, or soaptree, is a southwestern species with stiff, narrow, gray to blue-green leaves. Older plants develop several heads on erect trunks 10–20 ft. tall. (It needs a very big container if it reaches this size.) The branching flower stalks, 3–7 ft. tall, are covered with creamy white flowers in May and June. Other southwestern species include *Y. aloifolia,* or Spanish dagger, which has slender leaves on stems to 6 ft. tall; *Y. gloriosa,* also called Spanish dagger, is similar. *Y. baccata,* or datil, makes broad patches of thick-leaved rosettes and has short flower stalks. All are hardy to zone 7 or 6 and require well-drained soil.

Y. glauca, or bear grass, is common on the western Great Plains. It forms pincushion-like rosettes of narrow spiky leaves, gray-green with pale edges and about 2 ft. tall—ideal for containers. White flowers line a slender 3–6-ft. stalk in June. Zone 4.

Y. whipplei, or Whipple's yucca (pictured opposite), is native to southern California. It makes a 2-ft. rosette of gray-green leaves tipped with very sharp spines and bears pale yellow or creamy flowers on a thick stalk up to 12 ft. tall in May or June. The parent rosette dies after flowering but produces offsets at the base. Zone 7.

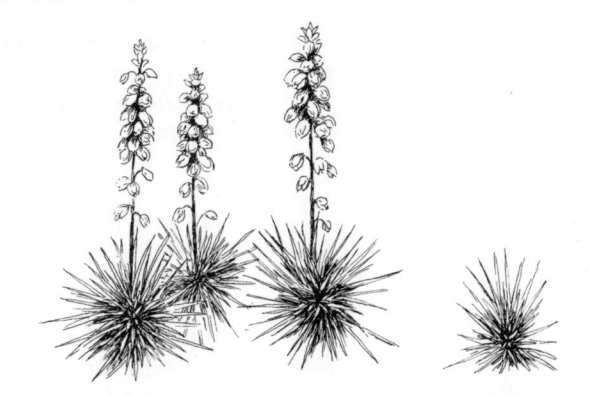

Y. flaccida, one of the hardiest yuccas, makes a 2½-ft. rosette of narrow leaves; the 4–7-ft. stalk bears white flowers that are fragrant in the evening.

The southeastern native *Y. recurvifolia* bears 2–3-ft.-long bluish gray leaves on a tall trunk and clusters of white flowers in June.

Zantedeschia
Zan-tee-des'kee-a. Calla
Araceae. Arum family

Description
Perennials with rounded storage rhizomes, large long-stalked leaves, and white or colored spathes that curl around the thumblike cluster of tiny flowers. Only 6 species, native to Africa.

■ *albomaculata* p. 159
Calla lily
Tender perennial often grown as an annual. Zone 8
Height: 24 in. Spread: 12 in.
Callas provide exotic flowers and foliage that make bold container displays. They are easy to grow, start blooming 6–8 weeks after the rhizomes are potted in late spring, and continue flowering until midsummer. The white spathes are about 4 in. long. The white-spotted leaves have long stalks and arrowhead-shaped blades. Grow with moisture lovers such as caladium or coleus. *Z. aethiopica*, the white calla, is a larger plant with white spathes up to 8 in. long. It is best for late-winter and spring display in southern areas, where its ever-

green foliage must be overwintered in a pot. *Z. rehmannii*, with yellow flowers and spotted leaves, is a good summer container plant. There are several new hybrid callas with pastel pink or yellow flowers; most are small plants with spathes less than 3 in. long.

How to Grow
Part sun; tolerates heat. Loam-based commercial soil mix. About the time of last frost, plant 1 rhizome 2–3 in. deep in a 10-in. by 10-in. pot; more rhizomes in bigger pots for a mass effect. Needs constant moisture; pots can be set in shallow water of a pond or "Chinese fish bowl." (Add aquarium charcoal to mix to keep water from smelling.) Feed every 2 weeks; stop after they cease blooming. Remove rhizomes from pot when leaves turn yellow or after frost in fall. Shake off soil and let rhizomes dry for a few days, then remove leaf bases and roots before packing rhizomes in dry peat, sawdust, or crumpled newspaper. Store in a dark place at 50°–60° F for the winter. Usually overwinters outdoors with no problems in zone 8 and sometimes survives in zone 7 or 6. Japanese beetles and spider mites attack the leaves.

Zinnia
Zin´ee-a
Compositae. Daisy family

Description
Annuals, perennials, and a few small shrubs with simple opposite leaves and showy composite flowers, often with bright-colored rays. About 20 species, mostly from Mexico.

■ *angustifolia* p. 123
(*Z. linearis*)
Annual. All zones
Height: 12 in. Spread: 12 in.
Once the weather warms up, this uncommon-looking zinnia billows from pots and blooms tirelessly until frost. It makes a loose mound of thin stems with sparse narrow leaves but blooms throughout the hottest weather and bears scores of blossoms 1–1½ in. wide. The species has golden orange rays, but new cultivars with white rays are more versatile. Combines well with grasses and as an underplanting for bolder plants such as spike dracaena or black-eyed Susan.

Z. haageana, or Mexican zinnia, is a similar but more upright species that also thrives in hot, dry conditions. It has bicolored flowers in shades of yellow, gold, red, mahogany, or maroon. 'Old Mexico' and 'Persian Carpet' are old but still-popular strains.

Creeping zinnia (*Sanvitalia procumbens*) is a smaller, spreading plant used in hanging baskets and other containers. Its colorful flowers bloom from midsummer to frost. Takes heat and drying out once established.

How to Grow
Full sun; tolerates heat. Loam-based commercial soil mix. Can be crowded in a mixed pot. Start seeds indoors 6 weeks before last frost. Doesn't grow well until the weather is warm. Requires no deadheading. Recovers from drying out. Japanese beetles eat the flowers; extremely mildew-resistant.

■ *elegans* cultivars *p. 123*
Common zinnias
Annuals. All zones
Height: 1–3 ft. Spread: 1 ft.

Zinnias are among the easiest annuals to grow, and their large vibrant flowers will enliven any patio. There are dozens of strains to choose from. Most have double flowers, ranging from 1 to 6 in. wide, available in all colors but blue. Plants range from 1-ft. dwarfs to cut-flower types that reach 3 ft. tall. Local nurseries usually grow mixed colors of different strains for spring planting. If you want one particular color, order seeds and grow your own plants. To soften their somewhat stiff appearance, combine them with plants of a looser habit, such as petunias, vinca vine, Madagascar periwinkle, or geraniums.

How to Grow
Like *Z. angustifolia*. They don't tolerate dryness—watch those planted in clay containers closely. Foliage is subject to mildew, which disfigures and weakens the plants. Don't crowd together with plants of similar height, so that air can circulate freely around the foliage.

Acquiring Plants

The urge to plant strikes most people in spring. With a supply of pots and soil on hand, the only thing missing is plants. You can grow your own from seed, cuttings, or divisions; you can purchase them; and you can get them from friends. However you acquire them, you want to have young plants ready when it's time to plant the containers.

Starting with Seeds

While it is possible to sow seeds (especially of quick-maturing vegetables such as lettuce) directly in their final pots, it's usually best to start and grow them into robust seedlings in other containers before transplanting into their final pots. This gives you more control of growing conditions and allows you to start more plants in less space, start them earlier, and have them ready when you need them. (Some seeds can be started indoors as many as 10 to 12 weeks before the last frost, so you'll have big, blooming plants as early as possible.)

Like school children, gardeners can start seeds indoors with no more than a cut-down milk carton, some soil, and a sunny window. A slightly more sophisticated approach, using plastic containers, commercial soil mix, and fluorescent lights, will greatly increase your capacity and improve your results. (See p. 391.)

Begin with a reputable seed-starting soil mix and some 3- to 4-inch plastic plant containers 2 to 3 inches deep. (Fine seed-starting mix can become waterlogged at the bottom of deeper containers and hamper root growth.) If you're reusing containers, scrub them with a soapy solution and a stiff brush to loosen and remove larger soil particles. Then soak them for 30 minutes in a solution of nine parts water to one part laundry bleach to sterilize them.

Moisten the soil mix in a clean bucket or pan. To check the moisture content, firmly squeeze a handful. The soil shouldn't fall apart when you release your fingers, but it should fall apart when you shake your hand. Fill each container to overflowing, working the soil into the corners, then lightly tamp to firm the seedbed to within 1/4 to 1/2 inch of the container's rim.

Now sprinkle, or "broadcast," seeds evenly across the surface of the mix. Unless the packet recommends otherwise, cover most seeds with soil mix to a depth two to three times the thickness of the seeds. Seeds are commonly inexpensive, so you can sow more than you need and choose the healthiest seedlings for growing on. In general, give seeds more rather than less room in a container, and sow only one species or cultivar to a container.

Sown in properly moistened mix, many seeds will germinate before additional water is required. You can cut down on evaporation by covering containers with sheets of plastic or glass or by placing them inside plastic bags. Check the mix in uncovered containers several times a day. Never let it dry out. When you need to water, immerse the container in a pan containing an inch or so of water; capillary action will draw the water up through the soil. Or gently wet the surface with a fine overhead spray. Use water that is room temperature or warmer; cold water can retard germination and growth. After watering, let the container drain completely.

Some seeds require light to germinate; others are inhibited by it. The seed packet will often tell you whether light is needed. Light falling naturally on a windowsill should be sufficient to germinate seeds that need light. (Don't put covered containers in direct sunlight, though; temperatures inside the covering can quickly reach levels lethal to seeds or emerging seedlings.) You can also place sown containers approximately 6 inches beneath 40-watt fluorescent lamps that are on eight hours or more a day. (Although special lamps are available for this purpose, ordinary fluorescent tubes work just fine.)

Different plants germinate at different soil temperatures. In general, some require soil above 70° F, whereas others prefer soil below that temperature. Seed packets may specify optimum temperatures; if not, you'll have to rely on experience. Many seeds will germinate at other than optimum temperatures—they'll just take longer to do so.

When seeds have germinated, remove any coverings and water as necessary by immersion or spray so that the seedlings, but not the soil, are dry by nightfall—this hinders the spread of disease. Allow all excess water to drain completely away rather than catching it in a saucer or pan beneath the container. As seedlings grow, water them less frequently, allowing the soil surface to dry slightly between waterings. Most seedlings grow best in daytime air temperatures between 60° and 80° F, depending on species, and in nighttime

Starting seeds in containers

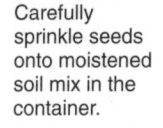

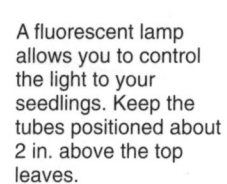

Carefully sprinkle seeds onto moistened soil mix in the container.

A fluorescent lamp allows you to control the light to your seedlings. Keep the tubes positioned about 2 in. above the top leaves.

After the first true leaves appear, transplant the seedlings to larger containers. Prick clumps out with your finger or a pencil and gently tease them apart.

Holding the seedling by a leaf, coax it into a hole poked in the mix in a new container. Put the new transplants under lights again and keep them well watered until they're ready to begin hardening off outside.

temperatures about 10° cooler. Normal room temperatures are usually acceptable.

The intensity and duration of light needed by seedlings also varies. Some thrive when subjected to continuous light, while others benefit from a daily period of darkness. If you are not aware of a species' light needs, place the seedlings several inches beneath fluorescent lamps for 16 hours or more per day and watch them closely. Spindly, weak seedlings are probably suffering from too little light. Those with "burned" or discolored leaves may be receiving too much light.

The small amount of nutrients in soilless mixes will soon be used up by the seedlings or washed out by watering and will need to be replaced. You can use almost any general soluble fertilizer containing approximately equal amounts of nitrogen, phosphorous, and potassium on seedlings. Some gardeners fertilize once a week; others do so each time they water. Unless the label specifies otherwise, you can dilute fertilizer to half or quarter the ordinary rate for once-a-week fertilizing. If you fertilize with each watering, you'll need to dilute to as little as one-tenth of the recommended rate. Either way, observe your plants. Weak, spindly growth often accompanied by yellowing of the leaves and increased susceptibility to disease can indicate nutrient deficiency. Too much fertilizer causes the leaf edges to "burn" and the stems to collapse.

When the tiny seedlings show their first "true" leaves (which resemble those of the mature plant), they are typically transplanted into roomier quarters to grow on until they're large enough to be put in their final container home. The soil mix you used for germinating the seeds will work fine. Choose a container size adequate for the plant's habit and rate of growth. You can transplant smaller plants into cell packs (usually containing four or six cells) or into flats, spacing the plants to avoid crowding as they grow. Plants that will grow larger can be put in individual pots, 2 to 4 inches wide.

The day before transplanting, water the seedlings well. Fill the new containers with moistened soil and tamp just as you did when preparing seedbeds. Then, with your finger or a pencil, gently remove seedlings from their original containers, individually or in clumps, lifting as much of the root system and its attached soil as possible. Holding only the leaves (not the stems or the roots), tease individual seedlings free of a clump. Disturb the soil adhering to the roots as little as possible.

Poke a hole in the soil in the new container. Then, aided by a finger or pencil, guide the roots into the hole so that all are buried. If the roots are too big for a narrow hole, hold the plant by a leaf in an empty cell and spoon soil around the roots. You can't go wrong positioning the seedling at the same depth it was growing, but many can be inserted farther to give the little stems more support. Water the seedlings by immersion or with a light spray soon after transplanting (this will settle the soil, too), and put them back under the lights.

As the seedlings approach a size suitable for their display container, you'll need to harden them off, gradually subjecting them to conditions similar to those outdoors. Start by setting them in a shady place out of the wind during the daytime. Then gradually expose them to sun and open air, finally leaving them out overnight.

Cuttings

A number of annual, perennial, and woody plants can be propagated by cuttings, a technique whereby a complete plant is generated from a shoot or root. Cuttings allow you to increase supplies of favorite plants and to overwinter others—rather than keep the whole plant, you pot up a few cuttings in the fall and enjoy good-size plants by next season. (Geraniums, heliotrope, and flowering maple are easy to grow from cuttings.)

The propagator's task is to take cuttings from those parts of the plant in which cells will most readily regenerate and to provide the levels of moisture, temperature, and light conducive to their doing so. Professional propagators leave little to chance in their procedures and equipment. Few gardeners have the resources or inclination to duplicate a professional propagating setup. But if you're willing to experiment—and to fail—you can have fun with a simpler, hit-or-miss approach.

In theory, propagating a cutting is easy. Just snip off a stem, strip the bottom leaves, stick it in potting soil, and keep it well watered. (See p. 394.) Although the failure rate is very high, gardeners have been propagating plants this way for centuries. If you take some measures to control the conditions in which the cutting roots—soil, moisture, temperature, and light—you can increase your chances of success.

When to take cuttings varies from species to species. For some, the soft succulent spring growth roots best, whereas others should be cut after the first flush of growth is past, and still others are made from mature, dormant stems. If you can't find out the timing for a particular plant, try taking cuttings at each stage. In general, take cuttings early in the morning from well-watered plants. Cut back from the tip of a healthy stem at least two nodes (the slight swellings where leaves attach). Cut with a very sharp, disinfected knife or pruners slightly below the node.

It is best to prepare and "stick" (plant) cuttings immediately. But you can refrigerate them in a plastic bag for sev-

New plants from cuttings

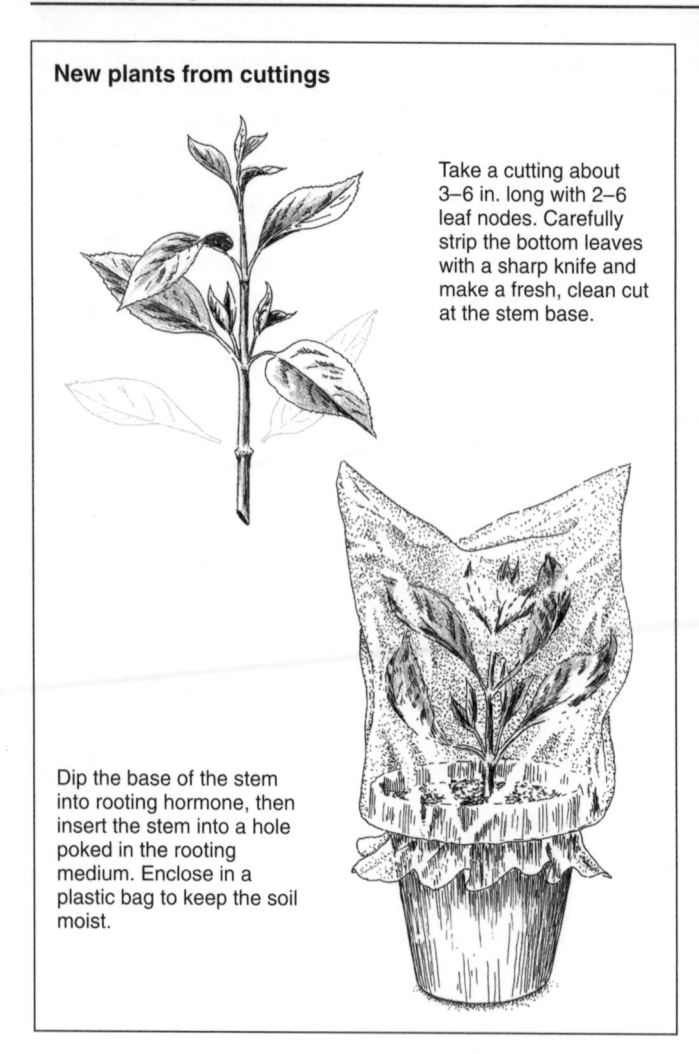

Take a cutting about 3–6 in. long with 2–6 leaf nodes. Carefully strip the bottom leaves with a sharp knife and make a fresh, clean cut at the stem base.

Dip the base of the stem into rooting hormone, then insert the stem into a hole poked in the rooting medium. Enclose in a plastic bag to keep the soil moist.

eral hours or, occasionally, for several days. Before sticking, strip the bottom leaves with a sharp knife. Make a fresh cut at the base of the cutting, then dip the base into rooting hormone, sold at garden centers as a powder. Tap the cutting to remove excess powder, which could harm the cutting.

Propagators root cuttings in various mixtures of sand, peat moss, vermiculite, pumice, and perlite. Perlite is a good, all-purpose material, but commercial potting soil may work fine. Put 2 to 3 inches of moist soil in a container, make a hole slightly larger than the diameter of the cutting and 1 to 2 inches deep, then insert the cutting. Gently push the surrounding medium into the hole and water thoroughly.

Ideal rooting temperatures are 70° to 80° F during the day and 60° F at night, but many cuttings tolerate a wider range. Unfortunately, there are no clear-cut ways of determining the best light level for cuttings. You'll have to rely on your own experiences and those of others, which are sometimes given in books. Moisture is critical. Too much can rot stems or leaves. Too little can kill a cutting quickly, sometimes within minutes. A clear plastic bag will retain moisture for cuttings in containers, but check it periodically. Remember that any transparent propagating tent quickly overheats in direct sunlight. Cuttings may take weeks or months to root. When the stem resists gentle tugging, transplant the cutting as you would a seedling into a larger temporary pot, or harden it off and plant it in its outside container.

Purchasing Plants

The easiest way to acquire plants is to buy them from a reputable nursery or be given them by friends. Nurseries sell most of their plants in plastic containers. Annuals usually come in small plastic pots or in packs of two, four, six, or more cells, linked like an egg carton. Perennials often require larger, individual containers that usually hold a quart or gallon of soil. (See below.)

Years ago, nurseries sold annuals before the plants developed flower buds or blossoms—very young plants suffer less transplanting shock and resume growth more quickly, so they soon catch up with older transplanted flowers. Then, to sat-

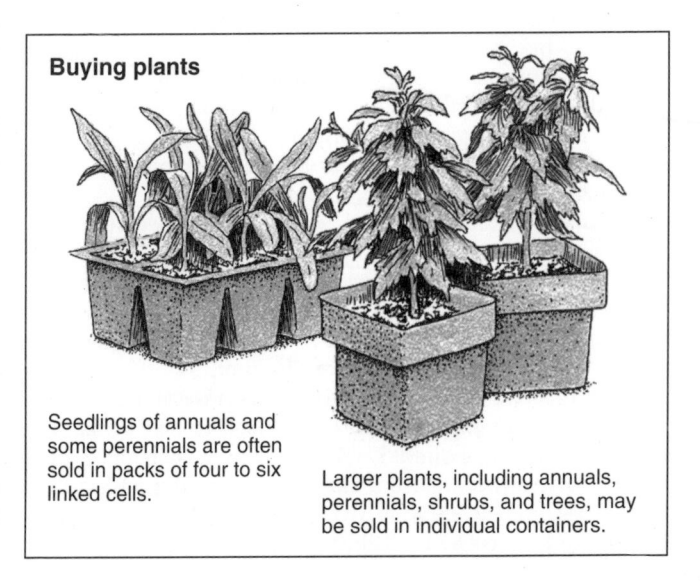

Buying plants

Seedlings of annuals and some perennials are often sold in packs of four to six linked cells.

Larger plants, including annuals, perennials, shrubs, and trees, may be sold in individual containers.

isfy a new generation of buyers who wanted instant color, growers began delivering older plants that were already in bloom. Soon any variety that was slow to bloom in containers disappeared from garden-center shelves. Today it's difficult to find garden-center annuals that aren't in early or full bloom.

Some plants, such as petunias, dwarf marigolds, and impatiens, are so vigorous that they hardly slow down when transplanted in full bloom. But others, such as celosia, put so much of their strength into forming large flower heads that if transplanted when in bloom they may barely survive.

For best results, then, choose the youngest annuals available. Look for plants with healthy green leaves all the way down to soil level. If the seedlings have begun to branch, all the better. Tall, wiry plants that are shedding their bottom leaves are probably suffering from lack of water and will take longer to establish in the display pot. Yellowed or discolored plants haven't been fertilized enough and may be permanently stunted. Look for signs of insects and disease, misshapen flowers, and distorted growth.

If you can, carefully pop a small seedling out of its plastic cell or tap a larger plant out of its pot and look at the root ball. A mass of roots spiraling around the container indicates a root-bound plant that will adjust slowly when you transplant it, no matter how carefully you untangle and spread out the roots.

Perennials are most often older than seedlings when sold. Grown in containers for up to a year (occasionally longer for some species), these larger, more mature plants can make a splash in your garden faster than plants grown from seeds or seedlings, but they're likely to be more expensive. Some perennials, such as irises and daylilies, are commonly shipped when dormant with bare roots or with roots packed in sawdust or a similar material to prevent dehydration. If you can't plant right away, be sure not to let plants shipped in moist material dry out.

The size of plants and containers varies considerably; pots range from 4 inches across to those containing 2 gallons of soil. Pot size doesn't necessarily correlate with performance. For a fast-growing species, a plant purchased in a 1-quart pot may be the same size at the end of a season in the container garden as one purchased in a 1-gallon pot.

Look for bare stems, discolored leaves, insects, and disease in container-grown perennials, too. A big plant in a small pot is likely to be root-bound. Look for exposed roots on the soil surface or protruding from the container's drainage holes. Perennials bought early in the season are less likely to be root-bound or stressed in other ways.

Potting Soils

Like their garden-grown counterparts, container plants need to be planted, watered, fed, pruned, and pinched. These processes will be familiar to gardeners who grow plants in the ground. But there are differences worth noting in the planting and care of container plants. In this and the next two chapters, we cover the basics of giving annuals and perennials in containers a good start and keeping them healthy over time.

Potting Soil

The most important ingredient in container gardening is soil. It doesn't matter how pretty the pot is or how artful the plant combinations, without a suitable soil, the result will be disappointing.

Although we say that plants grow in soil, it is more correct to say that plants grow in the spaces between soil particles. There roots absorb the water, oxygen, and nutrients that sustain growth above soil level. Soils differ in many ways, and one of the most important is in the size of the spaces between particles. Heavy clay soil has fine particles, with little space between them. It retains nutrients well but drains poorly—when it gets waterlogged, roots rot. Sandy soil is just the opposite. Its large, coarse particles are easily penetrated by roots and by water. Sandy soils are often nutrient-poor and difficult to keep moist enough. The ideal soil for many plants—in the ground or in containers—is a sandy soil liberally enriched with organic matter, such as rotted manure, leaf mold, compost, or peat moss. Organic materials act like a sponge, holding water and nutrients and making them available to roots.

Most garden soils are not suitable for direct use in containers. Dug and potted, clay soils compact into a dense, impenetrable mass; sandy soils lack the organic matter to hold nutrients and water. You can make your own potting soil by amending garden soil, but this can require some experimentation to get the right combination of amendments. If you need lots of potting soil for large planters and pots, making your own may be financially attractive.

Commercial potting soil

For many container gardeners, and particularly novices, commercial potting soil makes the most sense. Bought from a reputable manufacturer, it can be counted on to be a good growing medium, allowing roots to penetrate easily, aerating well, and holding enough, but not too much, water. It may come as a surprise that most bags of potting soil contain no real soil. Instead they are mixtures of organic materials, such as peat moss and ground bark, and lightweight minerals, such as perlite and vermiculite. Commercial soilless mixes contain few if any disease organisms and weed seeds. Some mixes also include lime (to balance the pH and to provide several important trace elements) and added nutrients of one sort or another.

Commercial potting soils vary, but most are suitable for container use. Some gardeners develop a preference for the texture of one or another; they find finer mixes useful for seed starting, coarser for large pots and planters. Some look for a mix with added nutrients; others are willing to add fertilizer themselves. You can experiment with several brands, or ask what type of potting soil your favorite nursery uses. They may buy in bulk and be willing to sell you some. Pre-bagged mixes are cheaper in larger quantities—if you have someplace to store a 40-pound bale, you'll save money in the long run.

You can grow a wide range of annuals and perennials in ordinary soil mixes. You can also amend them to suit the needs of particular plants or to accommodate local conditions. Oriental lilies, for example, do best when you add peat moss and sand or coarse perlite to the mix. Lily bulbs are susceptible to rot, and the sand or perlite improves drainage. Peat moss helps retain necessary moisture, inhibits bacteria, and lowers the pH—lilies prefer soil slightly on the acidic side. Some plants have very special soil needs. Cacti and succulents, for instance, thrive on a mix composed mainly of coarse sand and gravel, which imitates the soil of their native habitat. (In the plant encyclopedia in this book, we've suggested soil amendments or special mixes for certain plants. If you want to grow other plants with special needs, consult the nursery that sold them to you or ask your local Cooperative Extension agent for advice.)

Where rainfall is plentiful, you may wish to incorporate sand, small gravel, perlite, or vermiculite in commercial mixes to improve drainage. Where rainfall is scarce and container plants must rely on the gardener remembering to water for survival, you can add compost, peat moss, or other organic matter to increase water retention. The science of polymers has provided another amendment: nonorganic crystals that absorb and store water like tiny reservoirs within the soil. Gardeners are still experimenting with polymers, but these materials can help keep plants moist in hot, dry conditions without the gardener having to resort to the hose every few hours.

Homemade potting soil

Recipes for potting soil, like those for favorite foods, combine art and science and can vary considerably depending on the artist. A simple recipe for a "real soil" mix combines in equal parts three ingredients: good garden loam, compost or peat moss, and coarse sand. Pass the loam through a 1/4-inch mesh screen to remove debris, and buy the coarsest sand you can find—if it will pass through a window screen, it's too fine. Substitute perlite for sand for a lighter-weight mix. If you're uncertain about the quality of your soil, you can evaluate it using the simple method shown in the drawing. Loam, that ideal garden soil, can vary widely in its makeup. Loam soils contain less than 52 percent sand, between 28 and 50 percent silt, and 7 to 27 percent clay.

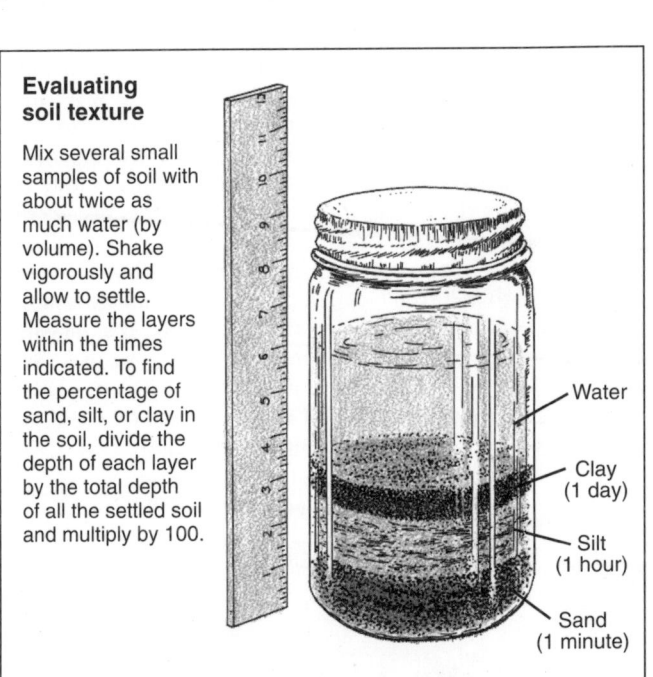

Evaluating soil texture

Mix several small samples of soil with about twice as much water (by volume). Shake vigorously and allow to settle. Measure the layers within the times indicated. To find the percentage of sand, silt, or clay in the soil, divide the depth of each layer by the total depth of all the settled soil and multiply by 100.

- Water
- Clay (1 day)
- Silt (1 hour)
- Sand (1 minute)

The success of any mix using soil depends on the soil's quality. If your soil contains too much clay or is otherwise poor, you can make a soilless mix. Jim Wilson suggests the following two mixes in his book *Landscaping with Container Plants* (Boston: Houghton Mifflin, 1990). The first, for plants in pots up to 8 inches wide, consists of equal parts moistened sphagnum peat moss and vermiculite, to which is added dolomitic limestone at $1/2$ ounce per gallon and triple superphosphate (a fertilizer) at $1/4$ ounce per gallon. You can also add gypsum at $1/2$ ounce per gallon to provide calcium. (Gardeners in areas where the water is alkaline can omit the limestone and gypsum.)

For larger pots and planters, the mix is equal parts coarse, medium, and fine materials. Wilson suggests small nuggets of pine or fir bark for the coarse; pulverized pine or fir bark for the medium; and moistened sphagnum peat moss for the fine. To these he adds the same amounts of limestone, superphosphate, and gypsum as for the other mix. You can alter these mixes for certain plants or conditions as suggested earlier for commercial mixes.

To mix a custom batch of potting soil, whether you're amending a commercial mix or starting from scratch, use a plastic pail or barrel, depending on the quantities. Add ingredients as you would to make a cake, stirring with a stick or your hands. As you proceed, add enough water to moisten the mix slightly. Some mixes wet more easily than others, and one that wets poorly is likely to cause problems. If allowed to dry out in the pots, it will always be difficult to remoisten.

Some gardeners reuse their potting soil from year to year. At the end of the season, you can dump the contents of pots in garbage cans or in large piles in the garden. (Include the plants if you're discarding them; stems and roots decay over the winter, adding to the organic matter in the mixture. Don't include diseased plants.) In spring, mix the soil and screen out the chunks that haven't decomposed. You can add store-bought mixes or other materials to balance the mixture. Reusing potting soil can cause problems—the soil may compact more easily and, worse, it may have picked up disease organisms or weed seeds. If you don't want to take the risk, put old potting soil on the garden compost heap.

Planting a Container

Pot size is largely a matter of common sense, based on how big the plant is at potting time, how big it is likely to get, and how long it will take to do so. Annuals grow to full size quickly and will likely not be around long enough to be potted up if they get too big. Some perennials also grow quickly. Fast-growing plants need to start out in pots that seem too big, lest the pot rapidly become too small. The half-dozen annual seedlings that look lost in a 3-gallon pot will soon engulf it.

Slower-growing perennials should be gradually upgraded to larger pots. Pick a pot that the plant can grow into in a season or so, rather than one large enough to accommodate its mature size three or four years down the road. Specimens sold in gallon containers will give good results the first season; younger plants (including those you start from seed) will be less expensive but will take longer to make a show.

The rule of thumb is to put a newly purchased perennial in a pot about 2 inches or so wider and deeper than the one in which it is growing. The problem with a pot that is too large is that the extra soil retains more moisture than the plant can use; soggy roots tend to rot. If you are careful about watering, you can plant in pots larger than the rule of thumb would recommend. This is handy for plants such as chrysanthemums that may be purchased as seedlings in the spring for fall display and for plants that grow rapidly. Instead of repotting several times during the season, you can put a plant bought in a 3-inch pot in its 8-inch display pot right away—provided you water with care until the plant begins to fill the pot with roots.

Of course, some pots will hold more than one plant, and some containers (window boxes, permanent planters) will hold a considerable number. Experience will help you develop judgment of how much crowding the pot-mates can take. Generally plants can be much closer in pots than in the garden, but too much crowding can affect growth rate (leading to leggy or stunted growth) and health (crowded plants are more susceptible to disease). Because you're concerned with only a season or a few months' growth for annuals, they are more malleable in this regard than many perennials.

As a rule, the smaller the pot, the greater the maintenance. Pots of 6 inches in diameter or less are of little use for any plants but drought-tolerant cacti and succulents—they lose moisture so rapidly that they are simply too difficult to keep watered. Shallow pots are most suitable for plants such as succulents that do not mind some drought and elevated soil temperatures. Deep pots benefit plants with extensive root systems. Remember that those plants that survive with little winter protection require containers that can also withstand the rigors of winter and cycles of freezing and thawing.

Found containers—glass bowls, ceramic pots, marble sinks, and so on—are handsome additions to a container garden. Their one drawback is their lack of holes for drainage. You can plant in them without drainage holes, but you must monitor your watering closely to make sure that the soil doesn't stay too wet—this can be difficult to judge in deeper pots. Alternatively, you can bore drainage holes. In wood or lightweight metals, this is easy to do with twist bits and a hand or power drill. Clay and ceramic vessels can be bored with masonry bits and a hand-held power drill, as can various cement and stone containers. Glass must be bored with a special bit; you can do it yourself, but the bits may be hard to find. Better to go to a glass shop and have them do it for you. These shops will often be able to bore holes in hard stone, too. Holes $1/2$ inch in diameter are easier to bore than larger ones; just remember to cover them with a screen to prevent clogging.

Planting Basics

We'll discuss procedures for planting different kinds of containers, but first a few pointers about handling seedlings and plants during this process. Before you begin transplanting, give the root ball a good watering, then let it drain thoroughly. A moist root ball will cohere much better than a dry one.

When removing a plant from an individual container, never pull it out by its stem. Rather, place one hand over the top surface of the root ball, fingers spread on either side of the stem, then turn the pot nearly upside down. (See p. 403.) Gently thump the bottom of the pot with your free hand, and slide out the root ball. You'll get the hang of it with a little practice. If the plant in a plastic pot is difficult to dislodge, lay the pot on its side on the ground or a table and push

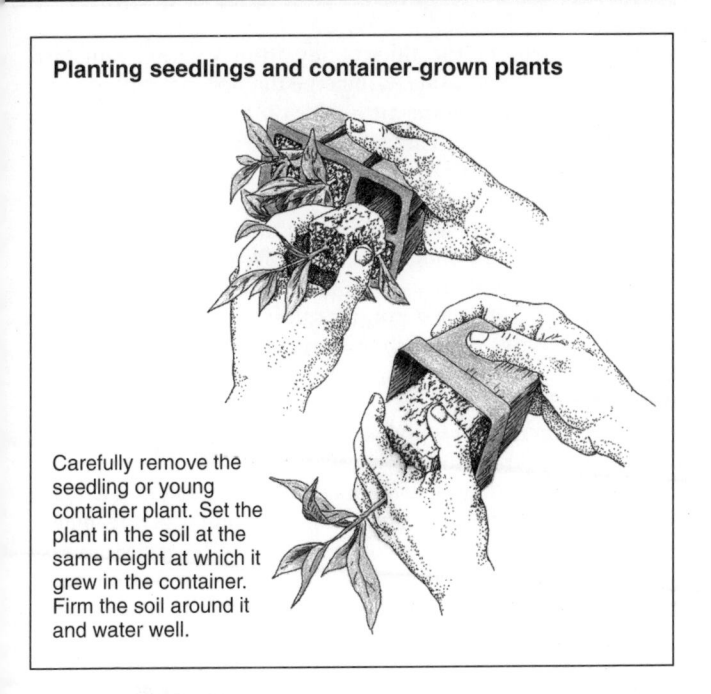

> **Planting seedlings and container-grown plants**
>
> Carefully remove the seedling or young container plant. Set the plant in the soil at the same height at which it grew in the container. Firm the soil around it and water well.

down on the sides as you roll it back and forth. Then try to slide the root ball out. Removing plants from six-packs is a snap in comparison. Simply push up from the bottom of the plastic cell with your thumb or finger. Cradle the root ball with your other hand.

Most plants can go directly into the display container, but those that have become pot-bound need some extra attention. You can tell if a plant has been in its container too long if the roots clog the drainage holes and have made a twisted mess on the surface of the root ball. Sometimes the roots grow in circles around the curve of the pot's wall. Trim off snarls of roots or encircling roots with a knife or scissors. This will encourage the formation of new roots when the plant is transplanted. In extreme cases, where a large portion of the roots needs to be trimmed, trim some of the top growth to relieve the burden on the roots.

Planting in Terra-Cotta

These classic garden containers have much to recommend them: earthy good looks, excellent drainage, and superb aeration. Air and water vapor pass readily through the porous walls; gardeners often say that a clay pot "breathes," an aid in preventing root rot.

To prepare a terra-cotta pot for planting, you must first

soak it to prevent the thirsty clay from wicking moisture away from the soil inside. Submerge the pot in a sink or pail filled with water until the air bubbles subside, indicating that the clay is saturated. This usually takes about 5 to 10 minutes. Old pots may look as though they're stained with white mildew. These stains are fertilizer salts deposited when water saturated with dissolved fertilizer evaporated through the pot walls. After soaking these pots, scour them with a stiff brush or pad. A thick buildup may require some elbow grease to remove. If you're reusing a pot, it's safest to "sterilize" it to kill soilborne diseases that might be lurking there. Just add bleach to the water in which you soak the pot—one part household bleach to nine parts water.

Before filling a pot with soil, cover its drainage hole to prevent loss of potting soil during watering. You can use a piece of broken pot just large enough to cover the hole, or a 2-inch-square piece of old window screen. Position large pots where you intend to display them before adding soil—it's much easier on your back. If you're concerned about moisture damaging the surface beneath a big pot, remember to place a plastic saucer under it now. (Water will saturate a clay saucer; you can buy plastic saucers in the same colors as clay.)

Begin by adding soil to the pot. For a pot holding a plant with a large root ball, add enough soil to position the top of the root ball about an inch below the rim of the pot. If the depth of the root balls of plants sharing a pot differ, plant the deepest first, add soil to accommodate the next deepest and so on, so that the top surfaces of the root balls will all be level. If the transplants are small (six-pack size), you can fill the pot to within an inch of the top and burrow into the soil with your fingers to plant.

As you add soil around larger root balls, firm it with your fingers so that the roots make good contact with the new soil. Firm small transplants with slight pressure to anchor them. Make sure all plants are positioned at the level they were previously growing, avoiding planting them too low or too high. The soil mix will settle somewhat after watering, so press with your fingers to locate "soft" spots between plants, and add small amounts of soil to even them out.

Immediately after planting, water thoroughly with a gentle stream of water, such as from a watering can with a fine spray. Add water in several stages, allowing it to sink in each time. Stop when it runs through the drainage hole. Any plants that weren't firmed in properly will lean, and small pockets will sometimes appear as soil fills air pockets below. Add small amounts of soil to make the surface level and to stabilize tilting plants. Not all pots require saucers, but they are especially helpful for smaller containers that dry out quickly.

Bare-root plants aren't handled much differently. Before planting, soak the roots in a solution of tepid water and dilute soluble fertilizer (about one-quarter normal dosage). Add soil to the bottom of the pot, gauging its depth to position the plant at the height it once grew in the field—you can usually see a little discoloration at the base of the stem indicating the previous soil line. Spread the roots and add soil, working it around the roots with your fingers to eliminate air pockets. Water the filled pot, then add soil where it has settled.

Planting in Plastic or Glazed Pots

This procedure is very much like the one just outlined. These pots aren't porous, so you don't need to soak them. But you should clean those you're reusing with the bleach solution to kill disease organisms that might have contaminated previous soil.

Plastic or nonporous pots generally stay cooler and lose less water by evaporation than terra-cotta pots. This can cut watering chores, but the soil in these pots is more likely to become too soggy, resulting in poor plant performance from oxygen-starved roots or from rot. It is particularly important that you fill large plastic or glazed pots with soil that drains very well. Because these containers retain moisture better, be careful if you put a small plant in a large nonporous pot. For multiple-plant pots, keep the proportion of new soil to root ball relatively low.

Hanging Baskets

Two types of baskets are commonly used for plants. One is essentially an ordinary pot suspended by wire, chain, or other means. Filled with plants that trail over the sides of the pot, it resembles a "true" hanging basket, which is a loose mesh of thin metal wire lined with sphagnum moss and filled with soil. Planted on the top, sides, and sometimes bottom, the traditional basket presents a floating mass of flowers and foliage.

Ample, regular moisture and fertilization are crucial for best appearance and growth of either type. Drying winds are the enemy of hanging baskets, and sphagnum baskets dry out even more quickly than plastic or clay ones.

Hanging pots

Planting this type of basket can be done as outlined above for pots. Plastic pots are popular because of their light weight, but you can use a wide range of containers, provided they have a drainage hole and plenty of room for soil and roots.

Filled with moist soil, any type of hanging pot can be quite heavy, so anchor them with suitable hooks into strong supports and make sure that the suspending rope, chain, or wire is up to the task as well. Special lightweight potting soil mixes make sense for large hanging pots. You can cut the weight of ordinary mixes by adding perlite. It is the rare hanging basket that gets overwatered, so the soil mix should usually be moisture-retentive, incorporating lots of organic matter. Drainage is normally not critical, unless you are growing succulents. It's worth considering adding polymers to the mix to retain even more moisture, especially if you live in a semiarid climate or one with extremely hot daytime temperatures.

"True" hanging baskets

Designed to be planted over their entire surface, these baskets have a full, lush look. You can make a wire framework yourself, but it's probably best to start with a store-bought one. Your local nursery should be able to provide the basket as well as the unmilled sphagnum moss to line it. Unmilled

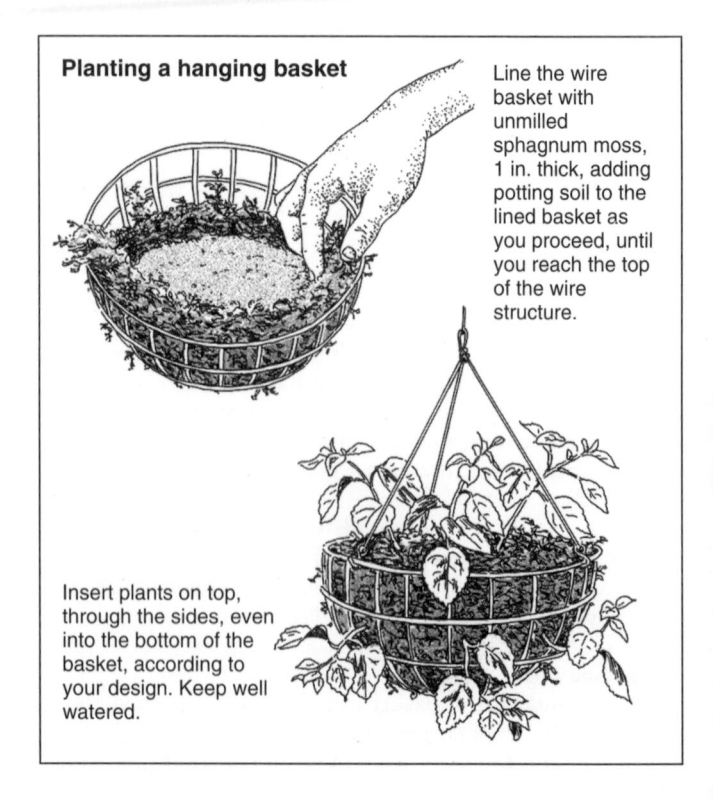

Planting a hanging basket

Line the wire basket with unmilled sphagnum moss, 1 in. thick, adding potting soil to the lined basket as you proceed, until you reach the top of the wire structure.

Insert plants on top, through the sides, even into the bottom of the basket, according to your design. Keep well watered.

moss has not been shredded, and its intertwined strands hold together to support the weight of the soil.

Start by soaking unmilled sphagnum moss for at least 10 minutes in tepid or warm water until it is well saturated. Then, working from the bottom up, line the basket with a 1-inch-thick layer of moss, adding rich, moisture-retentive potting soil as you go until you reach the top of the wire frame. (See p. 406.) You can cover the top of the soil with moss to keep evaporation to a minimum. In semiarid areas, some gardeners place a sheet of thin plastic between the moss and the soil to retain more moisture—sometimes this is the only way to keep the plants growing during midsummer. Hanging baskets can be heavy, too; select supports accordingly.

It's often easiest to plant a wire basket while it's already hanging. Planting on top is simple, but the sides and bottom take patience. Pull the moss aside gently to make a hole just large enough to insert the root ball of a six-pack-grown annual or a rooted cutting. Use your fingertips to firm the soil around the plant and to push the moss up to the protruding stem of the plant. Space the plants fairly closely so that they'll mingle as they grow, eventually giving the impression of a floating ball of foliage and flowers. A well-planted, well-maintained hanging basket is a beautiful sight.

Wooden Containers

Gardeners who wish to make their own containers usually turn to wood. Easy to cut and assemble, wood can be fashioned into many configurations to house plants—planters, tubs, window boxes, and hanging containers. Square or rectangular planters are the most common, but gardeners with superior carpentry skills can dream up all sorts of designs. Of course, there are also many commercially made wooden containers from which to choose.

Cedar, redwood, and cypress are resistant to rot and are commonly employed for containers. Pressure-treated construction-grade lumber for exterior use also resists rot; once the preservatives are thoroughly dry, they won't harm plants. (If the treated material is wet when you buy it, let it dry for a month before planting. Protect your skin and eyes when working with freshly treated lumber.) Old, reclaimed wood can have a charming look but may not last long once it comes in contact with wet soil.

The fasteners you choose to construct the box also affect its durability. Galvanized nails are perfectly acceptable, but screws will last even longer. A mass of wet soil in a big box can exert considerable pressure on fasteners; consider reinforcing the corners with L-shaped metal braces. If you hang boxes from windows or deck railings, make sure the fasteners are strong enough to support the box and a load of moist soil.

You can extend the life of any wooden container by coating its inside surfaces with some sort of water sealant or by lining it with flexible plastic. Rigid plastic liners are sold, too, and you can size your boxes to accommodate them. If you stain or paint the outside of the box for ornamental reasons, keep in mind that a dark color such as hunter green, brown, or black will absorb more heat than a pale color, which might cause problems for roots.

As with any container, drainage is essential. Drill holes in the bottom and cover them with crockery shards or screen. Plant wooden containers as previously outlined for terracotta. If you want to cut down on the weight of a large wooden container such as a half-barrel, you can fill it halfway with Styrofoam packing peanuts or similar material, adding soil mix on top. (This technique will, of course, work for large containers made of any material.)

Hypertufa: Lightweight Do-It-Yourself Stone

American rock gardeners have long admired the English use of antique stone sinks for containers. Carved from soft rock, the sinks have proved an effective and charming home for alpine plants. Those who don't grow alpines but like the looks of stone often plant sinks with cacti, succulents, and other plants.

Nice idea—if you can find an old stone sink. Not many of us can, but you can make a reasonable copy. Rock gardeners have been doing it for decades. These facsimiles are called hypertufa troughs. The first troughs imitated the look of the original stone sinks and were fashioned by applying a mixture of cement, peat moss, and vermiculite or perlite over chicken-wire reinforcement.

Modern trough makers have eliminated the cumbersome chicken wire, adding strands of a concrete reinforcement called Fibermesh to the recipe to provide the same sort of strength. A cottage industry producing hypertufa containers now flourishes in some areas, and you can buy these troughs at garden centers in some cities. The mix described here for making your own was developed by Ernie Whitford, an avid rock gardener in Colorado.

Making your own trough requires an afternoon of work and several weeks of patience as the mixture cures thoroughly. The ingredients are equal volumes of perlite, sphagnum peat moss, and dry cement, and about one handful of the fluffy Fibermesh per gallon of mix. (For the dealer nearest you, contact Fibermesh Company, 4019 Industry Dr., Chattanooga, TN 37416; 615-892-7243.) To color the "stone," add 1 ounce of powdered cement dye per gallon of mix. A trough 15 inches square requires about 3 gallons of mix.

Making the trough

Mix the ingredients in a large bucket or wheelbarrow. Protect your hands with rubber gloves and your lungs with a dust mask or scarf. When the dry ingredients are thoroughly mixed together, add just enough water to produce a slurry the consistency of cottage cheese—this doesn't take much water.

The mixture is often formed between two molds, an inner and an outer. (See pp. 410–11.) You can make these of wood or improvise with containers of the desired size. Two rectangular plastic tubs, one 4 inches longer and wider than the other, will nest together to produce a trough with sides 2 inches thick; a round container can be made by nesting the top 6 inches of a 7-gallon plastic nursery container inside the top 6 inches of a 10-gallon container. Sharp corners are easily chipped, so make or select molds with rounded corners. Before each use, coat the contact surfaces of the molds with linseed oil, which will act as a release agent.

Cover a worktable with a sheet of plastic and position the molds on it. Then, with gloved hands, pour the mixture and build up the bottom of the trough to about 2 inches thick. (Do this on the plastic sheet for bottomless molds.) Next, pack the mixture tightly between the inner and outer molds. Wait about 10 minutes, then remove the inner mold. You can form drainage holes in the bottom with a ½-inch dowel, and round the inner corners now, too. Without moving the mold and mixture, cover them with plastic so that the mixture doesn't dry too fast, and let it cure for 48 hours.

After curing, remove the outer mold. (If you've forgotten to make the drainage holes, do so now with a screwdriver.) Brush the outer surfaces of the trough with a wire brush to enhance the texture; don't worry about the "cat hair" look this will create. Cover the trough with plastic again and let it cure another two weeks; you can move it now, but pick it up by the bottom and handle it carefully to avoid hairline cracks. Wash the trough several times as it cures to leach out excess lime, which would otherwise affect the pH of your potting soil. Complete the trough after two weeks by burning off the "cat hair" with a propane torch. Take care not to let the torch heat any spot too much—damp pockets in the walls might burst, forming small pits or cracks.

If the mix is not runny, you can make a trough with a single mold, such as a cat litter tray, or make a free-form trough over a mold made of damp sand, the way sand candles are

Making a hypertufa trough

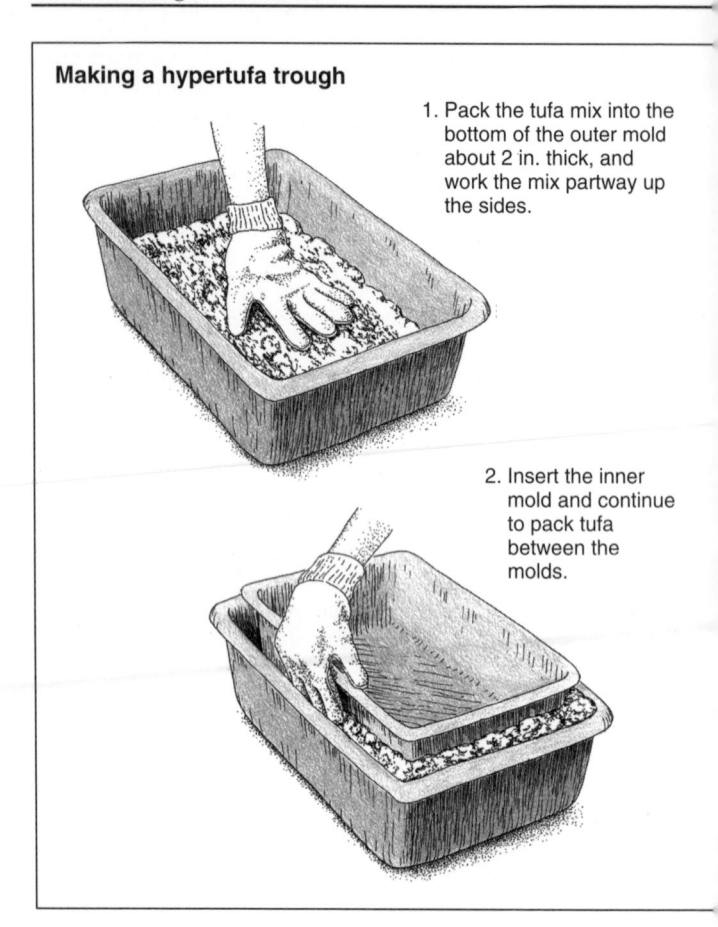

1. Pack the tufa mix into the bottom of the outer mold about 2 in. thick, and work the mix partway up the sides.

2. Insert the inner mold and continue to pack tufa between the molds.

made. Cover these molds with about 2 inches of the mixture, as evenly as possible. It is especially important not to skimp in the corners and rim. Follow the previous instructions for curing.

Planting the trough

Cover the drainage holes with crockery or wire screen. If you're planting alpines, the soil mixture should generally be both organically rich and well drained. Consult a nursery specialist to determine which alpine perennials grow best in your region. Choose plants with a slow growth rate. Young plants in 2¼-inch pots are an ideal size for starting out. (If you put other sorts of plants in troughs, plant them as described for terra-cotta.)

Fill the trough nearly to the rim with the soil mix. Arrange rocks, if you desire, on top. A rule of thumb is that rocks in

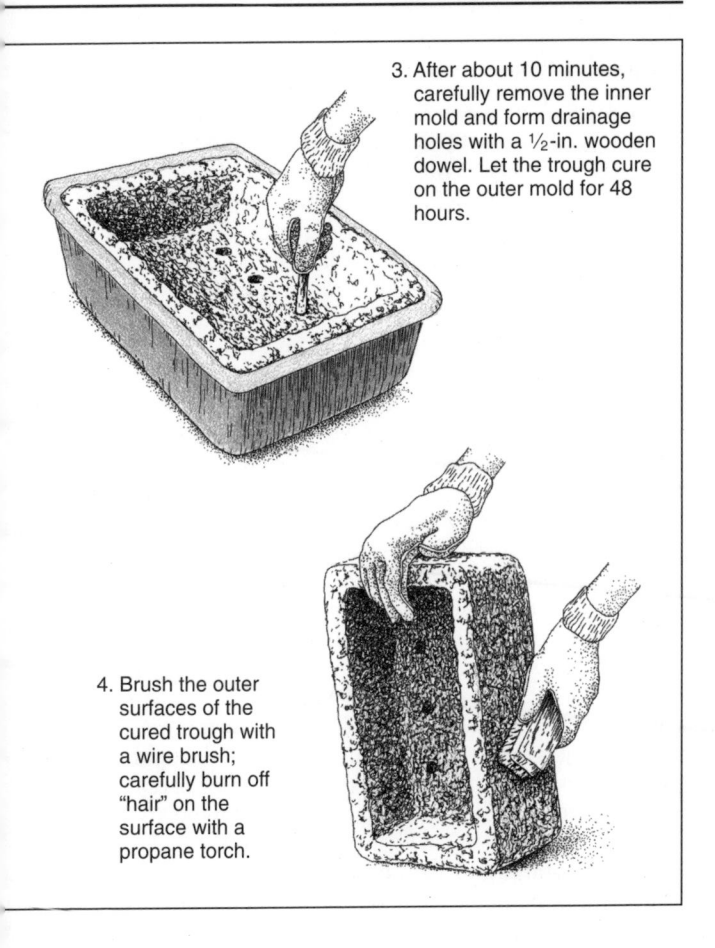

3. After about 10 minutes, carefully remove the inner mold and form drainage holes with a ½-in. wooden dowel. Let the trough cure on the outer mold for 48 hours.

4. Brush the outer surfaces of the cured trough with a wire brush; carefully burn off "hair" on the surface with a propane torch.

nature, like icebergs, are mostly below ground. For a "natural" look, bury up to two-thirds of the rock, or position the rock so that it looks as though there's more rock below, even if there isn't. Planting takes time, carefully scooping out holes between the rocks to position the plants. Spread a mulch of coarse gravel that matches the rocks (available at aquarium stores). Mulch fills crevices, prevents rot by keeping moisture away from the bases of the plants, keeps roots cool, and retards evaporation.

Because alpine plants suitable for troughs grow slowly, these little rock gardens are long-term projects. The plants can live outside throughout the year, even in cold climates, but they should be placed in the shade of a fence or building in winter to prevent the destructive freeze-thaw cycle from distressing both container and plants. They can also be overwintered in a bright, cool greenhouse or a cold frame.

Permanent Planters

Most permanent planters are constructed of brick, stone, or cement. Some are built of concrete blocks and then faced with stucco or a veneer of stone; others are made of landscaping timbers. Like any permanent structure, a planter needs a good foundation to ensure that it won't settle and buckle or crack under its own weight or as a result of the freeze-thaw cycle in cold-winter areas. Depending on the size, material, subsoil, and region, a foundation can range from tamped earth to poured concrete extending below the frost line. If you're building your own, consult with an experienced builder to determine the best foundation and construction techniques—this will save you time and money in the long run.

Nearly all planters are built without bottoms so that moisture can drain through the native soil. If your soil drains poorly, you'll want to add drainage holes in the sides of the planter or even a system of drainpipe underneath. Large, tall planters may hold enough soil to require additional drainage even if the native soil beneath drains well.

For most purposes, the soil mixture for a planter should be a rich garden topsoil. You can customize the soil mixture to meet the needs of the plants you intend to grow, adding compost or peat moss to make it more moisture-retentive, or sand and gravel to improve drainage for drought-tolerant plants. Consider that small trees, shrubs, and perennials will have to live in these close quarters for many years, not just months, so invest in good topsoil and amendments—it's a major undertaking to dig out and replace poor soil later.

Planting a permanent planter is not so different from planting in a garden. Let the soil settle for at least several days before you plant. Water it thoroughly to see if there are any low spots, and add additional soil to make it level. The final soil level should be several inches below the top of the planter; otherwise a heavy rainfall will wash out soil, exposing plant roots. A mulch of coarse gravel can also protect against this kind of planter "erosion."

Water Gardens

Technically, most home water gardens could be considered container gardens—the water is contained in a preformed fiberglass or plastic pool or in a flexible plastic liner. We'll restrict ourselves, however, to rather more modest aboveground water gardens. For these, anything that holds sufficient water is a candidate for a container—ceramic vessels, plastic tubs, wooden barrels, even terra-cotta pots whose drainage holes have been plugged.

Water gardening is a specialized pursuit, and we recommend that you consult local experts or read books devoted to the subject. In general, you'll need to tailor your water garden to your space and conditions. Most water plants require at least a half day's sunlight to perform well. Aquatic plants do best in different depths of water; hardy water lilies, for example, prefer the soil surface in which they are planted to be 6 to 16 inches beneath the water surface.

Plant aquatic plants in plastic if the pot is submerged or in terra-cotta if it rises above the water. A heavy loam garden soil is best—don't use soilless mixes or amend soil with perlite, vermiculite, or organic materials, which will float away. Position the plant's roots and crown in the soil as directed by the nursery or mail-order supplier (most include planting instructions), and cover the soil surface with a layer of coarse gravel to hold it in the pot when under water. Add fertilizer tabs specially formulated for aquatic plants. Fill the "pond" container (half-barrel, for instance) and let it sit for several days to allow any chlorine in the water to dissipate. Then lower the plants to the correct depth, using bricks or empty pots as platforms to adjust the height.

Aquatic plants need to be protected during cold winter months. Most can survive in a sunny window or porch during the winter; some, such as water lilies, can be packed in moist peat moss and stored in a cool place (approximately 35° to 50° F) over winter.

Caring for Container Gardens

To keep your newly planted containers healthy and flourishing, it's necessary to establish a maintenance routine. As for gardens grown in the ground, you need to attend to watering, fertilizing, and pruning. Most annuals excepted, container-grown plants also require repotting periodically. And, depending on your climate, you may have to take special measures in winter.

Watering

The most important chore of the container gardener is watering. No two gardeners face exactly the same conditions. You may need to haul out the watering can once a day to soak the potted geraniums on a sunny balcony, while your neighbor waters the containers on her shady terrace every third day and her husband checks his collection of cacti and succulents every Saturday. Your climate, the time of year, rainfall, and humidity, as well as the type of plants you grow and the sizes and types of containers in which you grow them, will determine how often you need to water.

A soft spray of water from a fine rosette on a watering can or an attachment to a hose is the best way to water containers. A strong stream of water can wash soil out of the pot and away from the roots. Water slowly so that you moisten the soil in the entire pot. Let the water percolate through the pot gradually until it begins to seep through the drainage hole. If only the top few inches of the soil get wet, roots will concentrate there, rather than making use of all the soil in the pot. Many gardeners like to fill the saucers underneath pots about halfway with fine gravel. Excess water collects in the gravel so that the pots aren't sitting in a pool of water. The water in the gravel evaporates during the heat of the day, increasing beneficial humidity around the leaves of the plant above.

Observation is the key to effective watering. Learn to recognize when your plants need water, and know that they need more water as the mercury climbs and as they increase in size. Be especially vigilant with hanging baskets and small containers in exposed areas during the heat of midsummer. A good rule of thumb is to water when the top 2 inches of soil in a pot feels dry. Moist soil is heavier than dry soil, so the weight of a pot is an excellent indicator of its moisture level. If the tips of leaves begin to brown, that's a symptom of water stress. Wilting is another blatant sign. It's also important to watch for signs of too much moisture, such as yellowing leaves, particularly for plants in very large pots made of a nonporous material.

Make it a habit to check containers in the morning, when plants should be at their freshest. It's normal to see a little flagging at midday during warm weather; plants wilt slightly when they shut down to conserve energy. Don't reach for the hose immediately. Wait to see if they perk up as the sun sets, especially if the soil in their pots is still moist to the touch. It will be even more difficult for most plants to absorb more water if their soil is soggy. To reduce midday stress on new transplants, mist the foliage or provide temporary shade.

If you are the forgetful sort, spend much time away from home, or have a great many containers, you may want to invest in a drip-irrigation system. Linked by a network of tubes, each container (including hanging ones) is served by one or more emitters that drip water onto the soil. Hooked up to a timer that doles out the water on a predetermined schedule, such a system is nearly foolproof.

It may take a summer to learn just how much water is ideal for your plants in your conditions. Experience is the best teacher. Everybody makes mistakes; who hasn't been distracted one hot day and ended up incinerating the marigolds?

Fertilizing

Container plants soon use up the nutrients in their limited supply of soil and need regular feeding. A well-balanced fertilizer is adequate for most container-grown plants. The ratio of the three most important elemental nutrients, nitrogen, phosphate, and potassium, is listed on the bag. A 7-10-7 fertilizer, for example, will contain, by weight, 7 percent nitrogen, 10 percent phosphate, and 7 percent potassium. In a balanced fertilizer, the percentages of all three are more or less equal. Some plants do best when fed a specific ratio of the three main elements, as well as other minerals in smaller amounts. Special fertilizers are marketed for roses, succulents, vegetables, and acid-loving plants. These can be used on their own or in combination with a more generic plant food.

Fertilizers come in several forms. Granular fertilizers are sprinkled on the surface of the soil, scratched in, and carried down to the roots during successive waterings. These are the least useful for container plants because they have a tendency to burn roots in the upper portions of the soil. Some gardeners, however, successfully mix granular fertilizers into the soil mix before potting.

Water-soluble fertilizers are dissolved in water and delivered to the plant by watering can or hose attachment. Their nutrients are absorbed not only into the soil but also by the leaves of the plants that are wetted by the spray. Before applying a water-soluble fertilizer, give plants a good soaking with plain water. Roots in dry soil are more likely to suffer fertilizer burn.

Slow-release fertilizers are a boon to busy people. Applied once at the beginning of the season, they break down gradually, delivering nutrients over a period of three to nine months or so, depending on the type and temperatures (the higher the temperature, the faster the release).

Fertilize first when you plant. Some gardeners apply a weak solution of a water-soluble balanced fertilizer before transplanting, with the hope that it will reduce the shock to plants of being moved. Others apply a similar dilute solution when the new transplants are first watered in their new containers. A "rooting and blooming" fertilizer—high in phosphate—applied at or near transplanting time promotes vigorous rooting and, ultimately, a more robust, floriferous plant.

After planting, feed container plants on a regular basis. The timing is up to you, but every two weeks throughout spring and summer is a good plan (unless you're relying on slow-release fertilizers). Pay close attention during hot weather in midsummer, when plants are growing quickly. Confined in tight quarters and competing for vital nutrients, they are especially vulnerable to stress by heat and drought. Timely feeding will keep them healthy and blooming.

Always follow recommendations for dosage on the fertilizer label. Never overdo it—too much fertilizer can harm or even kill plants. In addition, salt by-products in the solution can build up in the soil and on the surface of the pot. These salts can also injure roots.

CARING for Container Gardens 417

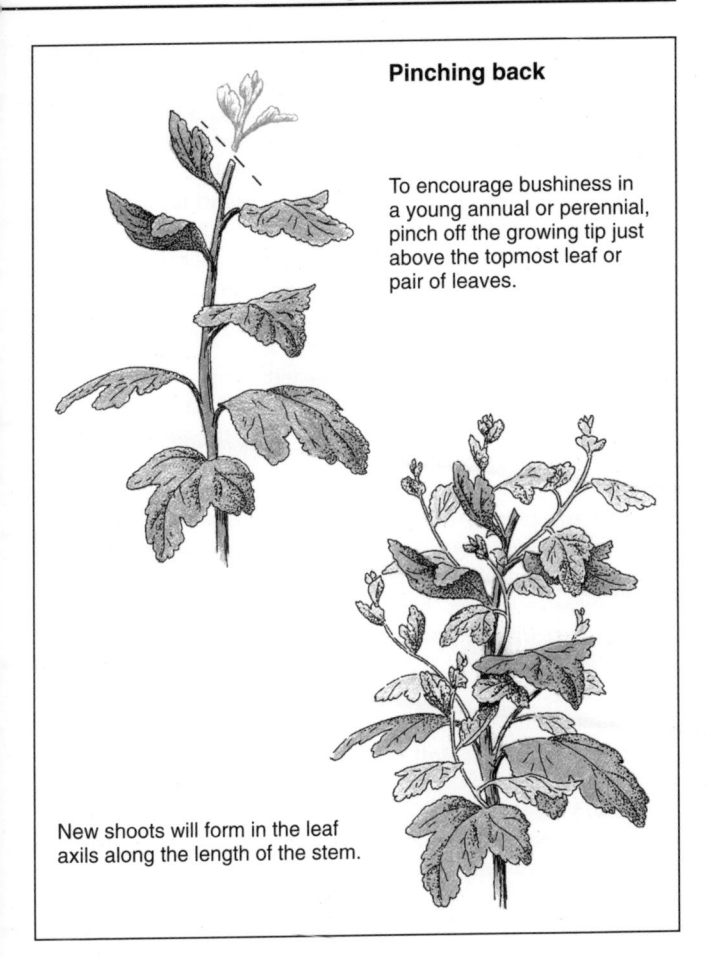

Pinching back

To encourage bushiness in a young annual or perennial, pinch off the growing tip just above the topmost leaf or pair of leaves.

New shoots will form in the leaf axils along the length of the stem.

Pruning

Many annuals and perennials benefit from pruning or pinching. Timely snips can promote bushy growth and more or larger flowers; they can encourage plants to flower a second time; and they can restore plants that are too leggy, have outgrown their allotted space, or have taken on unsightly shapes.

A number of annuals should be pinched when they are transplanted to their display pot. When the growth tip at the end of a stem is removed, the plant will form additional shoots on the stem, producing a fuller, bushier plant as shown in the drawing above. (Many perennials react the same way.) Removing flowers and buds at the same time allows the plant to concentrate its energies in forming shoots and roots. It may take some resolve to break off that first flower at the stem, but it will reward you a hundredfold in the months to come.

Petunias provide an excellent example of the benefits of early pinching. Left alone, a petunia will grow just a few stems with a few flowers on each stem. Properly pinched petunias have been known to produce more than a dozen stems with as many as a hundred blossoms at a time. Other plants that respond well to pinching at planting time include geraniums, coleus, marigolds, zinnias, calendula, salvias, ageratum, and dusty-miller. Some annuals, such as impatiens, form multiple branches on their own; these "self-branching" plants rarely need pinching.

During the course of the growing season, most flowering plants (annuals and perennials) benefit from the regular removal of spent blossoms, a procedure called deadheading. Using your thumb and forefinger, sever the spent blossom where it meets the stem. The biological mission of most annuals is to bloom profusely, set seed, and die. Deadheading prevents the plant from setting seed, thereby encouraging it to continue blooming. Annuals that benefit from deadheading include petunias, marigolds, salvias, geraniums, and calendulas. Some plants drop their blossoms unaided. Among these "self-cleaning" annuals are impatiens, Madagascar periwinkle, lobelia, zinnia 'Classic', sanvitalia, sweet alyssum, and portulaca.

At some point during the summer, many ornamental plants look leggy and worn out. To promote flowering, cut the entire plant back by half and fertilize immediately. Plants that appreciate this treatment include petunias, California poppies, lobelias, sweet alyssum, flowering tobacco, and pansies. If your plants are going strong and show no signs of slowing down, there's no need to cut them back.

Additional pruning for annuals and perennials is done to regulate growth, correct misshapen growth, or remove damaged or diseased material. (Turn plants regularly so that each side gets equal exposure to the sun; otherwise they'll become lopsided as they grow toward the sun.) Experience is the best teacher here; don't be afraid to wield the pruning shears, but learn from the consequences of your cuts. If plants have sufficient light, water, and nutrients, your pruning chores should be minimal.

Repotting

Most healthy perennials eventually grow too big for their containers. Some do so rapidly, in a single season or even sooner; others may live happily for years before suffering from cramped quarters. (If you've chosen containers for annuals with the mature size of the plants in mind, they won't need repotting during their single season of glory.)

It's time to repot when you see signs of overcrowding—roots growing through the drainage hole, reduced growth and flowering, and drought stress (a pot full of roots is difficult to keep moist). To confirm that a plant needs repotting, moisten the soil thoroughly, let it drain, then gently slide the root ball out of the pot. If it won't come easily, run a knife or thin spatula between the container wall and root ball and try again. Don't yank on the stem; in fact, don't handle it at all. Support the root ball as it comes out of the pot, and handle the plant by the root ball afterward. Extracting plants from larger containers or from containers filled with several plants can be trickier—try to disturb root balls as little as possible.

It's time to move to a larger container if the roots fill the entire container and are beginning to circle the outside wall. Cut away tangled or encircling roots with a sharp knife or pruning shears. If you remove more than a small fraction of the plant's roots, cut back the plant's top growth by a similar amount. Plants that aren't ready for repotting may benefit from "topdressing." Just remove the top few inches of soil from their pots and replace with rich, new soil.

As mentioned previously, the rule of thumb is that the new pot should be no more than 2 inches wider and deeper than the old. Soak terra-cotta pots as already described; cover drainage holes with clay chards or wire screen. Add enough soil to the bottom of the pot to position the top surface of the root ball at least an inch below the top of the pot's rim. Gently place the root ball on the fresh soil. Center it in the pot, and work fresh potting soil between it and the pot walls, tamping it firmly with your fingers. (If the plant was off-center or leaned in its old pot, position it in the new pot to correct those faults.)

If the transition is a smooth one—without the trauma of the root ball falling apart—you may not need to do any pruning, although you should consider pinching off buds and flowers so that the plant will concentrate its energies on developing roots and shoots. Water the already moist soil thoroughly with a weak solution of soluble fertilizer. Keep the plant out of direct sunlight and wind for a few days, and mist the foliage if you notice wilting.

At some point, you may wish to call a halt to the progression of ever-larger pots required by certain plants. A wide range of perennials—daylilies, hostas, primroses, black-eyed Susans, irises—can be divided when they grow too large for repotting. Just remove them from the old pot, split them into clumps of a size you're comfortable with, and pot them up as you would a new plant. (Spare divisions are often welcomed by gardening friends.) It's usually easiest to divide plants at the beginning or end of the growing season, before shoots and foliage have appeared or after you've cut them back. If you divide in the fall, make sure hardy plants have enough time to establish new growth and harden it off before the onset of winter.

Not all pot-bound plants need immediate repotting. Some succulents continue to thrive in what seem like inadequate quarters. Some bulbous plants, including alstroemeria, agapanthus, crinum, and amarcrinums, flower best when they are crowded. Even so, there comes a time over a period of several years when they need to be divided or moved up to a larger pot. That chore is normally best saved for late winter or spring.

Controlling Pests and Diseases

Potted plants are subject to the same pests and diseases as are plants in the garden. They are more vulnerable to some and less vulnerable to others. Some plants, no matter how perfect your care, are prone to various pests and diseases. You must decide whether it is worth the fight each year.

Vigilance—prevention, early identification of problems, and quick treatment—is critical for controlling pests and diseases. Pay attention to your plants, learn their growth habits, and become attuned to signs of stress. This sort of observation can be easier for container-grown plants than for those in the garden—there may be fewer plants, and in their separate pots, they are more readily seen.

In general, it's easier to discover the damage done by pests and diseases than to identify the culprits—the insect you see resting on the tattered leaf may not be the one that did the chewing. Likewise, different diseases often manifest similar symptoms. Knowledgeable nursery staff and county extension agents are invaluable assistants for identifying problems and providing specific solutions.

The container gardener who forgets to water regularly will soon discover that drought-stressed plants are more susceptible to insect damage. Insects commonly encountered on container plants include whiteflies, spider mites, aphids, earwigs, mealybugs, various caterpillars, and Japanese beetles. Other insects may pose problems for specific plants or in specific regions of the country.

Whenever possible, choose an environmentally safe method of treatment. Insecticidal soaps are the first choice of many gardeners to control most chewing and sucking insects. Some insecticides, such as pyrethrum and rotenone, are derived from natural sources. (While "natural," these products are often toxic to humans, animals, and birds and must be handled with care.) Systemic insecticides, which are absorbed into the tissues of the plant, are useful against most chewing and sucking insects. Don't use them on plants you intend to eat.

Biological warfare is sometimes possible, using products such as *Bacillus thuringiensis* (Bt), a toxin-producing bacterium that poisons various caterpillars. In addition, you can import or encourage beneficial insects such as ladybugs and praying mantises, which attack other pests. (Broad-spectrum insect sprays will kill the good insects as well as the bad and should be used only as a last resort.) Birds are also allies to be encouraged.

Plant diseases are largely caused by fungi, bacteria, and viruses. Symptoms appear on roots, stems, and foliage, depending on the disease and conditions. Fungal diseases are at their worst during hot, humid weather. These diseases flourish when foliage remains damp overnight, so try to keep plant leaves dry by watering in the morning and allowing the sun to dry them. A sulfur-based spray or powder, an organic treatment, can control an outbreak. Bacterial diseases are difficult to control; the best course may be to destroy affected plant parts or entire plants. When pruning off infected stems, be sure to sterilize the shears in alcohol after each cut. Viral diseases are best dealt with by controlling the insects that carry them; plants are often beyond help once they've succumbed. Wash your hands after disposing of infected plants so that you won't spread the disease.

Potted plants are somewhat safer from some garden pests than are plants grown in the ground. Handpick snails and slugs that reach your prize pots; use commercial bait or beer—whatever your favorite method of destruction—when conditions warrant. Check under pot rims and saucers where these pests might hide by day. Most containers are relatively safe from burrowing and tunneling animals such as moles, voles, ground squirrels, and mice. You may have to fence or adopt other strategies to thwart deer, raccoons, squirrels, and other pests of your region.

Wintering Over

Unless you live in one of the warmer areas of the United States, where temperatures stay well above freezing year-round, you are likely to want to grow plants that won't be able to survive the chill or freezing temperatures of your winter. Lucky is the gardener with a spot to keep these plants through the winter.

For some plants, overwintering isn't a concern. There's very little point in saving most annuals from the inevitable completion of their life cycle, although some can be temporarily reprieved, brought indoors for a few more weeks of flowering. On the other hand, tender perennials that are commonly grown as annuals in cold-winter areas are often worth saving. The most common is the geranium; others include various salvias, lavender, fuchsia, and heliotrope. All can be sustained through the winter in a greenhouse, sun porch, or solarium; on a bright windowsill; or even under lights. Many cacti and succulents and some herbs, such as rosemary, also must be moved inside when first frost threatens. Plants in large containers can be a challenge to muscle indoors and to find a space that will accommodate them. Give thought to your energies and accommodations before purchasing these plants.

Once inside, most plants will show signs of stress. Adjusting to lower light levels, reduced humidity, and shorter days, plants typically will drop leaves and cease flowering. Don't make the mistake of force-feeding them fertilizer—it's natural for plants to go into a resting state where little or no new growth is made. You can ease the transition by reducing watering by at least a third. Don't prune (other than removing dead leaves) or fertilize. Increase humidity around plants by setting pots on gravel-filled saucers full of water. Group plants together, mist the foliage, and use a humidifier. Place them away from heat sources such as furnace grates and away from drafts of cold air from outdoors. As spring approaches, increase water, fertilize, and carry out needed maintenance. Prune to rejuvenate and promote bushiness. Topdress, repot, divide, and take cuttings as needed.

Plants confined indoors should also be watched for outbreaks of pests. The most common are spider mites, aphids, whiteflies, and mealybugs. A soapy bath in the kitchen sink or shower should eradicate them. For large, hard-to-move plants, employ a pail and sponge or a spray bottle of insecticidal soap.

Many tender bulbous plants can be wintered over. Some can be dug and their bulbs, corms, or tubers stored in a dark, cool but frost-free basement or cellar. These include dahlias, montbretia, gladioli, acidanthera, cannas, and lilies. Others, such as agapanthus, tulbaghia, oxalis, crinum and amarcrinum, and alstroemeria, can be grown on indoors. Some can be treated either way.

Hardy perennials may weather the winter outdoors, but most need extra protection. Even bone-hardy perennials are more vulnerable to the ravages of cold above ground in their pots. The freeze-thaw cycle can be particularly damaging. Sometimes it is sufficient to move them to the shelter of the north side of a fence or building where insulating snow will accumulate and remain. You can mulch with straw, wood chips, pine boughs, or leaves all around the pot and between groups of pots. The idea is not to keep them warm but to keep them dormant. The roots may survive the cold just fine, only to have new top growth killed when it comes out too soon during a balmy spell in winter. Potted perennials in clay pots can be buried up to the pot rims in the vegetable garden and mulched.

A cold frame provides excellent storage for dormant perennials. Fill the spaces between the pots with mulch or Styrofoam peanuts. Lift the lid on warm days to keep plants from resuming growth prematurely; you can buy temperature-activated devices for cold-frame lids. A cool greenhouse, cellar, or garage can shelter dormant perennials, but make sure night temperatures drop below 50° F to keep them dormant. Finally, you can't forget watering, even in winter. Regularly check all potted perennials, wherever they're overwintering, to make sure they do not dry out completely.

Planting and Caring for Trees and Shrubs

Trees and shrubs usually require a long-term commitment of time (and often a healthy outlay of cash), so it is particularly important to choose plants that are suitable for your climate and for the specific conditions in which you wish to grow them. In some ways, the best advice is to buy plants from a reputable nursery with knowledgeable staff. Ask them which plants are likely to do best for you, and ask them how best to plant and care for them. That said, the following information, and that given in the plant encyclopedia about growing specific plants, will help you succeed.

Certain materials and practices are much the same whether you're growing annuals and perennials in containers or trees and shrubs. Rather than repeat some of these basics here, we recommend that you read the previous chapters on growing annuals and perennials before proceeding with this chapter.

Choosing the Right Plant

One of the attractions of container growing is portability—you can grow plants that wouldn't ordinarily survive local conditions if you have the energy to move them and someplace suitably protected from the elements to move them to. If you live in an area that regularly experiences freezing temperatures and have no sheltered storage space available, you'll have to choose plants that can survive outdoors in winter. Those in the hot, dry climates of the Southwest or the hot, humid climates of the Southeast should look for plants tolerant of those conditions.

Since you can't keep increasing the size of the pot indefinitely, you'll do best to choose trees and shrubs of smaller stature, including dwarf varieties. There's no sense in planting a full-size apple tree, for example, when a dwarf or semi-dwarf form will provide the same flowers, foliage, and fruit.

Some plants that are large at maturity may be suitable for containers if they grow slowly. You can get a lot of good years out of a Hollywood juniper before it gets so big that you have to water it twice a day. Conversely, fast-growing trees such as eucalyptus can provide several years of enjoyment before they outgrow their pots and your energies. Finally, if you're willing to prune regularly and water daily, many trees and shrubs can be trained and grown as bonsai specimens.

Start with healthy young plants sold in 1-gallon or slightly larger nursery containers. Inspect the specimens at the nursery, looking for damage to trunk and branches and for discolored leaves indicating disease or water or nutrient stress. Avoid any plant whose roots are growing out of the bottom of the container, or ask a staff person to slide it out of the pot so you can see if it's root-bound. Reputable nurseries not only offer healthy plants, they're also likely to guarantee their health for a period of time after purchase.

Choosing a Container

If you start with young specimens, most trees or shrubs will need to be repotted several times over the years. A newly purchased dwarf fruit tree growing in a 5-gallon plastic or fiber pot may eventually require a half whiskey barrel or wooden planter that holds as much as 30 to 40 gallons of soil. Along the way it will need a number of containers, each only inches wider and deeper than the last. Starting or repotting a tree or shrub in a container that is larger demands careful attention to watering to avoid problems.

Because trees and shrubs should never lack for moisture, the best containers are usually wood, which helps keep heat buildup and subsequent moisture loss and stress to a minimum. Planters constructed of rot-resistant woods such as redwood, cedar, or cypress and provided with adequate drainage holes are excellent choices. If you use wood treated with preservatives, make sure the preservatives are thoroughly dry before planting (wait a month if possible), and protect your eyes and skin when building the container. Square planters, either painted or left to weather to a silver-gray, are longtime favorites for larger tree and shrub specimens. These planters must last a long time—build them well.

For young plants and small mature plants, an old-fashioned bushel basket or nail keg is suitable. Large terra-cotta or ceramic pots are handsome, but they are more easily damaged when you're moving a heavy specimen around and are subject to cracking if left exposed to freezing temperatures. Cement or cast-stone containers work well and can have a pleasing appearance, although they make an already heavy combination of soil and plant even heavier. Plastic pots are lightweight but are often nondescript—you can hide one inside a more decorative container such as a wicker basket. Long-term exposure to the elements (especially sunlight) can make some plastics brittle.

When choosing or building a container, remember that you may need to move it to shelter in winter or summer. You can easily add heavy-duty casters or wheels to a wooden container before you add soil. It's nearly impossible to do so later. Some gardeners position the container on a sturdy but unobtrusive rolling pallet made of rot-resistant wood.

Potting Soil

A pot-grown tree or shrub depends on a relatively small amount of soil for all its needs, so it requires good soil. Soil recommendations for particular plants are noted in the encyclopedia section of this book; in addition, seek advice from the nursery from which you purchase the plant.

In general, commercial or homemade soilless potting mixes, which usually contain vermiculite or perlite for good drainage and peat moss for moisture retention, may not be rich enough to sustain growth over a number of years. To these, add anywhere from a third to a half of additional organic matter such as compost, leaf mold, or well-rotted manure. Adding large amounts of organic matter can retard drainage; supplement the mix with coarse sand or small gravel to restore drainage. Topsoil mixes vary widely; you may need to supplement them, but with what and how much depends on the nature of the mix and the plant it must support. Remember that plants with limited moisture needs require a more sharply drained mix than others.

Planting

Early spring is the best time to plant a tree or shrub. Deciduous and evergreen plants both are best potted up before they break dormancy; they will suffer less stress and will wilt less then. If deciduous plants have leafed out or evergreens have begun active growth, pot in a shady spot during the cool part of the day.

The planting techniques for trees and shrubs are similar to those outlined for annuals and perennials. Water the plant thoroughly before removing it from its current container. Soak a bare-root specimen for several hours in a solution of tepid water and about one-quarter the recommended dosage of a balanced, all-purpose liquid fertilizer. If you're planting in terra-cotta, soak the new pot in water so that it doesn't draw moisture from the potting soil.

Remove a container-grown plant from its pot, taking care to support the root ball as well as the trunk. Add enough soil to the new pot to position the top surface of the root ball at least 1 inch below the pot's rim, and position the root ball in the container. Work soil around the root ball and firm it in place; water thoroughly, then add more soil to spots that have settled. If you're transplanting a large, heavy specimen, take care not to damage the root ball, trunk, or branches—enlist some help to make handling easier. Set the root ball gently in the pot. Dropping it can collapse the root ball, damage roots, or crack the pot.

Bare-root plants are handled much the same way. When positioning the plant, be careful that the soil reaches no higher than it did in the growing field—usually the previous soil line is apparent as a ring around the base of the stem. This is especially important for fruit trees that have been grafted onto dwarfing rootstock. The graft, which appears as an obvious bulge on the trunk, should be 2 to 3 inches above the surface of the soil. Otherwise, the part above the graft may take root and grow, undoing the dwarfing characteristics of the rootstock. Once the plant is positioned, work soil around the roots to eliminate air pockets, firm in place, water, and fill in settled spots.

Watering

Watering chores will vary with the type of tree or shrub, the time of year, the soil mixture, and the size of the pot. While it may not be necessary to water on a regular schedule, particularly for large containers, you should check moisture levels routinely. Don't let the soil dry out completely between waterings. And don't let it get too moist—soggy soil can starve the plant of oxygen and can lead to root rot. To check, dig down several inches with your fingers to feel how much moisture is still in the soil. A large specimen in a large container will not have as much problem with evaporation as a small plant in a small pot. The larger tree or shrub will use more moisture to support its leaves, but the larger root ball will stay cooler.

When you water, do so slowly and thoroughly, letting the water sink in all the way to the bottom of the container. Avoid superficial sprinklings that moisten only the surface of the soil. You can conserve moisture and keep your watering duties to a minimum by mulching the soil surface with bark chips, large gravel, or similar material. A living mulch of annuals can also shade the soil. These plants will require moisture, of course, but they will root very shallowly and not interfere with the roots of the tree or shrub.

Continue watering during autumn and winter. Evaporation from soil is much slower during cool weather, but during unseasonable warm-ups in the winter months, unwatered plants will be stressed. The effects may not become apparent until they resume growth in the spring. Fall and winter water is especially important for evergreens, whose foliage continues to transpire, albeit at a reduced rate; the foliage is also vulnerable to drying winter winds. If your trees and shrubs are left outside, rain and snowfall may provide enough water; if not, you'll need to supplement what nature provides.

Fertilizing

A potted tree or shrub cannot send out roots in search of nutrients the way one in the garden can, so you must provide it a steady diet. Use a balanced fertilizer (a 5-10-10 formula, for example) or one designed specifically for the plant you're growing. Whether you opt for a granular fertilizer, a water-soluble fertilizer, or a slow-release type depends on your preference and the plant's. Granular fertilizers may burn roots near the soil surface. Liquid fertilizers are easy to measure and less likely to burn.

If you don't choose a slow-release fertilizer, which works for periods of three to nine months or so, you'll need to feed plants regularly. Some gardeners feed monthly; others feed every two weeks using half the monthly dose. Critical feeding times are when plants resume growth in the spring, when they begin to flower, and during the heat of summer when they are growing vigorously and are most vulnerable to stress. Monitor plants regularly for signs of nutrient deficiency, including slow or abnormal growth, discolored foliage, or failure to flower or fruit. Monitoring is particularly important for plants that flower almost continuously, such as roses or crape myrtles.

Stop feeding in mid-July in northern states and mid-August in southern and southwestern states so that the plants can slow their growth in preparation for winter. Evergreen and deciduous trees and shrubs wintering outdoors or indoors as well as tropicals that will winter indoors all need a rest.

Mineral salts from fertilizers accumulate in the soil and on the pot edges, and they can be damaging to roots and cause leaves to brown at the tips. If a buildup becomes apparent, you can flush these salts from the soil by trickling water from a hose slowly through the pot; let it run for as long as half an hour for a large pot. Scrub the salt residue from outside pot walls with a stiff brush.

Repotting

Trees and shrubs started as small plants will need to be moved to larger pots as they grow. How often you'll have to repot depends on how fast the plant grows; when growth begins to slow, check to see if roots have become overcrowded. They may be visible growing through the drainage hole, or you may have to slide the root ball out of the pot to check.

Procedures for repotting are much like those for potting a new plant. Water the root ball thoroughly and let it drain—a moist root ball holds together better than a dry one. Carefully remove the plant from the old pot; avoid pulling on the trunk or injuring the bark. You may require some help to maneuver the heavy root ball of a large specimen. Take great care not to scrape or otherwise damage the bark on the trunk of the tree. If necessary, disassemble the old container to preserve the root ball intact—knock apart a wooden box, cut through a plastic one, or break off a terra-cotta pot.

Feeder roots tend to cluster around the outside walls of the pot, and they may be a tangled mess. Trim tangled roots or those that circle the pot. Some "scruffing" of these roots is actually beneficial—it encourages active rooting into the new soil. If the roots are densely overgrown, you may need to slice off as much as 1 inch from the sides and bottom of the root ball with a sharp knife. (You can avoid this problem by monitoring the root ball regularly and transplanting before roots clog the pot.) When you trim or lose roots, prune a few inches from each branch to help relieve the workload for the roots as they begin to reestablish themselves in the new soil.

The new container can be 2 to 4 inches larger in diameter and several inches deeper than the old. The permissible increase in size becomes larger in proportion to the container. For example, if you're repotting a plant that has outgrown a box 2 feet square and deep, the next container might be 6 to 10 inches larger on each side. Use the same formula of soil mix in which the plant has been growing. Cover the drainage holes with shards or screen, and add enough soil to position the surface of the root ball about 1 inch below the rim of the pot. Avoid dropping the root ball into the new pot. This can cause the root ball to fall apart and injure delicate roots—the less jostling, the better. Add new soil on the sides and firm it in gently. Water immediately, slowly, and thoroughly, letting moisture percolate all the way down until it runs through the drainage holes. Add additional soil in settled areas. Trim any branches damaged during transplanting.

There comes a time when it is no longer possible or practical to move a near-mature specimen to a larger container.

The plant will need to remain in its present container, and you will need to compensate. Topdressing the soil will suffice for several years. In early spring, remove as much as 3 to 4 inches of soil from the top surface of the root ball and replace it with organically enriched new soil.

Later, perhaps six to ten years down the line, a tree or shrub may become root-bound and need further care besides annual topdressing. Growth will be very slow and the flowering may diminish significantly. Take the dormant plant out of its container in early spring and prune the roots back by approximately 20 percent. Cut the top growth back correspondingly. Remove as much soil as possible and replace with a fresh mixture. This should help rejuvenate the specimen and aid in encouraging it to flower or fruit better.

Pruning

Pruning of container-grown trees and shrubs is similar to that for their counterparts in the garden. Because growth may be somewhat slower in pots, and because the plants you grow may be dwarf varieties, pruning may not be as severe as for garden-grown plants.

You should prune to maintain shape, to remove dead and diseased stems and branches, and to promote vigorous, bushy growth. Some plants will require very little maintenance; others, much more. Most evergreens, for example, need little shaping unless you grow them as topiaries or prefer geometric shapes. Many deciduous plants are also at their best when allowed to assume their natural, graceful shape. These plants, such as flowering almonds or forsythia, are best pruned only to remove dead branches or to promote bushiness.

Some pruning can be avoided if you turn plants every few weeks during active growth so that they receive even amounts of sun on all sides. This helps prevent lopsided growth, bare spots, and leaning. Regular turning is especially important for evergreens, which may develop "bald" spots on a side that continually faces away from the sun.

The best time to prune most deciduous shrubs and trees is after they have flowered. Many of them set flower buds on old wood. If you prune them in spring before they flower, you are cutting off most of the current year's flowers. You can induce full, bushy growth in many trees and shrubs by pinching off the growing tips starting in the spring and, if necessary, continuing through the summer. Simply remove the bud tips on the main vigorous branches with your thumb and forefinger, much as you would for a petunia. This encourages the formation of new shoots both at the growth tip and farther back on the stem. Deadheading the spent flowers of ornamental flowering trees and shrubs, such as lilacs, spireas, or roses, helps the plant concentrate its energies on developing roots and shoots rather than seeds.

Controlling Pests and Diseases

Container-grown trees and shrubs are subject to the same ailments and pests that commonly afflict their garden-grown counterparts and will require about the same care. Because they are generally smaller, container-grown trees and shrubs can be simpler to monitor and to treat. To prevent fungal diseases, for instance, it can be easier to keep water off leaves, and you can move containers around to provide plenty of air movement around the foliage.

The comments on pest and disease control for annuals and perennials given in the previous chapter apply also to trees and shrubs. Remember that drought-stressed plants are most likely to be affected. Use the most effective, least toxic controls; don't use systemic pesticides on plants that bear edible fruit. Follow instructions on the labels. Don't forget that organic controls can be toxic to humans and animals; treat them with respect.

Wintering Over

Dealing with winter is probably the major concern of container gardeners who wish to grow trees and shrubs. It's one thing to stash a half-dozen pots of dormant perennials in your garage or basement, quite another to figure out what to do with a 10-foot-tall tree and its half-barrel and 200 pounds of soil. Even if you have the space, it's not an easy task to wrestle a huge container-grown specimen indoors. Some gardeners use dollies; some use teenagers.

You can, of course, choose plants that will survive your winters outdoors. But remember that the entire root ball of a container plant is exposed to rapid freezes and thaws throughout the winter. This can stress the plant, damage roots, and even heave the plant out and away from the sides of the pot. Winter winds can shake the root ball, damage limbs, and desiccate tissue. As mentioned in a previous chapter, some experts suggest that container-grown plants intended for overwintering outdoors should have a hardiness rating at least one zone and sometimes two greater than yours. (Zone 6 gardeners should choose plants hardy in zone 5 or 4.)

Classic "tub plants" such as oleander, citrus trees, hibiscus, bougainvillea, and other tropical and subtropical plants need to be moved indoors as winter approaches. Even gardeners in relatively mild-winter areas may have to move some plants indoors. Tropicals are often wintered over in greenhouses, solariums, or a bright window. Make every effort to increase humidity around them to ease the shock of the move. Many will drop some leaves or cease flowering. Don't be alarmed; they are getting ready for a well-earned rest. Most will not lose all their leaves but will shed some to compensate for lower light levels and correspondingly less energy output.

Trees and shrubs that are marginally hardy in your area, or those that survive a zone or two farther south, will also need indoor shelter. To thrive, some deciduous plants require two to three months in temperatures below 50° F; a cool basement or cellar might provide this. (A cool dormant winter is as important in the life cycle of deciduous plants as a warm summer—the rest revitalizes them in preparation for the production of flowers and fruit in the spring.) Nectarines and some peach varieties need this indoor cold treatment in more northerly areas. The trees and shrubs that require this indoor cooling vary from region to region.

Plants that move indoors are relatively easy to care for. Continue routine maintenance such as removing dead leaves and watching for outbreaks of spider mites and aphids. Don't apply fertilizer until after the first of the year, in most cases. Cut back watering as well, but don't let the plants dry out completely.

There are a range of measures you can take for the trees and shrubs you choose to winter outdoors. At the very least, move them to a shady spot, protected from wind. There, the soil will stay cold and thaw more slowly and gently when warmer weather arrives. In autumn after most of the leaves have dropped, wrap the trunks with a commercial tree wrap to help prevent loss of moisture and sunscald on the bark. If the plants can be moved, storage in an unheated shed or garage offers protection from wind and some moderation of temperature fluctuations.

Several additional steps of protection are prudent. Insulate the container by ringing it with bales of hay or bags of leaves. Stuff air pockets in the ring with loose leaves or straw. (You can also line the inside of a container with Styrofoam insulation when you plant.) Rather than pack pots in insulation, you can bury them up to their rims in a garden bed or bury the root ball itself; either way, mulch the surface generously.

To minimize damage from wind, pull the branches of deciduous trees together and bind them with twine or rope, or cover them with burlap. Evergreens such as upright junipers or spruces can be similarly protected from wind desiccation and damage. You can further decrease water loss in broad-leaved evergreens with an antitranspirant spray.

For complete outdoor protection, build a cage around each plant. Use strong posts to anchor the cage, and encircle the plant with chicken wire or chain-link fencing. Tie the branches together, erect the cage, then fill it with leaves or straw; a covering of burlap or cloth is optional. Moisture can penetrate from above, but trunks and limbs are protected from the extremes of weather.

Make it a weekly habit to check the moisture level of overwintering trees and shrubs, whether they're in the basement, in an unheated garage, or outside. Evaporation is slow during cold periods, but roots shouldn't be allowed to dry out. They mustn't be kept soggy, just barely moist. In spring, gradually remove the insulation around the plants. If the branches have been covered, expose them gradually to sunlight.

Appendices

Hardiness Zone Map

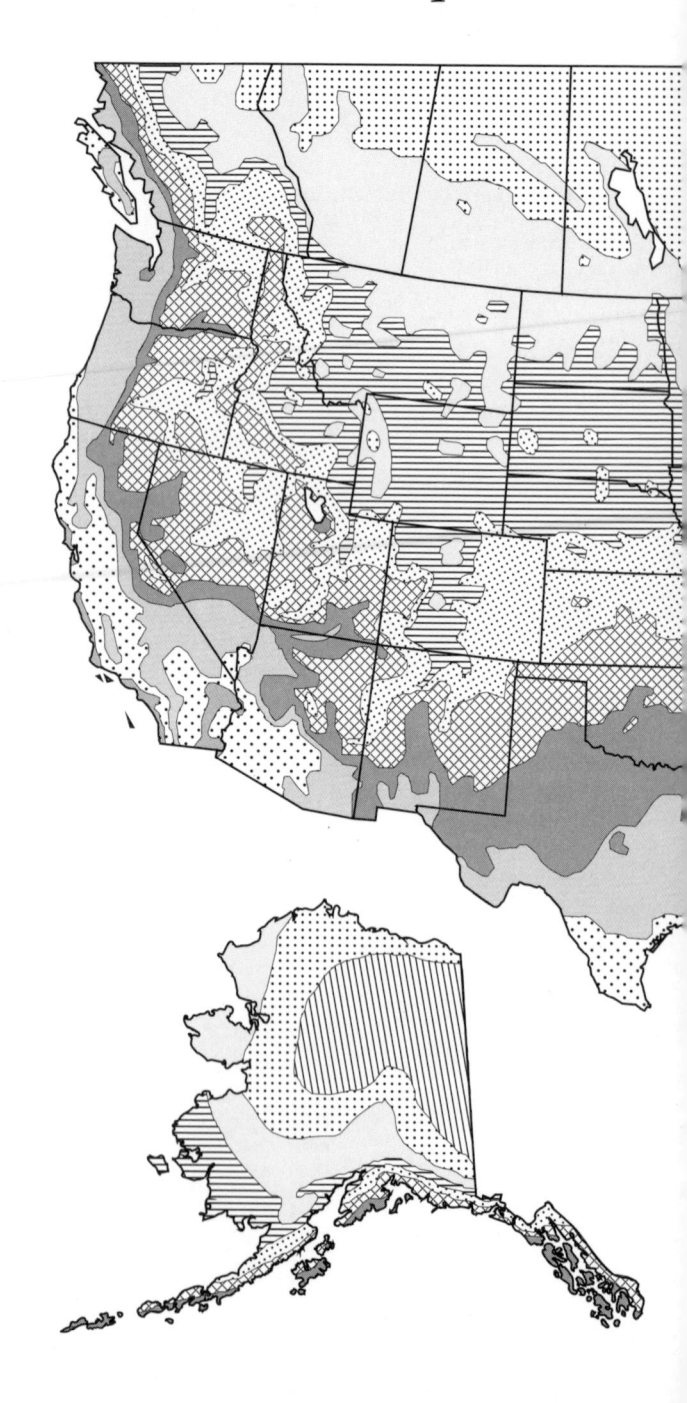

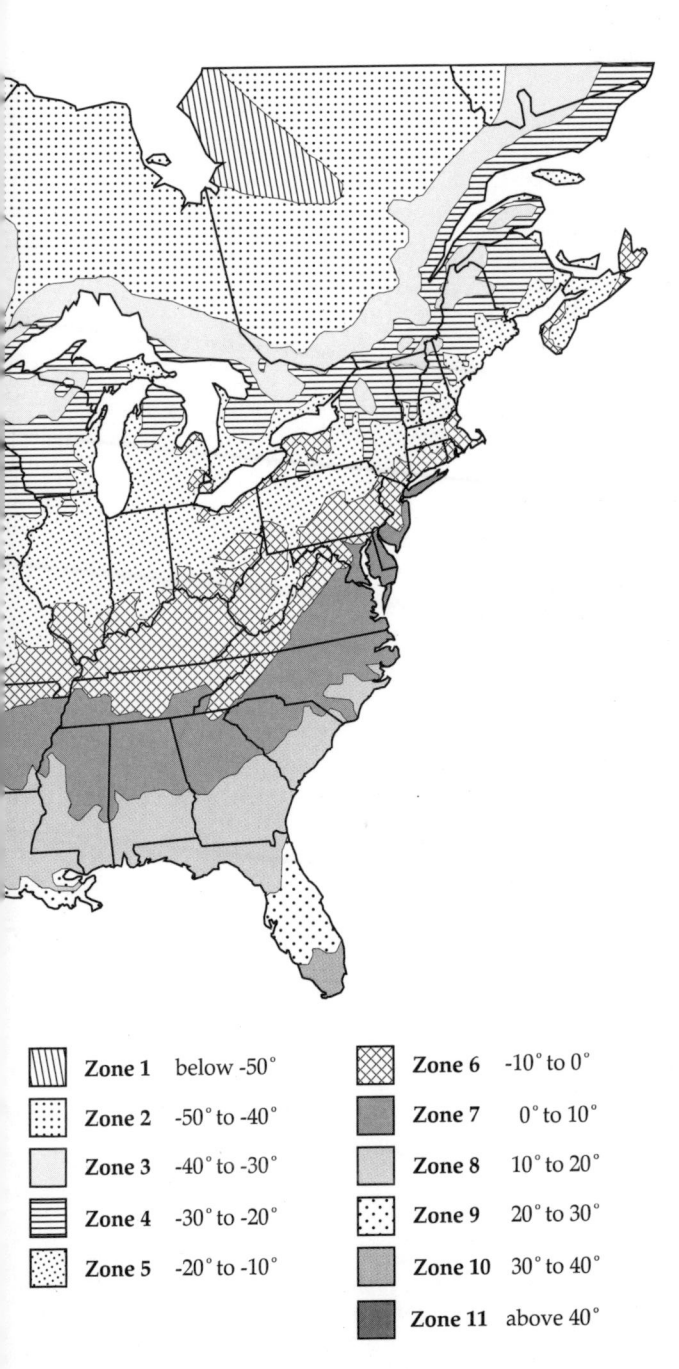

	Zone 1	below -50°		**Zone 6**	-10° to 0°
	Zone 2	-50° to -40°		**Zone 7**	0° to 10°
	Zone 3	-40° to -30°		**Zone 8**	10° to 20°
	Zone 4	-30° to -20°		**Zone 9**	20° to 30°
	Zone 5	-20° to -10°		**Zone 10**	30° to 40°
				Zone 11	above 40°

Photo credits

Allen Armitage: 127A, 129B, 136B

Liz Ball/PhotoNats: 141B, 143B, 180B

Rita Buchanan: 134B, 154A, 159B, 172B

Cole Burrell: 47, 129A, 130A, 140A, 152B, 170-171, 175A

Rosalind Creasy: 7, 10, 55, 75, 83, 87, 89, 90-91, 93A, 109A, 116B, 133B, 139B, 144B, 146B, 178A, 199B

Greg Crisci/PhotoNats: 153A

Michael Dirr: 191B

Wally Eberhart/PhotoNats: 155B

John Elsley: 21, 46, 70A, 112A, 128B, 138A, 151B, 159A, 162B, 176B

Tom Eltzroth: 12, 15, 20, 44A, 52, 66-67, 88, 100A, B, 101A, B, 103B, 104B, 105B, 108B, 112B, 115B, 116A, 118A, 119A, B, 120B, 121A, 123A, B, 147A, 154B, 156A, 158A, 163B, 165A, 167A, 169A, B, 179A, B, 184B, 185B, 188B, 194A, 198A

Derek Fell: 4, 5, 13C, 16, 17, 18, 22, 25, 32, 34, 35, 37, 44B, 50, 51, 59, 85B, 102A, 103A, 106A, 113B, 124-125, 130B, 150B, 158B, 160-161, 162, 164B, 168A, 175B, 176A, 182-183, 186A, B, 187B, 189A, 191A, 192A, 193A, 195A, 196B, 197B, 200A

Charles Marden Fitch: 71B, 94A, B, 98-99, 104A, 105A, 109B, 115A, 127B, 146A, 155A, 165B, 166B, 193B, 196A

Jennifer Graylock: 133A

Pamela Harper: 108A, 120A, 131B, 135B, 142A, 145A, 148-149, 150A, 156B, 166A, 167B, 174A, 177A, 181A, 184A, 188A, 197A, 198B, 199A, 201

Kristi Jones: 107B, 117B

Robert E. Lyons/PhotoNats: 142B, 152A

Charles Mann: 6, 9, 11A, B, 13B, 23, 36, 38A, 39, 43B, 54B, 63A, B, 65, 69A, B, 70B, 77, 78, 79A, 80, 81A, B, 82, 122A, 126A, 128A, 131A, 132A, 134A, 135A, 136A, 137A, 138B, 139A, 145B, 163A, 173A, B, 192B

Scott Millard: 144A

John Neubauer: 28, 31, 53, 68A, B, 74, 85A, 86A, B, 92, 111A

Jerry Pavia: 8, 38B, 45, 54A, 56-57, 58A, B, 64, 71A, 79B, 94C, 114B, 117A, 157A, 172A

PhotoSynthesis: 13A, 14, 33, 40, 41, 43A, 48, 49A, B, 72-73, 76A, B, 93B, 102B, 107A, 114A, 121B, 122B, 132B, 137B, 140B, 143A, 164A, 177B, 178B, 180A, 185A, 187A, 190A, 195B, 200B

Ann Reilly/PhotoNats: 106A, 110A, B, 111B, 126B, 141A, 151A, 174B, 181B

Robin Siktberg: 194B

Lauren Springer: 190B

Steven Still: 147B

George Taloumis: 113A, 118B, 153B, 168B, 189B

Virginia Twinam-Smith/PhotoNats: 157B

Linda Yang: 60, 61, 62

Index

Numbers in **boldface** *type refer to pages on which color plates appear*

Acanthus, artist's, 204
Acanthus mollis, **126**
   'Latifolius', 'Oakleaf', 204
Acca sellowiana, 263
Acer
   japonicum 'Aconitifolium',
      'Aureum', 205
   palmatum, **172**, 204–5
   palmatum 'Bloodgood',
      'Dissectum', 'Oshi Beni',
      'Sango Kaku', 205
   shirasawanum 'Aureum', 205
Achillea, 204–5
   clavennae, 206
   'Moonshine', **126**, 206
   taygetea, 206
   tomentosa, 206
Acorus
   calamus 'Variegatus', 272
   gramineus 'Ogon', 272
   gramineus 'Variegatus', **127**, 272
Acquiring plants, 389–96
Adam's-needle, **147**, 383–84
Adiantum
   capillus-veneris, 264
   pedatum, 264
Aeonium arboreum
      'Atropurpureum', 24
Agapanthus, 206–7
   africanus, 207
   orientalis, **150**, 206–7
   orientalis 'Alba', 'Peter Pan',
      'Headbourne', 207
Agave, **184**
   octopus, 208
Agave, 24, 207–8
   americana, 24
   attenuata, **184**, 208
   deserti, 208
   mayonensis, 208
   parryi, 208
   utahensis, 24
   victoriae-reginae, 24, 208
   vilmoriniana, 208
Ageratum, 42
   hardy, **135**, 260–61
Ajuga, 208–9
   pyramidalis, 209
   reptans, **127**, 208–9
   reptans 'Bronze Beauty',
      'Burgundy Glow', 'Catlin's
      Giant', 'Metallica Crispa',
      'Royalty', 'Silver Beauty' or
      'Variegata', 209
   'Tricolor', 228
Allium, 209–10
   schoenoprasum, **128**, 210
Allspice, Carolina, 84
Aloe
   candelabra, 24
   medicinal, 24
   tiger, 24
Aloe, 24
   arborescens, 24
   barbadensis, 24
   variegate, 24
   vera, 24
Aloysia triphylla, **100**, 210–11
Alsophila australis, 264
Alumroot. *See* Coralbells
Alyssum, 48, 49
   sweet, **114**, 312
Alyssum, 312
Amarcrinum, 23
Anemone, 23
Annuals, 19–20, **98–123**
   combined with perennials or
      vines, **6, 13**, 21–22, **23, 35, 44,
      57, 76**
   spacing of, 40
Antigonon leptopus, **162**
   'Album', 211
Antirrhinum, 211–12
   majus, **100**, 212
   majus 'Floral Carpet', 'Rockets',
      'Tahiti', 'Wedding Bells', 212
Arborvitae
   American, **200**, 369–71
   oriental, **201**, 370
Arbutus unedo, **184**, 212–13
   'Compacta', 'Elfin King', 213
Arctotis garden hybrids, **101**
   'Flame', 'Wine', 213
   stoechadifolia var. *grandis*, 213
Arrowhead, 84
   giant, 30
Artemisia, 214
   absinthium 'Lambrook Silver',
      'Valerie Finnis', 214
   'Powis Castle', **128**, 214

Artemisia (Cont.)
  stellerana, 256
  stellerana 'Silverado', 273
Arundinaria
  variegata, 217
  viridistriata, 217
Asparagus, ornamental (asparagus fern), 101, 215
Asparagus, 214–15
  densiflorus 'Myers', 101, 215
  densiflorus 'Sprengeri', 215
Aspidium capense, 265
Asplenium nidus, 265
Aster, purple China, 55
Astilbe, 84, **129**
Astilbe 5 *arendsii* hybrids, **129**, 215–16
  'Bressingham Beauty', 'Bridal Veil', 'Cattleya', 'Deutschland', 'Fanal', 'Glow' ('Glut'), 'Peach Blossom', 'Red Sentinel', 'Rheinland', 'Sprite', 'White Gloria', 216
Athyrium
  goeringianum 'Pictum', **129**, 263
  nipponicum 'Pictum', 263
  otophorum, 263
Avena sempervirens, 274
Azalea, 349–52
  Belgian Indicas, 351
  deciduous species, **178**, 350
  dwarf, 75, 84
  evergreen, **198**, 351–52
  Exbury, 350
  Girard, 351–52
  Glen Dale, 351
  Gumpo, 351
  "hose-in-hose," 351
  Knap Hill, 350
  Kurume 'Coral Bells', 'Hino Crimson', 'Hinodegiri', 'Snow', 'Ward's Ruby', 351
  Mollis, 350
  Northern Lights, 350
  North Tisbury, 352
  Robin Hill, 352
  royal, 350
  Southern Indicas 'Fielder's White', 'Formosa', 'George Lindley Taber', 'Pride of Mobile', 351

Balconies and rooftops, 60–62
Bamboo, 216–18
  black, **195**, 216–17
  clumping, 218
  heavenly, **192**, 322
  running, 216, 217
  yellow-groove, 216–17

Bambusa multiplex 'Alphonse Karr', 218
Barberry, 75, 220–21
  Japanese, **172**, 220
Barrel cactus, 27
Basil, 19, 87
  sweet, common, lemon, 115, 328–29
Bay
  California, **45**
  sweet, **191**, 305
Bear's-breeches, **126**, 204
Begonia, 13, 19, 53, **81**
  fancy-leaved, 83
  fibrous, 83
  strawberry, *see Saxifraga stolonifera*
  tuberous, 48, 83, **150**, 219
  wax, **102**, 218
Begonia, 218–19
  5 *semperflorens-cultorum*, **102**, 218
  tuberhybrida hybrids, **150**, 219
  tuberhybrida 'Non-Stop', 219
Bellflower, 231–32
  Dalmatian, 232
  Serbian, **131**, 232
Berberis, 220–21
  thunbergii, **172**, 220
  thunbergii 'Atropurpurea Nana' or 'Crimson Pygmy', 220, 228
  thunbergii 'Aurea', 'Bonanza Gold', 'Gold Ring', 'Kobold', 'Rosy Glow', 220
Bergenia, heartleaf, **130**, 221
Bergenia cordifolia, **130**, 221
  'Bressingham White', 'Rotblum', 'Silver Light' ('Silberlicht'), 'Sunningdale', 221
Black-eyed Susan, 14, 67
  vine, **169**, 371
Bluebeard, **173**, 234–35
Bonsai, 9, 94, 95, 351
Border jewel, 21
Bottlebrush, lemon, **185**, 229
Bougainvillea, **22**, 72, **162**
Bougainvillea, 221–23
  hybrids, **162**, 222
  hybrids 'Barbara Karst', 'Brilliant Variegated', 'Crimson Lake' or 'Mrs. Butt', 'La Jolla', 'Raspberry Ice' or 'Hawaii', 'San Diego Red', 'Texas Dawn', 222
Boxwood, 91, 225–26
  littleleaf, **185**, 226
Brain cactus, 27
Brassica oleracea, **102**, 223
Broom, Warminster, **174**, 252
Browallia, 83

Browallia speciosa, **103**, 224
Buddleia, 224–25
  alternifolia 'Argentea', 225
  crispa, 225
  davidii, **173**, 224–25
  davidii 5 *fallowiana* 'Lochinch', 225
  davidii 'Harlequin', 225
  'Nanho' series, 225
Bugleweed. *See Ajuga*
Bulbs, 23, **44**, 148–59
Buttercup, Persian, **158**, 347–48
Butterfly bush, **173**, 224–25
Buxus, 225–26
  microphylla, 226
  microphylla var. *japonica*, 226
  microphylla var. *koreana* 'Compacta', 'Green Beauty', 'Winter Beauty', 'Winter Gem', 226
  microphylla var. *koreana* 'Wintergreen', **185**, 226
  microphylla var. *koreana* 5 *sempervirens* 'Chicagoland Green', 'Green Gem', 'Green Mound', 'Green Velvet', 226
  sempervirens 'Suffruticosa', 226
Buying plants, 395–96

Cabbage, 19
  flowering, 223
Cacti, 24, **25**, 26–27
Caladium, 55, 83, **151**
Caladium, 227
  bicolor, 227
  5 *hortulanum* 'Candidum', **151**, 227
Calamintha, 227–28
  grandiflora 'Variegata', 228
  nepeta (or *nepetoides*), **130**, 228
Calamondin, 242
Calendula, 228–29
  officinalis, 89, 228
  officinalis 'Family Circle' mix, **103**
Calla lily, 23, 83, **159**, 385–86
Callistemon, 229
  citrinus, **185**
  citrinus 'Captain Cook', 'Little John', 229
  viminalis, 229
Calonyction aculeatum, 293
Camellia, 230–31
  Ackerman hybrids, 231
  hiemalis 'Shishi Gashira', 'Showanosakae', 231
  japonica, 230–31
  japonica 'Alba Plena', 'C. M. Wilson', 'Elegans', 'Glen 40',
    'Giulio Nuccio', 'Mrs. D. W. Davis', 'Pope Pius IX', 'Purity', 'Shiro Chan', 230
  japonica 'Eugene Lize', **186**
  oleifera, 231
  reticulata, 230
  sasanqua 'Jean May', 'Mine-No-Yuki' ('White Doves'), 'Yuletide', 230–31
Campanula, 231–32
  portenschlagiana, 232
  poscharskyana, **131**, 232
Canna, 23, 48
  water, 29, 84
Canna, 232–33
  5 *generalis*, 232–33
  glauca, 29
  hybrids, 29, **151**, 232–33
  hybrids 'Pfitzer Dwarfs', 'Striped Beauty', 'Wyoming', 233
  'The President', **151**, 233
Capsicum, 233–34
  annuum, 233–34
  annuum 'Aurora', 'Candlelight', 'Fiesta', 'Holiday Cheer', 'Holiday Time', 'Jigsaw', 'Maya', 234
  annuum 'Holiday Chili', **87**
  annuum 'Red Missile', **104**
Cardinal climber, 293
Cardinal flower, 84
Carex morrowii 'Aureo-variegata', **131**, 272–73
Carnation, 257
  border or hardy, 256, 257–58
  See also Dianthus
Carolina jessamine, **165**, 268–69
Carpet bugle. *See Ajuga*
Caryopteris, 236–37
  5 *clandonensis* 'Blue Mist', **173**, 235
  5 *clandonensis* 'Dark Knight', 'Longwood Blue', 'Worcester Gold', 235
Catharanthus roseus, 235
  'Magic Carpet Pink', **104**
Cedar
  Atlas, **94**
  Eastern white, *see* Arborvitae, American
Celosia, 67
Celosia, 236
  argentea, **105**, 236
  var. *cristata*, 236
  var. *plumose*, 236
Ceniza. *See Leucophyllum frutescens*
Centaurea cineraria, 364
Century plant. *See Agave*
Ceratostigma plumbaginoides, **132**, 236–37

Chamaecyparis, 237–38
　obtusa and cultivars, **186**, 237–38
　obtusa 'Coralliformis', 'Crippsii', 'Kosteri', 'Nana', 'Nana Gracilis', 'Torulosa', 237–38
　pisifera 'Boulevard', 'Cyrano-Viridis', 'Nana', 238
　pisifera 'Filifera Aurea Nana', **187**, 238
Chaste tree, **181**, 382–83
Chives, **128**, 210
　oriental, 89
Christmas fern, 265
Christmas rose, 278
Chrysanthemum, 48, **49**, **133**
　florist's or hardy garden, **132**, 239
Chrysanthemum, 239–41
　frustescens, 239
　morifolium, **132**, 239
　multicaule, **105**, 240
　nipponicum, 239
　pacificum, **133**, 240–41
　paludosum, 240
　parthenium, **106**, 241
　parthenium 'Aureum', 241
Cibotium glaucum (*C. chamissoi*), 264
Cinquefoil, Bush, **177**, 342
Citrofortunella mitis, 242
Citrus cultivars, **187**, 242–43
Cleistocactus, 27
Clematis, 243–44
　'Comptesse de Bouchard', 'Duchess of Edinburgh', 'General Sikorski', 'Guernsey Cream', 'Kermesina', 'Polish Spirit', 'Sieboldii', 'Silver Moon', 'The President', 244
　large-flowered hybrids, **163**, 243–44
"Climate," 51–52, 61
Clivia, 23, **152**
Clivia miniata, **152**, 245
Clock vine, 72
Clover, water, 84
Cobaea scandens, **163**, 245–46
　var. *alba*, 246
Cockscomb, **105**, 236
Colchicum, 23
Coleostephus myconis. See *Chrysanthemum multicaule*
Coleus, 19, 83, **106**, 234
Coleus blumei hybrids, 246–47
　'Fiji Red', **106**
Conifers, dwarf, 75, 84, 237. See also Cypress; *Juniperus*; *Taxus*
Conoclinium coelestinum, 260–61
Containers. See Pots and planters
Coralbells, 21, **138**, 281–82

Coral vine, **162**, 211
Coreopsis, 21
　thread-leaved, **133**, 247–48
Coreopsis, 247–48
　rosea, 248
　verticillata, **133**
　verticillata 'Golden Showers', 'Zagreb', 247
　verticillata 'Moonbeam', **235**, 247, 248
Corylus avellana 'Contorts', **174**, 248. See also Harry Lauder's walking stick
Cosmos, 17
　yellow, **107**, 249
Cosmos, 249
　bipinnatus 'Sonata', **235**, 249
　sulphureus, 236
　sulphureus 'Bright Lights', 'Diablo', 'Dwarf Klondike', 'Sunny', 'Sunny Red', 249
　sulphureus 'Lady Bird Orange', **107**
Crab apple, **177**, 316–17
Cranberry bush, European and American, 379
Cranesbill, 21
Crape myrtle, **94**, **176**
Crassula, 25
　arborescens, 25
　falcata, 25
　ovata, 25
Creeping Jennie, **140**, 315
Crocosmia, 249–50
　'Lucifer', **152**, 249–50
Crocus, 23
　autumn, 251
　Dutch or common, **153**, 250–51
　golden, 251
Crocus, 250–51
　ancyrensis 'Golden Bunch', 250
　chrysanthus 'Blue Pearl', 'Cream Beauty', 'Ladykiller', 'Snow Bunting', 251
　speciosus, 251
　vernus 'Little Dorritt', **153**
　vernus 'Peter Pan', 'Pickwick', 'Remembrance', 'Yellow Mammoth', 250
Crown-of-thorns, 25
Cup-and-saucer vine, **163**, 245–46
Cuttings, propagating from, 393–95
Cyathea cooperi, 264
Cyclamen, 23
　florist's, **153**, 251–52
Cyclamen persicum, **153**, 251–52
Cyperus, 84, 86
Cyperus
　alternifolius, 29
　papyrus, 29

Cypress
　false, 237
　Hinoki, 31, **186**, 237–38
　Sawara, **187**, 238
Cypress vine, 293
Cyrtomium falcatum, 264–65
Cytisus, 252–53
　'Allgold', 'Hollandia', 252
　5 *praecox* 'Warminster', **174**, 252
　scoparius 'Moonlight', 252

Daffodils, 23, 48, **64**, **157**, 323, 324–25
　cyclamineus hybrids 'February Gold', 'February Silver', 'Peeping Tom', 325
　double 'Cheerfulness', 'Golden Ducat', 'Tahiti', 325
　jonquilla hybrids 'Suzy', 'Trevithian', 325
　long-cup 'Binkie', 'Carlton', 'Ice Follies', 'Salome', 325
　poeticus hybrid 'Actaea', 325
　tazetta hybrids 'Geranium', 'Paperwhite', 325
　triandrus hybrids 'Hawera', 'Thalia', 325
　trumpet 'Dutch Master', 'Golden Harvest', 'Mount Hood', 'Unsurpassable', 324–25
Dahlia, **17**, 23, **107**
Dahlia, 253–54
　hortensis, 253
　hybrids, **107**, 253
　'Park Princess', 'Piccolo', 'Rigoletto', 253
Daisy, 54, 58, 78, 87
　African, 101, 213
　English, 19
　Gerbera or Transvaal, **109**, 269–70
　Shasta, 239
Daphne, 84, **175**
Daphne, 254–55
　5 *burkwoodii* 'Carol Mackie', **175**, 254
　5 *burkwoodii* 'Somerset', 254
　caucasica 5 *cneorum*, 254
　odora 'Aureo-Marginata', 254
Datil, 384
Davallia trichomanoides, 264
Daylily, 21
　hybrid, **137**, 279–81
Decks, patios and, 53–59
Delosperma, 255
　'Alba', 255
　cooperi, **134**, 255
　nubigena, 255

Dendranthema 5 *grandiflorum*. See *Chrysanthemum* 5 *morifolium*
Designing containers, 35–49
Dianthus, 75, 76
Dianthus, 256–58
　5 *allwoodii* hybrids, **134**, 256
　5 *allwoodii* hybrids 'Alpinus', 'Aqua', 'Doris', 256
　'Bath's Pink', 'Tiny Rubies', 258
　'Black and White Minstrels', 'Dwarf Fragrance', 257
　caryophyllus, 256, 257
　chinensis hybrids, **108**, 257–58
　deltoides, **135**, 258
　gratianopolitanus, 258
　plumarius, 257
Dicksonia antarctica, 264
Diseases, 421, 431. See also Pests and pesticides
Dogwood, 84
Donkey's tail, **71**, 363
Dracaena, 42
Drainage, 4, 8, 10, 11, 74, 402, 404, 406, 408
Duckweed, 86
Dusty-miller, 19, **41**, 42, **120**, 364

Echeveria, 25
Echinocactus grusonii, 27
Echinofossulocactus, 27
Edible gardening, 19, **20**, **63**, 81, 87–89
Eichhornia crassipes, 29
Elderberry, Red, **180**, 360
Elephant's-ear, 84
Entryways, 62–64, 65
Eonymus, 258–60
　fortunei selections, 164
　fortunei 'Coloratus', 'Emerald Gaiety', 'Emerald 'n' Gold', 'Gracilis' or 'Silver Edge', 'Kewensis', 'Sarcoxie', 'Silver Queen', 'Variegatus', 259–60
　fortunei var. *radicans*, 260
　fortunei var. *vegetus*, 260
Eupatorium, 260–61
　coelestinum, **135**, 260–61
　coelestinum 'Alba', 261
Euphorbia milii (Lomi hybrids), 25
Euryops pectinatus, 21
Exacum affine, **108**, 261

Fargesia
　murielae, 218
　nitida, 218
Fatsia, 261–62
　5 *fatshedera lizei*, 262
　japonica, **188**, 262

Feijoa, 262–63
  sellowiana, **188**
  sellowiana 'Coolidge',
    'Nazemetz', 'Pineapple
    Gem', 263
Ferns, 82, 84, 263–65
  asparagus, 84
  bear's-foot, 264
  bird's-nest, 265
  Boston, 83
  Braun's holly, 265
  Christmas, 265
  hare's-foot, 264
  holly, 264–65
  Japanese painted, **129**, 263
  leatherleaf, 265
  maidenhair, 264
  rock, 265
  soft shield, 265
  squirrel's-foot, 264
  sword, **142**, 264
  tassel, 265
  tree, 264
  Western sword, 265
Fertilizing, 40, 405, 415-16
  seedlings, 392
  trees and shrubs, 428
Fescue, blue, **136**
Festuca
  amethystina, 273
  ovina var. *glauca*, **136**
  ovina var. *glauca* 'Elijah's Blue',
    'Sea Urchin', 273
Feverfew, **106**, 241
Ficus, 266–67
  carica, **175**
  carica 'Brown Turkey', 'Kadota',
    'Mission', 266
  pumila, **164**
  pumila 'Minima', 'Variegata', 267
  repens, 267
Fig, 266–67
  common, **175**, 266
  creeping, 91, **164**, 267
Firebush, **136**, 275–76
Firethorn. *See Pyracantha*
Flax, New Zealand, **143**
Floribundas, 354–55
"Found" containers. *See* Pots and
    planters
Fringe tree, 84
Fruit trees. *See* Trees and shrubs
Fuchsia, 41–42, 76, 83
Fuchsia, 267–68
  'Gartenmeister', 330
  5 *hybrida*, **109**, 267–68
  'Lord Byron', **92**
  magellanica (or 'Riccartonii'),
    268
Funkias, 284

Gaillardia, 67
Garlic, society, **158**, 375
Gelsemium, 268–69
  sempervirens, **165**, 268–69
  sempervirens 'Pride of Augusta',
    269
Geranium, 19, 63, 79, 332–35
  combined with other plants, **22**,
    45, **48**, **54**, **55**, **70**, **72**, **83**
  common or zonal, **116**, 333
  ivy, **70**, **72**, **116**, 334
  Martha Washington, 333
  peppermint, 335
  rose, 335
  scented, **117**, 334–35
  strawberry, **145**, 361
Geranium, 332–33
Gerbera, 269–70
  jamesonii, 269–70
  jamesonii 'Happy Pot', **109**
Germination of seeds, 390
Globe amaranth, **110**, 271
Gloriosa, 270–71
  superba, **154**, 270
Goatsbeard, 84
Golden ball, 27
Gomphrena, **17**, 235
Gomphrena, 271
  globosa, **110**, 271
  globosa 'Buddy', 271
Grapefruit, 'Marsh' seedless and
    'Ruby', 242
Grape hyacinth, **156**, 320–21
Graptopetalum paraguayense, 25–26
Grass, ornamental, 39, 67, 76,
    271–75
  blue fescue, **136**, 273
  blue oat, 274
  Bowles' golden, 275
  clumping, 273, 274
  crimson or red fountain, **43**, 275
  fountain, 275
  hare's-tail, 275
  New Zealand flax, **143**, 274
  ribbon, **142**, 273–74
  variegated Japanese sedge, **131**,
    272–73
  variegated Japanese sweet flag,
    127, 272
Guava, Pineapple, **188**, 263
Gymnocalycium, 27

Hakonechloa macra 'Aureola', 274
Hamelia patens, **136**, 275–76
Hanging baskets. *See* Pots and
    planters
Hardiness zone map, 436–37
Harry Lauder's walking stick, 75, 84,
    174

Haworthia, 26
Hawthorn, Indian, **198**, 348
Hedera, 276–77
   helix 'Glacier', 'Goldheart', 'Needlepoint', 276
   helix 'Rochester', **165**
   hibernica, 262
Helictotrichon sempervirens, 274
Heliotrope, **110**, 277
Heliotropium, 277
   arborescens 'Iowa', 277
   arborescens 'Marina', **110**, 277
Hellebore, Corsican, 278, 279
Helleborus, 278–79
   argutifolius, 278, 279
   s *hybridus*, 278
   niger, 278, 279
   orientalis, **137**, 278, 279
Hemerocallis, 279–81
   'Black-eyed Stella', 'Condilla', 'Ed Murray', 280
   'Eenie Weenie', 'Hyperion', 'Joan Senior', 'Mary Todd', 'Pardon Me', 'Ruby Throat', 'Siloam Double Classic', 281
   'Stella d'Oro', **137**, 281
Hemlock, dwarf, 84
Hen-and-chickens, hens-and-chicks, **146**, 163–64
Herbs, 19, 87, 88, 210, 305–6. *See also* Basil; Rosemary; Thyme
Heuchera, 281–82
   americana 'Pewter Veil', 282
   'Bressingham Bronze', 282
   s *brizoides* 'Chatterbox', 'Coral Cloud', 'June Bride', 'Mount St. Helens', 'Pluie de Feu' ('Rain of Fire'), 'Tattletale', 'White Cloud', 282
   'Chocolate Ruffles', 282
   micrantha 'Palace Purple', **228**, 263, 282
   sanguinea, 281
   sanguinea 'Snowstorm', **138**
Hibiscus, **55**, 283
Hibiscus rosa-sinensis, **111**, 283
Hinoki cypress. *See* Cypress
Holly, **32**, 75, 288–91
   Chinese, **189**, 289, 291
   English, 329
   Japanese, **189**, 290
   lusterleaf, 290
   topal, 289
   Yaupon, 290
Holly fern, 264–65
Honeysuckle, 313–14
   gold-flame or everblooming, **167**, 313
   gold-net, 314
   Hall's, 314
   Japanese, 314
   trumpet, 314
Horsetail, 84
Hosta, 14, 84
Hosta, **138**, 283–86
   'Blue Cadet', 285
   fortunei 'Francee', 'Hyacinthina', 285
   'Ginko Craig', 'Gold Standard', 'Hadspen Blue', 'Krossa Regal', 285
   plantaginea, 284
   plantaginea 'Aphrodite', 'Grandiflora', 'Honeybells', 'Royal Standard', 285–86
   sieboldiana 'Elegans', 'Frances Williams', 285
   sieboldii 'Kabitan', 286
   'Sum and Substance', 286
   tardiflora, 285
   ventricosa 'Aureo-Marginata', 286
   venusta and *v.* 'Variegata', 286
   'Wide Brim', 286
Houttuynia, 84
Humata tyermannii, 264
Hummingbird bush, **136**, 275–76
Hyacinth, 23, **154**
   grape, **156**, 320–21
   water, 29, 84
Hyacinthus orientalis, **154**, 286–87
Hydrangea, 287–88
   arborescens 'Annabelle', 'Grandiflora', 288
   macrophylla 'Forever Pink', 'Mariesii', 'Mariesii Variegata', 'Nikko Blue', 'Pia', 287
   macrophylla 'Pink Supreme', **176**
Hypocyrta glabrus, 26

Ice plant, 26, 75
   hardy, 255
   purple, **134**, 255
Ilex, 288–91
   aquifolium, 329
   aquifolium s *cornuta*, 290–91
   s *attenuata*, 289
   'China Girl', 290
   cornuta, **189**, 291
   cornuta 'Carissa', 'Dwarf Burford', 'Rotunda', 289
   crenata, **189**
   crenata 'Compacta', 'Convexa', 'Glory', 'Golden Gem', 'Hellerii', 'Hetzii', 'Northern Beauty', 290
   latifolia, 290
   'Nellie R. Stevens', 290–91
   verticillata 'Sparkleberry', **32**
   vomitoria 'Nana', 'Pendula', 'Stokes Dwarf', 290

Impatiens, 19, 42, **43**, **54**, 72, 83, 112, 291–92
Impatiens, 291–92
 New Guinea hybrids, **111**, 291
 wallerana, 291–92
 wallerana 'Grand Prix', **112**
Ipomoea, 292–93
 alba, 293
 batatas, 292
 batatas 'Blackie', 293
 coccinea, 293
 s *multifida*, 293
 purpurea, **166**, 293
 quamoclit, 293
 tricolor, 293
Iris
 blue flag, 296
 dwarf crested, 295
 Japanese, 29, 84, 295
 Japanese roof, 295
 Louisiana, 84
 reticulated or violet-scented, **155**, 294
 Siberian, 295
 yellow flag, 295–96
Iris, 293–96
 cristata, 295
 ensata, 295
 kaempferi, 29
 laevigata, 295
 pallida, 295
 pseudacorus, 295–96
 reticulate, **155**, 295
 reticulata 'Cantab', 'Harmony', 'J. S. Dijt', 294
 sibirica, 295
 tectorum, 295
 'Variegata', 295
 versicolor, 296
 Xiphium hybrids, 295
Irish lace, 367
Ivy, **41**, 84, 91, 276–77
 English, **165**, 276
 ground, 72, 75, 84
Ivy geranium. *See* Geranium

Jack-in-the-pulpit, 84
Jade plant, 25
Jasmine
 Chilean, 318
 Chinese, 296–97
 Star or Confederate, **166**, **169**, 296, 373
 summer, 296
 yellow, *see Gelsemium sempervirens*
Jasminum, 296–97
 mesnyi, 296, 297
 nitidum, **166**, 296, 297
 officinale, 296
 polyanthum, 296–97
Jonquils. *See* Daffodils
Juniper, 91, 297–300
 alligator, 298
 creeping, **190**, 298–99
 dwarf, 84, 95, **190**
 Hollywood, 297
 Rocky Mountain, 298
 shore, 299
 weeping, 298
Juniperus, 297–300
 chinensis 'Mint Julep', 'San Jose', 'Torulosa' or 'Kaizuka', 297
 chinensis 'Pfitzerana', **190**, 297
 communis 'Compressa', 298
 conferta 'Blue Pacific', 'Emerald Sea', 299
 deppeana, 298
 flaccida, 298
 horizontalis, 298–99
 horizontalis 'Bar Harbor', 'Wiltonii' or 'Blue Rug', 299
 horizontalis 'Blue Chip', **190**, 299
 horizontalis 'Mother Lode', 300
 s *media*, 297–98
 procumbens 'Nana', 300
 sabina 'Broadmoor', 300
 scopulorum 'Blue Creeper', 300
 scopulorum 'Blue Heaven', 'Gray Gleam', 'Pathfinder', 'Wichita Blue', 298
 squamata 'Blue Carpet', 'Blue Star', 299
 virginiana 'Grey Owl', 298

Kaffir lily. *See* Clivia
Kalanchoe tomentosa, 26
Kale, flowering, 48, **102**, 223
Kumquats, 242

Laburnum, 84
Lagerus ovatus, 275
Lagerstroemia, 300-301
 fauriei s *indica*, 'Acoma', 'Hopi', 'Sioux', 301
 indica, 300–301
 indica, 'Crape Myrtlettes', 'Petites', 301
 indica 'Natchez', **176**, 301
Lamiastrum, 42
Lamium, 301–2
 maculatum, 301–2
 maculatum 'Beacon Silver', **139**, 302
 maculatum 'White Nancy', 302
Lampranthus, 26
Lantana, 45, 55, **112**

common, **112**, 302–3
trailing, **113**, 303
Lantana, 302–3
  camara, 302–3
  camara 'Variegata', **112**
  montevidensis, **113**, 303
Lathyrus odoratus, 304
  'Bijou Mix', **167**
Laurel, 304–5
  Cherry or English, **197**, 344–45
Laurus, 304–5
  azorica, 305
  nobilis, **191**, 305
  'Saratoga', 305
Laurustinus, 380
Lavandin, 306
Lavandula, 305–6
  angustifolia, 305–6
  angustifolia 'Hidcote', 'Jean Davis', 'Munstead', 306
  angustifolia 'Nana', **139**
  dentata, 306
  5 *intermedia*, 306
  officinalis, 305
  stoechas, 306
  vera, 305
Lavender
  English or common, **139**, 305–6
  French, 306
  Spanish, 306
Lemon, 'Eureka', 'Improved Meyer', 'Lisbon', 'Ponderosa', 242
Lemon balm, **141**, 318–19
Lemon bottlebrush, **185**, 229
Lemon thyme, **89**, **146**
Lemon verbena, **100**, 210
Lenten rose, **137**, 278, 279
Lettuce, 19, 87
  water, 30, **86**
Leucanthemum paludosum, 240
Leucophyllum, 306–7
  candidum, 307
  frutescens, **191**
  frutescens 'Compactum', 'Green Cloud', 'Silver Cloud', 307
Light and shade, 52
  night lights, 81
  for seedlings, 392
  shade gardening, 82–84
Ligularia, 84
Lilac, Summer, **173**, 224–25
Lilium, 307–10
  Asiatic hybrid 'Dreamland', **155**
  Asiatic hybrids 'Bull's Eye', 'Doeskin', 'Pink Floyd', 'Rodeo', 'Sugarpie Suzie', 309
  Oriental hybrid 'Casablanca', 310, 357
  Oriental hybrid 'Stargazer', **156**, 310

Oriental hybrids 'Imperial', 'Le Rêve', 310
Lily, 23, 47, **155**, **156**, 307–10
  calla, 23, 83, **159**, 385–86
  gloriosa, **154**, 270
  kaffir, *see* Clivia
  peace, 82
  plantain, **138**, 284
  water, **28**, 29–30, 84, **86**
  white Asiatic, 55
  See also Daylily
Lily-of-the-Nile, **150**, 206–7
Lilyturf, **140**, 310–11
Lime, 'Bearss' seedless, 242
Lippia citriodora. See Aloysia triphylia
Liriope, 310–11
  muscari, **140**, 311
  muscari 'Big Blue', 'John Burch', 'Majestic', 'Monroe's White', 'Silvery Sunproof', 310
  spicata, 310
  spicata 'Silver Dragon', 311
Lobelia, 19, **22**, 72
  edging, **113**, 311–12
  trailing, 43
Lobelia erinus, 273, 311–12
  'Blue Cascade', **113**
Lobivia, 27
Lobularia, 312–13
  maritima, **114**, 312
Lonicera, 313–14
  5 *heckrottii*, **167**, 313
  japonica 'Aureoreticulata', 'Halliana', 'Purpurea', 314
  sempervirens, 314
Loosestrife, purple, 84
Lotus, 29
Lotus vine, 72, 84
Lysimachia nummularia, **140**, 315
  'Aurea', 315

Mahonia, 75
Malus, 316–17
  hybrid crab apple 'Donald Wyman', **177**
  hybrids 'Coral Cascade', 'Red Jade', 'Red Swan', 'Weeping Candied Apple', 316–17
Mammillaria, 27
Mandevilla, 317–18
  5 *amabilis* 'Alice du Pont', **168**, 317
  boliviensis, 318
  laxa, 318
  sanderi 'Red Riding Hood', 317–18
Maple, 204–5
  Japanese, 84, 95, **172**, 204–5

Marigold, 19, **20**, 47, 87, 89, 366–67
  African, 367
  French, **121**, 366–67
  lemon gem, **87**, 367
  Mexican mint, **120**, 366
Matricaria capensis. See
    Chrysanthemum parthenium
Melissa officinalis, **141**, 318–19
Mentha, 319–20
  aquatica, 319–20
  ꜱ *piperita*, 319
  pulegium, 320
  requienii, 320
  spicata, 319
  suaveolens, 319
  suaveolens 'Variegata', **141**
Milium effusum 'Aureum', 275
Miniature plants, 12, **179**, 354
Mint, 88, **130**, 227–28, 318–20
  Corsican, 320
  pineapple, **141**, 319
Moneywort, **140**, 315
Monkey flower, 84
Montbretia. *See Crocosmia*
Moonflower, 293
Morning glory, **166**, 292–93
Moss rose, **118**, 341
Mother-in-law's tongue, 26
Mother-of-pearl plant, 25–26
Muscari armeniacum, **156**, 320–21
Myrtle, **192**, 321
  crape, **94**, 176
Myrtus communis, **192**
  'Compacta, Compacta Variegata',
    'Microphylla', 321

Nandina, 322–23
  domestica, **192**
  domestica 'Alba', 'Compacta',
    'Harbour Dwarf', 'Moyers
    Red', 'Nana', 'San Gabriel',
    'Umpqua Chief', 322
Narcissus, 323–25
  paperwhite, 23, 325
  pheasant's-eye, 325
  See also Daffodils
Narcissus, **157**, 323–25
  jonquilla, 325
Nasturtium, 67, 72, 89, **121**, 374–75
Nelumbo nucifera, 29
Nematanthus glabrus, 26
Nemophila, 19
Nephrolepis
  cordifolia, 264
  exaltata, **142**, 264
Nerines, 23
Nerium oleander, **193**
  'Algiers', 'Casablanca', 'Petite
    Pink', 'Petite Salmon', 'Tangier',
    326
Nettle, Spotted dead, **139**, 301–2
New Zealand flax, **143**
Nicotiana, **43**, **49**
Nicotiana, 326–28
  affinis, 327
  alata, **114**, 327
  alata 'Domino', 'Fragrant Cloud',
    'Merlin', 'Nikki', 'Sensation
    Mixed', 'Starship', 327
  rustica, 327
  sylvestris, 327
  tabacum, 327
Notocactus, 27
Nymphaea, 29–30

Ocimum, 328–29
  basilicum 'Cinnamon', 'Opal',
    'Purple Ruffles', 'Spicy Globe',
    328–29
  basilicum 'Fine Vert Nain',
    'Golden Bouquet', **115**
Oleander, **193**, 326
Olive, Sweet, **193**, 329
Orange, 'Chinotto', 'Owari Satsuma'
    mandarin, 'Valencia' and
    'Washington' navel, 242
Osmanthus, 329–30
  holly-leaf, 329
Osmanthus, 329–30
  aguifolium, 329
  ꜱ *fortunei*, 329
  fragrans, **193**
  fragrans 'Aurantiacus', 329
  heterophyllus 'Gulftide',
    'Variegatus', 329
Oxalis, **157**, 330
  acetosella, 330
  crassipes, 330
  deppei 'Iron Cross', 330
  purpurea var. *bowiei*, 330

Pachysandra, 75
Panda plant, 26
Pansy, 23, **81**, 89, **122**, 381–82
Papaver, 331
  nudicaule 'Champagne Bubbles',
    'Sparkling Bubbles', 331
  nudicaule 'Wonderland Pink
    Shades', **115**
Papyrus, 29
Parodia, 27
Passiflora, 331–32
  ꜱ *alatocaerulea*, **168**, 331
  caerulea, 332
  edulis, 332
  incarnata, 332
  'Incense', 332

Index 449

'Jeannette', 332
vitifolia, 332
Passionvine, passionflower, **168**, 331–32
Patient Lucy, 111, 291
Patios and decks, 53–59
Peach tree, **88**
Pelargonium, **117**, 332–35
  crispum, 335
  5 *domesticum*, 333
  graveolens, 335
  5 *hortorum*, **116**, 333
  peltatum, **116**, 334
  tomentosum, **117**, 335
Pennisetum
  alopecuroides, **362**
  alopecuroides 'Hameln', 'Little Bunny', 275
  orientale, 275
  setaceum 'Burgundy Giant', 'Purpureum' ('Atropurpureum'), 275
Pennyroyal, 320
Pepperbush, **181**, 382–83
Peppermint, 319
Peppers, 19, **20**, **87**, **88**
  ornamental, 63, **104**, 233–34
Perennials, 19, 21–22, 57, 76, **124–47**, 396
  in water garden, 84, **127**
Perilla, 234
Periwinkle, 380–81
  common, 381
  large, **147**, 380
  Madagascar, **104**, 235, 287
Persian violet. *See Exacum affine*
Pests and pesticides, 87, 89, 420–21, 422, 431
Petunia, 13, 41, 48, 54, 70, 72, **117**
  "balcony," 335
  Grandiflora and Multiflora, 335–36
Petunia, 335–36
  'Azure Pearls', 'Salmon Pearls', 273
  5 *hybrida*, **117**, 335–36
  integrifolia, 335
Phalaris arundinacea 'Picta', **142**, 273–74
Philodendron, 82
Phormium tenax 'Sundowner', **143**, 274
Phyllostachys
  aureosulcata, 216
  nigra, **194**, 216–17
Picea, 336–37
  abies 'Pendula', 337
  glauca 'Conica', **194**, 336–37
  glauca 'Densata', 'Gnome', 336
  pungens, **195**

  pungens 'Blueness', 'Blue Spreader', 'Fat Albert', 'Globosa', 'Hoopsii', 'R. H. Montgomery', 337
Pickerel weed, 30, 84, 86
Pillar cactus, 27
Pincushion cactus, 27
Pine, 337–40
  bristlecone, 339
  dwarf white, 339–40
  Japanese black, **196**, 338
  Japanese white, 339
  lace-bark, 339
  mugo, **195**, 338
  Scotch, 340
  tanyosho, 339
Pineapple guava, **188**, 263
Pineapple mint, **141**
Pineapple sage, 118
Pink
  cheddar, 258
  China, **108**, 257–58
  cottage or Allwood, **134**, 256
  maiden, **135**, 258
Pinus, 337–40
  aristata, 339
  bungeana, 339
  densiflora 'Pendula', 'Umbraculifera', 339
  mugo, **195**
  mugo 'Gnome', 'Mops', 338
  mugo var. *mugo*, 338
  mugo var. *pumilio*, 338
  parviflora, 339
  strobus 'Nana', 339–40
  sylvestris 'French Blue', 'Nana', 'Watereri', 340
  thunbergiana, **196**
  thunbergiana (*thunbergii*) 'Oculus-draconis', 'Thunderhead', 338
Pistia stratiotes, 30
Pittosporum, 340–41
  tobira 'Variegata', **196**, 340
  tobira 'Wheeler's Dwarf', 340
Planters. *See* Pots and planters
Planting, 401–13, 426–27
  and repotting, 418–20, 429–30
Platycladus orientalis, 370
Pleioblastus viridistriatus, 217
Plumbago, dwarf, **132**, 236
Polka-dot plant, 42
Polyanthas, 355
Polypodium aureum, 264
Polystichum
  acrostichoides, 265
  braunii, 265
  munitum, 265
  polyblepharum, 265
  setiferum, 265
  tsus-simense, 265

Pomegranate, 178, 345
Pontederia cordata, 30
Poor-man's orchid, **44**
Poppy, 67
  Iceland, **115**
Portulaca grandiflora, 341
  'Sunglow', **118**
Potentilla fruticosa
  'Abbotswood', **177**, 342
  'Goldstar', 'Katherine Dykes', 'Primrose Beauty', 342
Pothos, 82
Pot marigold. *See Calendula*
Potting soil, 397–400
  for trees and shrubs, 426
Pots and planters, 5–14, 56
  arrangement/grouping of, 35–49, 57–60, 77–78, 84
  concrete, 8–9
  "found" containers, 15, 56, 80, 84, 402
  hanging baskets, **6, 40, 57,** 70–73, 88, 264, 405–7
  hypertufa, 11–12, 408–11
  materials for, 6–15
  metal, 9–10
  permanent, 14, 73–76, 83, 412
  planting and repotting, 401–13, 418–20, 426–27, 429–30
  plastic or glazed, 8, 405
  stone, 10–11
  strawberry jars, 89
  terra-cotta, 6–7, 403–5
  for trees and shrubs, 425–26
  water garden, 84–87, 412–13
  window boxes, 66–70
  wooden, 12–14, 407–8
Primrose, 48, 342–44
  common, 343
  Japanese or candelabra, 344
  polyanthus, **143**, 342–43
Primula, 342–44
  acaulis, 343
  auricula, 344
  japonica, 344
  juliae, 343–44
  malacoides, 344
  obconica, 344
  5 *polyantha*, **143**, 342, 344
  5 *polyantha* 'Barnhaven', 'Cowichan', 'Hose-in-Hose', 'Pacific Giants', 'Regal', 343
  sinensis, 344
  vulgaris, 343
Propagation from cuttings, 393–95
Propeller plant, 25
Pruning, 417–18
  trees and shrubs, 430–31
Prunus, 344–45

  laurocerasus 'Otto Luyken', **197,** 344
  laurocerasus 'Schipkaensis', 'Zabeliana', 344
Punica granatum
  'Nana', **178,** 345
  'Wonderful', 345
Purchasing plants, 395–96
Purslane, 341
Pyracantha, 346–47
  coccinea, **197**
  coccinea 'Lalandei', 346
  'Gnome', 'Red Elf', 'Ruby Mound', 'Tiny Tim', 346
  koidzumii 'Santa Cruz', 346
  'Mohave', 347

Queen's-wreath, **162,** 211

Ranunculus, 347–48
  acris, 347
  asiaticus 'Bloomingdale', 347
  asiaticus 'Tecolote Hybrids', **158**
Rebutia, 27
Redbud, 84
Red or crimson fountain grass, **43,** 275
Red star vine, 293
Reeds, 84
Repotting. *See* Planting
Rhaphiolepis, 348–49
  indica, **198**
  indica 'Ballerina', 'Charisma', 'Clara', 'Enchantress', 'Snow White', 348
  umbellate, 348
Rhodochiton, 72
Rhododendron, 349–53
  dwarf, 75, 84
Rhododendron, 349–53
  carolinianum, 352
  catawbiense, 352
  dauricum, 352
  'Gumpo Pink' (evergreen azalea), **198**
  'Ironclads', 352
  moupinense, 352
  mucronulatum 'Cornell Pink', 352
  schlippenbachii (deciduous species azalea), **178,** 350
  yakusimanum, **199**
  yakusimanum 'Ken Janeck', 'Mist Maiden', 353
Rooftop gardens, 60–62
Rosa, 353–56
  floribundas 'Allgold', 'Angel Face' 'European', 'Iceberg', 354–55

miniatures, **179**
miniatures 'Red Cascade', 'Rise and Shine', 354
polyanthas 'Cecile Brunner', 'The Fairy', 355
shrub roses 'Bonica', 'Carefree Beauty', 'Gruss an Aachen', 'Sea Foam', 'Wife of Bath', 355
standard roses 'Cherish', 'Sunflair', **179**
standard 'Françoise Austin', 'Linda Campbell', 355–56
standard 'Showbiz', **91**
Rose, 18, 55, 75, 90, 95, 353–56
  floribundas, 354–55
  miniature, **179**, 354
  polyanthas, 355
  shrub, 355
  standard, **179**, 355–56
Rosemary, 89, **199**, 336
Rose-of-China, 111, 283
Rosette tree, 24
Rosmarinus officinalis
  'Arp', **199**, 356
  'Blue Boy', 'Blue Spire', 'Collingwood Ingram', 'Huntington Blue', 'Lockwood de Forest', 'Pinkie', 'Prostratus', 'Tuscan Blue', 356
Rumohra adiantiformis, 265

Sage, 357–60
  blue, 357
  cedar, 360
  cherry or autumn, **144**, 358–59
  garden, **144**, 359
  mealy blue, **119**, 357
  mealy-cup, 42, 271
  Mexican bush, 358
  pineapple, **118**, 357
  purple or Texas, 89, **191**, 307
  scarlet, 270, 360
  See also Salvia
Sagittaria montevidensis, 30
Salvia, 41, 42, 48, 49, **119**, 359–60
Salvia, 357–60
  coccinea, 270
  coccinea 'Lady in Red', 360
  elegans, **118**, 357
  farinacea, **119**, 235, 357
  gesneriiflora, 359
  greggii, **144**, 358–59
  guaranitica, 357
  guaranitica 'Indigo Spires', 271, 358
  leucantha, 358
  officinalis, **144**

  officinalis 'Compacta', 'Icterina','Purpurea', 'Tricolor', 359
  roemeriana, 360
  rutilans, 357
  splendens, **119**, 359
  splendens 'St. John's Fire', 'Scarlet Pygmy', 360
Sambucus, 360–61
  nigra 'Laciniata', 360
  racemosa 'Plumose Aurea', **180**, 360
  racemosa 'Sutherland Gold', 360
Sansevieria, 26, 82
Sanvitalia procumbens, 387
Sasa
  palmata, 217
  veitchii, 217
Saxifraga
  sarmentosa, 361
  stolonifera, **145**, 361
Schizanthus, 19, 44
Sedge, variegated Japanese, **131**, 272–73
Sedum, 361–63
  'Autumn Joy', **145**, 235, 362, 382
  brevifolium, 363
  confusum, 363
  'Indian Chief', 362
  lineare 'Variegatum', 363
  morganianum, 71, 363
  oxypetalum, 363
  sieboldii 'Medio-Variegatum', 36
  spathulifolium 'Cape Blanco', 'Purpureum', 363
  spectabile 'Brilliant', 'Meteor', 'Stardust', 362
  telephium, 362
  'Vera Jameson', 273
Seeds, starting with, 389–93
Semiarundinaria, 218
Sempervivum, 363–64
  arachnoideum, 363
  tectorum, **146**, 363
Senecio cineraria, **120**, 364. *See also* Dusty-miller
Serviceberry, 84
Shade. *See* Light and shade
"Shamrock," 330
Short pillar cactus, 27
Shrubs. *See* Trees and shrubs
Silver-dollar plant, 25
Snapdragon, 76, **100**, 212
Snowbell, Japanese, 84
Soaptree, 384
Solenostemon scutellarioides, 246
Sorbaria, 84
Spanish dagger, 384
Spearmint, 319
Specialties, 90–95

452 Index

Sphagnum moss, 67, 92
  in hanging basket, 6, 73, 405,
      406–7
Spiraea, 365
  s *bumalda* 'Anthony Waterer',
      'Coccinea', 'Crispa',
      'Goldflame', 'Lime Mound',
      365
  japonica, **180**
  japonica 'Albiflora', 'Goldmound',
      'Little Princess', 'Nana' or
      'Alpina', 'Shibori' or
      'Shirobana', 365
Spirea, 365
  blue, **173**, 234–35
  Japanese, **180**, 365
Spruce
  blue or Colorado, **195**, 337
  dwarf Alberta, **194**, 336
  Norway, 337
Standard plants, 55, 90, 92, 95
Star cactus, 26
Stonecrop, 361–62
Strawberry geranium or strawberry
      begonia. *See Saxifrage
      stolonifera*
Strawberry tree, **184**, 212–13
Strawflowers, 70
Succulents, 24–26, 39
Sweet bay, **191**, 305
Sweet flag, 86
  variegated Japanese, **127**, 272
Sweet olive, **193**, 329
Sweet pea, **167**, 304
Sweet potato 'Blackie', 234

Tagetes, 366–67
  erecta, 367
  filifolia, 367
  Inca series, 367
  lucida, **120**, 366
  patula, **121**, 367
  patula 'Janie', 'Naughty
      Marietta','Scarlet Sophie', 'Suzie
      Wong', 366–67
  signata, 367
  tenuifolia, **121**
  tenuifolia 'Golden Gem', 'Paprika',
      367
  tenuifolia 'Lemon Gem', **87**, 367
Tanacetum parthenium. *See
      Chrysanthemum parthenium*
Tangelo, 'Minneola', 242
Tangerine, 'Dancy', 242
Tasmanian tree fern, 264
Taxus, 367–69
  baccata, 368
  baccata 'Adpressa', 'Fastigiata' or
      'Stricta', 'Repandens', 369
  cultivars, 367–69
  cuspidata 'Nana', 368
  s *media*, **200**, 368
  s *media* 'Brownii', 'Greenwave',
      'Hatfieldii', 'Hicksii',
      'Sentinalis', 369
Thuja, 369–71
  occidentalis, **200**, 369–70
  occidentalis 'Aurea' ('Golden'),
      'Emerald', 'Hertz Midget',
      'Little Gem', 'Little Giant',
      'Nana', 'Rheingold',
      'Umbraculifera', 'Woodwardii',
      370
  orientalis 'Aurea Nana'
      ('GoldenBell'), **201**, 370–71
  orientalis 'Elegantissimus',
      'Juniperoides', 'Westmont', 371
Thunbergia, 371
  alata, **169**, 371
  alata 'Angel Wings', 371
  grandiflora, 371
Thyme
  common, 372
  lemon, **89**, **146**, 372
  woolly, 372
Thymus, 372
  s *citriodorus* 'Argenteus', **146**,
      372
  s *citriodorus* 'Aureus', 372
  pseudolanuginosus, 372
  vulgaris 'Aureus', 'Golden Dwarf',
      'Silver Queen', 372
Tiddlywinks. *See Exacum affine*
Tobacco
  flowering, 19, **114**
  woodland, 19
Tomatoes, 19, 81, 88, 89
  'Quickpick', 87
Topiary, 55, 62, 91–92, **93**, 95
Trachelospermum jasminoides, **169**,
      373
Trees and shrubs, 30–33, 39, 45, 55,
      57, 77
  deciduous, **170–81**
  dwarf, 61, 75, 84, 95, **194**, **195**,
      336, 338–40
  evergreen, **182–201**
  fruit and dwarf fruit, 88, 89, **178**,
      187, 242–43, 263, 345
  planting and caring for, 424–33
  shade-loving, 84
Tropaeolum majus, 374–75
  'Peach Blossom', **121**
Tuberoses, 23
Tulbaghia, 375
  fragrans, 375
  violacea, **158**, 375
Tulip, 23, 48, 76, 375–77
  cottage, 376

Index 453

Darwin, Parrot, Rembrandt, 376
garden, **159**
lily-flowered, 376
Tulipa, **159**, 375–77
Darwin hybrids, 376
greigii, 376

Umbrella plant, 29

Vegetables. *See* Edible gardening
Verbena, 19, 76
garden, **122**, 377
lemon, 100, 210
purple, **140**
Verbena 5 *hybrida*, **122**
'Homestead Purple',
'Imagination', 'Peaches and
Cream', 'Romance', 377
Viburnum, 378–80
deciduous, 378–79
evergreen, 379–80
Korean spice, **181**, 378
Viburnum, 378–80
5 *burkwoodii* 'Eskimo', 379
carlesii 'Cayuga', 378
carlesii 'Compactum', **181**, 378
davidii, 379
opulus 'Compactum', 'Nanum', 379
plicatum var. *tomentosum* 'Shasta', 'Summer Snowflake', 'Watanabei', 378–79
tinus 'Eve Price', 380
trilobum 'Compactum', 379
Vinca, 42, 72, 84
Vinca, 380–81
major 'Aureomaculata', 380
major 'Variegata', **147**
minor 'Argentea-variegata', 'Variegata', 381
Vinca rosea. See Catharanthus roseus
Vines, 22, **35**, 42, 72, 160–69
Viola, 382
Viola, 381–82
cornuta, 382
5 *wittrockiana*, **122**, 381–82
Violet
bush, **103**, 224
Persian, *see Exacum affine*
Vitex, 382–83
agnus-castus, **181**, 382–83
negundo var. *heterophylla*, 382–83

Wandering Jew, 72, 84
Warminster broom, **174**, 252
Watering, 6, **40**, **61**, 414–15, 423
cuttings, 393, 395

seedlings, 390, 392
trees and shrubs, 427–28, 433
See also Drainage
Water plants, 28–30, **79**, 84, 86, **127**
and water gardens, 84–87, 412–13
"Wildflower" garden, 67
Window boxes. *See* Pots and planters
Winter creeper, **164**, 259–60
Wintering over, 421–23
trees and shrubs, 431–33
Wood sorrel, European, 330

Yarrow, **126**, 205–6
Yew, 84, **200**, 367–69
AngloJap, 368
English, 368
Irish, 369
Japanese, 368
Yucca, 383–85
Whipple's, 384–85
Yucca, 383–85
aloifolia, 384
baccata, 384
'Bright Eyes', 384
elata, 384
filamentosa, **147**, 383–84
filamentosa 'Golden Sword', 384
flaccida, 384, 385
glauca, 384
gloriosa, 384
recurvifolia, 385
smalliana, 384
whipplei, 384–85

Zantedeschia, 385–86
aethiopica, 385–86
albomaculata, **159**, 385
rehmanii, 386
Zinnia, **16**, 19, 47–48, 67, 76, **123**
common, 387
creeping, 387
Mexican, 386
Zinnia, 386–87
angustifolia, 236
angustifolia 'Classic', **123**
elegans cultivars, 387
elegans 'Yellow Marvel', **123**
haageana 'Old Mexico', 'Persian Carpet', 386–87
linearis, 386

Titles available in the Taylor's Guide series:

Taylor's Guide to Annuals	$19.95
Taylor's Guide to Perennials	19.95
Taylor's Guide to Roses, Revised Edition	19.95
Taylor's Guide to Bulbs	19.95
Taylor's Guide to Ground Covers	19.95
Taylor's Guide to Houseplants	19.95
Taylor's Guide to Vegetables	19.95
Taylor's Guide to Shrubs	19.95
Taylor's Guide to Trees	19.95
Taylor's Guide to Garden Design	19.95
Taylor's Guide to Water-Saving Gardening	19.95
Taylor's Guide to Garden Techniques	19.95
Taylor's Guide to Gardening in the South	19.95
Taylor's Guide to Gardening in the Southwest	19.95
Taylor's Guide to Natural Gardening	19.95
Taylor's Guide to Specialty Nurseries	16.95
Taylor's Guide to Shade Gardening	19.95
Taylor's Guide to Herbs	19.95
Taylor's Guide to Container Gardening	19.95
Taylor's Master Guide to Gardening	60.00

At your bookstore or by calling 1-800-225-3362.

Prices subject to change without notice